SONG HONGBING

CURRENCY WARS IV
Age of the Warring States

ΘMNIA VERITAS®

Song Hongbing

Song Hongbing (born in 1968) is a young economic researcher who emigrated to the United States. He worked there as a consultant for the American pension funds Freddie Mac and Fanny Mae that will disappear during the financial crisis of 2008.

货币战争④战国时代

CURRENCY WARS IV
Age of the Warring States

Translated from Chinese and published by
Omnia Veritas Limited

OMNIA VERITAS

www.omnia-veritas.com

© Omnia Veritas Ltd – 2021

PREFACE

In September 2008, the financial crisis that swept the world awakened people's dreams of permanent prosperity, and the wave of globalization suffered its worst reversal in nearly 30 years; in 2009, Governments around the world adopted unprecedented fiscal stimulus and accommodative monetary policies in an attempt to turn the tide and continue the previous pattern of economic growth, and the world economy seems to have shown signs of significant recovery in the last three years. Thus, a sense of optimism began to permeate the "post-crisis era". It was not until 2011, when the United States debt woes and the European debt crisis again sounded the red alarms for the economy, that people suddenly realized that we were not living in a healthy economic recovery, but had begun the long journey from an "acute illness" to a "chronic illness" of the economy.

The lack of historical indulgence is a common phenomenon in today's short-sighted, impatient and quick-witted society, where people seem to find it difficult to extricate themselves from the high tempo of business and the hustle and bustle of affairs and to think calmly about the root of the problem. When the news media is filled with shocking headlines of all kinds, when confusion and anxiety cling to our minds, few are willing to take the precious time to take a comprehensive look at the root causes of the problems that shape our day.

Will the U.S. economy go into recession again, and will the 2012 U.S. treasury bond cap fight be repeated? Will the European debt crisis be in full swing? Is the euro system headed for collapse? Should China save Europe? Is China's real estate bubble about to burst? Will China's economy land hard or soft? Can inflation be effectively controlled? What exactly should China do with its huge foreign exchange reserves? What is the cap on the appreciation of the yuan? Can Renminbi Internationalization Work?

If we do not rely on any historical reference system, confronting such a multitude and complexity of issues is enough to bring the fragile brain to its knees.

In fact, there is nothing new under the sun, all of the above questions, history has long given the answers, and it is our task to find them and discover them from history. The importance of studying history is reflected in the clear articulation of today's predicament. While history will not be simple repetition, there is a striking similarity in the ever-repeating nature of humanity in history. After all, the history of economics and money is the history of mankind's constant quest for the great value of wealth and his attempt to control the power to distribute it, within the constraints of limited resources.

This book will follow the main line of world reserve currency hegemony, starting with the deliberate overthrow of the pound sterling hegemony by the US dollar, showing how the US monetary strategy masters have gradually eroded the pound sterling power, squeezed the pound sterling's international reserve currency status and trade settlement pricing power, and how the pound sterling power has counterattacked the US dollar through the "imperial preference system", and returned the US dollar to its original "isolationist" form. The fierce struggle between the dollar and the pound created a vacuum of world financial power in the 1930s that exacerbated the Great Depression worldwide.

The Second World War provided a historic opportunity for the dollar to eradicate the pound, and the Atlantic Charter and the Lend-Lease Act were all sharp scalpels in Roosevelt's hands, aimed at dismembering the British Empire's pound. Eventually, the United States established a "Bretton Woods dynasty" with a dollar-based system as regent by "holding gold hostage to the vassals".

Roosevelt's vigilance against the resurgence of the pound sterling cut far outweighed his fears about the Soviet Union. The outbreak of the Cold War had its roots in Truman's radical subversion of Roosevelt's grand strategy. The U.S.'s stalking of the Soviet Union forced Stalin to give up hope of joining the dollar empire and working with the United States to partition the world. The trigger for the Cold War was the Soviet Union's sudden reversal and abandonment of plans to join the IMF and the World Bank, which was the direct cause of George Kenan's 8,000-word long Cold War diatribe. From there, the dollar and the ruble began a thrilling showdown.

After the end of World War II, the French occupied the Ruhr and Saarland industrial areas of Germany, and the United States began the "Morgenthau Plan" to completely "castrate" German industry. The Soviet Union's refusal to join the dollar empire gave Germany a chance to reemerge, and Germany's 1948 currency reform, which directly stimulated the Soviet Union, triggered the Berlin crisis. At the beginning of the 1950s, when the German-French dispute over the Ruhr and Saarland was becoming increasingly heated, the French and Germans had even seen the danger signals that war between the two countries would be inevitable, but the "coal-steel alliance" of the "super-sovereign" saved the war crisis, and it was only then that the great historical reconciliation between Germany and France began. For both sides, placing coal and steel under a "supersovereign" authority would make future wars "unthinkable and impossible". This institutional arrangement of a tightly bound community of interests is the starting point for the EU and the euro today. At the time of the establishment of the Coal and Steel Union, the European ruling elite was already planning the road map for a "United States of Europe". When we look at how the European elite bloc has operated the European Monetary and Economic Union for the past 60 years or so, we will understand that today's European debt crisis will not lead to the disintegration of the euro and the EU, but will accelerate the birth of a "United States of Europe".

The conflict between the US and Europe began in the 1960s during the de Gaulle era, when France's gold run against the US dollar directly accelerated the collapse of the Bretton system, and in the early 1970s, when the US dollar and European currencies entered an era of conflict and confrontation, and by the end of the 1970s, when the US dollar empire was almost on the verge of its final collapse, the US was already preparing to replace the US dollar with a special drawing right (SDR), and the US dollar announced its worst-case scenario of "power down". Finally, the dollar was saved by the rapidity of the new Chairman of the Federal Reserve, Volcker, when, beginning in the 1980s, the United States launched a model of debt-driven economic growth in which 1 per cent of the wealthy took back the distribution of social wealth from the Government, thus beginning an unprecedented era of "neoliberalism" in which wealth was concentrated in the hands of a tiny minority, and the "Occupy Wall Street" movement in 2011, in which 99 per cent of the United States population launched a formal challenge to this irrational system of wealth distribution.

The 2008 financial tsunami was a total liquidation of 30 years of the wrong economic model in the United States and of the dollar system since the creation of the American debt empire in 1971. The highly indebted United States economy will see a "lost decade" for the United States economy over the next three long, highly overlapping cycles of painful economic unleveraging, shrinking consumption by the "baby boomers" and bottlenecks in productivity growth.

In the harsh external environment of a prolonged economic downturn in developed countries over the next decade, China and Asia face major challenges to their development models. During the 30 years of reform and opening up, China's economy has developed to the present day with the propulsion of a two-stage rocket, namely, rural industrialization in the first 15 years and the globalization of Chinese manufacturing in the last 15 years. The first stage rocket went off in the mid-1990s, resulting in a cooling economy and deflation in the late 1990s. Now that the second-stage rocket is in the process of going off, the third-stage rocket must be launched for China's economic growth to continue in the future. The third stage of the rocket must and can only be the second industrialization of the countryside, the explosion of a new agricultural economy with informationization, intensification, high-technology and urbanization at its core, is the right choice for China to emerge from its impending economic difficulties.

America's woes are economic, Europe's are political, and Asia's are history!

The basis of interest in the "China-America" economic marriage is fracturing and disintegrating. America's tolerance for China's booming economy was originally based on the model of Chinese production, American enjoyment, Chinese savings, American consumption. China's future economic transformation will inevitably require a shift in the main resources of the national economy from being tilted towards overseas markets to being tilted towards domestic markets, thereby reducing savings exports to the United States. This process would change the basic U.S. position of continuing to tolerate China's economic growth. At present, Hillary's declaration of "America's Pacific Century" signals a fundamental change in the strategic posture of the United States, and the increasingly acute problems in the East China Sea and South China Sea are the precursors of this change.

The key to China's ability to defuse the U.S. siege lies in its ability to unite Asian countries into a solid community of interest. Today,

China should demonstrate this wisdom by boldly drawing on the "coal and steel alliance" that led to the historical rapprochement between Germany and France, completely removing the fuse from the gunpowder barrels of war in the East and South China Seas, taking the supra-sovereign "oil alliance" as a starting point, promoting the establishment of an Asian economic community, replacing the internationalization of the yuan with an Asian dollar strategy, achieving economic integration in Asia and tightly binding the interests of Asian countries so that war between Asian countries is "neither imaginable nor possible". It is only by relying on a united Asia that China can establish a firm footing for its move to the world.

As the saying goes, if you give up, how can you get it?

The Germans gave up the mark in favour of a more powerful euro; the Germans gave up the protection of their own market in favour of a more extensive European common market! The great wisdom of the Chinese should not be lost to the Germans.

Some would say that Asian issues are too complex and history too tangled. The problem is that if a united Asia will give China's interests fundamental security, then the path is worth trying, no matter how hard it is. Don't ask whether uniting Asia is feasible, ask how much creative effort China has made to this end!

China's globalization is not Europeanization, but should be Asianization first and foremost.

Only with a foothold in Asia can China go global; only with unity in Asia can China's economy be successfully transformed; only with a unified Asian currency can it compete internationally with the dollar and the euro, and finally form a triple monetary warring states era!

Author.

Xiangshan, Beijing,

November 10, 2011

CHAPTER I

Ambition Begins, Dollar Fails the Expedition

The United States, as the ultimate challenger to the global hegemony of the British Empire, pushed Germany to the forefront of the battle for hegemony with Britain, while sitting on the sidelines of the European countries' power drain. After the First World War, the United States sank deep into the dollar debt quagmire by laying heavy war debts on Europe's head, forcing countries to dump their treasuries. The United States cleverly exploited Germany's war reparations problem by successfully implanting the dollar into the German monetary system, which then gradually penetrated the currency reserves of other European central banks.

America's war debt also deprived Europe of the credit it needed for economic development, thus creating a dollar-dependent Europe. In the vast overseas markets of the old colonial empire, the United States took advantage of the capital advantage, opened up territory, rode on the rampage, and in the trade settlement constantly expanded the territory of the dollar empire.

Under the circumstances of monopolizing the world's gold reserves, the United States formed the strategy of "holding gold hostage to make the lords", using the British eagerness to try to restore the gold standard to rebuild the hegemony of the British pound, the United States encouraged, financed and even forced the British pound to bind with gold as soon as possible, thus seizing the dominant power of economic development of the British Empire.

But the United States, after all, is an emerging hegemon, ill-prepared for sudden and historic opportunities. While the strategy of dollar hegemony is clear, the means of achieving it are crude and the tools contradictory, and the Great Depression of the 1930s was the result of the inherent contradictions of dollar strategy.

Attempts by the United States to replace the gold standard, which the United Kingdom had established in 200 years, with a dollar-based system in 20 years are bound to face the dilemma of having more than one heart to spare. The United Kingdom, on the other hand, was exhausted in its efforts to defend its financial supremacy by defending its gold standard. While the dollar is collapsing into a global contraction, the pound is in ruins and is powerless to return. After the world lost its lender of last resort, there was a vacuum in the power of money and the world was plunged into a dark depression.

The global trading system is broken, world capital flows are depleted, and the will to sustain the peaceful development of nations is lost. The United States, on the other hand, has retreated into isolationism, healing on its own while waiting for the time to rise again…

The dollar's first expedition to conquer the world ended in failure.

Pound overjoyed as Mark throws his arms around

At 10:00 p.m. on December 31, 1923, a full-bodied Schacht rushed from Berlin to London. A foggy, cold winter night does nothing to dissipate the enthusiasm of the British to celebrate the New Year. In the bars of the streets and alleys, people are having a good time enjoying the peace, having forgotten about the unprecedented war five years ago.

At this time Schacht's heart was unusually heavy, and his home country, Germany, was struggling with poverty, hunger and anger. The great shadow of World War I defeat, the grotesque humiliation of ceding $1/10^{th}$ of the territory, the extortion of the huge war reparations of $12.5 billion (equivalent to Germany's GDP in the year before the war) by Britain and France, the recent brutality of the French army's forcible occupation of the Ruhr industrial zone in Germany, and especially the super-inflation that has swept Germany this year, completely looting the wealth of the German middle class. The Germans wept and sighed as they watched the value of the German mark being thrown into hell. Schacht was well aware of the significance of this trip to the fate of the German mark, who had come to borrow money from the British.

Only a month and a half ago, on November 12, Schacht was urgently appointed chairman of the German Monetary Council, enjoying the status of a cabinet minister with final veto power over

Germany's currency, a status that could be described as the country's economic czar. Schacht, who was in danger, immediately threw himself into the task of saving the German mark.

The German mark, at this point, has fallen wildly from 1 dollar to 9,000 marks a year ago, to 1.3 trillion marks to 1 dollar! Mark's credit is completely broken and beyond repair. Schacht and the German government had to think otherwise. Due to the shortage of gold in Germany, they invented a new mark, called the "land-rent mark", which was collateralized by German land and all assets on it, in an attempt to regain the trust in paper money. In this way, Germany would have both marks in circulation, and the key to the success of the new mark would be to find the right moment to lock in the ratio of the old to the new mark, and then quickly complete the withdrawal of the old mark from circulation.

When the ground-rental mark came out, the already astonished Germans had no faith in either mark in circulation at the same time, and people were still frantically abandoning the mark for dollars. By November 14, the black market exchange rate mark fell to $1.3 trillion to the dollar, officials urged the Schacht to hurry to lock in the exchange rate of the ground rent mark to the old mark, the Schacht did not move. on November 15, the mark fell to $1: 2.5 trillion mark, officials are already anxious to go to the house, the Schacht still do not show a word. on November 20, when the old mark fell to $1: 4.2 trillion mark, the Schacht immediately ordered to lock in the ground rent mark to the old mark of 1: 1 trillion. Schacht has calculated carefully that this equilibrium will eventually return when people's panic is fully released. Sure enough, the old and new marks continued to fall due to market inertia, even to the tune of 11 trillion marks per dollar by November 26. But like an overstretched rubber band, the market miraculously saw a mark rally. By December 10, the dollar finally stabilized at the $1:4.2 trillion mark equilibrium against the mark. Schacht's judgement proved to be accurate and his timing was spot on. The market began to exclaim that Schacht were economic wizards! In the meantime, the German government, with all its might, finally balanced its budget in January 1924.

The ground-rent mark has finally stood its ground, settling in at the $1:4.2 trillion ground-rent mark line.

However, Schacht understood in his heart that the ground rent mark was only a stopgap measure. In his view, currency issued against land is a pure game of faith. Who would really believe that a farm in Bavaria, or a plant in Ruhr, had any real connection with the ground-rent mark they were holding? In his mind, the collateral for money must have three core elements: a high degree of liquidity, easy exchangeability and full international recognition, and the only collateral for money that also meets these conditions is gold!

But Germany is precisely short of gold. Pre-war Germany had $1 billion worth of gold, supporting the $1.5 billion Imperial Mark, which was fairly well supported among the four economic powers of the United States, Britain, Germany and France. But war payouts and hyperinflation in the five years following the war have reduced Germany's gold reserves to a mere $150 million, and the country is no longer able to support its huge economic body.

The solution to the Schacht's problem was to borrow gold or foreign currency with sufficient reserves of gold, which could be freely exchanged for gold when needed, and only gold and foreign currency could finally stabilize the value of the German mark. The question is, who to borrow from?

Of course the U.S. has the most gold, sitting on $4.5 billion of the Big Four's total $6 billion in gold reserves![1] But the United States was by this time notoriously miserly in Europe, and was denounced by the French and English as "Uncle Shylock". The industries of the British and French allies were severely damaged by the war, and millions of soldiers and civilians were killed and wounded; as a result, Britain owed the United States $5 billion and France $4 billion.[2] A business is a business, and not a penny owed can be less! The ruthlessness of the United States pissed Britain off and forced France to openly loot. Even to the Allies, Schacht felt that borrowing money from the Americans as a defeated nation was seriously untenable.

Not to mention France. The naive French always thought they would take a hard knock from the Germans, and initially the French Chancellor united with the British lion's share and demanded at least

---

[1] Liaquat Ahamed, *Lords of Finance*, The Penguin Press, New York, 2009. p. 162.

[2] Michael Hudson, *Super Imperialism – New Edition: The Origin and Fundamentals of U.S. World Dominance*, Pluto Press; New Edition (March 21, 2003), Chapter one.

$100 billion in war reparations from Germany, the equivalent of eight years of German GDP combined! It didn't seem right to me afterwards, but the $55 billion bite was the price! Or did the Americans come out to round up and persuade Britain and France to reduce the compensation to 12.5 billion. In fact, given the state of the German economy at the time, it was simply not realistic to repay this astronomical amount of compensation. Since the French were convinced that Germany's huge reparations were imminent, once the provinces of Lorraine and Alsace, which had been taken by Germany in the Franco-Prussian War of 1870, were recovered, $4 billion was spent on reconstruction, leaving the Government with a high fiscal deficit. The French repeatedly threatened Germany to take the money immediately, but Germany delayed in handing over the money, the French, in a fit of rage, actually armed robbery, and sent troops to occupy the German Ruhr industrial zone. At this point he went to ask the French for money, and Schacht felt that he might be immediately beaten out of his place by the French.

The only hope is the British. Moreover, Schacht knew that he could make an offer that Britain could not refuse, and he had the Englishman's little mind well thought out. He's going on a trip to England and he's going to get it!

A tall, bearded English gentleman with a sharp eye was standing in the cold night breeze as Schacht stepped out of Liverpool Street station in London. He came to Schacht's heel and held out his hand to introduce himself. To Schacht's surprise, it turned out that he was the world-famous Bank of England governor, Montagu Norman. Schacht was somewhat flattered to be greeted by Norman himself.

Norman, though far from England, had been following Germany's hyperinflation, and the vicious currency devaluation that occurred in Germany in 1923 was the worst and most dramatic paper currency collapse ever seen by mankind, and for all the central bankers who saw inflation as the number one evil, the experience of the Deutsche Mark was eye-opening. The fact that Schacht, who had never had experience in managing a central bank, had managed to contain the hyperinflation that had left everyone desperate and terrified in a little over two weeks, could not fail to impress Norman.

The next day was New Year's Day and the city of London was empty in the middle of the New Year, and Norman led Schacht on a tour of the Bank of England and then to Norman's office. After a brief courtesy, Schacht got right to the point when he raised the hope that the

Bank of England would provide the German central bank with a pound sterling loan worth $25 million. It's not really a big number, and Schacht is prepared to use that money as a seed, supplement it with $25 million from German overseas banks, and with $50 million as core capital, he'll have the certainty of securing a $200 million loan on the London financial markets, thus laying the solid foundation for the new German mark. It's clearly a masterstroke to make a big move with little, and the key is that the first $25 million must be in place for the later moves to be viable.

Norman listened quietly to Schacht's request, slightly surprised, then just silent. Norman thought to himself, "Want to borrow money? For what? A bankrupt country with a huge $12.5 billion war reparations on its back, and Schacht, who has only been in office for a month and a half and is not yet a serious central banker, comes up and has a big mouth.

Indeed, there was much controversy within the German government over the arrogant and insolent Schacht, and the current Governor of the German Central Bank, Rudolf von Havenstein, was very unhappy with him, and in May 1922, the victorious country passed legislation to make the German Central Bank independent from government control, and if Havenstein refused to resign, Schacht would not have been able to take over as Governor. It was precisely because the German government could not move Havenstein that it had to set up a cabinet ministerial "monetary committee", which was in fact a separate body, and as a result two central banks emerged in Germany at the same time, each issuing its own mark, which was a world spectacle. Of course, Schacht has done a good job of suppressing hyperinflation, and there is no substitute for competence and prestige. Havenstein's poor performance in dealing with hyperinflation is also well known to the world, and I'm afraid he himself is embarrassed to continue to rely on the position of central bank governor under enormous government and popular pressure.

Just as Norman thought about it and didn't know how to word his rejection, Schacht seemed to read Norman's mind. There was a pause for a moment, and Schacht threw out a trump card that he had pondered so hard, a temptation that Norman could not refuse. Schacht, in the name of the German government's currency policy makers, declared that the German Central Bank is prepared to use the pound as a currency reserve asset! Not only that, but the loans granted are also denominated in pounds!

That's a direct hit to the bullseye from Schacht! Norman didn't hesitate to say yes – to borrow money.

Britain's currency "water turned to oil": foreign exchange reserves landed

After the end of World War I, Norman's greatest anguish was how to stuff the pound into the reserve assets of other central banks. It was with this in mind that Schacht saw to it that the seemingly impossible task was accomplished with ease.

Today, it may seem common sense to have foreign exchange reserves as the monetary reserves of national central banks and to issue national currencies as collateral, but, in 1922, the concept was absolutely unthinkable! In the traditional gold standard, the central bank's main monetary reserve is the vast majority of gold and short-term domestic paper, and only gold assets can satisfy the three characteristics of high liquidity, ease of exchange and international recognition.

In the gold standard mechanism, central banks are primarily concerned with gold reserves and rarely, if ever, actively intervene in financial markets if not for huge market turmoil (such as massive gold outflows). In a gold standard, the price, interest rate, credit, fiscal and trade balances are largely self-adjusting. Each country's currency has its own legal basis for gold content, all currencies are on par with gold, and exchange rate fluctuations are virtually non-existent. From the beginning of the 19th century until the outbreak of World War I, the gold standard monetary system laid down by the British Empire greatly facilitated world trade and economic development. The industrial revolution and urbanization, in the first wave of globalization, quickly propelled the fruits of Western civilization to all corners of the world. In the absence of mass wars and revolutions for nearly half a century, new technologies, represented by railroads, shipping and telegraphs, have been rapidly changing, international trade has flourished and global capital has flowed freely. The gold standard pushed the West to the pinnacle of civilization as never before.

However, development is destined to be uneven. Germany surged, the United States came to dominate, and the British Empire of the early 20th century was already the oldest of the old. Increasing fracture pressures are building up in the seemingly stable strata, and the fires of the earth are screaming out. The First World War, was the total outbreak of this huge economic disruption energy. The productive capacity of society was largely redirected to military industry and then destroyed by each other in the heat of battle. Global trade collapsed, world markets were fragmented, and more importantly the global capital flows that kept the gears of the world economy turning stopped. The failure of the gold standard has led to a serious over-issuance of paper money in various countries, with prices rising in turn, and an extreme imbalance in the gold reserves of countries that were roughly in balance.

In 1913 the four pre-war economic powers – the United States, Britain, Germany and France – had a total of $5 billion in gold reserves, with the United States having the most at $2 billion, Britain at $800 million, Germany at $1 billion and France at $1.2 billion.[3] Note that these gold reserves are not all in the hands of central banks, and commercial banks and currency in circulation also account for a large proportion. Interestingly but reasonably, the distribution of the four countries' gold reserves is roughly comparable to the size of their economies, with the slight exception of France, whose total gold reserves rose to $6 billion in 1923 as gold production increased, but the distribution was sharply distorted. As a result of risk aversion during the war, a total of $2 billion of gold from Europe flooded into the United States, which saw its gold reserves soar to $4.5 billion, the United Kingdom slightly reduced, France lost more, and Germany lost the most.

The post-war European countries were one after the other preparing to return to the gold standard, and the British Empire was in the most awkward position. If London is to regain its position as the world's financial centre, the pound must return to pre-war levels of value, and only then will it be credible, the cornerstone of finance being credit. But the UK currency has doubled in size and, apparently, there is a surplus of sterling notes compared to gold reserves. In the face of the United States, where gold is absolutely dominant, the UK's financial hegemony can be said to be doubly stressed. If the pound continues to weaken, sooner or later the world's economies and trade finance will go to a stronger dollar, global capital will converge on New

---

[3] Ibid.

York, and the financial empire that has been so painstakingly run for 200 years will never be the same. The loss of financial hegemony, the British Empire's status as the organizer of global trade, the monopoly of internationally settled currencies, and the pricing privileges of commodity markets will gradually disintegrate, and even the continental Commonwealth system will be able to sustain itself, and the imperial navy will still have the financial power to protect the world's oceanic passages, all of which are in terrible doubt.

Norman, at the helm of finance in the British Empire, thought hard and thought long and hard about how to solve the gold shortage dilemma. Ultimately, his only way out was to stiffly treat the pound note like gold, persuading and forcing nations to accept it, adding the pound to their central bank money reserve assets, in addition to gold. In 1922, guided by this line of thinking, the financial committee of the League of Nations, a British-led organization, formally recommended to the nations at the Genoa Conference the new British currency, the pound sterling note, which was identical to gold. It's like the "water to oil" moniker in the world of money. Water can't be oil, and paper pounds can't be gold! Ultimately, paragraph 9 of the Genoa Conference resolution explicitly calls upon States to "establish a new international practice whereby foreign exchange may be held in currency reserves for the purpose of saving gold".[4]

For the first time in the history of world currencies, the concept of foreign exchange reserves made its grand debut.

Norman invented a new monetary mechanism, which was the gold exchange standard. As the name suggests, it is the gold plus foreign exchange (convertible gold) standard system. Henceforth, central banks and commercial banks of all countries, in the future, will create money and credit with gold and foreign exchange as collateral.

In fact, anyone with a good eye can understand that this is not a place where there is no silver for 300 taels? If the UK has enough gold, why increase foreign exchange as a currency reserve asset? Just use the gold and you're done. Because of this, the concept of foreign exchange reserves promoted by the Normans is not smooth, and everyone will be suspicious of the concept of this currency "water to oil". After several

---

[4] Jacques Rueff, *The Monetary Sin of The West*, THE MACMILLAN COMPANY, 1972. p. 22.

efforts, the rest of Europe did not immediately buy in, except for the colonial possessions of the British Empire and the small economies of Austria and Hungary, which were plagued by hyperinflation after the war.

How could Norman not be overjoyed when Schacht, representing Germany, Europe's largest economy, asked Mark to throw himself into the arms of the British pound at a fraction of the cost of $25 million?

However, Norman still has a glimmer of concern, the lack of gold has led to the weakness of the pound, while the dollar with gold reserves five times the pound is coveting the king of the currency.

The Americans are really here.

The dollar has taken over, and Mark is in love with the new big money

On November 30, 1923, just as Schacht's ground-rental-mark defense battle was beginning to bear fruit, the keen nose of the Americans sniffed out opportunity and American bankers Dawes and Owen Young strutted to Europe. As American representatives of the Allied "Compensation Commission", they had come to investigate why the simple matter of paying off debts was so complicated by the Europeans.

Dawes was a famous cannon barrel who was in charge of logistical resupply for the American Expeditionary Force in Europe during World War I. After the war, the U.S. Senate held hearings to investigate unclear and costly accounts for U.S. logistics supplies. At the hearing, Dawes was overwhelmed by the senators' questions and finally burst into a rage: "To hell with it, we didn't go there to get a perfect set of ledgers, we were bleeding to win the war!"[5] Dawes' swagger stunned the hearings and has since gained notoriety. In fact, his profession is that of a banker.

---

[5] Charles Gates Dawes, Wikipedia, World War I Participation.

In September 1915, Morgan led a $500 million "Anglo-French loan"[6] for the Anglo-French Allies, arguably an unprecedented deal on Wall Street, but American anti-war sentiment was strong and European war bonds were not selling well. Especially in the Midwest, only one bank in Chicago was willing to get involved in Wall Street's war bond underwriting, and that was Dawes' bank. Since then, he has been affectionately regarded by Morgan as "one of his own". Dawes has been in the news since he was in the European media, but the man behind him, Owen Young, is the one who gets down to earth and does his job.

Before Dawes was a dizzying bill of national revenues and expenditures to guide the development of war debt repayment plans. Before the war, the U.S. economy was the largest, with a GDP of about $40 billion, equivalent to the sum of Britain, France and Germany. The war reduced the economies of France and Germany by 30 percent, Britain by less than 5 percent, and the United States made war money. By 1919, the U.S. economy was 50 percent larger than the three nations combined. Since Germany's pre-war GDP was $12 billion, we can try to calculate the size of the economies of the four countries in 1913 and 1919, respectively. Every day these drowsy numbers drift past Dawes' eyes.

More complexity lies ahead. Britain spent a total of $43 billion in the war, of which $11 billion went to finance these poor friends of France, Russia. It raised $9 billion from tax increases, about 20 per cent of the cost of the war, and borrowed $27 billion at home and abroad, the remainder of which could only be printed. With a total war expenditure of $30 billion, the French are known as the most tax-resistant people in the world, and would rather die than raise taxes, thus contributing less than 5 per cent of the tax revenue. The French middle class hates taxes, but loves to save, and they have subscribed to the 15 billion national debt. Given the scale of the French casualties, the United States and Britain had the moral imperative to shed some blood and lend France a total of $10 billion, leaving the remainder of the difference to the printing of bills. Germany's war cost $47 billion, 10 percent of which was contributed by taxes, and lacking the sophisticated financial markets and strong financing capabilities of Britain and the

---

[6] Ron Chernow, *The House of Morgan, An American Banking Dynasty and the Rise of Mordern Finance*, Grove Press, New York, 1990. p197.

wealthy middle class of France, Germany ended up relying on printing money. During the war, there was twice as much British money in circulation as before the war, three times as much in France and four times as much in Germany!

In total, Europe spent an astonishing $200 billion in WWI!

Finally, Dawes finally got his head around the debt: 16 European allies owe the United States a total of $12 billion, with Britain owing $5 billion and France $4 billion. And 17 countries owe Britain another $11 billion, France $3 billion, and Russia $2.5 billion,[7] a debt that went down the drain after the October Revolution.

Germany, the main defeated country, paid a total of $12.5 billion in war reparations.

The Europeans would easily conclude from this comparison of numbers that Germany's war reparations were almost the total of Europe's debt to the United States, and that as long as the Germans could pay them back, we could pay them back to the Americans. Of course, since Germany couldn't afford to pay, we had to drag it out.

Americans are depressed when they think about it, why do you Europeans fight and we pay for it? The United States is not donating money for charity, but for business loans. How can a business loan be confused with war reparations, a business is a business. It's your problem if you don't get paid by Germany. You owe us money, not a penny less! You can't repay the loan, you have no credit, shame on you!

The British Empire, as the financial centre of the world, has more credit than life, and it is worse than killing the British for not keeping their word. Before the war, in the eyes of high-minded British bankers, their American counterparts were dirtbags with money and no taste. After the war, the wealthy Americans cursed the British for not repaying their money and credit, provoking both anger and resentment among the British. The British media deplored the fact that the United States had delayed in entering the war and had deliberately made war money while watching its allies suffer such great sacrifices for the cause of freedom, and that if the United States had morals and conscience, it

---

[7] Michael Hudson, *Super Imperialism – New Edition: The Origin and Fundamentals of U.S. World Dominance*, Pluto Press; New Edition (March 21, 2003), Chapter one.

should have taken the initiative to reduce its debt. Now you have the audacity to call on your comrades in the post-war depression, it's a modern day "Sherlock"! So "Uncle Sam" was spoofed by Europeans as "Uncle Sherlock". "Ninety percent of French people think the United States is a selfish, heartless and greedy country," reports the New York Times in Paris. American diplomats in London found that the vast majority of Britons found American policy to be selfish, vile and shameful.

The United States has historically been a country where pragmatism reigns supreme, and moral evaluation means nothing to pragmatists. When someone is in debt, the United States hates to take a knife and cut that person with a pound of flesh, but when it's its turn to owe money, it's just a matter of rolling around and printing money, as much as it can. In comparison, Old Gentleman Britain is a little more generous.

It's the Americans who suffer when they quarrel and don't get paid. Dawes is on this trip for one purpose only, to tie Europe to the waistband of his pants with dollars!

Although the United States officially refuses to acknowledge that the money owed by Europe to the United States has anything to do with German reparations, in reality, any substantial breakthrough in debt collection can only be achieved through German reparations, which is really a puzzle that can be cut and dried. The victorious nation forced the amount of compensation on Germany that Germany simply could not afford to pay, and the result of that force was that the German economy went bankrupt, and it did. In the four years after the war, the Allies had 88 German reparations meetings, and everyone was eventually dragged out. At this point, Dawes introduced a completely new concept, which is that "ability to pay" is most important. How does one define Germany's ability to repay? It's the tax burden. The tax burden of war debt borne by the Germans should be comparable to that of England and France. Dawes' strategy of "setting aside the total amount of the payout, with a roughly equal tax burden" has finally opened the impasse.

However, France has now become a clear stumbling block. The French were unusually entangled and obsessed with German reparations, since the defeat of the Franco-Prussian War had resulted in a huge French reparation of 5 billion francs to Germany, a debt that had been plunged like a sharp knife into the hearts of the French, a humiliation that had escalated into a national feeling. The Germans had to pay first or the French would never withdraw from the German Ruhr industrial zone. Obviously, without this coal-steel production centre in Germany, the whole economy loses its engine, and there is still no way to talk about payouts.

This time, the Americans are in a real hurry! Morgan, Dawes' "own man", had finally lost patience with French obstinacy. At this point, Morgan was no longer the little heel of the pre-war British bankers, but the financial bigwig of the hegemonic side. Strength dictates mentality, Morgan pats on the back, the Frenchman must give in! Soon, something happened to the franc!

Before the war, the dollar was 1:5 to the franc, in 1920 it was 1:15, and at the beginning of 1924 the franc fell to 1:20, and when France persisted and refused to withdraw, on 14 January the franc plunged 10 per cent a day! France still wouldn't budge, and on March 8, the franc fell to 1:27. French financial markets were in turmoil as traders, banks, and the middle class began to flee franc assets on a massive scale. The French government angrily slammed shameless foreign exchange speculators as allies in the conspiracy, and on March 13 it had to turn to JPMorgan to borrow $100 million to stabilize the situation. But JPMorgan let the wind out through the grapevine that the French government had to accept the Dowis plan. When the French government was forced to go soft, the franc immediately rebounded from 1:29 to 1:18, a wild 60% rise in two weeks! For the first time, people have seen the enormous power of financial weapons in international politics.

The Dawes Plan is finally out. The Americans offered quite generous terms: the total amount of the payout would be left aside, $250 million for the first year, then increasing year by year to $600 million a year by the end of the 1920s. In practical terms, this amounts to a reduction in total German compensation from $12.5 billion to $8 billion to $10 billion.

That's not really the point. The opponent in America's mind is actually the British!

Under the banner of "no destabilization of the mark", the Dawes plan proposed that the reparations should be raised by the German Government in marks and deposited in a special supervisory account of the German Central Bank, to be supervised by a commissioner appointed by the Commission on Reparations and to decide whether it would be possible to "safely" convert the marks into foreign currency or to buy German products to pay off the debt, and that the money could even be used to lend to German companies! Apparently, this commissioner's position is the equivalent of Germany's economic overlord! Who's going to sit in this chair? Britain, France, and Germany are in a debt-to-debt relationship, and it's unfair whoever is, only the Americans have no preconceived notions, so it's most appropriate. At the same time, the Americans promised to finance $200 million of the $250 million of German debt to be repaid in the first year, part of which was used to replenish the Bundesbank's monetary reserves to stabilize the value of the mark.

When the Englishman heard of this plan, he could not help but be furious and evil to his heart's content! Mark was about to swoop into the arms of the pound, but at the critical moment, he killed a dollar bill and robbed the German currency reserves of their power. This humiliation is like taking a wife! Just as it was about to kick in, the United States asked Germany, with a grin on its face, who would you like to follow?

Schacht immediately clung to the dollar lap and bargained with the US for as much independence as possible from the mark. The final scenario was that the Reichsbank would be independent of the government and that the government would have no authority to make personnel adjustments during the term of the governor; that the Reichsmark would replace the Rentenmark; that the Dawesian planned to provide 800 million Reichsmarks to replenish the Bundesbank's capital; and that the Bundesbank's currency reserves would consist of 3/4 gold and 1/4 foreign exchange, with currency reserves not less than 40% of all currency in circulation and total bank savings. The natural dollar rules in foreign exchange. The German central bank to engage in gold reserves, the United States does not oppose, because the gold chips are concentrated in the hands of the Americans, the dollar is equal to gold, "to lower the Han is to lower the Cao", subjugated to gold is also equal to subject to the United States. What's more, once the Dawes plan is launched, there will be a massive influx of US capital into Germany and the German commercial banking system will be flooded with dollars.

What makes the British even more angry is that this is not a compensation package, it is clearly a plan to finance Germany's rise again! German reparations collected in marks and deposited in the German Central Bank, when to exchange foreign exchange, can be "safe" to exchange, the Americans say. The Americans had every right to allow this so-called payout to be lent again to German industry, thus strengthening the German economy. Isn't the reason why Britain fought four years of war with Germany, because Germany wanted to challenge the hegemonic system of the British Empire? What on earth is the United States doing to defend Germany like this?

The Americans had another layer of calculations, and I'm afraid Britain didn't react at the time. The U.S. provided dollars to Germany, which Germany used to first develop its economy and then compensate Britain and France; Britain and France then used the dollars to pay off U.S. debts. The dollar leaves the United States, travels around the world and then returns to the United States, which may seem superfluous, but is actually the strategic layout of the United States. The fundamental purpose of the international march on the dollar is to dollarize the German mark, to penetrate the dollar into the European economies and to gradually develop dependence on the dollar.

What the US really wants is to tie Europe to its own belt with dollars!

Keynes discovered that the dollar is overturning the gold standard

"The power of economics, whether correct or not, is often unexpected. What actually rules the world is just these thoughts. Many of those who think they do not accept the influence of any ideology are often long slaves to some deceased economist."[8]
—Keynes

The UK is short of gold and is naturally an active advocate of the gold exchange standard. The Americans are not averse to the gold exchange standard, but are optimistic about its success, because the US gold dominates overwhelmingly, the dollar is stronger than the pound, and the dollar is certainly more favored than the pound when countries are increasing their foreign exchange as a currency reserve option, the natural result of which is that the dollar exceeds the pound as a

---

[8] John Maynard Keynes, *The General Theory of Employment, Interest and Money.*

proportion of countries' reserve assets, thus establishing the future hegemony of the dollar.

However, the massive influx of gold has also brought a "burden of happiness" to the United States. This is because under the traditional gold standard, a large increase in gold would lead to a problem of forced increases in dollar credit, which would induce inflation. This is the same as the current oversupply of foreign exchange reserves in China, which has resulted in the forced over-issuance of the yuan.

The essence of central bank money issuance and commercial bank credit creation is an act of buying assets. When $2 billion worth of gold fled from Europe to the United States, the U.S. banking system will actively or passively "eat" the gold, and "spit out" in dollar bills or bank credit. When these banknotes and credits come into circulation, they will push up prices because the supply of commodities has not yet had time to increase. Thus, during World War I, it was not the material losses caused by the war, but the increase in the money supply that pushed up prices in the United States by 60 percent. And after the war, with the European economy in the doldrums and gold still continuing to flow into the US, the Fed finally couldn't sit still.

And the actual power of the Federal Reserve is actually manipulated in the hands of 12 Federal Reserve banks, notably the Federal Reserve Bank of New York, which has the big name Benjamin Strong at its helm. Strang was the head of JPMorgan, and worked closely with the Governor of the Bank of England, Norman, and the Governor of the German Central Bank, Schacht, who were known as the "Three Musketeers" of the world financial world in the 1920s.

Strang watched as a shipment of gold arrived in New York by ship from Europe and then flooded into New York's bank vaults like a flood, with the result being flooded credit and skyrocketing prices. He is determined not to let the gold rush hit the dollar dike so hard that he must contract the money supply to ease the upward pressure on prices.

When the Fed was in its infancy, its primary means was to influence the credit environment by adjusting the discount rate. Any bank that joins the Federal Reserve system can apply for a loan from the central bank through the discount window, and the discount rate is the rate at which the central bank is willing to provide such a loan. When the central bank raises the discount rate, it discourages the urge of commercial banks to take money from the central bank because the cost is higher.

But this method didn't work well in the early 1920s. Because gold is coming so hard in Europe, banks throughout New York have been flooded with bullion, and gold is where the bankers make their money, so there is already too much money in the market for banks to have to go to the central bank's discount window to borrow money. Strang adjusted the discount rate but couldn't stem the flood of credit that kept being created.

He must find more effective ways to directly control the money supply. As a result, Strang pioneered a way for central banks to pull back the currency by selling their treasury assets to the market. Similarly, if the market is short of money, the central bank creates money to buy assets and inject dollars into the market. This is what is now known as open market operations.

What Strang did at the time definitely counts as treasonous. In the gold standard, gold is the most central asset, and its proportion should have an absolute advantage, while other assets (e.g., treasury bonds, commercial paper) are only ancillary assets. But the result of this "operation" by Strang will be an increasing share of Treasuries in central bank assets, which will fundamentally reverse the basic definition of monetary reserve assets.

Why must central banks rely primarily on gold for their monetary reserves? Under the gold standard, the gold content of money is determined by law, and when central banks create money to buy assets or sell assets to bring back money, if the assets are gold, the assets and money are always equal in value when exchanged. This principle that the exchange of assets and currency must be equivalent is in fact the cornerstone of the balance and stability of the central bank's assets and liabilities. Replacing gold with national debt, which is always subject to direct or indirect default, would fundamentally dismantle the core of monetary stability, creating a potential misalignment of the real price of the central bank's money in exchange for assets and a natural tendency for currency devaluation.

Of course, the banking system clearly welcomes such innovation. Also as a bank asset, gold is stable but has no interest income; national debt is unstable but has cash flow. The national debt is the collateral for the future taxation of the entire population, as long as people work, the government has tax revenue, and if tax revenue exceeds fiscal expenditure, the cash flow of the national debt is guaranteed. Bankers' support for national debt as a substitute for gold is heartfelt, and national debt, as a core asset of the banking system, provides both a basis for lending and an interest income. In this way they will have two sources of profit: one is the interest charged through lending and the other is the interest on the national debt which transfers part of the universal tax to the financial system.

In turn, when gold money metamorphoses into debt money, there will be a serious side effect of money in circulation, which is the problem of double interest costs. Not only did people have to pay interest on the borrowed currency, but they also had to pay interest again on the collateral for the currency. Under the debt-money system, money becomes a burden for economic development. Society has to pay interest costs to a few people in order to use public money. Deadlocking the national debt to the currency is a design that cannot be logically convincing. At the same time, it is also a monetary system that has "cancerous information" in its genes. The larger the currency issue, the larger the debt, the higher the interest costs and the greater the pressure on the population to be "indebted". Since interest is only related to time, monetary expansion presents an endogenous rigid demand with a natural tendency to devalue the currency, and inflation will be the ultimate corollary. The "invisible hand" of inflation, which leads to the redistribution of wealth in society, is responsible for the worldwide polarization of the rich and the poor.

There is no love in the world for no reason, and no hate for no reason. The bankers' hatred of gold is profit-driven and logical. They constantly proclaim the uselessness of gold to society as a whole through the media, and they spread the idea that gold is only a barbaric relic to generations of students through their schools. Their aversion to gold and love of debt is actually rooted in the amazing benefits they share in the debt monetary system.

Strang's open market manipulation acted precisely to take advantage of America's absolute superiority in gold, paving the way for the eventual subversion of the gold standard.

On the other side of the Atlantic, another man who is also keeping a close eye on Strang's innovations is the discerning Keynes. Keynes saw in Strong's move not only the dangers of a gold standard, but also the dangers of financial hegemony in the British Empire, and from 1922 on, Keynes warned repeatedly, stating clearly in A Tract on Monetary Reform, published in 1923:

"A dollar standard is being plucked from the foundation of material wealth. For the past two years, the U.S. appears to be defending the gold standard, but in fact, they have established a dollar standard."[9]

In Keynes's view, the United States is "holding gold hostage to its vassals". While the United States has 75 per cent of the total gold reserves of the four economic powers and the currencies of other countries are in gold famine, the United States is burying the role of gold through open market operations and the dollar is doing its own thing depending on its economic situation. The real purpose of the US urging everyone to maintain the gold standard is to have the currencies of the UK and other European countries follow the Fed's baton and eventually develop a dependence on the dollar. If it continues in this way, won't the financial hegemony of the British Empire fall to Wall Street?

It should be said that Keynes' fierce attack on the gold standard also contained concerns about the fate of the British Empire.

In fact, the dollar is not only subverting the pound on the front lines of the reserve currency, but it is also meandering away from the trade settlement flank.

Trade settlement, dollar flanking blow

The pre-war British Empire was a veritable "world banker", although the total economic volume of the United States has reached 40 billion dollars, roughly equivalent to the sum of Britain, Germany and France, but Britain controls a huge overseas assets of up to 20 billion dollars, including a large number of investments in the United States, Britain is the largest creditor in the world. Berlin, Paris, and New York are not the same financial centers as London. In addition, Britain had a vast colonial economic system in Africa, the Middle East, Asia, the Americas and Oceania, with vast natural resources at the mercy of the British, and a vast colonial market entirely open to British industrial goods. Britain also has the most powerful navy in the world, controlling almost every major waterway in the world. The ships of world trade

---

[9] John Maynard Keynes, *A Tract on Monetary Reform*, 1923.

traveled across the oceans under the protection of the British Empire Navy. The financial credit that drives international trade, 2/3 is pooled in London, with half of the world's long-term overseas investment originating in the UK.

Due to the size of the UK's international trade monopoly, London monopolized the world's commercial promissory note transactions, trade between countries is generally settled in pounds sterling, so that money orders can be quickly and cheaply converted into cash in London. The Bank of England's regulation of the credit markets is based precisely on the re-discount rate for commercial paper. In the early years of the Fed's existence, as the US international trade was much smaller than the UK's and the market for commercial bills of exchange had not yet developed, its discount window mainly served the lending of member banks, one of the biggest differences between the UK and US central banks.

Due to the early start and size of the UK commercial money order market and its obvious cost and reputation advantages, there seems to be no substitute for the pound sterling as a trade settlement denominated currency. But the outbreak of World War I instantly turned that pattern upside down. As the industrial and agricultural production capacities of the major European countries were increasingly destroyed by war, their demand for American industrial and agricultural products soared. At the same time, the war has led to a massive shift of financial capital to the military industry in warring countries and an increasing shortage of trade credit, with the result that European countries have turned commercial promissory notes to the well-funded New York market for discounting. Dollar-denominated commercial bills of exchange began to appear, and after 1915, when costly wars caused the value of the pound to fluctuate dramatically, and the dollar's huge gold reserves made the dollar more stable, traders, who instinctively loathed currency fluctuations, began to turn the pound settlement into a dollar settlement.

The United States has seized on this rare opportunity in a hundred years to actively encourage its banks to expand overseas. The government mandates that any U.S. bank with a capital of $1 million or more is eligible to establish an overseas branch and that U.S. banks must support U.S. trade going global. The law allows these banks to contribute up to 50% of their own capital to purchase commercial drafts.

At the initiative of the government, American banks embarked on an unprecedented international march. National City Bank of New York (the predecessor of Citibank) was first in line, and as soon as the war broke out, it immediately sent out a questionnaire to its 5,000 corporate clients, asking them to suggest where the bank's overseas branches would be most helpful to them in expanding their business locally. DuPont was interested in the huge arms business and was ready to build a plant in Chile, where the National City Bank immediately opened a branch, as well as branches in Brazil and Cuba, and further expansion into European and Asian markets through acquisitions. Other U.S. banks followed suit, and by the mid-1920s, it took just 10 years for U.S. banks to establish 181 overseas branches[10] with financial tentacles around the world. These overseas branches actively persuaded local importers and exporters, who had previously settled in pounds sterling, to settle in dollars instead, and to discount on the New York market. By this time, not only have European countries been using the dollar to settle their trade, but many countries in South America, Asia and Africa have also started using commercial bills of exchange denominated in dollars.

Massive volumes of commercial promissory notes eventually flooded New York for discounting, greatly exceeding the capacity of New York banks to carry the money. The so-called discount, that is, the holder of a commercial bill of exchange to the bank to get the bill of exchange for cash at a discount, the bank accepted the commercial bill of exchange, in fact, is the U.S. bank overseas branches of the guarantee has not been due and payable. The bank in New York buys at a discount, can hold it to maturity, and then go to the surety bank to collect the full amount, the discounted portion of this is profit. But a big problem arises here; New York banks also need to borrow money in order to eat such a large volume of money orders, and the cost of borrowing is often higher than the profit from eating it at a discount. Because U.S. investors are generally familiar with traditional commercial money orders, which are bills of exchange whose value is determined by the buyer and seller themselves and whose value depends on the credit of both parties, there is a greater risk of default and investors tend to

---

[10] Barry Eichengreen, *Exorbitant Privilege, The Rise and Fall of the Dollar and the Future of the International Monetary System*, Oxford University Press, 2011. p27-28.

demand deeper discounts, which leads to higher investment costs for money orders. However, the risk of a new type of commercial bill of exchange, with the bank as a third party guarantee, depends only on the credit of the bank, and the investor's risk is shared by the bank, the investment cost of such a bill of exchange, should be less than the traditional bill of exchange. As a result of this perception gap, the problem of bills of exchange stalling has become widespread, severely hampering the formation of a discounted market for bills of exchange.

Sensitively spotting the problem was Paul Warburg, the founder of the Federal Reserve. Warburg founded the "American Promissory Note Association" to educate investors on the fact that bankable commercial drafts are a very worthwhile new product that is less risky than traditional U.S. commercial drafts without bank guarantees, and that the cost of investing in such a low risk, high yield product should be lower. Warburg has worked on the scale and cost of capital entry into the commercial money order market, on the one hand, and the liquidity of the money order market, on the other. The Governor of the Federal Reserve Bank of New York, Mr. Strang, is the man he handpicked and groomed to be a great general, and Warburg strongly advised Mr. Strang to get involved in this market. Strang, after careful study of commercial drafts, found that in his open market operations, in addition to buying and selling treasury bonds, it was possible to add commercial drafts as a new monetary instrument, so that the control of the money supply would be more flexible.

The Federal Reserve Bank of New York turned on the full steam and ate the bills of exchange that had been silted up in the market on a large scale, allowing the banks to quickly dispose of the bills of exchange and the turnover of funds was greatly accelerated, thus increasing the banks' appetite for bills of exchange. The rediscount rate, as set by Strang, is the discount rate at which the central bank eats money orders from the banks to build a solid winning bottom for the money order market. As long as banks buy bills of exchange at a lower discount than they sell them to the central bank, the difference in the middle is the bank's profit. The intervention of the Federal Reserve Bank of New York has led to a faster turnaround of bank funds, which has greatly increased the level of profitability of banks buying and selling bills of exchange. Even national central banks have taken a fancy to this area of investment, and the Dutch central bank, at the request of its own flower and diamond exporters, has put $10 million of revenue from exports to the United States into the money order market.[11]

The rapid rise of the U.S. commercial money order market has made the U.S. dollar start to become a key currency in the international market. By the mid-1920s, more than half of U.S. import and export trade began using commercial drafts denominated in dollars. And the deep involvement of the Federal Reserve Bank of New York, so that the discounted cost of the New York bill of exchange is a whole percentage point lower than London, a steady stream of bills of exchange flew to New York like snowflakes.

After just 10 years, the formerly bustling London market for commercial bills of exchange is now cold in front of the door, while the formerly untold New York market is booming with a thriving crowd. By 1924, the total amount of commercial bills of exchange denominated in dollars had more than doubled that denominated in sterling.

Before the war, the dollar's foreign exchange quotient was not even as exposed as the Italian lira and the Austrian shilling, let alone the pound, in the financial markets of each country, and ten years later the dollar has surpassed all other currency competitors.[12]

The year 1924 was an important turning point in the history of currencies, when the dollar fully broke through the defenses of the pound on the frontal reserve currency front, and for the first time the dollar's share of the foreign exchange reserves of the central banks of the countries exceeded the pound. On the flank of trade settlement pricing rights, beating the stubbornness of the pound. Since then, the dollar has completed its closing against the pound.

Forcing countries to return to the gold standard, the U.S. wants to "hold gold hostage to the vassals"

> *"Wrong economic thinking makes it difficult to see where one's interests belong. Therefore, what is more dangerous than the benefits is actually the ideas."*

---

[11] Ibid.

[12] Ibid.

—Keynes

Keynes already saw that the ultimate goal of the Americans was to subvert the monetary hegemony of the British Empire with a dollar standard. Gold is just a "Han Xian Emperor" in the hands of the United States, once the conditions are ripe, the dollar standard will abolish gold and claim the empire itself!

The United States' motive for strongly calling for, and even coercing countries to return to the gold standard as soon as possible is clearly not simple. In 1925, Britain barely resumed the gold standard, but fell into the American trap.

In just four years of war, the world has changed dramatically. While Britain defeated its hegemonic challenger, Germany, it depleted the economic resources for world domination. Throughout the nineteenth century, Britain exported capital to the world as a "world banker", premised on the trade advantages and capital surpluses created by the strong competitiveness of British industry. Long-term stable industrial capital accumulation is the guarantee of UK lending to the world, i.e. long-term savings to support long-term lending and progressive control of world resources, productive capacity and the wider market, creating a positive cycle. But the industrial rise of the United States and Germany in the late 19th century weakened Britain's industrial competitiveness and dried up London's potential to export capital to the world. World War I, on the other hand, fundamentally shook the British hegemon of capital export. After the war, in order to maintain its position as the world's financial centre, the pound had to stiffen up and British industrial competitiveness declined further. At the same time, the military costs of maintaining hegemony abroad remain high and the fiscal balance has deteriorated. The legacy of the war's currency overdraft and inadequate economic output has resulted in UK prices being 10 per cent higher than in the US, which has further undermined the world competitiveness of UK products. Simply put, the costs of maintaining imperial hegemony have outweighed the benefits it brings.

The restoration of the gold standard in Britain in 1925 actually exacerbated this fundamental contradiction. The scale of British capital exports abroad has returned to pre-war levels, but at a time when "world bankers" are relying heavily on short-term hot money savings to support long-term external lending, the potential for risk is much higher. The bully pound has been hollowed out from the bones.

It was precisely at this point that the United States played a major role in pushing and coercing Britain to return to the gold standard.

A plan that is capable of being accomplished is an ideal, one that is less capable is called a dream, and one that is powerless is a fantasy. Norman, the Governor of the Bank of England, apparently failed to distinguish between ideals, dreams and fantasies. Trying to regain the world dominance of the pound was only his dream, and trying to round it off by restoring the gold standard left Norman with nothing but fantasy.

But Norman's fantasies were strongly encouraged by the Americans.

On December 28, 1924, Norman arrived in New York quietly. In order not to be discovered by the media, he used a false name on board the passenger ship, and later American magazines described his trip as "unnoticed by anyone, like a figure in the dark of night".[13] However, there is no impervious wall under heaven. When a British journalist asked a Bank of England spokesman why Norman had been found in New York and what his purpose was in going to New York, the Bank of England officials were stunned, and it turned out that they had no idea that the governor had played the disappearances to New York.

By the time Norman stepped onto the docks of New York, his old friend Strong had been waiting there long ago. In the two weeks since, Norman has been surrounded by Strang and Morgan bankers who are launching a powerful round of offensives to press for Britain to return to the gold standard as soon as possible. In addition to the bankers, the U.S. government joined in the pressure on Britain, with Treasury Secretary Mellon telling Norman unequivocally that in January 1925, "the time had come" to restore the gold standard.

How important it was for the pound that Strang didn't have to lobby Norman for a return to the gold standard, because that was Norman's "ideal". Strang has only repeatedly stressed that the UK must act quickly and that the UK has "a few weeks at most, and months at best". Strang argued that the timing of the pound's return to the gold standard was just right, with political support from within the UK itself

---

[13] Liaquat Ahamed, *Lords of Finance*, The Penguin Press, New York, 2009.

and a helping hand from American capital, and in order to support the UK, the Fed had eased up on credit by mid-1924. At the same time, Strong also warned Norman that the window of time for restoring the gold standard was not wide and that Britain was about to start paying its debts to the US, which was bound to weaken the pound. And with credit easing coming to an end in the US, it will be costly for the UK to attract international capital to restore the gold standard.

Strang's prescription for Norman is "shock therapy", the long pain is worse than the short pain, the gold standard will make the UK economy more painful in the short term, but in the long term, will force the pound to adapt and adjust its price in the world market competition, the future of the UK economy is bright.

In order to put Norman off his worries and act immediately, Strong also offered generous terms, if the pound encounters difficulties, the Federal Reserve Bank of New York is ready to provide a loan of $200 million, in addition to JPMorgan and other U.S. bankers also promised to provide $300 million in reserve support.

Fearing that American money was not taken for nothing and that it would be held hostage in the future, Norman made a condition that the United States not interfere with the economic policies of the Bank of England, such as the size of credit or the setting of interest rates.

Americans are full of promises to come down.

In fact, American bankers have their own reckoning. Until World War I, they were mere henchmen to the British bankers, following the boss around the world. But after a night of riches, the mentality has changed drastically, the old bosses have been weak, now the minions are strong as oxen. The emperor takes his turn and comes to my house today. Since the opportunity to be the boss has come, why not be moved? Like the triads, it is customary for new bosses to take advantage of the old ones if they want to make a name for themselves.

Keynes was a bit like Qu Yuan, who described the consequences for Britain of the restoration of the gold standard. His central point was that the size of the US gold reserves dominated overwhelmingly, locking the pound to gold was tantamount to tying the pound's fate to the dollar, and the end result could only be to hand control of the British economy over to Wall Street.

As a result, Norman swallowed the American gold standard "shock therapy" pill, the economy has been in shock for 15 years, the five-year economic express of the European and American prosperity from 1924 to 1929 did not catch up, and after 1929 decade of the Great Depression did not delay the ship of thieves.

Gold Exchange Standard: The Root Cause of Liquidity

The gold exchange standard system was originally Norman's way of coming to the rescue, mainly to deal with the dilemma that Britain's gold reserves were no longer enough to support its position as a world financial centre, but it caused great trouble for the economies of all countries.

The gold exchange standard is inherently an unstable monetary system. The famous French economist Jacques Rueff, who served as an advisor to French President Charles de Gaulle, experienced firsthand the dramatic impact of the gold standard on the French economy in the 1930s. This innovation has created the world's current predicament," he noted. This currency system, known as the gold exchange standard, has been adopted in many European countries at the urging of the Financial Committee of the League of Nations. Under the system, the central bank is authorized to include not only gold and vouchers denominated in national currency in the currency reserve, but also to increase foreign exchange. While the latter goes into the assets of the host country's central bank, it is naturally deposited in the country of its origin."[14] of which, the last sentence is precisely where Luff's insight lies.

The real killer problem with using sterling and dollars as reserves for other countries' currencies is that when these foreign currencies flow into the country, they are automatically deposited back into the UK and US banking systems. In other words, the real position in foreign exchange never leaves the issuing country, and the foreign exchange inflows to countries are simply an increase in the figures on a shadow account. It's a very unnoticeable and rather roundabout concept.

Under the traditional gold standard, capital outflows are eventually settled in gold, with the inevitable result of domestic gold outflows. And under the gold exchange standard, liquidation can be done in foreign

---

[14] Jacques Rueff, *The Monetary Sin of The West*, THE MACMILLAN COMPANY, 1972

exchange and does not necessarily mean the flow of gold. Foreign exchange clearing, on the other hand, relies mainly on account clearing, unless the country to which the capital flows requires cash transportation.

So, how does account liquidation work? It is actually the capital inflowing country setting up a bank account in the exporting country, the capital exporting country subtracting a number from one account and adding a number to the account in the importing country and you are done. Although the importing country account is located in the banking system of the sending country, its ownership belongs to the importing country. Thus, the banking system of the importing country can create its own money supply on the basis of this "shadow account" of foreign exchange reserves. But the problem is that the money is simply an increase or decrease between two accounts that occur in the same banking system, with a decrease in one account implying an increase in the other, with the same total capitalization. Thus, capital-exporting countries can recreate money based on the same money. This is the problem of endogenous double credit creation in the gold exchange standard.

The same capital is used by both importing and exporting countries as the basis for credit creation, which means that the scale of credit has expanded significantly worldwide. The more widespread the implementation of the gold exchange standard, the larger the scale, the more serious the degree of credit proliferation, the result is a decline in lending standards, speculation, asset bubble expansion. The "boisterous twenties" in Europe and the United States were based on the era of credit bubbles created by this monetary system, and the Great Depression of the 1930s was its price!

In 1925, when Britain reluctantly restored the gold standard, both the pound and the dollar were freely convertible into gold, they became known as the hard currency of foreign exchange and formed the currency core state. Other countries, with the pound sterling and the dollar as their main currency reserves, issued their own currencies, thus becoming Anglo-American currency satellite countries. In this system of currencies, gold is like the sun, while the pound and the dollar are planets orbiting gold, and their satellite systems rely on the gravitational pull of money to move in the orbit of the Anglo-American economy.

In 1926, France was the only major power in this galaxy that had not yet returned to the gold standard, and the crisis of the franc began when the franc could not find its own orbit.

Exchange Rate Shockwave and the Battle of the Franc

Lafayette, here we come! Now, it's time to collect our debts.
—French cartoons popular in the 1920s.

In 1777, the young French aristocrat Lafayette, strongly infected by the American Declaration of Independence, came to the New World at the age of 20, committed himself to the American War of Independence, and forged a lifelong friendship with the American Founding Father Washington. He fought in many battles with great merit and was awarded the rank of Major General by the United States. After the victory in the American War of Independence, Lafayette rose to European fame and was twice awarded the title of "Honorary Citizen of the United States of America" by the United States. Lafayette's selflessness and heroism have become a symbol of American-French friendship. In the First World War, when the American General Pershing led the Allied forces into Paris, he came to Lafayette's grave to pay his respects with his "Lafayette, here we come!" This famous phrase spread throughout the United States and Europe, stirring up long-standing historical echoes in the hearts of Americans and French.

On July 11, 1926, more than two disabled French veterans in wheelchairs or assisted by nurses flooded to the door of the U.S. Embassy in Paris at the foot of the statue of the first President of the United States, Washington, filled with wreaths brought by the veterans. They're not here to pay their respects to America, they're here to protest! America's inexcusability in war debt has left the French with a grudge. What's wrong with President Colin Coolidge's line, "We pay for them to go to war?" It is a chilling display of indifference to the millions of dead and wounded soldiers of European allies such as France. What made the French more angry was that the dramatic devaluation of the franc made Americans flock to the country to buy French châteaux, paintings, expensive jewelry and other precious treasures that had been passed down for centuries. In Paris at the time, there were a whopping 45,000 Americans living there, and for $100 you could enjoy luxury in France. In July, a bus full of American tourists was attacked by a mob in Paris, and American tourists were often mocked and provoked by hundreds of people in downtown. The French media have compared Americans to "harmful locusts". The antagonism in popular sentiment between the United States and France was enough to trigger a diplomatic crisis.

The French government feels no better about Britain and the United States than it does about folk, and although France has finally finalized its war debt repayment agreement with the United States, it is still indignant that Britain and the United States did not see fit to save the franc crisis at the beginning of the year.

In 1926, France's economic fundamentals were stronger than Britain's, the finances were back in balance, and everything seemed to be going in a good direction, but the franc was like a kite with a broken wire, washed up in the foreign exchange speculation market. Since the franc is the only currency of the major Western countries that has not yet returned to the gold standard, it has become the object of concentrated international speculative capital hunting. In the summer of 1926, the franc fell again to 1:30, and the pressure on the franc was exacerbated by the frequent turnover of the French government, which exceeded $10 billion worth of French short-term debt.

The dramatic devaluation of the French franc alarmed the wealthy French middle class, and it was the free fall of the mark three years ago that triggered the German hyperinflation, which turned its value into water and the German wealth into water, and the past is still fresh in our minds! The French are keen to save, and much of that savings is invested in French Treasuries, whose plummeting franc means that the wealth invested in Treasuries is shrinking dramatically relative to the dollar and gold. French savers began to get wrapped up in speculative forces and sold off the franc like crazy.

The vicious devaluation of the national currency vis-à-vis gold and foreign exchange directly set off the inflation bomb. Prices began to soar at a rate of 2% per month, and the nightmare of German hyperinflation in 1923 was upon us!

Moro, the Governor of the Banque de France, who is on the verge of being appointed, is racking his brains for a way out of the franc crisis. He argued that the franc was different from the German mark of 1923, that Germany, as a defeated country, had a fiscal deficit that had worsened beyond all recognition, that the Ruhr was under French occupation, that the money supply was wildly inflated and that the economy was extremely depressed. And the problem with the franc was mainly one of confidence, France had renegotiated with the US and

Britain respectively to pay the war debt, the Americans finally accepted the French offer, the $4 billion dollar debt was cut by 60% and Britain agreed to reduce the $3 billion debt to $1.2 billion. France's finances have eliminated years of stubborn deficits, the return of investment in Alsace and Lorraine, the recovery of industry in the war-devastated regions of northern France, the completion of this massive $4 billion project, a sharp reduction in government spending, and future gains that should increase substantially. The Bank of France has established a legal limit of 41 billion francs for the currency in circulation, ensuring the stability of the franc's value. The real problem is the short maturity of French bonds, with recurring political scandals and change of government making short-term bond rolls subject to frequent crises of confidence.

To solve the problem of confidence, Moreau first thought of his own just took over the Bank of France, France's gold reserves of up to $1 billion is here, this is the world's second largest gold reserves after the Federal Reserve ah, once used, confidence crisis is not difficult to bear. However, the French government had already begged the Bank of France before, and the answer was – no way!

Founded in 1800, the Bank of France, unlike the Bank of England and the Federal Reserve, is a true temple of aristocracy, with 200 prestigious French families as its main shareholders, 44 of whom are dominant, the so-called "Gothic" families, whose power derives directly from family succession. From among them, 12 more directors were elected to assume the real power of the Bank of France. Among them, the Mallet, Mirabeau and Rothschild families have held their positions rock-solid for over 100 years. In those 120 years, three revolutions broke out in France, the polity changed five times, the head of state came out as an emperor, three kings, twelve presidents, and one went from president to emperor, but all the emperors, presidents, parliamentarians, and revolutionaries came to a screeching halt at the gates of the Bank of France, a puzzling historical puzzle indeed.

The franc crisis is on fire, and the central government of France has begged the Bank of France to redeem its national debt with gold reserves to curb the spread of the currency crisis, which the Bank of France has contemptuously refused. Blocked out by his own central bank, the French government had no choice but to beg for loans from the US and Britain to save the franc, and Strang and Norman didn't even lift an eyelid. The desperate French had to go to JPMorgan and other big international investment banks to beg for loans, and the bankers were hooting and hollering, but just wouldn't let go.

Moreau always felt that something was strange, he met alone with the Governor of the Federal Reserve Bank of New York, Strang, and finally came up with the answer. Strang offered two conditions: first, that the French government explicitly respect the independence of the Bank of France, and second, that the French Parliament ratify the new war debt repayment agreement as soon as possible. Moreau reached Norman, the governor of the Bank of England, again, and the answer was unanimous. It finally dawned on Moreau that although France's economy was better than Britain's, it was still a second-class citizen in the financial world. For the United Kingdom and the United States, financial aid is a "commodity" whose price will soar in times of crisis. By July 1926, the franc had depreciated to 1:50 against the dollar, and the franc was in danger!

On July 21, Raymond Poincaré came to power to form a cabinet with the support of French industrial giants, and also served as finance minister. This Poincaré is no slouch, having been in politics for more than 40 years, and is the oldest of all French politicians. He served seven years as a wartime president in World War I and three times formed a cabinet as prime minister. He was a strong ruler with a strong nationalist streak and became the staunchest of France's main warring factions in World War I. It was during his tenure that the French military occupation of the Ruhr industrial zone in Germany in 1923 was carried out. Poincaré has a great inspiration in the hearts of the French people and can be called the Bismarck of France.

The news of Poincaré's third term as prime minister of the government greatly boosted the morale of the franc in the foreign exchange market, and the French middle class believed in him, even worshipped him. As a result, the franc rebounded strongly against the dollar from 1:50 to 1:35 in a matter of days, appreciating by as much as 40%! All the foreign speculators who were short the franc were stunned!

Immediately afterwards, Poincaré announced a series of tax cuts that stabilized the panic of the French proletariat. He appeased the interests of big capitalists by announcing programs to stimulate industrial development and reduce government spending. The French capital that has fled in the last two years has begun to flow back to France on a large scale, and the French no longer need the assistance of foreign capital and have won the initiative for financial independence. It was only after the situation stabilized that Poincaré began to gradually increase taxes and improve the French fiscal situation.

Faced with a sudden trend of franc appreciation, Moreau was at a loss as to what to do. That the weak franc, long ridiculed by England and America, should appear far more imposing than the pound, surprised not only England and America, but made it difficult for the French themselves to adapt. To cope with the new problem of the appreciation of the franc, Moreau called on the famous French economist Lister and his student Quesnay to help the Bank of France develop a strategy for the stability of the franc.

By the end of 1926, the franc had already crossed the 1:25 mark against the dollar, and in only six months, the franc had doubled in value! The depreciation of the franc and the strengthening of the competitiveness of French industrial goods led to economic recovery and employment growth, but too rapid a depreciation shook franc confidence, stimulated capital flight and induced hyperinflation. If the franc appreciates too quickly, it affects French exports and weakens the French economy. What kind of exchange rate is the best state of stability that promotes economic development and stabilizes monetary confidence at the same time? Lister and Quesnay are precisely the intellectual engines of the Bank of France. France's predicament back then is also China's problem today.

If the 1:25 exchange rate were to rise, the Bank of France would have to intervene! Lister and Quesnay began to think outside the box and strongly demanded that the Bank of France put a cap on the appreciation of the franc. Because their ideas are so out of this world, there is no precedent for central banks to intervene in the foreign exchange market in this way, and Moreau is unwilling to eat the crab. At this time, the influx of foreign exchange into France is no longer a trickle, become a rolling river, the franc is forced to climb every day, seeing that the French economy is about to repeat the British overestimation of the pound brought about by the depression and deflation, Liszt and Quesné not hesitate to resign as blackmail, and urge Moreau to take decisive action.

Or did bystander Keynes see the problem for what it was:

> "The level of the franc (exchange rate) is not determined by speculators or the balance of trade, or even the risk-taking of the Ruhr district, but by how much of their own income the

French taxpayer is willing to put out to pay the French profit eaters (bondholders)."

In fact, if wealth is defined as the conversion of natural resources into final goods and services by human beings through labour, then society necessarily forms two kinds of people: labourers and profit eaters. Laborers create wealth through their labor, and profit eaters share in the wealth of laborers by renting out land, productive resources, monopolistic assets, public facilities, and capital.

The nature of the exchange rate is not an external issue, but rather an external feature of the institutional arrangements for the distribution of internal benefits. There are two extremes here: one extreme is that the distribution of benefits is heavily tilted towards workers, but not to the detriment of asset owners, then asset owners will tend to transfer assets abroad, international capital is more reluctant to enter, resulting in the formation of the foreign exchange market capital outflow than capital entry, the result is the depreciation of the local currency; the other extreme is that if the distribution of benefits is heavily tilted towards asset owners, then domestic capital is reluctant to flow out, and international capital will actively enter to share this beneficial distribution of benefits, at this time, there will be more international capital entry than domestic capital outflow, which ultimately reflects the appreciation of the local currency. And the difference between domestic and international productivity reflects only the size of the shareable wealth cake, not the proportion, and ultimately the scale of capital flows in and out, not the trend.

Both extremes would frustrate economic development, with the former leading to capital outflows and weakening the foundations of economic development, while the latter would frustrate labour motivation and reduce social spending power, and growth would be unsustainable. Either extreme will lead to a depression and the disintegration of the value of the local currency.

The optimal exchange rate is to find a stable equilibrium between the two extremes. At this level, the distribution of benefits between workers and profit-seekers is roughly balanced, with workers passionate about creating wealth and profit-seekers actively investing more, and international capital pouring in to expand the scale of resource investment and thus share the corresponding benefits. At the same time, after accumulating abundant capital, domestic asset holders actively seek new profit opportunities abroad, forming a general balance between capital inflows and outflows, and ultimately achieving a stable balance between labour and capital.

Simply put, in a state of free movement of capital and no intervention, the appreciation of the local currency reflects that profit eaters have the upper hand in the distribution of wealth, while the depreciation of the local currency implies that the distribution of benefits is biased in favor of labor.

After the war Britain and Germany went to two extremes, the former protecting the creditors with an overvalued pound, but strangling the economy; the latter bloodbathing the domestic proletariat with a viciously devalued mark, again destroying the economy. France, on the other hand, has found a balance between the two extremes.

On 21 December 1926, the Bank of France began to buy foreign currency in local currency on a large scale to curb the appreciation of the franc. Lister's efforts to curb the excessive appreciation of the franc met with fierce opposition from Rothschild and other Bank of France directors, and rumours circulated in France in the 1920s that "any party forming a cabinet had to consult Rothschild beforehand."[15] But Poincaré is not averse to this, and as Moreau's general backstage, he strongly supports Moreau and Lister's foreign exchange intervention policy. Moreau, under tremendous pressure, continued to buy foreign currency during the two years of 1927 and 1928, pinning the franc to the dollar at a level of 1:25. The French Ministry of Finance undertook to the Banque de France that all financial losses arising from foreign exchange intervention would be reimbursed by the French Treasury. Rothschild and others resorted to various means to undermine Moreau's plans, and in August 1928 Moreau was surprised to find that his telephone calls to and from the office of the Governor of the Banque de France had all been tapped. Moreau's relationship with Rothschild began to deteriorate tremendously.

As the French economy began a strong recovery on stable franc expectations and exports beat the UK to the punch, there was a split within the Bank of France's board, with the franc appreciation faction, led by Rothschild and French steel magnate Wendell, ultimately failing

---

[15] Liaquat Ahamed, *Lords of Finance*, The Penguin Press, New York, 2009. p. 245–246.

to gain the support of a majority of directors. The two men then set out to break with the practice of the Bank of France and publicly express their views on monetary policy in the hope of attracting international speculative capital to France on a large scale, thus forcing Moreau to abandon intervention in the market and allow the franc to appreciate. Rothschild even personally ordered the family's largest French railway company to buy the franc vigorously in an attempt to force it to appreciate, already suspected of violating restrictions on insider trading by Bank of France directors. In more than two years of intervention in the foreign exchange market, the value of French foreign exchange reserves, mostly sterling assets, has soared to $600 million.

What a turn of events, now it's Britain's turn to be ashamed. The French franc's fixed exchange rate strategy, French products have the world's strongest competitiveness, the British traditional market has been broken by French goods; and France's domestic price stability, economic prosperity, a great scene. The situation for the pound is getting worse, with a severe recession accompanied by high unemployment and accelerating capital flows from the UK to France. Norman strongly urged Moreau to come up with practical action to lower market expectations of the franc's appreciation and ease pressure on UK capital outflows. Morrow, on the other hand, suggested that the UK should raise interest rates to attract capital, which would clearly make the UK's decline even worse. Moreau pressed further, preparing to exchange the pound's foreign exchange reserves for British gold, and the pound became an instant surprise. Norman was furious and prepared to offer the French immediate repayment of their $3 billion war debt. The British and French were in a fight of attrition.

That's when the Americans whitewashed it again. As the peacemaker who mediated the Anglo-French currency dispute, the Americans suggested a truce between the two sides. Strang offered the U.S. proposal: that France still keep part of its sterling reserves and that the other part be exchanged for gold to France on the London market by the Federal Reserve Bank of New York and the Bank of England together. There are few conditions, only one, and that is a future increase in France's foreign exchange reserves, which must be shifted from the pound to the dollar. Americans are taking every possible opportunity to promote dollar reserves around the world.

France's economic and financial strength has been greatly enhanced by the correct application of the stabilization of the franc exchange rate, free from the traditional monetary theory.

By 1929, France's finances had improved dramatically, the Government had paid off all its debts to the Bank of France and the value of its bonds had doubled; in 1926 the French Government had a surplus of only 1 million francs, and in 1929 the accumulated fiscal surplus had reached 17 billion francs. France's currency reserves include up to $1.45 billion in gold and $1 billion worth of foreign exchange. Moreau and Lister were victorious in the battle for the defence of the franc. France's economic growth tenaciously resisted the first two years of the Great Depression, and it was not until the second half of 1931 that it was swept into a world recession.

Sliding down the economic rift valley, a vacuum of money power

"As long as the United States continues to lend generously to the world, thereby providing them with purchasing power that they do not possess themselves, Britain can continue to import from the United States and maintain exports to other countries. But as soon as anything happens that causes American investors and bankers to stop their lending to foreign countries, the UK's situation will become precarious. If Britain's credit runs out, its purchasing power will fall below the equilibrium limit of exports and debt service, and other countries will then experience the full consequences of the impoverishment of the German people."[16]

—Giorgio Pia

The economic crisis that swept the world in the 1930s was caused by only one thing: an unprecedented debt bubble created by an unprecedented monetary expansion, and the ultimate means of repayment was gold. Using limited growth gold to deal with infinitely inflated credit and debt will face liquidation sooner or later. The more severe the currency flood, the more staggering the eventual debt implosion will be. It is not a question of will and won't, but when and in what way a crisis will break out.

A major contributor to the proliferation of monetary credit is the gold exchange standard created by the UK to compensate for the

---

[16] Michael Hudson, *Super Imperialism – New Edition: The Origin and Fundamentals of U.S. World Dominance*, Pluto Press; New Edition (March 21, 2003), Chapter 3.

shortfall in gold reserves. Under this system, the dollar, pound sterling and gold are directly convertible, while other currencies are mainly held in reserve in dollars and pounds sterling, indirectly linked to gold. The fundamental problem brought about by the entry of foreign exchange reserves into national currency issuance, is the dual credit creation effect, foreign exchange exporting countries and foreign exchange importing countries respectively with the same capital to create their own credit, thus greatly increasing the total size of monetary credit worldwide. The inherent instability of this mechanism is reflected in the fact that when a crisis erupts in the most vulnerable peripheral countries, investors will race to sell their assets for scarce gold and foreign exchange; when gold runs out and foreign exchange is squeezed, this will inevitably trigger panic in the currency centre countries, which in turn will stimulate them to start selling assets for cash. Since the size of the asset bubble was much larger than the real cash flow, a sharp fall in its price would create a wild run on cash, where banks that had already been heavily leveraged could withstand the run, resulting in massive bank failures and a liquidity depletion. Bank insolvencies add to the perception that cash is insecure, thus accelerating the pressure on the entire banking system to run on gold, and the banking system that loses its currency reserves will react in chains, pulling down other banks in pieces. This led to a great depression in which companies went bankrupt and unemployment worsened significantly.

The United States is bound to face the dilemma of having more than enough to spare when it attempts to replace the gold standard that the United Kingdom has built up in 200 years with a dollar-based system that took 20 years. The United Kingdom, on the other hand, was exhausted in its efforts to defend its financial supremacy by defending its gold standard. While the dollar offensive has collapsed into a global rout, the pound has been left with no way back. With the loss of the world's lender of last resort, there is a vacuum in the power of money, the global trading system is broken, world capital flows are depleted, and the will to sustain the peaceful development of nations is lost. Like a society that has lost its government, that is limited in its mutual assistance, that is closed in on itself, that is robbed, and that is struggling to maintain its space, the world is in a state of total chaos. The hearts and minds of globalization have been dispersed and society has not been able to return to normal order for a long time. It was not until the outbreak of the Second World War that the will and passion of the Allies was revived.

The establishment of the dollar standard requires that nations must develop a demand for dollars, and the primary way in which this demand is developed is by insisting that Europe's war debt to the United States be paid. The United States had in fact abandoned the moral principles of President Wilson's participation in World War I, when Wilson's original words were, "We don't want to achieve any selfish goals, we don't want to conquer, we don't want to rule, we don't ask for reparations, we don't ask for any material compensation for the sacrifices made by freedom." It is estimated that the warring allies of Europe were moved to tears upon hearing this declaration of righteousness. It is not so much that the United States has fallen from a moral angel to "Uncle Shylock", but rather that the United States considers itself to be the result of a clever dollar strategy. With an initial face value of up to $20 billion, these debts already far exceed the total value of the world's gold reserves, a debt that in practice would be theoretically unpayable. And the strategic core of the dollar standard is to make it impossible for Europe to ever pay off its dollar debt in order to embed U.S. national debt into national monetary systems in the future.

To repay the U.S. debt, dollars are needed, and they can be obtained in several ways: (1) direct investment by the U.S.; (2) hot dollar inflows; (3) export surpluses to the U.S.; (4) borrowing more dollars from the U.S., creating a larger dollar liability. The dilemma for European countries is that direct investment in the dollar in a Europe that is extremely short of funds means that the dollar will sweep across Europe's industry cheaply and will make Europe a vassal of the United States in the future, and is therefore undesirable. And the dollar hot money, will undermine the financial stability of countries and even endanger the security of national currencies, which is a suicidal act to quench the thirst. When the first two options were ruled out, Europe could have relied on exports to the United States and traded goods for dollars to pay off its debts, but the sophisticated Americans had already seen this coming, so from 1921 to 1923, when Europe was ready to start paying its debts, the United States not only did not lower tariffs but kept raising them; in May 1921, the United States increased the emergency tariff on agricultural products, and in May 1922, the Forney tariff was introduced, raising the tariff on durable goods to 38 percent, more than double that of 1920. This keeps European goods out and blocks a third option for Europe. The last, and most hoped-for scenario for the United States, is that Europe keeps borrowing more and more dollars from the United States.

Private individuals or companies may go bankrupt, but the state will not, at least Americans were convinced of that in the first place. The Dawes plan was an elaborate US debt trap for Germany. As start-up capital, the $200 million loan from the United States to Germany in the first year not only grabbed the pound's exclusive hold on Germany's currency reserves, but also firmly held the throne of Germany's monetary and financial supremacy. The $3 billion of private capital that followed over the next two years made a big plunge into German industry. The entry of the dollar and the pound, under the new system of the gold exchange standard, became an important cornerstone of the German banking system to expand the mark credit, the larger the scale of the foreign exchange influx, the more amazing the German credit expansion. Behind the boom generated by the massive credit creation is a huge debt burden. In order to find more lending opportunities, American bankers "went to great lengths" to penetrate into Germany, persuading cities to take on dollar-denominated debt and build swimming pools, cinemas, stadiums and even opera houses. Witnessing the deepening of the dollar debt and the massive waste on projects that simply cannot generate dollar revenues to pay it off, German Central Bank Governor Schacht was anxious, knowing that Germany's short-lived false prosperity was in fact spawned by the dollar debt bubble and that Germany's real industrial capital accumulation under the pressure of war reparations and foreign debt could not be talked about. It will all end in economic ruin. Germany, the "subprime lender", has since become an important trigger for the crisis.

The most fundamental difference between the dollar standard and the gold standard is the way in which the native currency is cleared after international flows. Under a gold standard, dollar outflows would lead to gold outflows, with the result of weakening the size of U.S. monetary reserves and inhibiting domestic credit creation in the United States. The dollar standard would upset this equilibrium, with dollar outflows not reducing the domestic credit creation base, while dollar inflows increase foreign exchange reserves in countries, thereby expanding their money supply.

The Dawes project, which began in 1924, opened up a dollar loop game. The dollar flows into Germany, the mark will inflate, and there will be a brief economic boom, while German debt is amplified. Germany compensated the dollar to Anglo-French, which increased its foreign reserves and expanded its credit and debt simultaneously. By repaying U.S. debt in dollars again, the U.S. would receive more total principal and interest, which in turn would increase domestic credit and debt creation. Then the dollar flows abroad again, starting a new cycle. Each cycle brings more money supply in the countries through which the dollar flows, accompanied by a larger scale of debt, and the US itself is no exception.

It seems like a wonderful idea of perpetual motion. As long as American bankers are willing to lend generously to the world, the world economy can continue to prosper, and no one cares that the countries that borrowed the money are actually incapable of paying it back. This is a game of international "subprime" lending in the 1920s.

On July 7, 1927, Strong convened a secret meeting of the Federal Reserve Bank of New York on Long Island, New York. He didn't invite anyone from the Fed headquarters in Washington, where he will make a major decision to cut interest rates from 4 percent to 3.5 percent, prompting gold to flow to Britain. At this time the British gold reserves were being depleted and the gold standard was on shaky ground. And the US must not tolerate the collapse of the British gold standard. The unilateral decision to cut interest rates angered the Federal Reserve in Washington, which has the power to veto the decision of the Federal Reserve Bank of New York, but cannot force the Fed to change its policy, resulting in a split within the Fed. Not ignoring the Fed's infighting, Strang acted directly, injecting $200 million into open market operations from July through September, bringing the discount rate down to 35 percent. Wall Street boiled over, the stock market rushed to its final frenzy, and in the fourth quarter of 1927, foreign bond sales made history in the United States, and the dollar rushed abroad on an even greater scale.

All financial crises are debt crises, and all debt crises are prelude to a break in the funding chain.

By July 1928, the U.S. stock market had gone into a frenzy, with Wall Street making leveraged loans to stock investors of up to $7 billion at a dizzying 10% to 20% interest! The Federal Reserve Bank of New York, seeing that the bubble had reached an unmanageable point, had to immediately raise interest rates by 1.5 percentage points and interest rates soared to 5%. At this time the dollar overseas was stunned, the United States interest rates are so high, Wall Street usury is even more tempting, the dollar began to flow back sharply. The ring of dollars that supported the world's prosperity has finally broken.

The naked Germany was immediately exposed and the German economy immediately fell into the abyss of recession. Germany had to start controlling capital outflows while limiting imports. Immediately, London's financial markets panicked as Britain, with up to $1 billion in investments in Germany and Central Europe, now faces a freeze. The sudden high interest rates in the U.S. immediately started a massive outflow of gold from London, and the U.K. was forced to raise rates to ease that pressure. The decline in the UK has been even more severe.

By October 1929, the United States was finally at the point where its own debt bubble collapsed. At this point, the total debt size of the United States economy has reached 300 per cent of GDP. This pyramid of debt has to swell to stay afloat, and the scale of this debt payment has far exceeded the means of payment that gold can provide, and the American debt game has become a classic Ponzi scheme. As the peripheral countries fell into crisis and recession one after another, U.S. banks found out the problem was not good, and when they were ready to start recovering such a huge pyramid of debt, stock prices crashed. The U.S. economy is in a long recession.

After the first round of crises in 1929, the world economy entered a short period of silence, an even more frightening silence, with only a crack in the debt-damaged lake, and in May 1931, the general dike broke. With the collapse of Austria's largest bank, the German banking system was instantly overwhelmed by a flood of run-offs. Immediately afterwards, the British gold standard collapsed, France was finally swept into a vortex of decline by the crisis, and one after another crises broke out in Japan, Italy, Central Europe, South America, and other countries of the Commonwealth.

From 1914 to 1933, the dollar's first expedition for world currency hegemony ended in failure. The dollar, while defeating the global hegemony of the pound, was powerless to establish a new system of monetary domination. After the Great Depression, the countries suspended the war debt repayment, resulting in a dramatic decline in the control of the dollar on Europe; the break in the world trade chain, making the dollar in the international settlement of the influence of the serious shrinkage; although the dollar controls the gold "Han Xian Emperor", but the pound is rid of the gold, no longer recognize the "Han Dynasty".

The pound, although no longer the king of money, was still a major ceded vassal with its own army. After Britain abandoned the gold standard, the Commonwealth countries spread over all continents, including Sweden, Denmark, Norway, Finland, Portugal and Greece in Northern Europe, Egypt in Africa and Japan in Asia, as well as South American countries that maintained important trade relations with Britain, followed in Britain's footsteps and broke away from gold, which in fact formed an enormous "pound sterling area". They no longer listen to the dictates of the United States gold "Emperor Han Xian", but under the free-floating pound as an ally, to establish a strong intraregional trade system. They still control the world's supply base for raw materials, energy, monopolize a huge share of the world market, hold the main sea lanes of the oceans, and the mighty British Navy remains their protector. When America came to its senses, it was not the dollar that surrounded the pound, but the pound that surrounded the dollar around the world! The pound is now freer and stronger.

The dollar's nascent ambitions have suffered a serious setback! The Americans have finally figured out that the dollar cannot finally dominate the world without completely smashing the powerful pound zone system!

CHAPTER II

The regency, the pound sterling

In 1931, the British pound was freed from the shackles of the gold standard, relying on the "imperial preference system", formed a strong pound sterling power, spread from the three British islands to Africa, North America, Asia and Oceania, the vast colonial possessions, if you include Britain's major trading partners, such as Sweden, Denmark, Norway and Finland in northern Europe, Portugal and Greece in southern Europe, Iraq in the Middle East, Egypt in Africa, Asia and South America, the vast size, population and resources of the pound sterling area, constitutes a serious challenge to the world hegemony of the dollar.

Since the Great Depression, the United States has been left to fend for itself, and isolationism has been more of a realistic option for the United States than an active relinquishment of world leadership. The root cause of the delay in the recovery of the American economy was a misunderstanding of the nature of the crisis and the wrong response to it; when Roosevelt came to power in 1933, he was faced with 13 million unemployed, while in 1941, on the eve of America's participation in World War II, Roosevelt was still plagued by 10 million unemployed. Quantitative monetary easing (QE) was not an invention of today's Bernanke; the US had three rounds of QE stimulus in 1930, 1932 and 1933, and after a brief economic boom, waited for a second recession in 1937. The unemployment problem in the United States would have persisted for a long time if the war had not conscripted 30 per cent of the employed population into the war and turned them to the military industry.

The Second World War presented a good opportunity for the dollar to rise again. During the war, the United States deliberately weakened Britain's economic potential, and its fears of a comeback of the British Empire outweighed even those of Soviet expansion. With the Lend-Lease Act, the United States defeated the British "imperial preference system" and launched a general offensive against the pound sterling zone, taking advantage of the lethal conditions of post-war loans to Britain. Even the British themselves admit that if it had not been for the deliberate and planned arrangements of American policy, Britain would not have declined so quickly and so completely.

Eventually, the dollar finally took control of the world's currencies and established a Bretton Woods dynasty in which "the golden weak ruler ascended the throne and the dollar ruled the world".

The gold standard collapsed and the pound sterling district became independent

In the summer of 1931, the atmosphere in the City of London was extraordinarily depressing, with bad news coming one after another from all over the world, and there was already a growing sense that a financial storm was coming.

Since the beginning of the year, a wave of German bank failures is sweeping the world. Hungary's banking system was completely shut down, major banks in Romania and Poland went bankrupt, a massive bank run broke out in Egypt, a financial panic erupted in Istanbul, bonds in Bolivia and Peru defaulted, Chile's external debt began to default, and Mexico was forced to switch to the silver standard as its gold standard fell apart. London's long-established investment banks, such as Longyear and Schroeder, are struggling and are waiting for a Bank of England bailout.

On July 13, the British government released the Macmillan Report, the problems of the British banking system were revealed, the UK's short-term external debt was as high as $3 billion! It was a heavy bombshell that instantly sent the London financial markets into a frenzy. Mind you, the size of Britain's direct investment into the world was only $500 million a year, which was half of the world's total investment before the war! How could such a huge deficit be owed? As "world bankers", the British had long been accustomed to exporting capital to the outside world and had not expected to be so heavily in debt.

The bad news is compounded by the banking crisis in Germany and Central European countries, which has forced governments to tighten controls on foreign exchange flight, and by the fact that nearly

$1 billion in British investments could turn into bad debts that are difficult to recover.

Panic-stricken investors around the world immediately began pumping money out of London. In just two weeks, the Bank of England has lost $250 million worth of gold, which is half the total gold reserves! The Bank of England was forced to raise interest rates sharply from 2.5 per cent to 4.25 per cent, but it still couldn't keep the gold from rolling out. In a hurry, Norman turned to the United States and France for help with $250 million in foreign exchange, only to find that the money was invested like a stone bull into the sea, and was quickly drowned in a torrent of cash. Both the US and French governments have reached the end of their rescue, only to watch the Bank of England run out of gold.

Norman's body and nerves were finally completely broken. He had to wearily leave London to convalesce.

On the evening of August 22, the King of England abruptly cancelled a three-week leave of absence and secretly returned to Buckingham Palace. The British government's cabinet ministers have all given up weekends to gather at the Prime Minister's residence in Downing Street, the first time they have given up weekends off since World War I. In the small garden, the prime minister and ministers paced back and forth, ashtrays filled with cigar butts, various newspapers scattered on the floor, all anxiously awaiting a reply from the American JPMorgan consortium.

It was the US Government and JPMorgan that pushed for Britain to return to the gold standard in the first place, and now that the golden fortress of the pound is about to fall, the US Government is legally constrained from providing new funding. Instead, the French made it a condition of willingness to borrow, that the loan be denominated in francs. After all these years, the French have come to understand that the franc is an international reserve currency like the pound or the dollar, and that all transactions are settled in the franc, how beautiful it would be! As a result, the British said, don't dream it, Britain will never take a loan in francs!

The last hope is Morgan. At this moment, it is as if the fate of the entire British Empire hangs in the balance at the whim of Wall Street. Keynes' prophecy actually came true, and the gold standard did put the fate of the pound and even the entire empire in the hands of the Americans.

The American bailout was conditional on the requirement that the UK must cut $350 million in government spending, including life-saving money for the unemployed, and $300 million in increased taxes, and how that money is spent is subject to Morgan's advice. The British Government has never in its history suffered such a pittance, which is more like the terms of a payout for defeat than it is the terms of aid! But nowadays, one has to bow one's head when one is under the roof. After much haggling, the British Prime Minister made a final offer for help. Because of the controversy, the prime minister didn't even tell all the cabinet members. At this point, the only thing he could do was wait for the American verdict on the fate of the pound.

At 8:45 p.m., Morgan's telegram finally reached the Bank of England. The already impatient vice-president seized the telegram and hurried to 10 Downing Street. As he rushed into the small garden of the Prime Minister's residence, all eyes were immediately fixed on the telegram in his hand. The Prime Minister came forward and grabbed the telegram and rushed into the office, followed by other officials. A few minutes later, the roar from the house nearly shattered the glass of the windows, and the ministers, who did not yet know the contents of the articles, nearly tipped the table. The Cabinet was so badly divided that the Prime Minister had to ask the King to resign overnight, and the Labour Cabinet collapsed. The next day, the British press, under the headline "Banker's Extortion", denounced the American bankers for opposing the evils of the British working class.[17]

The new cabinet still made fiscal reforms under Morgan's terms, and the UK fell into a deeper recession, with cuts in unemployment benefits making domestic consumption even more depressed. The $400 million bailout from the US and French bankers arrived, but only lasted three weeks.

On September 19, the Bank of England had lost $1 billion in gold reserves and the UK's gold was finally depleted and the gold standard collapsed! What followed was the dashed dream of the pound regaining world monetary hegemony.

Day, did not collapse.

---

[17] Liaquat Ahamed, *Lords of Finance*, The Penguin Press, New York, 2009.

Although the pound has endured a huge dump in international markets and the exchange rate has depreciated by 30 per cent, the UK economy is free from the shackles of the gold standard and the pound has regained its freedom. The competitiveness of British industry has recovered strongly, and American and French products have been fiercely challenged in international markets by British goods. The British were beginning to taste the sweetness of the French devaluation of the franc in 1926, and it was the turn of the Americans and the French to grumble.

As international competitiveness improved and overseas investment opportunities diminished, UK capital began to shift to internal investment, a large number of new factories began to be built, machinery and equipment were renewed at an accelerated pace, the consumer industry flourished and housing demand soared, and the UK economy experienced a "mini-spring" after a long and bitter cold. The policy of cheap money and the repatriation of funds has led to a significant reduction in the level of short-term interest rates in the UK to 2 per cent, and the cost of long-term loans of up to $8 billion has been cut from 5 per cent to 3.5 per cent, significantly easing the cost pressure on the huge debt. It was not until the outbreak of the Second World War that the cost of financing British Treasuries fell further below 3 per cent. In contrast to the high financing costs of World War I, this reduction in financing costs continued throughout World War II. The United Kingdom has effectively waged a "war on 3 per cent interest" by financing its national debt.

Shortly after sterling's departure from the gold standard, the British Empire led its large colonial dependencies and important trading partners to establish a formidable sphere of sterling domination, the "imperial preference system" established at the 1932 British Empire Conference in Ottawa. Within the "pound sterling zone", there is a reciprocal reduction in tariffs or exemptions on imports between member countries, and high tariffs on imports from outside the member countries, to prevent the penetration of the vast market in the pound sterling zone by the exporting power of the United States and other countries.

Britain was once known as the Empire of the Sun, with one quarter of the world's population being subjects of the Empire and one fifth of the Earth's land area being its territory. Spreading from the British Isles to the Gambia, Newfoundland, Canada, New Zealand, Australia, Malaysia, Hong Kong, Singapore, Myanmar, India, Uganda, Kenya,

South Africa, Nigeria, Malta and countless other islands, 24 time zones on Earth are covered by the British Empire.[18] The international order under British hegemony has been called "peace under British rule". The global map of the British Empire, published by Britain, usually marked the empire's territory in red, gives a clear picture of the global reach of this vast empire. If you include the major trading partners of the United Kingdom, such as Sweden, Denmark, Norway and Finland in Scandinavia, Portugal and Greece in Southern Europe, Iraq in the Middle East, Egypt in Africa, Asia and South America, the market size, size, population and resources of the pound sterling area are large enough to pose a serious challenge to the hegemony of the dollar.

The British economist Jevons once described the economic influence of the British Empire this way: the plains of North America and Russia are our corn fields, Canada and the Baltic Sea our woodlands, Australia our pastures, Peru our silver mines, South Africa and Australia our gold mines, India and China our tea base, the East Indies provide us with sugar cane, coffee and spices, and the southern United States our cotton plantations. The new core strategic resources of the 20th century, such as oil, iron, aluminium, lead, zinc, copper, nickel, rubber and other raw material bases, are also largely controlled by the British Empire.

After the First World War, the dollar, riding on the moment of great wealth and relative European shrinkage, used the baton of war debt to launch a ferocious attack on the pound from the front of the reserve currency and the flank of the trade settlement, which, while ultimately defeating the pound's global system, was far from completely destroying the economic and wealth potential of the British Empire. Strategically, rather than the dollar surrounding the pound, it is the pound that surrounds the dollar around the world.

Once the pound broke free of the gold shackles, it also meant that the pound shed the dollar's restraints and won the strategic initiative. The pound was based on the "imperial preference system", which established a dominant influence in the sterling area. The sharp depreciation of the pound allowed the UK to begin a powerful counterattack against the dollar in various trade battlefields.

---

[18] British Empire, Wikipedia.

The dollar had to make a strategic retreat on a global scale. America's relapse into isolationism is not due to a lack of willingness to lead the world, but rather to a prolonged economic depression that has constrained its ability to do so.

The Fed nearly disintegrated, and the dollar was in shock for 48 hours

Since the collapse of the pound's gold standard in September 1931, the world began to fear that the dollar would also be forced off the gold standard. The massive devaluation of the pound has immediately cost the Bank of France a staggering £125 million in foreign exchange reserves of £350 million, seven times its own capital! Such losses, if it were an ordinary commercial bank, would have died several times over. The Dutch central bank lost all of its own capital, while Sweden and Belgium, countries that had been the Norman "water to oil" pound reserves, are now in tears. In Europe's powerful Bank of England Governor Norman, the Bank of Europe central banks have boasted that the pound and gold is as good as gold and lulled everyone into saving gold is not as good as saving the pound, this time it is really "bare-assed pushing mill – turn around to disgrace".

The Europeans, who have been shocked by this, are in a state of limbo, and the pound is so unreliable, how good can the dollar be? It's the heavy gold that feels solid in your hand. The day after the pound announced its departure from the gold standard, the Bank of France immediately asked the Federal Reserve Bank of New York, politely, if it could convert some of its dollar reserves into gold, now that it was short on cash. The Americans replied, no problem, we have American gold. As a result, the French immediately converted $100 million in reserves into gold. The Swiss central bank took a look at the French taking the lead and also asked for $200 million in gold, which the Americans still don't mind. Immediately after, the Belgian central bank exchanged 130 million and the Dutch central bank wanted 77 million, crying out for gold from the United States more and more. In just five short weeks, Europeans converted $750 million of their dollar reserves into gold.

This time, the American people don't feel right.

Gold of this magnitude has been pumped out of the U.S. monetary system, severely weakening the credit base of American banks. Without credit collateral, the large number of loans released had to be repaid immediately, and now that everyone is short of money, lenders simply can't repay the loan, only forced to jump off the building to sell the asset, everyone throws together, and as a result no one can run. And so, within 5 weeks of the Europeans siphoning off the gold, 522 American banks failed on a massive scale! By the end of 1931, the number of bank failures had reached a staggering 2,294! 20,000 U.S. banks that have gone bankrupt by 1/10th, while losing $1.7 billion in savings to ordinary people.

Faced with an unprecedented wave of bankruptcies, American savers suddenly realized that their lives were in danger of total destruction at any moment and immediately began to withdraw their deposits from various banks. In just six short months, $500 million in cash flew from banks into the mattresses of thousands of homes. The crisis in the banking system is on the verge of extinction, and bank credit in the United States has shrunk by 20 percent compared to 1931. The dramatic contraction of monetary credit has led to falling prices, increased indebtedness, business bankruptcies, worsening unemployment, sluggish consumption, increased bad debts and run-offs, and a vicious circle in US finance.

Originating in the U.S. dollar debt bubble, the resonant effect of this crisis of confidence induced the U.S. stock market crash of 1929 after Germany led the way in rupture in 1928. After the panic subsided temporarily for more than a year, Austria and Germany experienced another more complete banking system collapse. The second round of the financial crisis was far more deadly than the first, which swept through the British gold standard dike and then crossed the Atlantic again, sweeping through the American banking system in 1931–1932.

In February 1933, the cloud of the dollar crisis began to build over New York. At the center of this storm is the very heart of the dollar system – the Federal Reserve Bank of New York!

Since late February, the Federal Reserve Bank of New York has lost $250 million in gold in two weeks, a quarter of its total reserves, although the Fed as a whole has more than enough gold reserves, but as these gold resources are spread across 12 separate Fed banks, which are facing a run on banks in their respective jurisdictions, the banks have long lost out. Coupled with the long-standing style of the Federal Reserve Bank of New York, not only the Fed's headquarters in Washington, D.C. are full of grievances, other Fed banks are equally indignant. The Federal Reserve Bank of New York, in a time of crisis, is already in a quandary of being alone.

Instead of abating, the tide of bank bankruptcies is getting worse.

By March 2, the Federal Reserve Bank of New York's gold reserves had fallen below the lower limit set by law, which is 40 percent of its money-issuing reserves.

For the next 48 hours, the crisis was rapidly worsening on an hourly basis. The Federal Reserve Board in Washington has sensed that the entire US central banking system is in danger of disintegrating!

After Strang's death from illness in 1928, Harrison inherited the mantle at the Federal Reserve Bank of New York. But his luck is too bad, the scenery decent good day did not live, every day busy in the "disaster and fire fighting" on the front line. The last option to save the Federal Reserve Bank of New York and himself is to close all the banks in the country! But a move of this magnitude is, after all, something that has never happened since the founding of the United States.

It is at this critical juncture that the change of government between the old and the new comes at an awkward juncture. Roosevelt has been elected, but will not be sworn in until March 4. President Hoover is already a lame duck in power. Harrison was able to persuade the Federal Reserve Board in Washington, as well as President Hoover, who had deep ties to Wall Street, but he could not persuade Roosevelt. It is not that Roosevelt was unaware of the seriousness of the problem, but that he had to look on the wall at this point.

In the face of the banking crisis, President Hoover has long since jumped to his feet in a hurry, if the nation's banking system is not shut down, the Federal Reserve will fall apart and the US economy will collapse! He, Hoover, will also go down in history as the first president in American history to bankrupt the nation's economy, fearing to leave a bad name in the history books! Anxious, Hoover repeatedly urged Roosevelt to work with him on contingency plans as soon as possible, but Roosevelt was free and unhurried.

Roosevelt was not in a burdened mood at the moment, the economy was in shambles, that was the incompetence of his predecessor, and that was why he was elected, "the people need change". It would be politically unwise to join forces with Hoover on any plan, and to get involved in such a mess at this point would make it difficult for him to get out of it in the future, and he wouldn't do such a stupid thing to wipe someone's ass. When the situation is completely rotten, once he takes the reins, he'll get all the credit, or else, the blame can be placed on the unlucky President Hoover, while Roosevelt himself is undefeated.

On March 3, the Federal Reserve Bank of New York lost $350 million in one day! Of that amount, $200 million was an international run and $150 million was a cash run by the general population. It is now short of reserves by a whopping $250 million! The Federal Reserve Bank of New York finally put down its shelves and looked around for help. Other Federal Reserve banks let out a chilling burst of cold laughter. The disintegration of the Federal Reserve is no longer a distant imagination, but a harsh reality close at hand. Since the Federal Reserve Bank of New York is a private company, not a government department, the risk of its bankruptcy is real.

This day, and President Hoover's last working day, is tomorrow's Roosevelt era. As is customary, that afternoon, a calm Roosevelt invited President Hoover to his home for a cup of tea and a chat. How could Hoover be in such a mood, he was here to make a last-ditch effort. After some official courtesy, Hoover offered to talk to Roosevelt in private. Roosevelt smiled and motioned Hoover to the study, where the Federal Reserve chairman, the Treasury secretary and Roosevelt's aides were waiting. It was an arduous negotiation, and Hoover was almost pleading with Roosevelt: "Will you and I jointly sign a joint statement tonight announcing the closing of the bank?" For his part, Roosevelt replied uncompromisingly, "If you don't have the guts to take the consequences yourself, I will wait until the president is inaugurated to do it (what you should have done)." When I saw it, Hoover had to leave like that.

Hoover is anxious, the Fed is even more anxious, and it is JPMorgan who is most anxious. The Federal Reserve Bank of New York is the main instrument of the international bankers to call the world's lords, and it is unacceptable in any case that the collapse of the last hundred years of the dream of gold power is about to dash.

Throughout the night of March 4, the phone calls at Roosevelt's home could not be stopped for a moment. In 1922, he was involved in the establishment and president of the United European Investment Company as a director, international financial giants such as the German financial giant, the Warburg family's head Max Warburg, his brother is known as the "father of the Federal Reserve" of Paul Warburg, and Paul's son James, is the main financial adviser after the

Roosevelt administration. Max's other brother was a partner in that year's No. 1 Wall Street investment bank, Kuhn Loeb & Co. which was a key node in a network of Jewish financial relationships around the world. It was during his time in office that former German Chancellor Cuno, also an advisor to Roosevelt, exploded into German hyperinflation. Roosevelt, the company's largest individual shareholder, had made a fortune when the German mark plunged. Roosevelt was also no stranger to the JPMorgan bankers in general, and it was Ramon, JPMorgan's sharpshooter, with whom Roosevelt's personal friendship ran deep, and it was Ramon who arranged Roosevelt's accommodations and introduced Roosevelt to various relationships when the young Roosevelt arrived in Washington at the beginning of his political career.[19]

The gods and goddesses were all talking, but the issue of the closing of the banking system was so much on Roosevelt's mind. The Fed chairman was even a major lobbyist, calling both sides frantically all night to close the gap between Hoover and Roosevelt's positions. In the end, Roosevelt was so annoyed that he had to talk to Hoover three times, and kept breaking down the differences between the two positions until 1:00 a.m., and still could not reach a compromise. Roosevelt finally just had to leave it at that and it was time for bed.

While Roosevelt slept, the Fed chairman couldn't sleep. In order to make a statement for himself in history, the President decided to convene the council meeting overnight. Those already asleep at home, sick in their beds, attending cocktail parties, the Fed's governors braved the wind and rain to arrive on the slippery roads. The meeting continued until 2 a.m., culminating in a written statement recommending that the president close all banks in the country immediately. Knowing that Roosevelt had gone to bed, everyone played a mind trick and ordered the statement to be shoved through the door of the Roosevelt house. It was delivered in a timely fashion. Early the next morning, Roosevelt was about to go to the inauguration when he found this announcement at the door and was so angry he almost fainted. Isn't it obvious that the Fed is setting itself up for this!

---

[19] Chapter V of *The Currency War*.

In fact, the Federal Reserve is also being pushed to the brink. If the banks don't close, the New York Fed Bank will run out of reserves on Monday! If the central bank of the United States of America is shut down by the people and foreigners, the credit of the dollar will collapse! Any talk of a global strategy for the dollar or a competition with the pound for supremacy would be for naught. There must be a rush to close the doors of the nation's banks before the Federal Reserve Bank of New York is forced to close. That's a different story, the Fed was run and shut down, turning into the government forcing the banking system to overhaul. The defendant turned into the plaintiff! The Fed will act as the executive of the cleanup from on high, not the object of the cleanup!

Bankers do things and never have to prepare Plan B, let alone for such a major event.

Plan B is that if it doesn't make sense for Roosevelt to shut down the nation's banks, it would be to shut down banks in New York State and the Chicago area of the Central Financial District first. This will win precious time and ease the pressure on the two major Fed banks, New York and Chicago, to run. The executive order to close the bank had to be issued by the governor, and the governor of Illinois, where Chicago was located, was not afraid to pick this head himself, offering to follow suit as long as New York State acted first. The hordes of bankers killed off again to the home of the governor of New York State. The governor was no one else, none other than one of the famous Lehman banking family's own, Herbert Lehman. The Lehman Brothers Company at that time, but a hegemon of Wall Street, in March 1933, the most critical moment, was Lehman Brothers in the rescue of the Federal Reserve Bank of New York. As a result, in September 2008, the Federal Reserve Bank of New York did nothing to save Lehman Brothers. The insidiousness of the financial underworld and the insidiousness of the bankers' hearts is evident from this!

It wasn't until 2:30 a.m., when news of Roosevelt's refusal to budge, that Governor Lehman officially announced that all banks in New York State would be closed for three days beginning Monday. An hour later, the Illinois governor announced a follow-up. Massachusetts and New Jersey, which had originally been negotiated, announced the order to close the bank in the early hours of the next day. The governor of Pennsylvania turned out to agree, but at this point could not find anyone. He planned to attend the presidential inauguration, the man was in Washington, but was staying at a friend's house and could not be reached for a moment. The Fed, in a pinch, had to send someone to the door to wake the governor, only to fall back to sleep after the sleepy Pennsylvania governor issued the order.[20]

On March 4, Roosevelt was inaugurated as President of the United States. On that day, the nation's banks were ordered to close and consolidate for ten days. This is the first time in U.S. history, and in the history of world money, that the world's largest economy will be living completely without banks and money within ten days.

Three rounds of quantitative monetary easing and the U.S. is not out of the Great Depression

In a developed, industrialized country, can the economic system still function once the currency is lost, just as a modern city is suddenly cut off from running water and electricity?

The answer is: can!

Human societies are so adaptable that they often exceed people's imagination!

When the American banking system was shut down, there was no mass rioting in society as expected. On the contrary, the social order is surprisingly well organized. This is the hope of Roosevelt's New Deal on the one hand, and the natural resilience of people on the other.

American malls are flexible and continue to offer goods to customers on credit. Doctors, lawyers, auto body shop owners, accept personal debt notes as a means of payment. Classes at the university are as usual, and the canteen is booked for students to eat. The Broadway show box office, which also accepts personal notes of indebtedness, must show a bank savings book to prove that it has money to pay back in the future. Hundreds of local governments have issued local vouchers, and states have had their own experience of issuing "colonial vouchers" as early as the American War of Independence. In other places, direct collection of goods as a means of payment has been adopted. A boxing match, such as the one in New York, was priced at 50 cents, and spectators could buy tickets with hats, soap, cigarettes, and even shoes of comparable value. However, there are limits to credit,

---

[20] Liaquat Ahamed, *Lords of Finance*, The Penguin Press, New York, 2009. p. 448.

small amounts are fine, and too large an amount can cause trouble. Even without the currency, Americans are not delayed in having fun, and as a result more than 5,000 tourists are stranded in Florida because their overdraft limit is exceeded.

When Roosevelt came to power, the focus was of course on saving the economy, but his New Deal was prescribing the wrong medicine; in 1933, Roosevelt had 13 million unemployed when he took office, and by the end of 1941, before the United States entered World War II, he was still facing more than 10 million unemployed, and had it not been for the fact that World War brought one third of the American workforce directly into the war effort or into the war system, it is feared that unemployment would have continued into the mid to late 1940s.

Roosevelt determined that the crisis was rooted in falling prices. He argued that falling prices had led to the loss of industrial profits, an increased debt burden, low willingness to invest, insufficient production starts and high unemployment. At the same time, the sales price of agricultural products has contracted severely over the years, causing farmers to lose money and reducing their spending power. The collapse of asset prices has left Wall Street in a state of shock, paralysing the banking system, severely weakening financing capacity and making it difficult to fund the economic recovery.

Thus, Roosevelt's central idea was to do everything possible to bring prices back up and out of the misery of deflation. Eighty years later, the Bernanke and Obama administrations largely followed Roosevelt's thinking and responded to the financial tsunami by "reflation of assets". This is also the main reason why the United States is still unable to walk away from the crisis. Roosevelt, after a brief period of prosperity with the New Deal, fell back into the 1937–1938 recession in his fourth year in office, while Obama faced the same danger of a second recession in his fourth year in office. Roosevelt's inability to fix unemployment is just as much of an economic nightmare for Obama as it is for him.

The mistake made by both is almost identical, giving birth to a disease of the heart and taking medicine for a headache. To have a debt crisis on the dollar, but to have a fiscal deficit to solve it, and more debt to solve a crisis brought on by debt, is in itself a paycheck. Price inflation or asset inflation, the only way to alleviate debt pressure is by devaluing the currency. The most extreme example of this is the German hyperinflation of 1923, where the total collapse of the mark did wipe out Germany's domestic debt, but also the value of money and the people's trust in the government. In the end, the Weimar Republic of Germany paid this debt of good faith at the cost of its collapse. The United States today, using the dollar's reserve currency status as a gamble to force the dollar's international creditors and domestic taxpayers to share the losses and penalties that should have been inflicted on Wall Street. If the dollar devaluation's deadbeat strategy goes too far, the result will be world-wide hyperinflation and the complete bankruptcy of the dollar's integrity.

The fall in prices is the result, not the cause, of the shrinking of bank credit created by the massive debt implosion. Attempts to use price recovery as a key to solving the crisis can only open the door to cheap money and deficit finance. Cheap money will destroy people's savings and real purchasing power, while deficit finances will increase the eventual pressure on consumers to go into debt, which is completely antithetical to a healthy economic recovery and increased employment. How can such an economic policy, with its logic reversed and the cart before the horse, achieve sustainable results?

Hoover had already messed with QE twice before Roosevelt started his monetary easing policy.

From November 1929 to June 1930, in an effort to save the Wall Street stock market from the October crash and crisis of confidence, the Federal Reserve Bank of New York conducted its first round of QE, steeply reducing interest from 6 percent to 2.5 percent and injecting $500 million into the banking system. The Fed's bold move was also quite unorthodox, with so-called counter-cyclical monetary policy, a novelty idea that was still unheard of at the time. The Fed is also in a mess of internal arguments. Due to the lack of theory and practice, we can only rely on hazy and plausible metaphors, the result is naturally a donkey's lips cannot match the horse's mouth.

The Fed's money printing, combined with falling prices, led to a rise in real money stocks, which rebounded strongly by 50 percent in the first half of 1930. The economic crisis didn't seem so scary, confidence was greatly restored, and the bull market adjustment theory began to be accepted by many. But the good times were short-lived, the economy continued to slide, and the stock market was bearish again into the second half of the year.

In February 1932, the Federal Reserve lobbied Congress to pass a bill that would allow U.S. Treasuries to serve as a monetary reserve, thereby taking away the rigid constraints of gold against the dollar. Since the establishment of the Federal Reserve in 1913, dollar issuance has remained under a gold spell, with a $40 gold collateral behind a $100 issue, and the remaining $60 collateral being primarily short-term commercial paper. While the Fed can buy and sell Treasuries in the open market, using Treasuries as its primary asset and, in effect, using purchased Treasuries to inject liquidity into the banking system, U.S. Treasuries do not legally serve as a monetary reserve for the dollar. U.S. Treasuries don't even hold a candle to commercial paper in terms of dollar issuance. The reason is that the U.S. Congress is very wary of the Fed's monetary powers and is very worried that one day the Fed will monetize the national debt, contribute to the government's fiscal deficit, and use monetary power rent-seeking to corrupt and bind the government, thereby subverting the intrinsic value of the dollar. However, this "secret order" of Congress to control the monetary power of the Federal Reserve, in the crisis was cleverly repealed by the Federal Reserve.

The Fed can finally eat into Treasuries through massive open market operations, embedding Treasuries at the heart of dollar issuance. The national debt, as a core reserve for the dollar, would objectively force it to increase with economic development, which can only be achieved through fiscal deficits. The Fed's use of increased issuance of treasury bonds both served to tempt the government's insatiable desire to overspend and to coerce it into a prolonged period of deficits that would otherwise lead to the economic hardship of monetary contraction. This reliance on debt was the source of the Fed's power and the means by which the US later dealt with the UK. How ingenious of the bankers to devise such a subtle monetary trap! Congress has been taking advantage of the economic crisis to easily flank the Fed's elaborate monetary "Maginot defense line", which was designed by the bankers.

After the passage of the new law, the Federal Reserve immediately started printing money, started QE2, massive buying of treasury bonds, injected another billion dollars into the banking system, the U.S. stock market in 1932 after the start of QE2, should be nearly double!

As it turns out, when the new bill was passed in February 1932, it was the same time that the U.S. stock market had been superbly bottomed since the 20th century!

The stock market has bottomed out, but the economic recovery is far from over. What Roosevelt is about to launch is precisely QE3.

Roosevelt originally had a senior financial advisor, he is James Warburg – the "father of the Federal Reserve" Paul Warburg's son, if counted by generation, should be the Fed's brother generation. James was 25 years old when he served as vice president of the International Acceptance Bank, followed his father Paul opened up a new world in the U.S. commercial promissory note market, established the dominant position of the dollar in international trade settlement made a gigantic battle; at the age of 37, he became the youngest financial giant on Wall Street, serving as vice chairman of the board of Manhattan Bank (the predecessor of today's JP Morgan Chase Bank). It turns out that Roosevelt had been prepared to give him the key position of Treasury Secretary as a bridge between Roosevelt and Wall Street, but he preferred to be the President's personal adviser. James's character was not very stable, probably due to his premature teenage ambition, and he later developed a fierce emotional confrontation with Roosevelt, even openly trolling the state of Roosevelt's New Deal in the press, making his political future suffer greatly.[21]

After the president alienated James, the Roosevelt-era heavyweight, Treasury Secretary Morgenthau recommended his teacher, George Warren, a Cornell University professor of agricultural economics, to be the president's economic adviser. Roosevelt was quite appreciative of Warren's theory of price re-inflation, and although the president himself didn't understand economics, his rather questionable instincts told him that rising prices were the way out of the crisis. Warren's thinking fits perfectly with Roosevelt's expectations.

Warren spent a decade painstakingly investigating the roots of the decline in prices of agricultural products since the 1920s, and in 1932 published his magnum opus, "Wholesale Prices from 1720 to 1932: 213 Years on. The conclusion reached is that there is a clear correlation between gold and commodity prices, more gold is a price increase, less gold is a price decrease. This conclusion in itself is nothing special, as gold is the cornerstone of credit expansion, and an increase in gold will

---

[21] Ron Chernow, *The Warburgs, The Twenty Century Odyssey of a Remarkable Jewish Family*, Random House, New York, 1993. Chapter 27.

lead to an expansion of monetary credit and a natural increase in commodity prices. But in the early 1930s, monetarist ideas had not yet sprung up, and Roosevelt found them very refreshing to hear. More explosive point is that Warren proposed a "secret recipe" to solve the price decline: since the increase in gold can make the price rise, then the devaluation of the dollar to the price of gold, is equivalent to an increase in the total amount of gold, the crisis is not resolved? With such a simple approach, Roosevelt instantly found a sense of economic "prophecy". The President is determined and ready to solve the problem of the Great Depression in one fell swoop by devaluing the dollar against the price of gold.

In fact, the two currency increases of 1930 and 1932, and Roosevelt's devaluation of the dollar against gold, both of which attempted to solve the serious debt problem by manipulating the value of money from two perspectives (the former from quantity and the latter from quality), were unfortunately unlikely to succeed. In a severe debt crisis, the most effective way to do this was to write off the debt completely, allow the large banks to go bankrupt, and the government to take over monetary power and inject money directly into the economy, so that the economic situation would rapidly improve with virtually no debt, and then allow the banks to gradually recover on their own. In 1933, the German Schacht used this therapy to completely turn around the German economy, which was far worse than that of the United States, in only four years, eliminating 30 per cent of the unemployment rate and achieving virtually full employment.

The essence of the Great Depression was that there were massive resources and production facilities idled on one side and a serious labor force idled on the other, and as long as money combined the two, the economic engine was bound to restart. However, the banking system is unable to provide and unwilling to risk credit when it is most needed due to the serious problem of bad debt. It is difficult to solve the dilemma of how money enters the real economy simply by devaluing the currency to fund commercial banks. Because banks create credit on the premise that someone has to lend money and no one does, or that banks are afraid to lend, then the dollars that are cheaply created by central banks do not automatically flow into the real economy. Mass unemployment in the Great Depression left consumers without purchasing power and banks afraid to extend consumer credit to them, while businesses were afraid to hire people to start production on a large scale because the consumer market was sluggish. And the way out of this dead cycle is to start with a massive increase in employment, which is the only way to bring about consumption growth. While the Roosevelt New Deal made some effort in this regard, it fell far short of the enthusiasm for devaluing the currency.

The Roosevelt initiated QE3 included, getting off the gold standard, the dollar falling from $20.67 to $35 for an ounce of gold, and the dollar depreciating dramatically against gold!

The French can't figure out why a country with the most gold in the world would choose to leave the gold standard. The British are grasping at straws, the pound was forced off the gold standard and the US is voluntarily giving it up, what is the US up to? For Americans, the question is very simple, since most countries do not recognize the gold "Han Dynasty authentic", I still take gold as a bodhisattva, why? Gold is originally a tool of the United States to restrain others, if everyone gets rid of gold, then the dollar insists on the gold standard, not only can not control people, but is subject to people. However, the United States, after all, the United States has left an extra heart, although temporarily abandoned the gold standard, but due to the overwhelming dominance of the United States gold reserves, perhaps in the future can again use gold to hold other countries. So Roosevelt ostensibly abolished the gold standard, but did not allow folk to hold gold, forcing ordinary people to sell all their gold to the Federal Reserve at the low price of $20.67, and then causing it to appreciate, which is tantamount to robbing folk of their money and then funneling the benefits to the banking system.

Later, when the Bretton Woods system was established, the United States really brought out the gold "Emperor Han Xian", and all countries had to bow down again. Even after the U.S. decoupled the dollar from gold in 1971, up to 8,000 tons of gold were still stored. The United States is a country that always leaves something to chance.

Once Roosevelt's QE3 was announced, Wall Street applauded and stocks surged 15%. Another member of JPMorgan, Grand Admiral Ruffinwell, paid tribute to Roosevelt on behalf of Wall Street, "Your move away from the gold standard saved a nation on the verge of total collapse". When it comes to gold, the president and Wall Street are supposed to be on the same page.

Spurred on by QE3, US wholesale prices rose 45%, stocks doubled, and debt costs were cut significantly. The economic recovery has seen the light of day, with a 100 per cent increase in heavy equipment orders, a 200 per cent jump in car sales and a 50 per cent expansion in industrial production.

Roosevelt is enjoying the wonderful joy of success at this moment. But, the president forgot, can a recovery in jobless growth be sustained? The bankers are saved, the capitalists are happy, and the common people? Without a substantial increase in their ultimate ability to consume, everything is ultimately an illusion. Sure enough, in 1937, Roosevelt again faced a "recession" in the midst of a depression.

"My destiny, I'm in charge!"

In June 1933, the London Economic Conference became an international event of worldwide interest. Countries around the world, struggling in a declining swamp, have pinned their hopes on the straw that holds the London Conference. It was a conference that was destined to go downhill. Because instead of overlapping, the US and UK focus on each other.

For the British Empire, the separation of the pound sterling area gave the British economy a firm footing, and if it was to regain its hegemony over the pound it would need to expand international trade, with Britain's foreign trade accounting for over 20 per cent of national income and the financial sector heavily dependent on trade. If international trade is not well-functioning and the financial sector is not restored, the economy will be unstable. It is therefore necessary to bring the trade maps of the dollar and franc zones under the umbrella of the sterling zone. But the bad news is that the US dollar is also off the gold standard and is depreciating even harder than the pound, and the franc is not afraid because it does not understand the situation and is still clinging to the gold standard. It is imperative that the exchange rate between the pound, the dollar and the franc be stabilized as soon as possible. Only by stabilizing the currency can the recovery of international trade and the strengthening of the pound's position be guaranteed. Of course, war debts also have to be forgiven. Britain therefore has only two points to make: first, that monetary stability is a prerequisite for world economic recovery, and second, that war debt can be reduced if it is reduced.

The United States thinks of something else entirely. The United States believes that the dollar is currently weak, with thousands of banks failing and the recession worsening, so it must first revive the economy and build up its strength and wait for the dollar to rise again. Unlike Britain and other European countries, the U.S. market is self-reliant, with foreign trade accounting for only 2 to 3 percent of national income, so Roosevelt's focus was on domestic economic recovery rather than external stability of the dollar. What's wrong with a depreciating dollar that addresses falling domestic prices while also boosting exports, increasing employment and hitting the pound? As for war debt relief, don't even think about it!

At the table, the Anglo-American conversation was about who had the higher priority of monetary stability and economic recovery, while the two sides at the table were kicking the shadowless leg of the currency.

On the opening day of the conference, British Prime Minister Macdonald, in his welcome speech, made a deflected reference to the Allied war debt, which the Americans immediately protested as a violation of Britain's prior commitments.

When the British mentioned monetary stability, Roosevelt instructed the U.S. delegation, on hearing the news, not to dwell on the issue and for the United States to focus on the economic recovery. But the British will not let go of the problem of the dollar's inability to depreciate excessively. As a result, Roosevelt had to enlighten the British with nothing but facts.

Before the meeting, the British got word that the US might devalue the dollar to the £1:3.50 level, but during the meeting, the dollar fell sharply to 1:4.18 and the British began to call out sharply. By June 27, the dollar had fallen further to 1:4.3, the lowest exchange rate since the American Civil War, and the British were crying out in their voices. The next day, the dollar fell to 1:4.43, this time never to be heard from the UK again in protest.

> "Roosevelt's bargaining strategy between June 17 and 20 was more successful than he could have imagined himself to be, Foreigners are finally convinced that Americans will not commit to a stable currency. They just have to accept that as fact. All they are asking now is for some kind of gesture from the US, even if it is some kind of insignificant gesture, a gesture that in no way limits his freedom of action on the dollar, but still curbs

the frenzied exchange rate speculation of the previous three weeks."[22]

Despite Roosevelt's dominance of the conference, he found that some in the American delegation were not on his side! Among them are his financial adviser James Warburg and Harrison, the governor of the Federal Reserve Bank of New York. Roosevelt affirmed repeatedly that don't talk about monetary stability, I'm devaluing the dollar, re-inflating prices, and I want whoever wants to discipline my devaluation policy to look good!

But international bankers have a unique penchant for private "small meetings". Bank of England Governor Norman, Bank of France Governor Monnet (Morrow's successor), New York Fed Bank Governor Harrison, and others, shunned the spotlight of the General Assembly and secretly found a place to continue discussing options for monetary stability. They almost reached a private agreement that the pound should remain unchanged relative to the 30% depreciation of gold; that the dollar should rally and remain at the same level relative to the 20% depreciation of gold; and that the franc should continue to hang on to gold and remain in value. Such an arrangement is relatively favourable to the pound, while at the same time setting the stage for the infinite devaluation feared by the franc, with the dollar depreciating moderately, rather than substantially. It was a compromised consensus of central bankers on several sides.

But such a private agreement violates Roosevelt's great taboo! What Roosevelt hated most was not quite what they discussed, but the way in which this secret agreement was made. It's the equivalent of central bankers setting the tone and then going back to convince or coerce their respective governments to agree to these agreements. Where has Roosevelt put me with such a perverse act? Of all bosses, there is nothing more disgusting than having one of their own men secretly conspire with others behind their backs, and disagree with their own words. It's like eating from the inside out!

Word leaked out about the secret currency stability agreement!

---

[22] Michael Hudson, *Super Imperialism – New Edition: The Origin and Fundamentals of U.S. World Dominance*, Pluto Press; New Edition (March 21, 2003), Chapter 3.

Roosevelt, in a fit of rage, got the White House to make a public statement about what Harrison et al. were doing that the US government neither knew nor would allow! To underscore his outrage, Roosevelt let out some really hard words, and a White House spokesman deliberately stressed to reporters that Harrison was not a representative of the U.S. government, he was simply representing the Federal Reserve Bank of New York, which is an entity separate from the U.S. government!

As a private company, the Federal Reserve Bank of New York is naturally not part of the U.S. government, and Roosevelt knew this for a long time; but by saying such harsh words at this moment, he is clearly knocking the mountain and warning Harrison and the Federal Reserve Bank of New York, who is the real boss!

Roosevelt was not a child of a poor family who rose to the presidency by personal effort. Those presidents who have no roots are not really the Establishment, and they must rely on the interest groups that support them in power. But American history does have strong presidents with real power in their hands, and Roosevelt was one of them.

Roosevelt's great-grandfather, James Roosevelt, founded the Bank of New York in 1784, arguably one of the oldest banking families in the United States, which was run by his cousin, George, until Roosevelt ran for president. Roosevelt's father, also named James, was an American industrial tycoon who owned a number of huge industries such as coal mines and railroads, and was the founder of the Southern Railway Securities Company, which was the first securities holding company in the United States to merge the railroad industry. Roosevelt himself is a Harvard graduate, a lawyer by training, and his main clients include JPMorgan & Co. Backed by a strong banking background, Roosevelt became Assistant Secretary of the U.S. Department of the Navy at the age of 34. Roosevelt also had an uncle who was president, Leonardo Roosevelt. His other cousin, George Emmanuel Roosevelt, was also a prominent figure on Wall Street, having reorganized at least 14 railroad companies in the era of the great railroad mergers, and being a director of the Guaranty Trust Investment Company under JPMorgan, Hanover Bank, and the New York Savings Bank, the list of other companies on which he served could be typed up in a pamphlet. Roosevelt's mother, the Delano family, was also a hairpin family and nine presidents were related to their family. No president in recent American history has had greater political and banking resources than Roosevelt.

Harrison saw the news and was simply stunned, he had never thrown such a spectacle at anyone before. He had no face to stay in London for meetings anymore. The feeling, he later told a friend in New York, was "like being kicked in the face by a donkey".

Watching Harrison get his nose smacked by Roosevelt, Warburg had to go and make a fool of himself. This time he stepped in personally, again engaging the British with the French to continue discussions about currency stability.

This time Roosevelt's lungs are blown! He just doesn't get it, first Harrison, then Warburg, and then a couple of times blatantly playing opposite him. He has decided to completely overturn the entire London Economic Conference! Apparently, the tone of this meeting had been set beforehand by the international bankers, and these people in the US delegation were not the President's own people, they were not going to negotiate for the President, they were going to negotiate for themselves in his name!

On 2 July, Roosevelt sent a personally drafted combat diatribe against monetary stability to the United States delegation in London: "It [monetary stability] seems to me to be a disaster, a tragedy of universal proportions... If the aim of nations at this greatest event is to bring more real and permanent financial stability to the masses of all nations, then the purely artificial and experimental monetary stability programme devised by those few is the antiquated way of the international bankers". The contents of this telegram were publicly revealed to all participants, and the London Economic Conference had been doomed to failure. Warburg flip-flopped with Roosevelt.[23]

Roosevelt shares the same character trait as all strong characters, which is to always be in control of your own destiny.

The Forgotten Truth About America's Rise

The drawback of the Smith doctrine is that it is, in reality, a private economics doctrine, involving only individuals in a country or in the world, and that this private economy will form and develop naturally in

---

[23] Ron Chernow, *The Warburgs, The Twenty Century Odyssey of a Remarkable Jewish Family*, Random House, New York, 1993. Chapter 27.

a certain situation. What is assumed here is a situation in which there are no nationalities or national interests with clear-cut boundaries, no distinct political organization or cultural stages, no wars or hatred between nations. The doctrine is nothing more than a theory of value, nothing more than the theory of an individual shopkeeper or businessman. It is not a scientific doctrine, and it does not show how the productive forces of a nation can be generated, grown and continued in the special interest of the cultural welfare, power, survival and autonomy of the nation.

The path to America's rise is precisely the choice to strongly dominate its own destiny.

Roosevelt was able to ignore the external stability of the dollar and focus on domestic economic recovery because the United States has a low degree of external dependence, with foreign trade accounting for only 2 to 3 percent of U.S. national income. Europe's emphasis on monetary stability has taken precedence over domestic issues, given that external trade accounts for 20 to 30 per cent of the income of the major European countries, the unstable external monetary environment and the lack of a rapid recovery of international trade have made it impossible to talk about economic recovery within Europe.

Roosevelt's hegemony stemmed from the fact that the United States did not have to rely on the European market, and Europe could not help but beg for American money. Ultimately, it is America's own huge market size that lays the foundation for its economic independence. The rise of the U.S. economy has been described as a miracle in the history of the world economy. A backward, predominantly agricultural former colony, far from European civilization, surprisingly surpassed the economies of the major European powers combined in a hundred years. It cannot be ruled out that there is an element of luck in this, but the main determining factor is the US's own policy choices. Among them, never handing over one's destiny to another, is the most central belief in the rise of America.

The path of rise of the United States is clearly different from that of the United Kingdom. Britain was the first to colonize, then develop trade, then the Industrial Revolution and finally establish world hegemony. The colonial conquest brought to the British Empire a vast reserve of labour and an abundance of natural resources, overseas trade won the raw capital and potential markets needed for the Industrial Revolution, which in turn brought about an unprecedentedly effective integration of labour, natural resources, global markets and industrial capital, thus establishing a whole set of principles and doctrines for the organization of production, principles of trade, market transactions, and capital flows. This is the idea of free trade that Britain is trying to sell to other latecomers, and at its core it is about perpetuating and institutionalizing the advantages that the first countries have already gained. Under such an institutional arrangement, the British would be the controllers of the machine of world economy and trade: the raw materials and basic commodities of the world would be priced by the British; the principal industrial products of the world would be supplied by British factories; the semi-finished and auxiliary products of the world would be arranged by Britain for production in other countries on the principle of comparative advantage; and the sale of various products in the world market would be distributed by Britain on the basis of profit. At the same time, the UK will provide funding to keep the whole system up and running. In addition, the Imperial Navy would be on standby to fight any potential challengers to the established system.

For the Americans, the whole point of the War of Independence was to get rid of their dependence on Britain. Specifically, freedom from dependence on the world market under British control, dependence on British capital and dependence on British industrial products.

After the War of Independence, it became clear to the Founding Fathers of the United States that the main source of future growth of social wealth would be the industrial capacity of the country. But until 1800, the United States remained a typical agricultural country, with only 8 out of 326 joint-stock companies investing in manufacturing, a mere 2.4 percent of the total. To develop industry, the most important things are technology, equipment, talent and capital, and the UK banned the exodus of machine equipment and technicians long ago. In the face of the dumping of British industrial products, the United States is still in infancy, the manufacturing industry is facing a catastrophe.

The Napoleonic Wars broke out in 1807, when Britain, fighting Napoleon, ordered the forced conscription of any British on board a neutral ship, and in June, intercepted and shelled the USS Chesapeake off the coast of the United States to conscript its seafarers. This stirred strong anti-British sentiment in the United States, and in December 1807, the United States Congress passed the Embargo Act, which prohibited all ships from leaving the United States for foreign ports.

While the embargo has caused modest losses to U.S. exports and the maritime industry, it has won valuable growth opportunities for the manufacturing sector. The embargo winds allowed American manufacturing to temporarily avoid competitive pressure on British industrial products, and manufacturing profits soared. At the same time, the financial and trade consortium in the north of the United States, due to the depression of navigation and trade, had to put a large amount of capital into the manufacturing industry, which led to the rapid development of industrial production in the United States, by 1810, the manufacturing product reached 120 million U.S. dollars. In 1812, the outbreak of the second war between Britain and the United States, the British industrial products in the United States market greatly reduced, once again to the United States manufacturing continued to provide a natural opportunity for the development.[24]

During this period, the most severe difficulties facing the U.S. manufacturing industry in its infancy, namely advanced equipment, technology and talent dilemmas, began to ease. The proliferation of industrial technology in the UK is hard enough to legislate. After the war of 1815, with the resumption of trade with Britain and Europe and the resurgence of British goods, U.S. manufacturing remained vulnerable, more than half of the factories closed down and a large number of workers lost their jobs, triggering the U.S. economic recession of 1818.

The disruption of British trade by the two wars and the great post-war impact of British products on American manufacturing finally made Americans determined that foreign industrial products must be kept out of the American market by high tariffs in order to create good external conditions for the rise of American industry.

At the urging of the American industrial complex, Congress passed the Tariff Act in 1824, raising tariffs on products such as textiles, wool, pig iron, and flax. The Harrisburg Convention, on the other hand, provides for lower tariffs on imports of products that cannot be

---

[24] Michael Hudson, *America's Protectionist Takeoff 1815–1914, The Neglected American School of Political Economy*, Garland Publishing, Inc., New York & London, 1975.

produced in the country and higher tariffs on certain special products, such as up to 90 per cent on wool and up to 95 per cent on pig iron.

Throughout the 100 years of America's industrial rise in the 19th century, the U.S. tariff rate was over 40 percent in most years and 20 percent in the low years. By 1900, American industry was dominating the world. Without the protection of high tariffs, this miracle would be unthinkable!

In addition to high tariffs, there is one other notable feature of the rise of American industry, and that is high wages! In free trade theory, it's an incredible freak. High wages mean high costs, and high cost products mean elimination from the world market in the doctrine of comparative advantage. But Americans don't believe that! For the primary purpose of American production of industrial goods is not to satisfy the enjoyment of foreign consumers, but to improve the standard of living of their own people.

Since colonial times, labor costs in the U.S. have been more than 1/3 higher than in continental Europe, a natural consequence of the scarcity of labor that has made the new continent attractive to European immigrants. When the United States began to push for industrialization, the issue of high wages had sparked a 30-year-long debate between the pro-British school within the United States and the American school. The pro-British school of thought, which strongly believes in British free trade theory, believes that industrialization and high wages are incompatible. Using the example of European industrialization, they point out that workers in European countries have low costs and difficult living conditions, and that the United States could not succeed without a labor price advantage if it competed with European products. But the American school of thought was tit-for-tat,

> *"The success of American industry has been achieved not by depressing the wages of its workers, but by the more advanced organizational management and greater efficiency of the labor force, which has maintained a higher standard of living. Higher wages will mean better food and living conditions for workers, which will make America's workers more workaholic and have more creative energy. High-wage countries are beating their 'cheap labour' rivals in all fields".*

The American school of thought holds that labor is a capital, not just a cost. Investment in the workforce will result in more productive returns. A higher quality of life, better education, and more energetic physical, energy, and intellectual strength will provide better products and services that will inspire more invention and creativity! This notion is distinctly different from the static view of labor as a cost, as opposed to profit, which Li Jia Tu used.[25]

Is it labor costs, or human capital? The great debate between the pro-British school and the American school has allowed American policy to end up leaning toward the high wage strategy option.

It is because of trade protection that American industry has gone from weak to strong. It is the very idea of labor as a form of capital that makes American workers pay much higher wages than in Europe, and higher productivity and more inventions give capital a return that far exceeds its input. It is the development of its own powerful industry that has created the largest number of industrial goods and services in the world, and it is the large middle class with high wages that has created the largest consumer market in the world. It is because of the enormous size of the domestic market in the United States that it is finally able to keep its own destiny firmly in its own hands!

The rise of American industry has adopted a strategy of high tariffs, high wages, strong industry, heavy technology, and big markets.

The U.S. takes British assets at its peril

After the unhappy London Economic Conference of 1933, the United Kingdom and the United States parted ways, the United Kingdom focused on operating its own vast pound sterling area, while the United States continued to be "isolated" in its own economic difficulties.

The outbreak of World War II in 1939 finally broke the fragile and dreary balance of the world. The war instantly inflamed the blood of all nations. The Nazi victory in Germany, which wiped out Europe, showed the United States the perfect opportunity to make a comeback.

Americans never thought that these street punks from the German, Italian and Japanese Axis countries could really make a big deal out of the fact that the GDP of the United States alone is 50 percent higher

---

[25] Ibid.

than the three countries combined. After all, wars are fought with money and food. The Axis countries were latecomer industrial countries, lacking the military bases and raw materials provided by overseas colonies, and the final battle of the world wars was resource consumption. The British, French, Soviet and Chinese powers alone would be enough to deplete the human, material and financial reserves of the Axis powers, while the vast overseas resources of the British Empire would provide war supplies incessantly, and a prolonged war would be more and more beneficial to the allies, and eventually the United States would have an overwhelming advantage in entering the war.

The United States, like a shrewd businessman, dials the balance of power and calculates when it is in America's best interest to enter the war. Americans weren't really worried about the eventual victory of Germany or the expansion of the Soviet Union, on the contrary, the United States was more apprehensive about the strength of the postwar British Empire. So, the United States wanted to weaken Britain as much as possible in the war so that the post-war world would be one America.

The British Empire, faced with two challenges from Germany, had an increasingly difficult time coping. Just as Britain did not expect France to be so unbeaten in the war, the United States was equally surprised that Britain's decline was far more severe than the United States had estimated. The UK was the first of the industrial countries to come out of recession, thanks in large part to the large market in the sterling area. By 1938, Britain actually had a whopping $4 billion in gold and dollar reserves, four times more than in the early 1930s! But just a year after the war broke out, Britain's gold and foreign exchange reserves plummeted to $1 billion by September 1940. By November, Churchill had to tell Roosevelt privately that "the time for a break in Britain's cash flow was not far off". Although Roosevelt was secretly surprised by the speed at which the war was consumed, he would not believe Britain's story lightly. While Roosevelt declared that "the United States is the great arsenal of democracies", he implied that it still costs money to buy arms.

Faced with Churchill's crying poverty, Roosevelt was in no hurry to suggest that it would not be easy to convince Congress that the British had indeed exhausted all their resources and that the United States must reach out immediately to help. If the situation in the UK is really urgent, there is a quick way out, and that is to sell off the British holdings in major US industrial companies.

The bankers understand that the UK has tens of billions of dollars of "idle assets" overseas, and it is time for the UK to use the money to force the UK to jump off the block and sell, and the bankers will make a fortune.

In March 1941, just as Congress was discussing the Tenant Frontier Act, Roosevelt informed Britain that some of its most important corporate shares must be sold immediately to the Americans. Among the businesses that Britain was forced to sell was the American Viscose Company, the super money-making machine of the Courtaulds textile empire in the United States, which had 18,000 employees and seven factories in the United States and was the largest rayon enterprise in the world at the time. The Americans only gave the British government 72 hours to announce the sale of the business. When the representative of the British Government announced this decision to Cortez with a sinking heart, the veteran English gentleman simply asked, "Is this decision in the national interest, regardless of the pain it will cause me and my company?" Upon hearing the affirmative answer, the old gentleman slumped back in his seat. He had only 36 hours to convene the board to announce plans for the sale of the business. That's arguably the shortest record in the history of corporate M&A in the world. The business naturally went to JPMorgan, which gave the Englishman $54 million and changed hands for $62 million on the market. After the war, Churchill claimed in his Memoirs that the company's tangible assets alone were worth more than $128 million and that "Cortez, the assets of this great British company in the United States, were sold cheaply at the request of the American government, and then again at a high price in the capital markets, from which Britain did not benefit." When J.P. Morgan saw this account, it was so shocked that it hastened to unclog through various connections, hoping that Churchill would not be so harshly harsh.[26] To Churchill's dismay, this is just the tip of the iceberg of British assets being blackmailed by the US.

In support of the war on democracy and freedom, news of the American demand that the British sell their assets cheaply went viral in the United States, and a large number of American speculators were

---

[26] Ron Chernow, *The House of Morgan, An American Banking Dynasty and the Rise of Mordern Finance*, Grove Press, New York, 1990. p. 462–463.

excited to sleep through the night, including the amazing Dr. Hamer. A student at Columbia Medical School, Hamelbon became a millionaire while a student due to the natural business acumen of Jews, who began dumping drugs while he was a student. He later traveled alone to the Soviet Union shortly after the October Revolution, where he befriended his great mentor, Lenin, and has since been trading in the Red Soviet Union. After making a fortune, he made a fortune again by buying many artworks from the Soviet Union and buying them back in the United States on the cheap. When he heard the news that British assets would be sold off, he quickly figured out a big deal that even a big international investment bank like JPMorgan wouldn't dare think about. That's selling off British military bases in the Western Hemisphere!

Hammer did the math, Britain's war debt to the United States in 1925 was $5 billion, and by 1940 there was $3.5 billion unpaid. The United States was so frightened by its debt that it passed the Johnson Act in 1934, which provided that any country that did not pay its World War I debts would not get another penny from the United States. In fact, the United States has been the most harsh to Britain, even the Axis countries such as Italy, the United States has received half of the debt relief generosity, Germany even received a large investment in dollars, France has also been greatly reduced debt, only to Britain is particularly stingy, the United States to Britain's scruples, as can be seen from the depth of. It was the Johnson Act and the Neutrality Act that prevented the United States from directly assisting Britain in World War II. It's also because of this that there's room for Hammer to make a big splash. Hammer argued that there was no way Britain could take the $3.5 billion it needed to pay the US debt first, but the war was burning money. Therefore, the UK only has to liquidate its assets to offset US debt.

What he had in mind was Britain using its colonial territory to pay off its debts. Of course, America has never been interested in colonies, because there is a cost to ruling, and instead of laying out such a big stall as England did, it's better to sell products to these places, to make money anyway. The tastes of Hammer merchants fit right in with the American business nature. After careful analysis, Hammer listed areas of possible interest to the United States, such as Honduras, the Falkland Islands, Guyana, some islands off the coast of Newfoundland, etc. The U.S. has no interest in direct rule, but cannot be uninterested in leasing these areas and establishing military bases. War was imminent, and the United States would likewise need military bases around the globe after the war, when it would inevitably take the place of the United Kingdom as it is now, and the global order could not be maintained without military bases overseas.

Hammer darted about in his head, first giving Britain the same treatment as Italy, which would cut Britain's debt in half, then putting a number of islands on 99-year leases at $25 million each, and Britain's debt would be paid off, with the extra money available to buy American weapons, such as the 50 destroyers about to be retired. Later, Hammer called the plan "a destroyer-for-military base".[27]

Act immediately when you have a plan. Hammer looks around for connections, pushes his programs, and is exhausted but excited every day. Finally, his proposal to acquire British island territories "by lease or otherwise" was introduced into Parliament. However, the bill was shelved because Congress did not want to offend domestic anti-war public opinion. Hammer is not discouraged, it's not that simple in a business of this size. In order to find "evidence" of public opinion in favour of the United States aid allies, he hired a collection of editorial pages of major newspapers in recent times and found that 92 per cent of editorial pages were in favour of the aid allies. That's public opinion evidence!

With his newspaper clips, Hammer met Roosevelt through connections; after all, he had contributed money to the Roosevelt campaign. Roosevelt flipped through newspaper clips with interest while listening to Hammer's rhetoric about how critical Hammer's "destroyer-for-military-base" would be to the future of the United States. Roosevelt saw the value of the Hammer program, that is, America's future plans for global hegemony. Roosevelt understood that a true hegemonic state with a carrot in its hands was not enough, it needed a big stick. Later, Roosevelt famously said, "Be gentle in your words, but carry a big stick in your hand."

Hammer's plan worked! Britain received 50 American destroyers, which were instrumental in Britain's persistence in the naval battle of 1941.[28] However, in his memoirs, Hammer never mentions how much

---

[27] Armand Hammer, *Hammer*, *G. P. Putnam's Sons*, New York, 1987, Chapter 16.

[28] Ibid.

he has gained from this huge business. The fact that the United States has been able to manipulate national territory and the war machine is a disgrace to China's maoists.

"The Lease Act," "The Butcher's Solution to the British Empire

On March 11, 1941, the United States finally passed the Lease Act. This bill is arguably tailored to dismember the British Empire's economic system. The central issue that Congress has been considering from the beginning is the counter-offer of the lease! What the Americans want is a commitment from Britain, and other recipient countries, to cooperate in the post-war reconstruction of multilateral trade. This commitment is, to put it bluntly, the abolition of the "imperial preference system" and the dissolution of the pound sterling area. The Americans don't forget about multilateral trade, that's because the pound sterling zone is too powerful, if the British don't take advantage of the fact that the British are being driven to their knees by Germany, will the British give in easily? Americans don't even forget business when they go to war, or more accurately, America goes to war for business.

Even before the passage of the Lend-Lease Bill, Churchill had his eye on Roosevelt's pound sterling zone, knowing how important it would be for the pound to resist future aggression by the dollar, with the "imperial preference system" as its cornerstone. But Churchill, after all, was a strategist, and he could not have chosen to fight two formidable enemies on different battlefields at the same time; Hitler's pressure on the military battlefield had almost overwhelmed Britain, and to fight Roosevelt on the economic battlefield at this point would have been the end of Britain. As a result, he has deliberately kept his vague commitment to the United States. Churchill stressed the opening of the raw material markets of the European colonies to all allies, the ending of discriminatory provisions in the import markets and "full respect for the preferences we now enjoy". This was a fallback for Churchill, which was to retain the "imperial preference system" and the British monopoly on the colony's raw material resources. Roosevelt was no good at muddling through, having left this sentence out of the Lease Act.

As a result, in Section 7 of the Lease Act, the ambush of the dispute between the parties was laid. This article provides that "① the expansion of production, employment, exchange and consumption of goods, which are the material basis for the freedom and welfare of all peoples, through appropriate international and domestic measures, ② the elimination of all forms of discriminatory treatment in international commerce, ③ the reduction of tariffs and other barriers to trade." When Keynes saw this article, he was indignant that it was "Mr. Hull's foolish proposal" and that he believed that Britain could only impose more severe financial and trade controls after the war.[29]

Clearly, the price of the Lend-Lease Act was to end the British Empire's poundage cession.

In late 1943, U.S. Treasury Secretary Morgenthau and White emphasized that Britain's reserves "had grown so much that Britain now had to pay in cash for some of the items supplied to it from its rental accounts. When British officials pointed out the need to keep sufficient reserves for the post-war period, Morgenthau assured them that Britain's post-war needs would be met later by special measures." In fact, the United States has been forcing the United Kingdom to always be in a state of "wiping out its family money", the United Kingdom's reserves can not exceed the pre-war $1 billion. The US strategy was that the lower Britain's wartime foreign exchange reserves, the greater its dependence on the US in the future, and the easier it would be to force Britain to abandon the "imperial preference system". This means that the UK will have to turn to the US repeatedly in the future, and God knows what price the US will offer again then. The throat of Britain's fate was already stuck tightly in the American's, and the more it struggled, the tighter the American hand got.

In addition to the U.S. government jamming Britain's neck in front, the U.S. Congress was not idle, and it gave the British another hard kick in the back. The head of the Senate War Investigation Committee, and it was later President Truman, who declared that "the purpose of leasing was never to serve as a means for allies to pass on the costs of war to the United States. If the beneficiary country is unable to repay in dollars, they can transfer part of their international holdings,

---

[29] Michael Hudson, *Super Imperialism-New Edition: The Origin and Fundamentals of U.S. World Dominance*, Pluto Press; New Edition (March 21, 2003), Chapter 3.

such as oil reserves and metal reserves, to that country."[30] Britain deserved it when it ran into an economic rival like the United States. Hitler was born fierce, but after all, not so much a thief's eye.

As the war reached its final stages, Britain became increasingly uneasy because the Tenancy Act would be terminated as soon as the war was over, when it would enter liquidation. Liquidation would have been an economic bomb for the British, and the great depletion of the war forced Britain to stockpile large quantities of war materiel before eventual victory, and once the war was over, those remaining materiel would be commuted into Britain's debt to the United States. With a serious shortfall in foreign exchange reserves, the UK has a huge post-war reconstruction to face, costing money everywhere. More grimly, Britain's debt to the United States, along with the cost of the war to the colonial vassal states, must add up to a disastrous figure. Britain will once again go from being the victor of the war to the loser of the debt.

Britain had expected Japan to drag its feet in the Pacific for another year, and the British Government was confident that "the Japanese would not let us down", a period that would allow Britain a little room to manoeuvre financially. Unfortunately, after the war in Europe ended, Japan held out for only three months before surrendering.

The British Empire immediately fell into a bottomless abyss of debt.

The Bretton Woods dynasty: gold is weak, the dollar regulates the world

Americans had been envisioning the future dollar age since 1941, when they had just entered the war, and America's confidence in winning the war was unquestionable. Numerous academic seminars, policy advice, and congressional hearings gradually shaped America's postwar financial strategic plan, which was the Bretton Woods system established in 1944.

The Bretton Woods system is simply this: one centre, two basic points.

---

[30] Ibid.

One center would be a world monetary center with gold as the weak lord and the dollar as the real power. The US dollar is pegged to gold, while national currencies are pegged to the US dollar, and we all embrace the kingdom of gold. Under such a system, the United States dollar and gold would serve together as the monetary reserve for each country to issue its own currency, and the dollar would be deeply embedded in the monetary credit of each country, and as long as the world economy was developing, the demand for the dollar would naturally increase, and the dollar would reap the fruits of each country's development through increased currency issuance. It was nothing more than an upgrade of the gold standard of 1922, with the dollar crowding out the pound and its application extended to the globe. The problem of dual credit creation has not been solved, and it is bound to reignite a liquidity flood and a larger currency crisis around the world.

Since the United States has already accounted for half of the world economy after World War II, and its military power is even more arrogant, why doesn't the United States directly establish a dollar dynasty, and why does it still need to invite the gold that has been abolished from the throne to become a puppet emperor? Cao Cao has never dared to usurp the Han dynasty for self-reliance. It is not that Cao Cao does not have enough strength, nor is it that he does not have this ambition, but the time is not ripe for him to do so. The United States shares similar concerns that the universal legitimacy of gold, still embraced by all peoples, cannot be extinguished in the short term. The Second World War was not yet over, and post-war reconstruction was all the more necessary to rally hearts and minds. The United States is also a traditional isolationist country, the first time as a protagonist to ascend to the stage of world hegemony, still lacking in leadership experience, at this time to abolish gold and set up its own dollar, lest the trick will be a mistake. The deeper fear is that the hidden danger of the pound sterling's fragmentation has not yet been eradicated, that the Soviet Union's power is growing, and that if the imposition of the dollar standard on the world is immediately proposed, the complex situation of the pound sterling reasserting itself as king, the rouble dividing itself and the franc overwhelming itself cannot be ruled out.

If one embraces gold, the problem is much simpler, not affecting the monetary dominance of the United States on the one hand, and the selflessness of the United States on the other hand, to collect the hearts and minds of the world. The United States owned 70% of the world's gold reserves after the war, and a drop in gold is a drop in America. The

United States controls the real power of the world's currency, Britain is deeply dependent on American debt, and it is only natural to ask Britain to support gold; France's gold reserves are second only to the United States, the franc zone in the 1920s is a group of gold-loving European countries and their colonies formed a trading system, France is bound to support gold; the Soviet ruble has always adopted a gold standard, under the lure of American aid, has sent a delegation to the Bretton Woods Conference. If the Soviets were told directly that the world would adopt the dollar standard in the future, Stalin would immediately flip out, while gold could pull the Soviet Union into the US-dominated world monetary system. In this way, the world of money will not be difficult to unify. When the time comes to cut the dollar's link to gold again, the world will have gotten used to the dollar long ago and the rally will be much easier to control.

The dollar chose Cao Cao's way of thinking, abandoning vanity and seeking only real profit. Wait for the right time, scrap gold to stand on its own!

The gold exchange standard created by Bretton Woods is a dollar standard in the name of the gold standard.

In addition to the monetary center of the "Gold Rush, Dollar Regency", the first fundamental point is the International Monetary Fund (IMF).

In the 1920s, the world currency "Three Musketeers" – the Federal Reserve Bank of New York's Strang, the Bank of England's Norman, the German central bank's Schacht, and later the Bank of France's Moreau, is the core of stabilizing the exchange rate of countries. In the form of private parties, they hammer out the monetary value relationship between countries behind the scenes and then demand acceptance by their respective governments. After World War II, the U.S. wanted the IMF to play a role that would replace the functions of the Big Four that year, with a more legal, regulated and standardized process to achieve exchange rate stability in each country.

Why has exchange rate stability, which Roosevelt once disdained in 1933, now become a major issue that the United States must face? In World War II, the United States, in support of a war that consumed so much, fully activated the economic machine, essentially achieving full employment and escaping the high unemployment of the Great Depression. When peace comes, the United States will have to deal with a huge overcapacity problem, and the war has made it heavily dependent on foreign needs. By the end of the war, the United States had realized that 60 million jobs must be maintained to achieve basic employment in society, and that the nightmare of high unemployment would befall the United States again if there were no overseas markets to absorb the vast productive capacity at home. At this point, the resumption of international trade is of strategic importance to the United States.

In order to achieve a stable monetary system, national currencies have to establish a pivotal relationship with the United States dollar, which commits $35 to 1 ounce of gold, so that national currencies indirectly achieve a locked-in relationship with the value of gold through the dollar. And the IMF is the kind of fund that ensures the stability of this currency parity relationship. When a country's currency deviates too much from the established exchange rate, it may overdraft a portion of its own funds from the Fund to intervene in its currency to bring the exchange rate back within the established range.

The initial establishment of this fund, the United States naturally contributed the bulk of the money, with $2.8 billion at 27% and the British Empire as a whole at 25%, because various resolutions require an 80% majority to pass, so both Britain and the United States have a veto, which is also a way for the United States to give Britain a face, and everyone to jointly rule the world monetary system, but the United States is clear that it is impossible for Britain to pool the votes of all the autonomous states under the empire at the time of the vote. Therefore, it is still the United States that calls the shots.

The British had their own considerations about the role of the IMF at first. For the currency standard, British negotiator Cairns suggested that an international monetary unit, the Bancor, should be created, instead of dollars and gold, and that everyone should borrow money to pay back the world dollar. Also, the IMF is supposed to be a world central bank that assumes the role of lender of last resort, i.e. in times of crisis, unlimited money creation. The UK's little abacus is clanging, and since the UK is over-indebted and desperate for funds, it wants the IMF to be an ATM that can overdraft and spend money, but doesn't want to be specifically indebted to a national currency, so it comes up with an ambiguous banker. And the one who ends up paying the bill for this fuzzy currency debt is apparently the United States, which is running a massive surplus.

It's a daydream, the American mind thinks. No more dollars, so haven't all those years of America worked for nothing? Scrap the gold? The dollar's not even that bold. Does anyone believe in that half-man, half-god Banker that Keynes made up? You want to fuck the World Central Bank? So the Fed is going to drink the northwest wind? Want to use the IMF as an ATM and the Americans end up paying for it? That's too much of a wishful thinking, isn't it?

The Americans dismissed Keynes' proposal article by article, insisting that the IMF is not a bank, but a fund. Everyone has to contribute money up front, can borrow transfers as needed, and then have to repay, or the shares will be reduced accordingly. The UK had to accept the US terms, the currency boss back in the day, but now it's a phoenix in the air, worse than a chicken.

The second fundamental point of the Bretton Woods system is the World Bank. The World Bank's original intention was to finance post-war reconstruction, and later took into account the financing of development in less developed countries.

In practical terms, the United States uses World Bank loans as a lollipop to reward countries that are willing to submit to the Bretton Woods dynasty, abandon the notion of self-sufficiency in economic development, cut tariffs and trade protections, and be willing to be good citizens of the dollar empire. Anyone who does not join this United States-dominated global system is economically choosing "self-imposed exile".

The United States had by this time completed its transition from being a staunch trade protection practitioner to an aggressive free trade advocate. The fundamental nature of the United States is businessmen, businessmen are pragmatic, do not believe in the so-called doctrine, what is good for me, resolutely use, what is not good for me, resolutely abandon, contempt for all others to judge!

Precisely because the rise of the United States relies on trade protection, so the United States especially taboo other countries to rejoin "their old ways. This is just like the Song Dynasty emperor Zhao Kuang Yin who ascended to the emperor's throne in a yellow robe, and whoever wants to wander around in front of him in a yellow robe must be guilty of his big mistake.

Although the United States had completed its regency, the hidden danger of the pound being divided had not yet been cut. The dollar still has work to do to cut the feudalism.

A killer to the pound, a poisonous dollar, no husband

> *"It is outrageous that in return for the loss of a quarter of our national wealth in the common anti-fascist cause, we are to burn incense for half a century to those countries that have become rich from war."*[31]
>
> —*The Economist* (UK)

The vast colonial system of the British Empire provided Britain with nearly unlimited credit overdraft power during the war, the colonial and Commonwealth countries provided the British army with all kinds of resources, food and raw materials, and also included the cost of the British army fighting in Egypt and India, even the cost of the American army on the ground was counted against Britain, as well as the cost of the Indian army assisting the British army fighting overseas, etc. They subscribed to British Treasuries and built up large reserves of pounds sterling, which was an important reason why Britain was able to withstand the depletion of the war and eventually win. The British colonial system and other trading partners supplied Britain with supplies in exchange for pound sterling reserves, while Britain and its allies depleted dollar reserves to buy arms from the United States, with the result that the total size of the pound in national reserves after the war was double that of dollar reserves. On the face of it, the pound has larger reserves than the dollar and remains the world's most dominant currency, but 2/3 of those reserves are concentrated within the pound and are under a high degree of instability.

Sterling accumulated heavily in sterling-area countries, not because it was more valuable, but because Britain froze their wartime options for converting the pound into other currencies. The presence of the US dollar makes the pound under great threat of being sold off by the countries in the pound zone at any moment. Prior to World War I, the UK's overseas assets were much higher than its liabilities, so the stability of the pound's value was unquestionable. But the UK now has

---

[31] *Economist* 1945.

a net external debt of $15 billion, six times its gold and foreign exchange reserves! If the pound were to lift its foreign exchange freeze, countries would be scrambling to convert their pound reserves into dollars and the pound would immediately face a catastrophic avalanche of value.

Britain should have continued to freeze foreign sterling reserves, and then use British exports to gradually repay these foreign debts, this can pull British employment, out of the shadow of the post-war recession, but also to stabilize the value of the pound, the most important thing is to maintain the existence of the pound sterling zone, as long as there is this economic base, rise again later is not impossible. If the freeze is lifted, the pound sterling zone will be turned to the dollar, not only to help the United States to expand exports and strengthen the sphere of influence of the dollar zone, but also the pound sterling zone will be fundamentally disintegrated and doomed.

Just after the end of the Second World War, Keynes, as the core brain of the British economy, went to the United States on behalf of Britain to negotiate the post-war loan issue, but on this big issue of the survival of the pound sterling area has a serious lapse of judgment, fell into the trap set by the United States, thus personally buried the pound sterling 200 years of hegemony.

The Americans proposed to Keynes that the United States could provide a $3.75 billion line of credit to Britain, adding to the $1.25 billion that Canada could provide for a total of $5 billion. But on one condition: the UK must unfreeze its foreign reserves of pounds by July 15, 1947!

The super-conceited Keynes, who originally thought that the United States and Britain were both allies and brothers of the same language and blood, and that the United States would be generous in relaxing the terms of the loan, was prepared to discuss with the Americans the wonderful idea of the future joint domination of the world by Britain and the United States, but was completely unprepared for the United States to put forward such a "too soon for each other" terms. Keynes really didn't understand the political machinations of America, and he actually said yes!

Commenting on this Keynesian loan, the British Economist pointed out pointedly,

> *"Not many people in this country would believe the Communists' theory that the destruction of Britain and what it stands for in the world was a premeditated, conscious purpose of American policy. But the evidence at hand can be read as follows: if every grant of aid is conditional, Britain will be caught in the inescapable inevitability of having to ask again for more aid, which can only be obtained at the cost of Britain's further self-denigration and self-diminishment. The result, then, is clearly what the communists had speculated."[32]*

Sure enough, on July 15, 1947, the hegemony of the pound collapsed completely.[33] After the war, Britain had counted on the resurgence of the pound zone, but the Americans were not going to give the British Empire a chance to die.

Germany's powerful pound hegemony, which was untouchable in both world wars, was easily destroyed by the United States with a mere fraction of the $3.75 billion loan.

One wonders, if the United States has any illusions about Britain, an ally who once rolled in the trenches and is still a brother of the same race, being so bitter to kill for power, can any other country have any illusions?

---

[32] Ibid.

[33] Barry Eichengreen, *Exorbitant Privilege, The Rise and Fall of the Dollar and the Future of the International Monetary System*, Oxford University Press, 2011. p40-41.

CHAPTER III

Currency Cold War, Rejecting the Dollar is Rejecting Peace

The Soviet Union's rejection of the Bretton Woods system was not the result of the Cold War, but precisely the cause of the Cold War. Roosevelt's scruples about the resurgence of the pound in World War II far outweighed concerns about the expansion of the ruble. In order to create the most favourable international environment for the United States after the war, Roosevelt was determined to break down all trade barriers in the world, completely eradicate the respective monetary zones, liberate the colonial raw material bases under British and French control, connect the resources and labour supply of the Soviet Union and Eastern Europe, absorb China, Japan and other Asian countries into the world market, and establish a "permanent peace under American rule" with the United States as the core of political power, the dollar as the monetary and financial basis and the goal of unifying the world market. After Roosevelt's death, the originators of the Cold War in the United States overturned his general policy and forced Stalin to finally reject the Bretton Woods system and instead establish his own Ruble Empire, thus beginning the Cold War.

In Lenin's New Economic Era, the ruble established the gold exchange standard, known as the Golden Ruble. During the Stalinist era, the rouble evolved into a "planned system", which was no longer a medium for active participation in commodity transactions, but a passive measure of the turnover of "barter" under the planned economy.

Stalin's 10-year plan to catch up with Western industrial powers in the 1930s, like the 156 key industrial projects that China built with Soviet aid in the 1950s, would not have succeeded without massive technological diffusion and the raw accumulation provided by the countryside. And at the time the only country that could provide the proliferation of Western technology was Germany, which was defeated in World War I. In fact, it was with the support and funding of the German military that the Soviet Union was able to learn and learn from modern advanced industrial technology.

After the war, the Soviet Union, with its great military might and national power, fought a fierce battle against the dollar in the currency circulation domain around the world. It was not until the mid-1960s that the ruble gradually developed into a permanent confrontation with the dollar due to the stagnation of the Soviet Union's own economy.

The oil crisis of the 1970s led to the discovery of a powerful economic weapon in the United States, which was the oil trade. It was the effective use of oil, the deadly "dollar dagger", by the United States in the mid-1980s that plunged a knife into the heart of the ruble empire.

Stalin rejects the dollar, Kenan drafts Cold War diatribe

The Bretton Woods system is nothing more than a "Wall Street outlet".[34]

—Representative of the USSR,
United Nations General Assembly, 1947

In February 1946, the weather in Moscow was cold and dry, with severe influenza spreading everywhere. American diplomat George Kennan also contracted wind chills, high fever, toothache, and side effects of medication that weakened Kennan. In the absence of U.S. Ambassador to the Soviet Union Harriman, the Embassy's big and small affairs were temporarily presided over by Kenan, who had to carry on with his illness and take care of various affairs. One of the main tasks is to deal with telegrams coming and going from various parts of the United States Government.

On February 22, bedridden Kenan had his secretary deliver Washington's call to his bedroom, and while going through the calls, a telegram from the State Department to the Treasury Department caught his attention. Treasury Department officials seem to be feeling increasingly anxious about the Soviet Union's delay in agreeing to the terms of the charters of the International Monetary Fund (IMF) and the

---

[34] Edward S. Mason and Robert E. Asher, *The World Bank since Bretton Woods*, The Brookings Institution, Washington, D.C., 1973. p. 29.

World Bank, and hope that the U.S. Embassy will soon figure out the Kremlin's true intentions.[35]

At the Bretton Woods Conference in 1944, the Soviets also sent a delegation, and there was a great deal of enthusiasm for the new world monetary system. In the August 1944 issue of Bolsheviks, the Soviets argued: "The Soviet Union is interested in this post-war cooperation because it allows the United States to promote and facilitate the process of recovery of our national economy and allows us to move forward quickly along the path to greater socio-economic development. At the same time, our allies and neutral countries are equally interested in developing trade with our country, since the Soviet Union was able to buy and consume large quantities of surplus manufactured goods from those countries. The Soviet Union always met its obligations scrupulously, as is well known." An article published in Planned Economy in 1944 similarly illustrates the Soviet attitude,

> "Our country is importing goods from abroad and exporting our products. After the war, our trade with foreign countries will increase considerably. Thus, the Soviet Union identified with the stability of the capitalist currency and the restoration of economic life in other countries. Short-term credit from the IMF, as well as long-term credit from the World Bank, will contribute to the development of trade relations between the Soviet Union and other countries. The Soviet Union was just as interested in this as any other country."[36]

The initial enthusiasm of the Soviets for the Bretton Woods system was understandable because they didn't really get the spiritual substance of Roosevelt's grand dollar strategy.

In Roosevelt's view, what Bretton Woods had established was actually a dollar dynasty, and while still retaining the nominal status of gold, the dollar would become the de facto master of monetary power in the world. In the future, countries around the world will adopt dollar-centric currency reserves and base their national currency issuance on dollar reserves. As Keynes saw it in the 1920s, the system was designed

---

[35] George F. Kennan, *Memoirs 1925–1950*, Pantheon Books, New York, 1967. p. 292–295.

[36] Michael Hudson, *Super Imperialism – New Edition: The Origin and Fundamentals of U.S. World Dominance*, Pluto Press; New Edition (March 21, 2003), Chapter 6.

to lead inevitably to the ultimate fate of nations' economic development, which would be in the hands of Wall Street. The main potential threat to this dynasty, according to Roosevelt, came not from the economically bankrupt Soviet Union after the war, but from the British Empire, which could at any moment zombie up.

Since coming to power in 1933, Roosevelt has spent much of his time in office battling the economic crisis, with his most bitter feelings being the 12-year Great Depression and the nightmare of unemployment for over 10 million people. World War II, which destroyed the European economy at the same time that the U.S. economy soared by 90 percent, and the future fate of America's excess production capacity and large employed population will be tied to the postwar world trade boom. To this end, he is determined to break down all barriers to trade in the world, completely eradicate the respective monetary zones, liberate the colonial raw material bases under British and French control, connect the resources and labour supply of the Soviet Union and Eastern Europe, absorb China, Japan and other Asian countries into the world market, and establish a "permanent peace under American rule" with the United States as the core of political power, the dollar as the monetary and financial basis, and the goal of unifying the world market.

Roosevelt was convinced that the British Empire waiting to make a comeback was a major obstacle to American strategy, and that the Soviet Union, whose economy was almost completely destroyed by war, was completely different from Britain. The Soviet Union had no overseas colonial system, its industry was far from adequate to compete with the United States, agriculture was a huge market for American agricultural products, and the Soviet Union posed no threat in terms of foreign investment. Through the grind of war, Roosevelt saw Stalin as a trustworthy world leader with no immediate impulse to subvert the world capitalist system; on the contrary, Roosevelt was unimpressed by Churchill's narrow-mindedness and frequent petty actions. To this end, it is consistent with the ultimate strategic goals of the United States to make the necessary political compromises and economic assistance to the Soviet Union and to integrate it into the American world system.

American bankers believe that the phenomenon of the U.S. and Soviet Union occupying vast continents at each end of the planet, controlling vast resources in areas where they do not compete with each other, must be seen as a dominant and dominating force in the course of future history. Both the Soviet government and American financiers have an abiding interest in maintaining a managed gold standard, because both the United States and the Soviet Union have the largest gold reserves and are potentially the largest gold producers. Although the economy of the Soviet Union was controlled by the state, it was not an expansionist theorist. In contrast to the UK, the Soviet Union in no way threatened US exports and international investment plans. The huge domestic demand in the Soviet Union would result in its resources being used primarily for domestic needs and not for economic penetration of other countries.[37]

But Kenan and most American politicians are far from the strategic vision and panache of Roosevelt. Roosevelt's death from illness on the eve of his war victory in April 1945 interrupted established U.S. strategic planning. Vice President Truman, who had been living in the shadow of the great president, was finally "set right," sensitive and paranoid, especially squeamish about comparing his policies to Roosevelt's, and unusually keen to demonstrate his decisiveness and self-confidence. Truman not only swapped out all the White House interiors that made him feel Roosevelt's presence, but in turn swapped out officials who adhered to Roosevelt's strategy.

Kennan could not understand why, in the highest Allied decision-making circles in Europe, the Americans were always deeply guarded against the British and instead more friendly to the Soviets; why General Patton, the most radical of the anti-Soviet forces, was repeatedly sidelined by the top brass of the American military.

What infuriates Kenan even more is that American aid to the Soviet Union was far better than it was to Britain. On August 13, before the war was over, the U.S. military stopped sending military supplies to Britain without waiting for the President's order; on the day Japan announced its surrender, without consulting Britain beforehand, it unilaterally terminated the Lease Act's aid to Britain and began to liquidate it, converting the supplies left in Britain into a debt of $532 million, and the supplies still in transit made the British owe another 118 million. The United States, on the other hand, was very lenient with the Soviet Union, providing it with up to $250 million in aid until the end of October, when the war was long over.

---

[37] Ibid.

The most unpleasant thing for Kenan was the pro-Soviet policy of the U.S. Treasury, which in June 1943 offered the Soviet Union a share of $763 million in the future International Monetary Fund (IMF), and later talked about $1.2 billion. The U.S. started with a share of 2.5 billion, the U.K. was about half, and the Soviet Union and China were third and fourth. Treasury Secretary Morgan Sow proposed to Roosevelt that the post-war aid loan to the Soviet Union be as much as $6 billion, with a 30-year repayment period and an interest rate of only 2.5%, which is far better than the disgraceful $3.75 billion aid loan that Keynes negotiated for Britain. Later, Morganzo's men, White, the U.S. chief negotiator for the Bretton Woods program, suggested in a memorandum to Roosevelt that the U.S. make a $10 billion aid loan to the Soviet Union, with repayment terms of 35 years and interest reduced to 2 percent.

Because he could not understand the pro-Soviet tendencies of the United States government, Kennan wrote repeatedly to the government, stating that he could not hope in the Soviet Union and concluding that the Soviet Union was necessarily expansionary in nature. But during Roosevelt's administration, Kenan's views were synonymous with short-sightedness and superficiality and certainly would not have been taken seriously.

However, the shift in international strategic thinking during the Truman era presented Kenan with a historic opportunity to make his mark.

In the Yalta system established by the Troika of Roosevelt, Stalin and Churchill in February 1945, Stalin proposed that Eastern Europe should be included in the Soviet Union's sphere of influence, while Churchill had run to Moscow beforehand to make a deal with Stalin whereby Britain recognized Soviet spheres of influence in Romania and Bulgaria, while the Soviet Union recognized British prerogatives in Greece, since the Mediterranean was the maritime lifeline of the British Empire, and Eastern Europe was the Soviet security buffer zone. When Roosevelt heard the news, he was taken aback. Britain did this, apparently in order to maintain the vast system of the British Empire, while the Soviet Union, by placing Eastern Europe under its protection, would create another dominant force. In this way, would not Roosevelt's ideal of destroying monetary domination and establishing a unified world market be destroyed in one fell swoop? The contradiction focused on Poland, where the Anglo-Americans certainly wanted a pro-Western government in power, but the Soviet Union liberated and occupied Poland, and Stalin demanded that the Polish government must obey the Soviets. The final compromise between the two sides was that Stalin promised to place pro-Western officials in the Polish government to represent Western voices. Roosevelt felt unsatisfied but barely able to accept it, after all, there is a difference between an ideal and reality. As long as the Soviet Union enters the Bretton Woods system, the United States will be the ultimate winner, and some partial compromise will be necessary for that.

The trouble was that after Roosevelt died, Truman wanted to flip the case. Without Roosevelt's prestige, opposition to the American "policy of appeasement" against the Soviet Union began to emerge, and Truman, who definitely did not want to become a second Chamberlain, decided that he had to be tough on the Soviet Union. Harriman, the U.S. ambassador to the Soviet Union, began to let loose, linking economic aid to the Soviet Union and Poland to the problems of Eastern Europe. Wasn't it out of line for Stalin to start getting wary? Is it that once Roosevelt dies, American policy will change? Stalin rejected Truman, noting that the American demands contradicted the spirit of the Yalta resolution. Of course, Stalin did not want to bog down the issue and finally suggested that the quota of Polish pro-Western officials be increased by a few more. Truman reluctantly agreed.

But the ensuing Soviet-American feud over a range of issues, including Turkey and Iran, left Stalin with deep doubts about America's ultimate intentions. Many of the original Soviet doubts about the Bretton Woods system are now fermenting again. "In the discussions of the Bretton Woods agreement, the Soviets expressed their apprehensions about the White plan, which allegedly proposed to abolish all restrictions on trade, currency in the near future. It seems very obvious to them that under contemporary capitalist conditions, especially in the post-war period, such a path would be impossible for many countries to adopt. Because their economic independence is under serious threat if state regulation is not applied." The Soviet representative made it clear: "They are not participating in this most brutal war ever fought to make the world safer for American and British exports." Stalin finally saw that the pressure being exerted by the United States to push for free trade was ultimately aimed at taking economic control of Eastern Europe and even the Soviet Union into American hands. The Soviet Union did not refuse to join the IMF, "just to tell U.S. officials that Moscow needs more time to consider the terms of the agreement".

The Soviet Union is waiting and watching for the American attitude.

On February 22, the U.S. Treasury Department sent a telegram to Kenan precisely in the hope of understanding the real motives for the Soviet Union's delay in joining the IMF.[38] Kenan, on the other hand, took the opportunity to write an 8,000-word telegram, which elevated his negative personal judgment of the Soviet Union over the years to the theoretical level of "the two sides of the coin", and provided the ideological ammunition for Truman's urgent political gesture of refusing to be "Chamberlain's second", which won him an ovation in the suddenly changed political atmosphere in Washington. Kenan also became a hit and was later called "the originator of the Cold War".

In the months that followed, instead of seeing American aid loans, the Soviets waited for Churchill's "Iron Curtain speech". Disappointed, the Soviet Union declared its refusal to join the IMF and World Bank and parted ways with the Bretton Woods system.

America's dream of trying to bring the Soviet Union into the dollar empire by means of currency and trade has finally been dashed. A cold war that lasted for more than 40 years, cost $8 trillion, cost hundreds of thousands of lives and divided millions of families, has kicked off.

From then on, the Soviet Union chose to part ways with the dollar dynasty and set about building its own ruble empire.

The Golden Roubles and the New Economic Policy

The financial history of Tsarist Russia is a history of the long-term devaluation of the ruble and the repeated rampant inflation.

From the 17th century until the end of the 19th century, the ruble was changed from copper to silver, from silver to paper money, and from paper money to finally gold. The establishment of the Tsarist gold standard in 1897 made the gold ruble one of the five strongest currencies in the world, and successfully survived the two shocks of the Russo-Japanese War of 1904–1905 and the Russian Revolution of

---

[38] George F. Kennan and John Lukacs, *George F. Kennan and the origins of Containment, 1944–1946*, University of Missouri Press Columbia, 1997. p. 9–10.

1905–1906. The outbreak of World War I forced Tsarist Russia to abandon the gold standard, and Tsarist Russia burned a total of 67 billion rubles in World War I, 25 percent of which was raised through taxes and 29 percent was backed by long-term loans, with British loans to Tsarist Russia accounting for a significant share, but after the October Revolution, British loans were refused to be repaid by the Soviet government, which was a significant reason for Britain's subsequent war debt to the United States. In addition, the national debt was financed by 23 per cent, leaving the rest of the money to be printed. From 1914 to 1917, the amount of money in circulation in Tsarist Russia increased 15 times, and so did the price of goods!

From 1914, when Russia participated in World War I, until 1921, Russia was involved in a seven-year war and experienced a period of unprecedented hyperinflation; after the outbreak of the October Revolution in 1917, the 14 Western countries joined forces with domestic rebels in an armed attack on the fledgling Soviet regime and soon occupied large swathes of Soviet territory, cutting off the most important sources of food and fuel in Russia. Factories in the Soviet Union were shut down, people were starving, supplies were scarce and the new regime was in danger. In order to win the war, the Soviet regime had to maintain the huge size of the 4.5 million Red Army under extremely difficult economic conditions. In order to support the costly war, the Soviet regime, on the one hand, began to issue its own Soviet rubles and, on the other, had to resort to the extreme measures of wartime communism: these included the provision of all rural foodstuffs, with the exception of rations, which had to be handed over to the State to support the war; the provision of foodstuffs, daily necessities and consumer goods for the urban population, all of which were supplied by State quotas; the compulsory participation of citizens who could afford to work; and the complete nationalization of industry and commerce. The wartime communist policy imposed quotas on almost all products of industry and agriculture.

After three years of civil war, the Soviet ruble, which was severely overstretched, had completely lost its credibility. From 1913 to 1921, prices in Russia rose a total of 49,000 times! At its worst, the Soviet ruble had depreciated to the appalling extent of 5 per cent per hour.

In 1921, when Russia finally achieved a decisive victory in the war, it was confronted with a severe economic depression, a scarcity of commodities, famine and a near-collapse of the rouble. The American Hammer witnessed this critical period with first-hand accounts. It was in this year that Hammer, at the age of 23, finally arrived in Moscow after a great deal of trouble. The Soviet Union he saw along the way was ramshackle and dilapidated; rail transport was almost crippled, public transport overcrowded and dirty; people were dressed in rags and hungry; shops were empty and the streets scattered. The Columbia University School of Medicine graduate, curious and passionate about the world's first socialist country, volunteered to help the local people with the epidemic of typhus, but the reality was like a basin of ice water that woke him up to his dream.

When Hammer arrived in Moscow, he carried with him a large amount of dollars, which he had expected to be free from worry, but in Moscow he found his dollars completely useless. With the closure of the National Bank by government decree in 1920 and the transfer of all banking operations to the Ministry of Finance, the formal financial system ceased to exist. Hammer wanted to buy something, but he couldn't pay the dollars, so he was taken to the Treasury for a replacement voucher. What Hammer got was a large piece of paper worth $10 with several small vouchers printed on it, and when you needed to buy something, you tore one off to pay. Hammer spent half the day milling around the streets of Moscow, buying nothing at all except buttons, shoelaces, and apples that the vendors were hawking. Tired and hungry, Hammer returned to the inn, and what awaited him were swarms of mice and bugs, and then there was the greasy, dirty bed and quilt. The hotel does not provide meals and he has to go to get a food supply card. With these food cards, you can go to a State supply point and pick up some bread, meat and vegetables, provided they are available. When Hammer arrived at the food point, it turned out that hundreds of people were lining up for the so-called food, only what appeared to be black bread made from a mixture of dirt and sawdust and a few moldy potatoes.

That's what life was like in the capital, Moscow, at the time!

When Hamer arrived in the Urals, he was simply stunned. The severe drought had nearly wiped out the local food supply, and thousands of farmers flocked to the railway line, boarding the trains as soon as they saw them, filling even the roofs. The children were starving to the bone, their bellies bulging from eating indigestible grass and leaves. At Ekaterinburg station, the bodies of those who had been killed by disease and hunger piled up in the waiting room. They were transported to a nearby cemetery for burial, and the clothes on the bodies were stripped off, as it was too bad to waste. The wild dogs and crows ate fat in those terrible days. Hamer was puzzled by the abundance of natural resources in the Urals, and he had seen with his own eyes how the region, which had a great deal of precious raw materials, such as platinum, gems and furs, as well as a large number of high-quality asbestos mines, had been driven to desperation by the famine that was guarding its great treasures. The business gene in Hammer's bones immediately sparked wealth, and he proposed to the local government that his company buy $1 million worth of grain in the United States, ship it to the local disaster relief area, and in return, the local specialties of the raw materials would be exchanged for their sale by him back in the United States, which the local Soviet government immediately agreed to.

By the time Hamer returned to Moscow to raise the "food for raw materials" deal, Lenin's new economic policy had begun to take hold. Merchants were allowed to engage in free trade, farmers could sell their surplus grain after paying taxes, small businesses were returned to private owners, and foreigners were encouraged to invest. Later, the story of Hammer's food deal that saved a large number of disaster victims reached Lenin's ears as a prime example, and Lenin received and encouraged Hammer as the first American businessman to take the rights to the Urals asbestos mine.[39]

With the implementation of the new economic policy, the market in Moscow is like a juggling act, a variety of goods on the shelves, in addition to a wide variety of food and delicious, the best French wine, pure Havana cigars, the quality of English wool, the price of French perfume, in a lined counter.

A stable currency is a basic prerequisite for the implementation of new economic policies and the promotion of trade. The Soviet ruble, in which the people have lost faith, is clearly unable to carry the weight of the new economic policy. In October 1921, the Soviet National Bank of Russia was reorganized and in 1923 it was renamed the National Bank of the USSR, and the central bank was reestablished. However, to stabilize the currency, it was necessary to have strong wealth power, and at that time it was impossible to rebuild people's confidence in

---

[39] Armand Hammer, *Hammer, G. P. Putnam's Sons*, New York, 1987, Chapter 12.

monetary stability, either in industrial and agricultural production capacity, or in domestic savings, foreign exchange and gold.

At this moment of crisis, the Soviet regime, which was already poor and clanging, suddenly made a fortune.

After the Russian October Revolution, the Tsarist army in Siberia, led by Admiral Gorczak, marched on Moscow and seized Kazan, the treasury of the Tsarist central bank, with a whirlwind capture of £80 million worth of gold reserves. He was then defeated in the advance on Moscow and finally fled eastward along the Siberian Railway with the gold. In winter, the cold in Siberia completely destroyed the morale of this defeated army, which had just run to Irkutsk and was in disarray. Among the defeated army were also a large number of mercenaries from the Central European countries, who, in order to return home alive and safe, were willing to make a deal with the Soviet government to hand over Kolchak and that gold to the Soviet government, which in turn guaranteed their personal safety and allowed them to return to Europe by boat from Vladivostok.[40]

In the end, the Soviets got about £50 million worth of gold. At that time, one pound was about 10 taels of silver, which was a huge sum of 500 million taels of silver! The Japanese extorted 230 million taels of silver from China through the Sino-Japanese War and succeeded in establishing a gold standard yen system after the British partially exchanged it for gold. This huge reserve of gold laid a solid foundation for the Soviet government to successfully stabilize the currency.

In 1922, the Anglo-American, French, German and other countries held an economic conference in Genoa, and Soviet Russia sent a delegation. On 11 October 1922, the People's Committee authorized the National Bank to issue bank notes called "Chevron" with not less than 25 per cent of gold and foreign exchange as currency reserves. Despite the severe lack of foreign exchange in the Soviet Union, this did not prevent the establishment of a gold exchange standard. Each Chevron contains 7.74234 grams of gold, equivalent to 10 gold rubles in the Tsarist era.[41] At the same time, old roubles, which had previously

---

[40] Maurice, Collis, *A Centennial History of HSBC*, China Books, 1979, p. 109.

[41] Xu Xiangmei, *A Study on the Transformation of the Russian Banking System*, China Finance Press, 2005, pp. 33–37.

been issued by the Soviet government and which had been severely devalued, were in circulation, and the government regularly published the value of the Chevron to paper roubles.

It is often said that "bad money expels good money", but this conclusion is premised on the fact that bad money prevails when the people have no choice. There is no choice, that is, the government forces the people to have no choice, and when the control of the regime declines and there is no ability to enforce the law, there is bound to be a situation where the market is willing to accept good money but not bad money. For example, when the Kuomintang suffered a major defeat in the second half of 1949, the people of the southern provinces refused to accept the National Government's golden vouchers and automatically began to circulate Yuan Dao. When the government is determined to protect the interests of the people and takes the initiative to introduce stable good coins, then the bad coins will disappear faster.

At the beginning of 1923, Chevron accounted for only 3 per cent of the total amount of money in circulation in the whole of Soviet Russia, which gradually increased to 83.6 per cent by February 1924. In 1924, the Soviet Union issued new roubles, and the monetary reform was completed, with the Chevron being the currency of account and the new roubles in circulation, one Chevron being equal to 10 new roubles.

The new Soviet gold ruble is born!

The stable gold ruble soon eliminated the rampant inflation, greatly accelerated the development of commodity trade, and contributed to the success of Lenin's new economic policy.

The Soviet Union's development model is in dispute

Lenin's new economic policy was undoubtedly a great success, saving the 1921 crisis of confidence in the regime, averting the collapse of the peasant-industrial alliance, with widespread support from peasants, workers, craftsmen, merchants and foreign investors, and a great development of production and trade. The prestige of the Soviet regime was consolidated in the hearts of the people. In 1927 the Soviet economy finally recovered to its pre-war level of 1913.

However, after Lenin's death in 1924, the question of what model of development the Soviet Union should adopt sparked a fundamental controversy that eventually degenerated into a bitter power struggle.

The economic policy of any country is, by its very nature, the art of maximizing economic output and rational distribution within the boundaries of limited human, material and financial resources. At the same time, economic output and distribution must reflect different priorities and focuses in different historical periods and in different external environments. The choice of economic policy, largely reflecting the will of the state and government, whether it is the establishment of British hegemony, the industrial rise of the United States, or the economic catch-up of Germany, clearly highlights the important influence of the state in economic development. In fact, the world has never had an absolute market economy and free trade, and that kind of economic environment, which is formed spontaneously by independent individuals, does not really exist in the real world; the so-called market economy is, in essence, a national market economy.

The Soviet Union was then faced with the choice of whether to continue to develop a market economy or to move towards a planned economy.

Until 1926, 82 per cent of the Soviet population was still agricultural and only 7–8 per cent of the labour force was engaged in industry, which made the Bolsheviks, with their strong working-class leadership at their core, unbearable! In the eyes of the Americans and the British, the Soviet Union was only a typical developing country, not even as good as Brazil and Argentina, with an economic gap of 50 to 100 years from the major Western countries.[42]

As the first socialist country, the social goals and economic programme of the Soviet Union were not acceptable to the ruling class of the entire world. Since 1918, foreign armed intervention and economic blockades have been the order of the day, and it has been almost impossible for the Soviet Union to develop its economy normally.

How to develop the economy and strengthen the country in an abnormal state, so as to effectively ensure the survival and development of the Soviet regime? Two schools of thought were formed in the Soviet Union.

---

[42] Armand Hammer, *Hammer, G. P. Putnam's Sons*, New York, 1987.

One school of thought: Lenin's new economic policy should not be a short-term expedient, but rather a fundamental strategy for the economic development of the Soviet Union. On the premise of the continuous improvement of the people's standard of living, take into account the coordinated development of agriculture, light industry and heavy industry, oppose the treatment of agriculture as a "domestic colony", and obtain the primitive accumulation necessary for the rapid development of industry at the expense of farmers.

The other school of thought believes that, in order to succeed in establishing a socialist state in the face of the siege of the capitalist world, priority must be given to the development of heavy industry and the acquisition of the necessary base for military industry at the earliest possible pace. They had learned from the lessons of past armed interventions and economic blockades by the West that future wars would be inevitable, and that heavy industry at that time had made little visible progress in the New Economic Policy, and that a strong heavy industry could not be built in a short time without concentrating the human, material and financial resources of the country. Therefore, the New Economic Policy must be abandoned in favour of a model of rapid industrialization with a five-year plan at its core.

From later historical facts, without the acceleration of industrialization, the Soviet Union would certainly not have been able to withstand the powerful attacks of Nazi Germany, with the result that the Soviet regime would have collapsed and the Soviet Union would have become a German occupied zone. Backed by the resources of the Soviet Union, Germany's war power would be further strengthened. It is feared that the entire outcome of the Second World War, and indeed world history to the present day, will be a different story. Perhaps the British government would go into exile, the United States would have to hold North and South America, and China would be permanently occupied by Japan.

Finally, Stalin's strategy of rapid industrialization became the model for the development of the Soviet Union. He proposed that the Soviet Union should catch up with Western industrial powers within 10 years. From a micro point of view, the development of Soviet industry is relatively inefficient, but from a macro point of view, Soviet industrialization can be described as rapid progress. By the end of three five-year plans, the Soviet Union had built up a strong industrial system of aircraft, automobiles, tractors, steel, chemical and defence industries, and had become the world's second largest industrial power after the

United States. It should be stressed that the short and large scale of the industrial rise of the Soviet Union was unprecedented in the history of the world economy, and that it was an astonishing leap forward in the external environment of the Great Depression of the world economy, under conditions of total dependence on domestic resources. In the 1930s, before the outbreak of the war, the Soviet Union produced 4,000 aircraft a year, and during the war it reached a staggering 30,000. Even the strong manufacturing capacity of German industry was gradually unable to resist the growing industrial power of the Soviet Union, which had come close to the strength of the United States in terms of military production capacity.

But the potential pitfalls of the Soviet Union's industrialization are just as daunting.

Any investment in economic development must be provided by savings, and before the industrialization of the Soviet Union there was neither sufficient domestic nor borrowable foreign savings, and the only thing that could provide for capital accumulation was agriculture, which constituted a major part of the national economy. High-speed industrialization demanded labor and food from farmers, but the strategy of prioritizing heavy industry resulted in light industry failing to provide farmers with consumer products in exchange for their food. The massive shift of labor from agriculture to industry and cities made it necessary for farmers to provide more food and keep a smaller portion for themselves. At the same time, it was necessary to feed the increasingly large Red Army, and the situation of the peasants was getting worse.

Under normal market economy conditions, peasants who owned land could reject such unequal exchanges and demand reasonable prices, which is exactly what happened; between 1923 and 1927, the prices of industrial products were considerably higher than those of agricultural products, leading peasants to be reluctant to sell food to the State; in 1927, peasants sold only 13 per cent of the total harvest, whereas in 1913 the proportion was 26 per cent. In this way, the peasants maintained a high standard of living, but the accumulation of industrialization cut off the source.

Under these circumstances, Stalin decided that the traditional agricultural model was not sufficient to support the cumulative demands of industrialization and that compulsory collective and State farms, with communalization of land, means of production and livestock, were necessary to force peasants to produce and tolerate a lower standard of living. The result is that farmers would rather kill their livestock than give it to collective farms without compensation. From 1928 to 1933, during the period of implementation of collective farming, the Soviet Union's cultivated cattle fell from 30.7 million to 19.6 million, sheep from 146 million to 50 million, and horses from 33.5 million to 16.6 million, and the farmers' enthusiasm for production was seriously frustrated.[43] From then on, until the collapse of the Soviet Union, agriculture became a major problem for the Soviet Union, which often failed to feed its own population in such a vast territory. A major exporter of food in the Tsarist era was increasingly becoming a food importer in the middle and late Soviet period. By the post-1970s, the scale of Soviet food imports had become a serious threat to the stability of the Soviet political economy. Ultimately, the food crisis has become a major cause of commodity shortages, privilege, popular discontent, trade imbalances and economic collapse.

German power, Soviet industrialization accelerates

Industry, especially heavy industry and the military industry, in addition to the huge financial investment, it is more important to have complex production technology, advanced organization and management, comprehensive supporting equipment, all kinds of professional talents, the speed, depth and breadth of the penetration of the industrial revolution into the countries of the world, which determines the fate of these countries in the 20th century.

Only in the mid-1920s, the Soviet Union was a typical agrarian country and a socialist country under a tight economic blockade by the West. After seven years of severe international and domestic war, the economy has only just picked up a bit, and the industrial base only has some almost abandoned industrial equipment and long-outdated technology left over from the Tsarist Russia era.

---

[43] Carroll Quigley, *Tragedy and Hope: A History of The World in Our Time*, The Macmillan Company, New York, 1966. p. 392–402.

When Hamer began his asbestos mining contracting adventures in the Soviet Union in the early 1920s, he couldn't imagine how far behind Russian industrial technology and equipment had fallen.

> *"I've never seen mining done in such an archaic way in my life, The workers used clumsy hands to drill through the ore, and it usually took about three days to drill a hole large enough to place the explosives. The fried ore was packed in baskets and carried on human backs up high steps, where workers sat in rows and rows and used small hammers to crack the stones. After the ores are cleaned, they are transported by the farmers in small carts to a railway station ten miles away."*

Primitive artisanal mining represented the level of industry prevalent in the Soviet Union at the time, which was thousands of miles away from modern industry! The first thing Hammer did was update the equipment, he brought in a generator, brought in a pneumatic drill from the United States, replaced the small hammer with a pounding machine, and the mechanized operation became a local sensation. He used a chainsaw to replace the traditional miter saw, a few minutes to complete the work of the previous day to complete the felling of trees sawing board, 50 miles around the Russian people are coming to see the hustle and bustle, they hauled the wood from home, just to see for themselves what the "table knife cut cream" chainsaw is hiding something weird.

The proliferation of technology is firstly the introduction of equipment and secondly the cultivation of human resources. Hammer brought in tractors made by Ford, and he brought in Ford engineers to train the Russians on how to use the tractors to pump water, saw wood, drive generators and plow the land. As their 50 tractors drove haphazardly from the port into the city centre, causing great panic, the Russians assumed it was American and British tanks that had started the invasion. Later, when it was learned that the tractors were for plowing the land, thousands of farmers gathered along the way to watch the novelties being shipped in from the United States.

No wonder Lenin said that Russian industry was 50 to 100 years behind the West.

The Soviet economy in 1927 was roughly equivalent to China's in 1953. The 156 large-scale industrial projects built by the Soviet Union in the 1950s laid a solid foundation for industrialization in China. For an agricultural country, the technology and equipment of industry and the immense productivity they bring is magical and incredible, and learning and using these technological devices already takes a considerable amount of time to digest and assimilate, let alone to produce and manufacture these complex industrial devices. This requires not only deep theoretical knowledge, but also practical experience in mass production and the ability to organize and manage production. Without the $2.4 billion loan provided by the Soviet Union and the socialist countries of Eastern Europe at that time, and the more than 18,000 experts sent by the Soviet Union to China with drawings of all the machinery and equipment of all the factories and handed them down to Chinese engineers and skilled workers over a period of 13 years, could China have laid the foundation of heavy industries such as iron and steel metallurgy, non-ferrous metals, petrochemicals, machining, automobile and shipbuilding, electronics industry, aircraft manufacturing, etc. in 10 years' time? The significance of this Soviet-style industrial technology proliferation aid is that it helped China form its own industrial hematopoietic function, which is far more significant than $2.4 billion or even $10 billion in cash aid!

By the same token, on the basis of the Soviet Union in the mid-1920s, Stalin's goal of catching up with Western industrial nations in 10 years would have been impossible to achieve without the massive proliferation of foreign technology. So who, given the historical conditions of the time, was able to provide such assistance?

The answer is Germany, which, after World War I, was always ready to overturn the injustice of the Treaty of Versailles and to make a clean slate.

As early as the early 1920s, the German military regarded the restrictions imposed on the German army by the Treaty of Versailles as a disgrace; Germany was unable to develop an air force, a navy, heavy equipment such as tanks, large calibre artillery and anti-tank guns, and the army was limited to 100,000 men. The inherent arrogance of the German nation, tormented by the defeat and humiliation of unequal treaties, inevitably led to a strong rebellion against the will. And the German military and arms industry giants are a direct expression of this rebellious will. But they understood that the Anglo-French power was overwhelming at the time and that confrontation was clearly not going to work, but secretly, Germany did not stop for a moment from trying to "save the country on the curve". That's when the Soviet Union became the best partner.

At the Genoa Economic Conference in 1922, the British-led League of Nations was working to sell the Norman-invented gold standard to the world's central banks, and Germany and the Soviet Union sent their own delegations to the Genoa Conference. The two orphans of the international community, however, were not able to intervene at the meeting, feeling that they were "the same as the rest of the world" and sympathizing with each other. At this meeting, the Soviet-German Treaty of Rapallo was signed to cancel each other's war reparations claims, fully restore diplomatic relations between the two countries, and establish a close trade alliance.[44] Britain and France were shocked by it.

Germany soon became the largest trading partner of the Soviet Union.

Germany was oppressed by Britain and France, and faced with strong hostility from Poland, befriending the Soviet Union not only benefited each other in trade, but also played an important role in weakening Poland and reducing pressure from Britain and France, both politically and militarily.

General Hans von Seeckt, later known as the "Father of the Wehrmacht", was the initiator of the military and industrial cooperation with the Soviet Union. Sektor became, in fact, the soul of the German army after World War I. Although the German staff headquarters was abolished by British and French compulsion, Sektor kept the staff headquarters, the essence of the German army's superior combat power, in the name of the Bureau of Military Affairs. His response to the 100,000-strong IDF was to turn every soldier into the seed of a future army, every officer with the capabilities of a future general and marshal, and once the war machine was activated, the 100,000 men would immediately be able to train and build a million strong army. Many of the famous generals of World War II, such as Marshals Rommel, Burke, and Longstedt, came under Sektor's account. Later, he also traveled to China and became Chiang Kai-shek's military advisor, proposing three major military-building ideas that influenced his life: the army as the basis for ruling power, the army's power lies in its

---

[44] League of Nations Treaty Series, Volume 19 327 L 1923.

excellent quality, and the army's combat potential comes from the cultivation of the officer corps.

In fact, Sektor's elite Wehrmacht army of 100,000 during the Weimar Republic era was indeed a decisive factor in whether the regime could be consolidated. Even Hitler, who wanted to consolidate Nazi power when he came to power, had to cooperate with the Wehrmacht and even destroy his own troops. It was because Hitler did not trust and could not ultimately control the Wehrmacht that the Nazis formed their own SS to check the Wehrmacht's power.

This is how Sektor judged the Soviet-German Treaty of Rapallo,

> *"Although (trade with the Soviet Union) was good for Germany, its (the treaty's) economic value was not the main aspect, the political significance was the key. The progress in Soviet-German relations is the greatest and only increase in power that peace has achieved so far in Germany. The progress of this relationship, in general, deserves to start with economic cooperation, but the strength of (Soviet-German) cooperation is that this economic interaction will pave the way for future political and military cooperation."* [45]

In early 1921, Sektor formed a section in the Wehrmacht code-named "Group R", headed by a close friend, von Schleicher (who became Chancellor of Germany in 1932 and was the leader of Hitler and the Nazis), to establish secret German assistance to the Soviet military industry, docking with the Chairman of the Soviet People's Committee for Foreign Trade, Grazin, and in September 1921, Soviet and German representatives began secret talks in Schleicher's apartment and agreed on implementation details for German financial and technical assistance to the Soviet military industry. Of course, the Soviet side also had to give back to the Wehrmacht, which was to allow the German military to set up the arsenals and training bases needed for military industry in the Soviet Union.

In March 1922, the first German military industrialists arrived in the Soviet Union. A month later, the German aircraft company Junker began construction of a modern aircraft manufacturing plant in the Fili region on the outskirts of Moscow, and Krupp Arms began construction

---

[45] Wheeler-Bennett John, *The Nemesis of Power*, London: Macmillan, 1967, p. 133.

of a heavy artillery production plant in the southern Soviet Union. Subsequently, German military flight training schools, tank testing academies, chemical weapons production plants, and submarine construction bases began to be built one after another in the Soviet Union.[46]

A large number of German military-industrial technologists were sent to the Soviet Union to help Soviet engineers, hand in hand, set up a series of manufacturing plants for aircraft, tanks, large-caliber artillery, chemicals and more. The establishment and operation of these factories, on the one hand, enabled the Soviet Union to acquire extremely valuable advanced industrial technology and to train a large number of engineers for the military industry, while at the same time acquiring the refined production management skills of German industry, significantly reducing the technological gap between the Soviet Union and the industrialized countries; on the other hand, these factories enabled Germany to test new technologies and inventions in practice, to produce all kinds of heavy equipment and military aircraft prohibited by the Treaty of Versailles, and to maintain the world-leading level of German military technology to a level that was not outdated. Germany, under cover of the Soviet Union, evaded checks by Anglo-French inspectors on the compliance of German military industry with the requirements of the Treaty of Versailles during a five-year-long military-industrial cooperation.

The honeymoon period of more than five years of Soviet-German military-industrial cooperation, from 1922 to 1927, was also a crucial period in the Soviet Union when the road to industrialization was debated within the country. It was with the help of the German military industry that the Soviet Union acquired the technology, equipment, experience and talent needed for industrialization. When the Soviet Union began its first five-year plan in 1928, it only took a few dozen times the proliferation of these valuable industrial technologies to rumble the wheels of industrialization.

---

[46] Ibid.

The Expansion of the Ruble Empire

> *"Moscow's rejection of participation in the Bretton Woods monetary system and the reduction of trade barriers in areas under its control is not the result of the Cold War, but its cause."*[47]
>
> —Gaddis

After the war, the American dream of bringing the Soviet Union and Eastern Europe onto the map of the dollar empire was dashed. The United States decided to sentence the Soviet Union and Eastern Europe to "economic exile" and "life imprisonment" for political and military containment. When the United States began its "dollarization strategy" against Europe in 1947, the Soviet Union and Eastern Europe were rejected in disguise.

The "Marshall Plan" was essentially a substitute for German war reparations, which dealt a severe blow to the process of reconstruction of the Soviet economy while at the same time achieving the domination of European reconstruction by American financial power blocs. The Yalta Agreement and the Potsdam Proclamation made it clear that the Soviet Union would receive war reparations from Germany, which could be paid in the form of German machinery and equipment, industrial enterprises, cars, ships, raw materials, etc., at a time when the Soviet Union had suffered so much war damage that it had almost lost its ability to earn foreign exchange from exports, so that German war reparations would become the most important external resource in the process of Soviet economic reconstruction. The core of the "Marshall Plan" was the disguised abolition of German war reparations to the Soviet Union and its replacement by United States financial assistance to Europe. Although the aid was ostensibly open to both the Soviet Union and Eastern Europe, the Marshall Plan set out conditions for economic liberalization that were incompatible with the planned economic system of the Soviet Union and thus "forced" it to exclude the Soviet Union and Eastern Europe from its scope.

The Soviet Union, on the other hand, by dismantling heavy industrial equipment on a large scale in Germany and sweeping up

---

[47] Michael Hudson, *Super Imperialism – New Edition: The Origin and Fundamentals of U.S. World Dominance*, Pluto Press; New Edition (March 21, 2003), Chapter 6.

everything of value, "recovered" about 66 billion marks in war reparations, more importantly, the Soviets did not forget the most creative wealth in the proliferation of industrial technology – talent, although the Americans took the first step to get rid of Germany's best 120 rocket experts, but the Soviet Union still managed to retain the remaining 3,500 engineers and excellent technical workers, these people are the core backbone of the missile business of which the Soviet Union is proud.

Without the aid of the dollar, the Soviet Union, relying on its own efforts, achieved a rapid economic recovery in just five years, and in 1950 industrial output exceeded pre-war levels. With the recovery of economic strength, in the face of the U.S. policy of "economic exile", the Soviet Union began to "dig the wall" counterattack war. From the early 1950s, the Soviet Union launched an economic offensive against the weakest regions of a series of dollar empires.

For the dollar empire, every time the Soviet Union expanded its economic power to another region or country, the United States lost another normal market.

The establishment of a new China deprived the United States of the largest dollar-occupied area on the west coast of the Pacific, and the massive Soviet aid to China in the early 1950s meant that China's industrialization would accelerate significantly, creating a potential threat to the dollar empire.

At the same time, the Soviet Union began a subversive offensive in the pound sterling area of the Middle East, and in 1956 the Suez Canal crisis severely weakened Anglo-French power in Egypt by the United States, which did not hesitate to impose severe sanctions on all Anglo-French attempts to restore the imperial colonial system. But before the dollar could get in after the blow to Anglo-French, the ruble pounced at a breakneck pace. By 1958, the Soviet Union had driven a wedge in the ruble in Egypt, Syria and Yemen.

For Egypt, ruble aid is in the long-term interest of its economic development. Egypt had developed its own five-year plan, covering all areas of the modern economy, and the Soviet Union was there to help whenever Egypt needed it. Of course, there were no free lunches, and the Soviet Union was not a charity. Since the United States, through the Bretton system, had built a dollar empire, the Soviet Union had to build its own ruble empire in order to break the blockade of the dollar zone. At the heart of economic assistance is the expansion of the ruble's sphere of influence and the erosion of the dollar zone. Thus, the Soviet Union provided Egypt with a long-term loan in rubles, worth $178 million, with a time limit of 12 years, at an interest rate of only 2.5%, half that of Western commercial loans.[48] The Soviet Union spared no expense in occupying the ruble bridgeheads in North Africa. In the Egyptian desert, modern Soviet oil rigs are already producing, and plans for future oil refineries for Egypt are in full swing. In order to economically integrate Egypt into the ruble zone, the Soviet Union also for Egypt's main export of foreign exchange-earning fist product cotton, opened the door to the domestic market, at a time when Egypt's cotton exports are being rejected by the West, which can be said to be a blessing for Egypt. Not only that, but the Soviet Union sent food and fuel that Egypt was in desperate need of. The Egyptians felt no loss, it gained valuable technology proliferation, an export market for the Soviet Union, an acute shortage of vital supplies, and at the same time won the political-military protection of the Soviet Union.

The Soviet import price for Egyptian cotton was considerably higher than the world market price, making the Western market less attractive to Egypt. After hoarding cotton in large quantities, the Soviet Union had the energy to disrupt Western markets and harass the normal economic order of the dollar empire by selling it. The United States is carrying the burden of maintaining world market order, while the Soviet Union's market guerrilla warfare has left the United States in a frenzy. The Soviet Union's economic calculations were no less impressive than those of the United States, where cotton was purchased at a high price and then compensated for by the profits of industrial equipment sold at a high price.

In Syria, Soviet engineers were busy surveying the entire country and selecting sites for future aid aircraft manufacturing plants. Soviet oil experts are already making final preparations for oil extraction in the desert region of the Northeast. More to the delight of the Middle East, the Soviet Union was ready to install nuclear reactors in the region and provide a large ruble loan for future nuclear power plants.[49]

---

[48] Howard K. Smith, *The Rubble War: A Study of Russia's Economic Penetration versus U.S. Foreign Aid*, Columbia Broadcasting System, Inc., 1958.

[49] Ibid.

Not only was the Soviet Union on the move, but the Eastern European countries were also following closely the Soviet ruble expansion strategy. The Czech Republic built Africa's largest arms production system for Egypt and opened the site of Africa's largest ceramic production company near Cairo. In Yemen, Soviet engineers are building the largest modern port on the Red Sea, the first major public project in Yemen's history. China, with the coordination of the Soviet Union, was not idle either, helping to build the road through Yemen from Sana'a to Hodeida.

In Jordan, a direct confrontation between the ruble and the dollar erupted. Since the withdrawal of the pound's power in 1957, the dollar has stayed. But how much of a role the United States can play in such a small Jordan remains uncertain. For the Soviet Union, fly meat is meat too, and to pry open any piece of the dollar zone's territory in the Middle East would mean one more beachhead position for the ruble, and there would always be a chance in the future to connect these scattered ruble bases into one big ruble zone. Jordan itself has a majestic dream of industrialization, and the key to fulfilling that dream is a transport artery that connects the country. Just as the United States hesitated, Yugoslavia and Poland killed in with the ruble, and Jordan finally ran out of patience as it waited through the long process of approving aid loans in the United States. The ruble district is the next city.

Asia plays a pivotal role in the battle between the dollar and the ruble. Asia is not only a vast region with a quarter of the world's population, but also the largest and largest European colonial system, rich in resources and raw materials, it is both a strategic focus of the United States to prevent the resurgence of the pound sterling area, but also the front line of resistance to the Soviet ruble economic infiltration. Since the post-war reconstruction, the United States has spared no expense in the Asian region, pouring $1 billion in aid. The United States is not only providing economic assistance, but also opening its markets to Asian countries for the sole purpose of tying China, Japan, South Korea and countries in Southeast Asia under the Kuomintang to the dollar zone. By the mid-1950s, Asia had become a veritable dollar-occupied region. No wonder, after the withdrawal of the Kuomintang from the mainland, the United States issued an exclamation of "who has lost China", which is actually more accurately expressed as "who has lost the Chinese territory of the dollar empire".[50]

When the Soviets had eased their economic difficulties in the recovery phase of the war, they began a major ruble offensive in Asia in the mid-1950s. From China to North Korea, from Southeast Asia to Afghanistan, Soviet experts and engineers were everywhere.

Neutral India, became the main battleground for the dollar and the rupee in Asia. Although the Soviet Union put in less than half the size of the U.S., its successful ruble influence operation greatly offset the strength of the dollar. At India's largest steel company, Bilai Steel, it plans to complete its second five-year plan to produce 1 million tonnes of steel, or one-fifth of India's national steel production, and employ up to 50,000 people. The Americans paid the most money, but it was the Indians who gave the impression that the Soviets were the main contributors to the project. The reason for this was that a large number of Soviet engineers were on site, who, unlike the American experts who complained about the harsh living conditions and were paid half as much as the Americans, were enthusiastically and patiently helping their Indian counterparts to master and digest the technical difficulties as quickly as possible. In most cases, Soviet engineers did not simply advise, as required by the contract, but worked directly with the Indians on specific engineering details. It is no exaggeration to say that the Soviet Union mobilized the greatest potential and initiative in the offensive to break the dollar siege.

The ruble has not only launched a "counter-encirclement" campaign against the dollar in Eurasia and Africa, but has also put its "black hand" directly in the backyard of the United States – Central and South America. Since the Monroe Declaration, Central and South America has been drawn into its own sphere of influence by the United States. The Soviet Union was later to strike at America's backyard and at the same time more covert. In order not to irritate the United States so drastically, and in more cases, the will of the Soviet Union was manifested through Czech and Polish aid, and in 1958, when the Chilean president was ready to visit the United States in good faith to seek more market opportunities, the United States coldly dropped the

---

[50] Ibid.

word that it was about to begin resuming high tariffs on imports of copper products, the lifeblood of Chilean trade. The United States, without showing mercy, forced the Chilean President to cancel his planned visit to the United States. Chile's trade was facing a huge crisis at a time when the Soviet Union and East Germany had emerged just in time to buy Chilean copper products in large quantities, with hints that more orders were still to come. Although the Soviet Union did not promise future purchases, it has already stirred up a huge Soviet frenzy in Chile. It was a brilliant move by the Soviet Union to play the levers of influence.

When Argentina was in desperate need of 15 million barrels of oil and was shy of buying from the United States in dollars, it was the Soviet Union that played the role of Prince Charming, promising not only to sell its oil to Argentina, but also to sell it below international market prices. No dollars? It didn't matter, the Soviet Union accepted payment for raw materials, and Argentina was worried that they wouldn't sell. The Soviet Union simply became Argentina's great savior.

Argentina's neighbor, Uruguay, is facing economic bankruptcy and its largest export, wool, is being forced out of business by special high US tariffs on wool. At the same time, the dumping of food by the United States in the food market has left Uruguay's agriculture in dire straits. And the oil, modern industrial equipment and transport infrastructure that Uruguay desperately needs cannot be purchased because of the lack of dollars. Uruguay denounces the Americans for trying to bring down the current government and replace it with a more pro-American administration in the run-up to the elections. The Soviets were now descending like the Bodhisattva of the Goddess of Mercy, first purchasing $18 million in wool, paying not roubles but hard currency pounds, and then selling 1.25 million barrels of oil to Uruguay to solve its coal burning problem, still below the international market price.[51] The Uruguayan nation hailed the Soviets for their righteousness.

Immediately afterwards, there was another big show in Brazil: before the elections, Brazil's top export commodity, coffee, was

---

[51] Ibid.

suddenly stalled, inventories were backlogged and the foreign exchange balance deteriorated dramatically. Coffee is to Brazil what copper is to Chile and wool is to Uruguay. And the power to price these commodities is in the hands of the United States, and if the president of any country in Central and South America does not listen, the United States will only have to resort to economic means that will be enough to cause the country's economy to deteriorate dramatically and lose in the general election. But the Soviet Union came in and stirred things up so badly that the U.S. was smashing up the show. Brazil, like other countries in the South-Central United States, is rich in a variety of agricultural products and raw materials, but lacks oil and dollars and suffocates the domestic economy once it runs a trade balance deficit. The Soviet Union, as usual, traded oil for Brazil's coffee, cocoa, cotton and raw materials, turning around Brazil's economic woes in one fell swoop. At this time, Brazil had not even established full diplomatic relations with the Soviet Union. Since then, Brazil's enthusiasm for the Soviet Union has been high.

The purpose of diplomacy is to expand a country's sphere of influence. The so-called sphere of influence is the limit of the currency's reach, within which it can effectively influence the local economy and politics. In international relations, there is never purely political influence, but only economic influence in a political sense, that is, the power of money!

Economic aid and ruble diplomacy had become the Soviet Union's weapons of mass destruction against the dollar empire.

The food crisis, the consequences of rapid industrialization

The ruble's most powerful period against the dollar was the 1950s, when the successful and rapid post-war economic recovery of the Soviet Union set the stage for a massive expansion of the ruble's territory. However, the Soviet economy did not fare well for long, and as we entered the 1960s, Soviet economic growth became sluggish, restraining the ruble's expansionary momentum. The dollar entered a strategic hold phase with the ruble, while in the 1980s the dollar launched a decisive counterattack.

The first area of the Soviet economy to be exposed as problematic was agriculture. It is indeed inconceivable that an empire as large as 1/6 of the Earth's land mass, with a population of less than 300 million, would have to rely on increasing food imports to feed itself for most years after the 1960s. Russia is not incapable of self-sufficiency; in fact, until the beginning of the 20th century, it remained the world's largest food exporter, accounting for 45% of the world's total food exports. The mid-1960s were an important watershed in the deterioration of the food problem in the USSR.[52]

Indeed, the 1930s-50s were the golden years of economic development in the Soviet Union, and the industrialization of the country as a whole was a remarkable success. To sum up Churchill's assessment of Stalin, "The Soviet Union was merely an agrarian backwardness when he came to power, but a world superpower equipped with the atomic bomb at the time of his death". However, extreme skewed development necessarily hides extreme growth pitfalls.

Gaidar, who was Acting Prime Minister of the Russian Government, summed up the Soviet agricultural problem thus:

> *"Collectivization, depriving peasants of their freedom of movement, choice of work and place of residence, forced unpaid labour, and the necessity to support their families through personal sideline work, all amount to a return to serfdom. The difference is simply that instead of acting as one of the serfs, the state became the sole lord. In the absence of moral restraint and in the possession of modern means of monitoring and perpetrating violence, the Government is convinced that what happens in the countryside is irrelevant compared to the increase in investment in industrial infrastructure. All of this is a breakthrough in the maximization of resources from farmers, which is unique to agricultural societies, and the scale of redistribution of funds from rural to urban areas is unprecedented in world history. If labor in the countryside is compulsory, if it becomes some form of servile land rent, then it will inevitably restore the moral standard of labor in Russia before the abolition of serfdom as depicted in Russian literature."[53]*

---

[52] E. T. Gaidar, *The Demise of Empire: Lessons from Contemporary Russia*, Social Science Documentation Press, 2006, chapter 4.

[53] Ibid.

"Only fools love to work" is a true reflection of the Soviet rural labour ethic, and the enthusiasm with which people work for themselves and their families and the slowness with which they work for the public have been repeatedly tested in many countries and societies. The lazy work attitude, the social treatment of second-class citizens and the meagre income level have forced the most educated, capable and strongest labour force of the rural population to run to urban life at all costs, and this impulse and pressure to "jump the dragon's gate" has deprived the rural areas of their most productive essence.

In the era of the industrial revolution, the most critical development of a country depends on the scale of industrial technology diffusion, and the core element of industrial technology diffusion is talent. Only the creative involvement of people can integrate technology, equipment, capital, and raw materials into the final product. In the industrialization of the Soviet Union, it had succeeded in focusing on the effects of industrial technological diffusion; in the development of the agricultural economy, it had neglected that agricultural growth also required technological diffusion, and that agricultural technological diffusion could only be implemented by agricultural personnel of the same quality as industrial talent in order to produce the same investment benefits. The loss of large numbers of agricultural talent, both active and passive, created a dilemma that the Soviet agricultural problem could not be alleviated with greater investment.

In the United States or Western Europe, there is no class status gap or clear income gap between farmers and urban populations, and the choice between farming or urban settlement is often determined by personal life preferences, so that the quality of the agricultural population in developed countries enables them to carry the high returns expected from high capital inputs.

When the Soviet government realized that it could no longer continue to exploit agriculture, the accumulation of industry also had the capacity to feed it. The Soviet Government began to increase its investment in agriculture year by year from the beginning of the 1960s, from 14.3 per cent of the total investment in the Soviet economy in 1960 to 20.1 per cent in 1980; due to the expansion of the total economy, the scale of investment in rural areas, both in absolute and relative terms, has reached a rather alarming level, but in most years the Soviet Union was unable to meet domestic demand for food; in 1960 the Soviet Union was able to export some food, but in 1970 it had to import 2.2 million tons, and in 1982 it increased dramatically to 29.4 million tons, and in 1984 it reached 46 million tons!

As Andropov said in the 1960s: "Agriculture is particularly bad, and it will no longer be possible to tolerate a situation in which even the State cannot feed itself and has to import more and more food year after year. Any more of this and we'll soon be starving for a living." In 1963, due to a poor agricultural harvest and a severe shortage of foreign exchange in the USSR, the USSR had to sell 372.2 tons of gold to buy grain on the international market. The Soviet Union lost nearly one-third of its gold reserves at once, which Khrushchev regarded as a great disgrace. By 1965, the Soviet Union had to sell 335.3 tons of gold again to buy food, and this time everyone was used to it. It's getting numb after that.

Why did the Soviet Union run such a huge food deficit? The direct cause of this situation was the rapid industrialization and urbanization of the 1930s. Industrialization has made people's wage income constantly increase, and more and more urban population's demand for food supply quantity and quality has also increased, especially the pursuit of meat, eggs, milk and other high nutritional value food, resulting in more food being crowded out by livestock feed, which makes the food shortage problem even worse.

In the mid-1960s, cheap meat was lost in State shops; in the early 1970s, queues for food were increasingly common in major cities; and in the 1980s, even food supplied with tickets was difficult to come by. All of this has seriously undermined the people's trust in the government. This, coupled with the various phenomena of privilege that have arisen in the distribution, has added to popular discontent.

On the one hand, the industrialization of the Soviet Union has led to a long period of weakness in the agricultural economy and the inability to feed itself; on the other hand, deformed industrialization has squeezed the resources of the light industrial sector, making it difficult to produce products that are competitive on the international market and cannot be exchanged for foreign exchange. As a result, in order to ease the food shortage crisis, the Soviet Union had to rely mainly on oil exports for hard currency.

At last, the Soviet Union exposed its economic weakness to the United States, which was waiting for a chance to make a move.

Peak Oil, Soviet Union Falls into the Abyss

The Soviet Union has always been a major producer of oil and gold, because the annual production of gold is not enough to support the growing food deficit, oil has become the last hope of the Soviet Union in exchange for foreign food. I didn't expect this road to be the end of a dollar ambush to bury the stumbling block!

The Soviet Union's heavy dependence on oil for both industry and agriculture made it impossible to export on a large scale to generate foreign exchange, as the production capacity of the original Soviet oil fields could only meet the needs of domestic and satellite countries in the ruble region.

The discovery of the great Siberian oil fields in 1960 became the starting point for the Soviet Union's dream of a path to food abundance and political stability. Throughout the seventies, Siberian oil, as a gift from God, was stuffed into the Soviet treasury, and the disintegration of the Bretton Woods system in 1971, the decoupling of the dollar from gold, severely shook international markets, and the severe depreciation of the dollar accelerated the soaring prices of gold and oil. The outbreak of the two oil crises has made oil prices soar like wild horses on the run. The Soviet Union was like a rich man who had won the jackpot, spending endless amounts of silver and enjoying endless glory. The petrodollar has temporarily filled a huge deficit in food. In anticipation of an infinitely better future for oil prices, the Soviet Union embarked on a nuclear weapons confrontation with the United States, intensifying the arms race and thus plunging into the quagmire of the Afghan war.

The 1970s were the last time that the ruble went head-to-head with the dollar. When the United States took over the oil-exporting countries such as Saudi Arabia, fixed the basic national policy of the petrodollar, and then adopted the high interest rate trick to suppress the two tigers of inflation and the dollar crisis, the dollar difficulties finally carried through.

The US is finally freeing up its hands and ready to pack up the ruble.

In March 1977, the U.S. Central Intelligence Agency (CIA) submitted a secret memorandum to the U.S. government, The Impending Soviet Oil Crisis (ER 77–10147), in which the CIA stated that "the peak of Soviet oil output will come in the early 1980s, and in the next decade [referring to the 1980s] the Soviet Union will find itself, not only unable to provide exports of the present magnitude to Eastern Europe and the West, but also forced to compete with the OPEC countries for its own oil supplies. This marks a reversal of the current situation (referring to the huge Soviet oil trade surplus), with oil exports to the West accounting for 40 percent of Soviet hard currency revenues." The memorandum clearly states that "when oil production stops growing, and even before that, the Soviet Union's domestic economy and international trade relations will be profoundly affected."[54]

The CIA's memo is based on peak oil theory. "Peak oil" is said to have originated from the so-called "bell curve" pattern of mineral resources discovered by the famous American petroleum geologist Harbert in 1949. In 1956, Harbert boldly predicted that U.S. oil production would peak in 1967–1971 and then decline. His statement drew a lot of criticism and ridicule when the US oil industry was booming, but then the US did reach peak oil in 1970 and history proved his prediction correct.

It was the arrival of peak oil in the United States in the early 1970s that made the two Middle East oil embargoes powerfully lethal to American economic industries to a far greater extent than the U.S. government ever imagined. If the high resilience of the American market economy makes it difficult to resist the enormous impact of the oil shortage, the closed and rigid economy of the Soviet Union is bound to be hit even harder by the impact of the oil crisis. In particular, because of the important impact of oil exports on the Soviet food supply, oil could become a strategic weapon that could seriously destabilize Soviet politics.

What matters is not whether the "peak oil" theory is correct, but that the United States has recognized that it can not only influence market expectations, but that such expectations can be used by the United States to achieve its own important strategic objectives.

In the early 1980s, when the Reagan administration came to power, the CIA memorandum clearly influenced the U.S. government's

---

[54] CIA, *Intelligence Memorandum: The Impending Soviet Oil Crisis*, March 1977.

thinking on policy choices, which was to use the oil strategy to combat the fragile economic balance and political stability of the Soviet Union.

In 1979, the Soviet Union, in order to gain access to the Indian Ocean from land and to the United States for hegemony, and to obtain the rich oil resources of the Persian Gulf, brazenly launched the war in Afghanistan and within a week took control of the main cities and arteries of transportation throughout the country, cutting off the main corridors on Afghanistan's borders with Pakistan and Iran. Faced with strong pressure from the Soviet army, the oil-producing countries of the Middle East were alarmed and began to rapidly adjust their relations with the United States.

In April 1981, CIA Director Casey made a secret visit to Saudi Arabia. Casey worked productively in the economic warfare against Germany in World War II. Both sides began to plot how to use oil weapons against the Soviet Union.

In 1985, for the first time in history, Soviet oil production began to decline, and the long-awaited moment of "peak oil" in the United States finally arrived.

At the behest of the United States, Saudi Arabia announced more than a twofold increase in the scale of oil exploitation, which immediately triggered an unprecedented plunge in oil prices, and the revenues generated by Soviet oil exports fell into the abyss. Oil aid to Eastern European countries was unsustainable, and Eastern Europe, which was heavily indebted, was immediately plunged into economic recession and political instability. The Soviet Union's hopes of importing tens of millions of tons of food were dashed; the extreme shortage of social food increased the people's anger against the Government; the new construction stalls, which had been spread out on a large scale, were paralyzed by the difficulty of importing foreign equipment without foreign exchange, which, coupled with the enormous consumption of the war in Afghanistan, led to a serious deterioration of the fiscal balance; the massive foreign debt borrowed to support the new construction put the Soviet Union in a difficult position to repay; the military-industrial complex suddenly ran out of funds urgently needed for an arms race with the United States, leading to a surge in military discontent.

The Soviet Union has slipped to the brink of a full-blown regime crisis in a perilous environment of internal and external crisis, high debt, endangered finances and alienation.

The dollar has dropped its oil dagger and the ruble has returned to the west

After 1971, the dollar standard has shifted from nominal gold to the US treasury bond in essence, while the ruble has been on a "planned standard" in the name of gold since the 1930s.

In the world of the dollar, the essence of all economic activity consists of a series of exchanges, and the exchange that takes place is the process by which money changes hands with commodities. Thus, money is deeply embedded in all spheres of economic activity, and it is commodity transactions that create the demand for money.

In the early days of simple transactions, the buyer and seller were based on the principle of paying money in one hand and delivering it in one hand, and the expansion of the size of the transaction occurred in parallel with the growth of the currency. At this point, money exhibits a "rigid" quality, behind which money represents a commodity that already exists, and its main form is gold and silver. As the distance of the transaction increases, the buyer and seller, out of concern for transportation and convenience, gradually accept the credit method, from which commercial credit arises, i.e., the transaction has occurred and the money has not been paid. Commercial credit acts as a substitute for money to facilitate the transaction, and this deferred payment takes the form of a commercial money order. With the expansion of the scale of commercial credit, commercial bills of exchange and money together form the money supply to facilitate commodity transactions, and money increasingly reflects the "elastic" characteristics. This is the main feature of the first era of Western capitalism – the monetary credit of commercial capitalism.

The rise of the industrial revolution marked the advent of the second era of capitalism – industrial capitalism. Industrial technology has brought about the explosive growth of commodity production, the long and large capital cycle required for industrial development, the war over resources and markets has generated a greater demand for money, industrial credit, national credit, commercial credit and money together constitute a larger money supply to facilitate the huge commodity trading process of the industrial age. Since both industrial and national credit is a commitment to future payments and spans a larger time horizon than commercial credit, the "debt component" of the money supply is more prominent.

However, the planned economy model established by the Soviet Union institutionally denied private ownership and indirectly excluded the idea of commodity trading. The need for ruble no longer stems from the deal, but is a product of the plan.

If the State were to draw up uniform production plans for all sectors of the economy, which would be sufficiently precise and cover all the details of economic activity, then all the products created by the productive sectors would meet the needs of the consumer sector and economic activity would be as precise as a clock. The essence of money is to facilitate transactions, and if the quantity and variety of products required by the parties to a transaction is fully calculated beforehand, then the essence of the transaction becomes barter, and money is merely a statistical unit of measurement in which transactions occur.

Based on the idea of a planned economy, the ruble is created strictly according to the prior planning of economic activity, created by the national banks and directly stuffed into the chain of economic functioning, not as an active participant, but as a passive recorder. What Ruble is counting is only the total amount of product turnover.

From the point of view of issuance, the ruble is a typical "planned standard" currency.

In the early 1930s, when the Soviet Union completed the planned economy model, commercial credit between enterprises was first abolished in the financial sphere and direct bank credit was implemented, since commercial credit was an act of "private transaction" between enterprises, and the credit expansion effect of such transactions interfered with the precise calculation of product turnover in the planned economy. At the same time, the Government abolished the circulation of commercial paper between the old economic organizations, leaving the National Bank as the sole institution for the non-cash settlement of enterprises, in view of the fact that the former commercial paper settlement organizations, in the course of the settlement of paper, would have forced enterprises to deposit a considerable amount of money for settlement preparations, and that this scattered currency would have also interfered with the accurate functioning of the economic clock; in 1931, the funds of the various sectors of the domestic economy were gradually concentrated in the National Bank's clearing account, with which the National Bank made 73 per cent of its short-term loans.

Under the planned economy model, the functions of money and banks have greatly shrunk, forming the pattern of "big finance, small banks". The Soviet Union retained only four specialized banks for long-term investments, in addition to the National Bank, and the central bank essentially became a supercashier, responsible for simple operations such as currency issuance, short-term loans, and settlement.

In the first five-year plan, the banking system increased long-term investment in the national economy by a factor of 1 and short-term loans by a factor of 1.4, resulting in a 1.3-fold increase in industrial production and a 1.4-fold increase in total commodity transactions over the same period. The ruble is basically in sync with the economic clock.

However, as the economic system has evolved, the number of industrial categories has grown and the interrelationships have become more complex, and the difficulty of planning has soared geometrically. The State Planning Commission of the USSR plans only for the most important products, but also produces a complex balanced schedule of at least 2,000 products, on the basis of which other subordinate departments calculate detailed plans for 20,000 products, which are then issued down the chain.[55] The variables of economic activity are so numerous and the practical difficulties faced by enterprises are so varied that the plan makers are unable to provide forecasts for all the details of economic activity, let alone to monitor the productivity and quality of all enterprises. Instead, companies focus on completing plans and lack the underlying motivation to improve processes, improve quality, increase profits and strengthen competitiveness.

In Stalin's time, a plan was the law, and the consequences of failing to plan were the same as breaking the law, with the possibility of punishment, sentencing, or even shooting, so that the discipline of its execution was fairly guaranteed. But from the Khrushchev era onwards, the authority of the government declined, the execution of plans became a process of "bargaining", and the economic clock became increasingly inaccurate.

The failure of the plan is reflected not only in the difficulty of putting the plan itself in place, but also in the inability to make effective

---

[55] Xu Xiangmei, *A Study on the Transformation of the Russian Banking System*, China Finance Press, 2005, p. 26.

prior human arrangements for the evolutionary traits inherent in the economy.

The trouble is that, although the production plan is frequently difficult to complete, the ruble is being spent in strict compliance with the plan. Thus, the unfinished plans of economic activity are reflected in the shortage of goods and services, while the "precise expansion" of the money supply in accordance with the plan creates a surplus of roubles with no physical counterpart. Inflation in the Soviet Union was not initially manifested in the form of rising prices, but more primarily in the form of material shortages. On the surface, the income level of Soviets was growing, while in reality, the money was not enough to buy the food and consumer goods needed. At the same time, the Soviet Union's lack of various investment products in the financial markets made the excess ruble an even greater political burden.

The contradiction between the ruble's "plan-based" system and the failure of the plan formed the root cause of the incurable Soviet currency crisis.

The United States dollar, as a currency in circulation worldwide, allows the United States to effectively integrate global resources. The use of the dollar for most international trade settlements forced the Soviet Union and countries in the ruble zone to export oil and raw materials in order to obtain hard currency to import food and Western technical equipment.

In 1985, when Soviet oil production fell, the United States deliberately depressed world oil prices and created an artificial Soviet foreign exchange shortage, forcing the ruble-zone countries to borrow heavily from the West to meet import demand. The rigid demand for imports is reflected in the fact that a cut in food imports would trigger social contradictions and intensify the regime's crisis, while a halt to imports of foreign equipment would widen the technological gap with the West and fundamentally weaken the economic potential of the ruble region. More importantly, the main engine of economic growth in the Soviet Union and Eastern Europe is not the competitiveness generated by technological innovation, but the expansionary force created by the constant expansion of the scale of production by new construction projects, large-scale projects that require the introduction of huge foreign imports of equipment, and the cessation of imports means an unbearable waste of huge investments. Even at the end of 1989, when the Soviet Union's finances were at their end, the scale of unfinished projects reached 180.9 billion roubles, which, against the backdrop of the country's deep fiscal and monetary crisis, swallowed up 4/5 of the fiscal revenue.

The oil revenue crisis in the Soviet Union rapidly affected food imports and the fiscal balance, and the fiscal deficit triggered external debt difficulties and economic contraction, which in turn led to a decline in Soviet foreign aid to the countries of the ruble region and increased centrifugal forces within countries.

The "oil dagger" of the United States to deal with the Soviet Union, just a knife in the ruble on the key, even the United States itself did not expect the effect would be so good.

In 1988, when Soviet oil production declined again, the United States repeated the same tactic, this time with fatal consequences.

In 1988, the total external debt of the Soviet Union and Eastern Europe had reached $206 billion, and its total size was such that even without the addition of new external debt, the mere cost of debt would have led to an escalating total debt. By 1990, the Soviet Union would have had to use up all the proceeds from energy exports in order to repay the principal and interest on its foreign debt.

The Soviet Union had lost the magic wand of oil aid, was itself in a deep food crisis, had run out of hard currency and was no longer able to sustain other countries in the ruble region that needed emergency relief. When the monkeys scattered, the Soviet Union's half-century of hard-earned economic cooperation disintegrated, and the Soviet Union's half of the foreign trade market collapsed at the same time. The satellite nations have remarried to the West.

Political reforms under the economic crisis weakened the centripetal force of centralization and accelerated the sovereign independence of the Soviet Union republics. The unified market formed by the originally highly integrated internal economy provided the Soviet Union with half of its total economic turnover, and with the successive independence of the countries, the economic bloodline linking the Soviet Union as a whole was artificially severed, the domestic market was paralysed and the economy eventually collapsed completely.

The Soviet Union, a once invincible empire, suffering from internal economic ills, finally fell apart under the devastating external blow of the dollar.

CHAPTER IV

The Rise and Confusion of the European Currency

Today, there is a dizzying array of problems with the euro, and one after another with European debt. Do the Chinese need to save the euro? What is the attitude of American financiers towards the euro? Will the euro disintegrate? Will we see a United States of Europe? What exactly is the role of the yuan between the euro and the dollar? The purpose of studying history is not to rote memorize people and things that have passed, but to find living wisdom in these past historical experiences.

To gain insight into Europe today, one must know the German and French past; to know the future of the euro one needs to look back to the origins of the European Monetary Union; to understand today's ECB initiatives one has to study the ins and outs of the German central bank alone.

There have been so-called shadow governments in post-World War II Europe, without which the EU and the euro would not be what they are today, and the euro was not born as a result of European integration, but as a means of building a world economy, with the ultimate goal of creating a "United States of Europe". The euro or the European debt crisis that we are currently witnessing is the process that must be undergone to create this United States.

The attitude of the United States towards the "United States of Europe" (which is still fully realized) has been completely different in different periods of time, from strong support in the 1950s and 1960s, to gradual prevention. The U.S. needed to use European power to wall off the Soviet Union, and the U.S. likewise needed European market power to boost exports, provided that Europe was a docile little heel. It was de Gaulle's dissatisfaction with American bullying that allowed him to unite with other nations to attack the dollar and ultimately overturn the entire Bretton Woods system.

After 1971, the world currency entered the era of the dollar standard. As with the Bretton Woods system's full exchange rate standard, the dollar standard has the same insurmountable inherent contradictions.

History is today's reality, and reality is tomorrow's history! To focus on reality is to shape the history of tomorrow.

German industry was nearly "castrated", Roosevelt's death saved Germany!

In 1945, just before the end of the war, one thing that haunted Roosevelt was what to do with Germany after the war to ensure that the future "permanent peace under the United States of America" would not be challenged by the re-emergence of Germany.

In maintaining the world order under their rule, both the former British hegemon and the later American leaders are most worried about the "peace destroyers" like Germany, who have a "backbone" with explosive potential. In the 25 years from 1914 to 1939, Germany challenged the world order twice, both times breaking the world's bones, and Roosevelt had to weigh in carefully on whether there would be a third time. If the first two dragged down the British Empire, the third time would be against the United States. After the First World War, Germany was placed in the shackles of war reparations, which it could never break free of, and the severe restrictions of the Treaty of Versailles tightened the grip of the German military industry. Under such harsh conditions, it took Germany a mere 20 minutes to beat the old British and French colonial empires again, and Roosevelt's heart aches at the thought.

In Roosevelt's post-war design, the British Empire would be dismembered and the Soviet Union would be a trading partner of the United States, and what about this trouble-loving Germany? It would be better to have "industrial castration" and never have any consequences. Just as Cao Cao had captured Lv Bu at the White Gate House, Lv Bu screamed that the ropes were too tight, and Cao Cao said back, "The tiger must be tied in a hurry." At the behest of Roosevelt, Secretary of the Treasury Morgenthau devised the "Morgenthau Plan" to completely destroy Germany's heavy industrial base and return the German economy to the agricultural era of 100 years ago.

After Roosevelt's sudden death in April 1945, President Truman and a large number of opponents of Roosevelt's strategy joined forces to promote post-war "revisionism", which subverted Roosevelt's post-war strategy and began to press the Soviet Union, forcing Stalin to give up hope of cooperating with the United States and refuse to join the Bretton Woods-dominated dollar system, thus being forced onto the path of the Cold War.

Who is the main driver of the US-Soviet confrontation strategy? It's obviously England! Churchill was always a vanguard against the Soviet Union because he understood that if Roosevelt insisted on dismantling the colonial system of the British Empire, then British power would be compressed back to the British Isles, world hegemony would be impossible to negotiate, and even the status of a European ally would be untenable. Simply put, the UK will be completely marginalised. If the Soviet tree becomes the main target for the US, and the Soviet Union is used to replace Germany, then Britain will become the most important ally of the US and Britain's interests will be negotiable.

Churchill's plan was to eradicate Germany at the hands of the United States and then, as in the aftermath of World War I, to gradually exclude American power. Given enough time, with the resources of the vast pound sterling area, Britain will eventually recover and the world will still be the British Empire. At least in 1941, that's the direction Churchill saw the post-war world should be heading.

Roosevelt couldn't see past the little ninety-nine in Churchill's belly when, on 13 and 14 August 1941, before the United States entered the war, Roosevelt and Churchill were in Argentina discussing the Atlantic Charter, with the focus on the pound sterling area created by the British imperial preference. Eliot Roosevelt, Roosevelt's son, has a vivid record of the arguments on both sides.

Churchill said seriously:

> *"The British Empire's trade arrangements were..."*

Roosevelt immediately interrupted Churchill,

> *"Yes, the imperial preference system is an example. Those colonized peoples in India and Africa, and in the Near and Far*

East as a whole, remain (precisely because of imperial preferences) in their present backward state. "

Churchill's neck rose red and he reached out to question,

"Mr. President, Britain does not at present intend to discuss the question of preferential treatment within the imperial system. Trade makes the British Empire strong, and this policy should continue, and that is the condition that British ministers prescribe. "

Roosevelt replied slowly,

"You see, there is a difference of opinion on this issue. I firmly believe that if we are to have a stable peace, we must promote the development of backward countries ... and the 18th century (colonialist) approach certainly did not work ... no matter what policy your ministers suggest, that approach of looting raw materials from the colonies and denying them to the local people in return does not work ... the 20th century approach was to help those countries to industrialize..."

Churchill snarled in exasperation,

"You mean India!"

Roosevelt said calmly,

"Yes. I do not believe we can wage a war against fascist slavery without emancipating people in colonies around the world enslaved by backward colonial policies. "

Afterwards, Roosevelt taught his own son,

"We're going to make it clear to the British from the beginning that we're not going to be that 'helpful Charlie' who gets used up by the British and leaves it behind forever. "[56]

Roosevelt apparently felt that his policy toward Britain and toward the Soviet Union had been strongly resisted by the State Department, and at the end of 1943 he revealed his suspicions in this way:

"I have found many times that the men of the State Department have tried to hide information from me, either by delaying or by

---

[56] Jacques Cheminade, *FDR and Jean Monnet*, Summer-Fall 2000 of FIDELIO Magazine.

obstructing it, because the diplomats of these professions do not share my views. They should go and work for Churchill. In fact, for a long time, they did help the British... I was advised 6 years ago to cleanse the State Department completely. It is too much like the Foreign Office of the British Empire. "[57]

After Roosevelt's death, the British got their way! Truman, spurred on by State Department forces, finally targeted the Soviet Union as the number one enemy of the United States.

The Germans, on the other hand, were given an unexpected chance to be reborn. From 1945 to 1946, the U.S. occupation forces in Germany were carrying out the "Morgenthau Plan" to "castrate" German industry, which involved the dismantling of more than 1,600 factories, the loading of military bases with explosives and the dull explosions; a large number of factories were being dismantled and equipment was being shipped away; the docks in Hamburg, the Krupp arms industry, the Mercedes-Benz car factory, the Junkers fighter jet production line, the chemical base at IG Farben, and even the entire Ruhr industrial zone were in danger. The Morgenthau plan was far more complete than the destruction of German industry by the Allied heavy bombers.[58]

In 1947, there was an abrupt change in US policy towards Germany. The dismantling of German industrial facilities was essentially halted, the "de-Nazification" of Nazis among former government officials was screened, the selection process to absorb the ruling elite of the Third Reich into the new government was transformed into a selection process, the punishment of German war criminals was greatly weakened, arms barons such as Krupp were amnestied, financial cadres such as Schacht were accommodated, and the rolling dollars of the Marshall Plan of Aid would replace the smoke from the destruction of German industry by Morgenthau.

So, how much industrial power was left in war-torn Germany, especially in the midst of the massive and continuous Allied bombardment of the ruins?

---

[57] Elliott Roosevelt, *As he saw it*, Duell, Sloan and Pearce, 1946.

[58] Frederick H. Gareau, *Morgenthau's Plan for Industrial Disarmament in Germany*, The Western Political Quartely, Vol. 14, No.2, 1961, p. 517–534.

In their strategic bombing of Germany, the Allies targeted the bombing primarily on transportation, rather than on the German factories themselves. This was because Hitler had sufficiently evacuated the productive capacity of German industry to finally allow military equipment to be effectively put to war simply by centralized assembly. The Allies found the cost of decentralized bombing to be prohibitively expensive and extremely inefficient, and simply bombing Germany's transportation system would have prevented the eventual export capability of German military industry, a transportation target that was obvious and easily destroyed.

According to US Bombardment Command estimates, the bombardment destroyed only 6 per cent of German steel production, coal production only 2 per cent, coke 4 per cent, machine building 15 per cent, and metalworking machines 6.5 per cent, and on 12 December 1945, Colonel Burstein reported to a panel of the US Senate Armed Services Committee that "German industry is 75 per cent safe and sound and can be easily recovered under any circumstances."

In the case of Volkswagen, for example, Hitler paid great attention to the "National Automobile" project and even took part in the design of the "Beetle" cars, which were not produced in large numbers during the war, but the size of the plant and the advanced equipment at a cost of DM 2 billion were among the largest in the world, which was 50 per cent larger than the wartime plant of the Ford Motor Company.

At the end of 1939, Volkswagen completed the first phase of 80 per cent investment in plant, machinery and equipment. Despite the German Government's full financial support for the project, investments of this magnitude still appear to be financially inadequate, and the Government has had to make it compulsory for a quarter of Germans to pay DM 25 per month for the purchase of unproduced "national cars" in installments. By the end of World War II, 336,000 Germans had advanced DM 2.67 billion and did not get a car because VW was forced to turn to the production of military cars. The construction of mega plants with such amazing investments is unimaginable for entrepreneurs throughout Europe and even in the United States.

The damage done to the VW megafactory by the Allied strategic bombing was greatly overestimated and the damage to production capacity was not serious. The Allies did not dismantle the plant and, as a result, VW's car production capacity was quickly restored. It produced an average of nearly 30 Beetles per day in 1946 and 1947, more than 300 per day in 1950, more than 1,000 in 1955, and a total of 8,000 by the end of 1960. By this time, Volkswagen had exported nearly half a million vehicles to the United States. The Germans would not have been able to build such a large and well-equipped factory in the years after the war without the modern plant, which had been built over five years at great expense before the war. Neither the Marshall Plan nor the Oxfam Plan can be said to be an economic revival without the strong industrial power that Germany has accumulated over the years.

The Morgenthau plan did not hurt German industry too badly, mainly because the American occupation forces had to take on the heavy daily work of repairing urban infrastructure, clearing debris, rescuing civilians, maintaining order, etc., and had not freed up enough manpower to dismantle German industrial facilities. It is estimated that only a small percentage of the more than 1,600 blacklisted factories have suffered irreparable damage, and most are ready for normal production after a few months of repairs. In the end, German industry was dismantled at less than $1/10^{th}$ of its production capacity.

Thus, during and after the war, Germany retained about 70 per cent of its industrial strength, from its production organization system to its engineers and skilled workers, who, having eaten their fill, replenished their stocks of raw materials, and had sufficient energy supplies, were ready to turn on their machines and equipment and re-produce technologically advanced and high-quality industrial products just as orders came in.

This is the real basis of the German revival!

One more pressing issue that needs to be addressed before the German economy can get on track is the currency woes.

The Mark has changed, the Soviet Union has changed its face

While the United States, Britain and France occupied the western part of Germany, the Soviet Union controlled the eastern part of Germany, with the four great powers subdividing German territory and the capital, Berlin, under quadruple administration. The Soviet-occupied region is a traditional food supply base in Germany, and daily life in the East German region is pretty good. As the U.S. tightened its grip, the cloud of the Cold War was already looming over Germany, and the Soviet Union, in an effort to counter the aggressive U.S., began to tighten food exports from East Germany to West Germany, which put the Lower West in a tough spot.

In February 1946, the "Cold War Telegram" drafted by Kenan from his hospital bed in Moscow not only sent a whirlwind of confrontation through Washington and Moscow, but also starved the Germans. In the winter of 1946, the coldest winter of the 20th century, the Germans finally experienced what it was like for the people of Leningrad to be besieged by hunger and cold for 900 days, when the workers in the Ruhr industrial zone were fed only 1,000 calories a day, less than half the normal standard.

As was the case in the Soviet Union at the beginning of 1921, the German market in 1946 had an extraordinary shortage of commodities, even for the same reasons, namely the rationing of basic necessities and the severe devaluation of the currency; at the same time, the devaluation of the currency compounded the difficulties of the rationing system. In the post-war economic shortage, commodities and food disappeared clean from the shelves not because they no longer existed, but because they were hoarded. The so-called koochie is the pursuit of profiteering, and in an environment of severe currency devaluation, the koochie will bypass the currency and directly engage in bartering to get the most out of it.

Thus, the black market became the most active way of trading outside of rationing.

In West Germany, where food is undoubtedly the most scarce commodity, all wealth is a floating cloud compared to starvation. Peasants who had suffered less from the war and still had food left in their homes naturally became big winners in the black market trade. The city's rich and middle class flocked to the city, trading their homes for gold and silver treasures, paintings, and even furniture and clothing for flour, eggs, meat, and butter, and the peasants were suddenly extravagant with golden porcelain and high-class furniture. The black market in the city was also highly developed, and even the Allied occupation forces were enthusiastically involved in the popular trade. U.S. Army supplies were provided by the government, and the cigarettes, soap, razors, coffee, cans, and chocolates became sought-after in the market. Among these commodities, the cigarette was the most prominent, and with its high currency acceptance, liquidity, portability, easy division, and high homogeneity, the imperial mark began to play a formal role as currency in an era when it was a scrap of paper. The U.S. military naturally became the curiosity of this most scarce monetary commodity. They bought cigarettes from the army supply house for a dollar a piece, which could be exchanged in the market for various kinds of gold and silver jewelry worth thousands of imperial marks.[59]

The U.S. Army traded cheap cigarettes for the Germans' expensive Lycra cameras and grand pianos, which is essentially the same as the U.S. trading valuable commodities of nations today for dollar pieces of paper that are less valuable than cigarettes. Back then, the American occupation forces were surprisingly a little embarrassed, after all, this predatory trading made the solemn trials of Nazi war criminals at Nuremberg look more like the victors' share of the spoils.

It was clear that the "cigarette standard" could not be relied upon to re-establish normal market order in Germany, and since the Reichstag had completely lost its credibility, monetary reform had become a top priority. Still in line with the Soviet monetary reform of 1922–1924, the old currency was to be replaced by a new, more stable currency, but that year the Soviet Union had a gold reserve of 50 million pounds, and the Chevron and gold rubles were exchanged for less, and successfully replaced the Soviet paper ruble. The trouble was that in Germany in 1948, the economy had already gone bankrupt, gold was not available, the dollar had not arrived, and the Third Reich had left behind a large national debt, which amounted to 400% of the German GNP in 1939!

The 1948 monetary reform, again faced with the dilemma of the 1923 Schacht, the new mark reform will once again sing the "empty city" of the currency reserves, but this time the director-in-chief has been replaced by an American. The Americans were already ahead of the Germans in the field of money, so they did not go to the former German "economic czar" Schacht. The American strategy consists of three acts, which are the currency act, the issue act, and the exchange act.

---

[59] Vincent Bignon, *Cigarette Money and Black-Market Prices during the 1948 German Miracle*, 2009.

The Currency Act establishes the legal tender status of the Deutsche Mark (DM) to replace the Reichsmark; the Issue Act establishes the central bank status of the West German Federal Bank (Bank Deutscher Lander), which after 1957 became the famous Bundesbank; and the Exchange Act addresses the exchange rate between the old and new marks, as well as the implementation details.

The first question facing monetary reform is what is the most appropriate exchange rate for the old and new marks. This means that while the currency was over-extended fivefold, the total amount of goods and services on the market shrank by almost half, and the ratio of money to goods and services was nearly 10:1. Therefore, if the price indicator was set at the pre-war level of 1935, money circulation would need to shrink by 90 per cent, so the Americans decided to set the old and new mark exchange rate at 1:10.[60]

The key issue is in the banking system. The bank is like a flat burden, picking up the savings of the common people on one side and the loans released on the other, the savings are a liability to the bank because when people withdraw money, the bank is obliged to provide the full amount of cash. The loan is the bank's asset, the loan generates interest income and the bank makes money as a result, the money earned becomes capital money for the bank. Bankers are like pickers, balancing assets and liabilities on both ends, with their own capital money in their pockets. When you're done, take some silver from the asset side and put it in your own pocket; if you lose money, take some silver from your pocket and put it in the liability side. In short, always balance the ends of a flattened stretcher. After the monetary reform, 10 old marks for 1 new mark on the savings side shrank by 90 per cent, and the burden was out of balance, so the lending side also had to shrink, in the same proportion. There is a big problem here, a lot of bank lending was done during the war to Nazi governments at all levels, and now those governments are gone and the loans are uncollectible, with the result that the liabilities are high and the assets are low, and the banks' burdens are unbalanced, which means that the whole banking system could go bankrupt due to insolvency. The Americans said that it didn't matter, that the loans to the Nazi government would be

---

[60] Martin Pontzen and Franziska Schobert, *Episodes in German Monetary History-Lessons for Transition Countries*, 2007-04-13.

nullified, and that the asset hole in the middle would be covered by the national debt of the future newly created federal government, guaranteeing that everyone would be balanced and have some money left in their pockets. Thus, Americans and bankers rejoiced.

The population is required to deposit all the old marks in cash into a bank savings account within a certain period of time and to void them upon expiry. Bankers split each savings account in two, with half of the savings exchanged for 10 old marks for 1 new mark immediately, and the other half waiting 90 days depending on prices before deciding how. In addition, in order to ensure the normal conduct of business and life, the occupation authorities provided the Germans with the new marks necessary for their daily lives, exchanging 40 old marks for new marks at a rate of 1:1 per person, and the employer received 60 new marks for the basic living expenses of each employee.

Those who do not understand the mystery may think that this approach is fair, but in fact, there is a deep learning in the looting of wealth.

The main form of wealth of the rich and proletariat in Germany is stocks, real estate, gold bullion, jewelry, paintings and other forms of physical assets, while the main assets of the poor and middle class are all in bank savings. If you are rich, congratulations, your purchasing power will not be damaged by the monetary reform, if you are an industrialist or a big businessman who has taken a huge loan from a bank and purchased land, property, commodities or raw materials, then even more congratulations, your debt has been reduced to 10% and the rest will be paid for you by the poor. If you are poor and middle class, sorry, the vast majority of your wealth has been transferred to the rich. With high market prices for commodities, real estate and assets, monetary reform has robbed the poor and middle class of 90 per cent of their purchasing power, in effect a redistribution of social wealth, increasing the wealth of the rich by preying on the poor and middle class.

No wonder Schacht screamed viciously:

"This is a deliberate attempt to undermine the social fabric of Germany, with consequences even more sinister than the super-inflation of 1923... It is an attempt to harbour a scourge."[61]

I wonder if Old Schacht was so bitter because he was involved in the murder of Hitler and was thrown into jail by the Nazis, confiscating the family's assets and left with nothing but his retirement savings.

In the course of its implementation, the occupation authorities, in order to compel enterprises that had accumulated supplies to sell their products to the market as soon as possible to stabilize the market, provided enterprises with only the equivalent of 17 per cent of the new mark issued to the population, a move that indeed served to increase market supply and consolidate the credit of the new mark.

When the conversion of the old and new marks was completed, the total amount of money in circulation shrank by 93.5 per cent, slightly deviating from the target set.

Many see the monetary reforms of June 1948 and the introduction of free market economic policies as the main reasons for the take-off of the German economy, when in fact the complexity of the modern industrial system is not as simple as the free trade of a floor stall, and while market principles can be established in a relatively short time, strong industrial production capacity requires a long accumulation. The economic environment of free trade can never be a substitute for the foundation of a productive economy.

The root cause of Germany's industrial miracle was the strength of its strong industrial base, while monetary stability, a market economy and the Marshall Plan created favourable external conditions, and even with these conditions, the economic miracle required strong external opportunities. in 1949, Germany again experienced severe inflation of 38 per cent, forcing the newly established Central Bank to put an emergency brake on the economy. By early 1950, Germany's balance of payments deficit had worsened so badly that the United States had to lead the OECD to rescue Germany. It was the outbreak of the Korean War in 1950, which lasted three years with huge orders for military supplies, that really propelled the German economy to full capacity and finally put the German industrial machine into a high-speed take-off

---

[61] Hjalmar Schacht, *The Magic of Money*, Oldbourne, 1967.

orbit. Otherwise, German industry will have to rely on the slow recovery of the domestic and European markets.

On June 20, 1948, when the Americans officially launched the New Mark in Western Germany, the Soviet Union immediately realized the United States' intention to try to divide Germany unilaterally. Although West Germany has yet to form a federal government, the new currency and the new central bank have signaled that a new government is coming.

At least until then, the Soviet Union still had illusions of cooperation with the United States, and after four years of brutal war, the Soviet Union was desperate for respite and had neither the ability nor the desire to engage in a larger war again. Stalin was not a fanatic who wanted a global "export revolution", but a cold realist. Stalin's consistent advocacy of building socialism in one country is fundamentally different from Trotsky's thinking that he hated the idea of a global revolution together. Stalin also supported the communist movement in China and other countries, but the starting point was to create a larger strategic security buffer for the Soviet Union, not to overthrow the capitalist system globally. Realism made him realize that, in the face of the more advanced and developed productivity advantages of the West, the Soviet Union had to strategically defend itself, then develop, and then become strong.

Roosevelt adopted the Huairou strategy against the Soviet Union and Stalin was cooperative; Roosevelt recognized the Soviet Union's sphere of influence and Stalin agreed to join the Bretton Woods system. Stalin always placed the national interests of the Soviet Union above the mission of socialism. By funding Chiang Kai-shek's Northern Expedition in the 1920s with 30 million gold rubles and cultivating the power of Feng Yuxiang of the Northwest Army, he was trying to weaken the pro-Western warlords in northern China and the pro-Japanese Zhang Zuolin in the northeast and ease the imperialist pressure on the Soviet Far East. During the Soviet Civil War of 1918–1921, Japanese and Western imperialist forces entered Siberia precisely from the east, posing a great threat to the survival of the Soviet regime, a menacing spectacle that is still vivid in Stalin's mind. By supporting the Kuomintang while consistently suppressing the Communist Party's development of its own military power, he was afraid of undermining his overall strategy. Zhang Xueliang admonished Chiang Kai-shek, and Stalin, thinking that China's resistance could hold Japan back and make it unable to advance north, insisted that Chiang be released back to

Nanking. Even as the PLA was about to cross the river to liberate the country, Stalin was still mindful of his promise to Roosevelt that year and suggested that China should rule by river.

Stalin was so coldly realistic that he did not want to be an eager pioneer in challenging American hegemony. However, Stalin was not a negative defender either, and he firmly believed that the best defense was the offense. The essence of the Soviet defense was reflected in a tough offensive posture under Truman's stride.

Germany's monetary reform, without prior agreement with the Soviet Union, was a unilateral act that undermined the tacit understanding between Roosevelt and Stalin and would have made the Soviet Union increasingly passive in Eastern Europe if left to Truman's whims. Thus, Stalin had to give Truman a head-on blow.

The Soviet Union immediately sent a protest note to the United States for the start of the issuance of new marks in West Germany, stating that the introduction of separate currency reforms in the West was intended to divide Germany. When West Germany started issuing new marks, the old marks were still legal tender in the Soviet Union, and the old marks were flooding into East Germany, the savings of the people of the Soviet Union were instantly wiped out, inflation immediately soared, and the markets were in chaos. A few days later, Sokolovsky, the Soviet military commander in Germany, announced that the Soviet-occupied and Greater Berlin districts would introduce currency reforms and issue marks with special symbols from eastern Germany to protect the Soviet-occupied economy from the destruction of the Western occupation currency system. With the emergence of the two marks issued by the two occupation authorities in Germany, the division of the country was inevitable.

On the fourth day of the West German monetary reform in the United States, the Soviet Union announced the world-shaking "Berlin Blockade", which would cut off all land and water traffic between West Germany and Berlin as of 24 June 1948. In practice, the Soviet Union left room only for cutting off land and water traffic, and the three air corridors from Hamburg, Hannover and Frankfurt to Berlin remained open.

Germany's currency war, which finally sparked a real cold war.

Coal and steel union, the cradle of EU and euro dreams

When the German economy began to accelerate after the Berlin crisis in May 1949, an increasingly pressing reality constrained the rapid expansion of industrial production, namely a huge shortfall in the supply of energy and raw materials for German industry.

Germany's industrial energy relies mainly on coal, while at the same time industrial development is in urgent need of steel, without which German industry would not be able to develop, and coal and steel come mainly from the Ruhr and Saar regions of Germany. Saar was taken from France as early as 1947, and Ruhr became the fat meat that France was eager to swallow. But the Americans could not allow an economic collapse in Germany, which was at the forefront of the Cold War. The result of this compromise of interests was that the Ruhr Industrial Estate was co-managed by the IAR (International Authority for the Ruhr), which was set up by the Allies to determine how much of the coal and steel share Germany could get. In this way, the lifeblood of the German economy was stuck dead in the hands of the French.

Germany's most urgent task was to establish its own federal government as soon as possible, without which there could be no development in Germany without an end to the domination of everything in Germany by the occupation forces. And the French made the Ruhr commune an important condition for agreeing to the founding of a federal Germany, which the Germans had no choice but to accept. As the German economy grew stronger, the conflict between Germany and France was gradually intensified. It was as if one could smell the German-French tensions again after World War I.

The root of France's fear of Germany lies in the fact that France has been invaded by Germany three times in the 70+ years since 1870 and has never defeated Germany on its own. The industrial revolution in France began much earlier than in Germany, but the frequent revolutions and wars that constantly interrupted the development of French industry led German industry to take over later. The austere stereotypes of the Germans seem more suited to the rigorous, complex and precise running of the big industry than the romantic casual French. Although both wars resulted in the French claiming to be political and military victors, economically, France soon became Germany's underdog again. France no longer has the ambition and boldness of the Napoleonic era of the European continent, if not for the alliance of Britain and the United States, the French and Germany, the tiger as neighbors, will always be worried.

France strongly supported the Morgenthau plan to permanently "castrate" German industry, and personally cut off the two biggest problems of Saarland and Ruhr. However, as the Cold War atmosphere thickened, the United States began to lean more and more on Germany, but on the contrary, it looked at France more and more unpleasant, especially the "de Gaulle Doctrine" prevailing in France, which was even more disgusting to Britain and the United States. At the heart of De Gaulle's doctrine is the idea that France's destiny must be in its own hands.

As the political scales in the United States gradually tilted to the German side, France felt more and more strained to face an increasingly powerful Germany alone. France had to come up with a comprehensive strategy that would both put an end to the consequences of the war and effectively contain the tiger. After much deliberation, the French finally came up with a brilliant plan, the Schumann Plan!

On 9 May 1950, at a press conference, French Foreign Minister Schumann unexpectedly proposed the creation of a "supersovereign" economic entity under which the French and German coal and steel production capacities would be placed, shared resources, developed and managed together, and the structure would be completely open and any European country could apply to join. This is what became known as the "Coal and Steel Coalition" (ECSC, European Coal and Steel Community). Since both coal and steel are indispensable resources for states to wage war, placing coal and steel in the hands of a new entity that exceeds the authority of the German and French states would fundamentally eliminate the intention and ability of both sides to wage war. No wonder Schumann hailed the coal-steel alliance as "making war not only inconceivable, but also materially impossible".[62]

The Schumann Plan first obtained the strong support of the United States, in order to deal with the Soviet Union, the Western camp of Germany and France reunited, pulled out the fuse of future wars in Europe, the coal-steel alliance formed by the common market, also helped the recovery of the European economy, overall conducive to the strategic objectives of the United States, the United States in 1950, is the era of national power, it is now anxious European economic

---

[62] Treaty establishing the European Coal and Steel Community, ECSC Treaty.

recovery is not fast enough, the United States does not export enough goods, the European resistance to the Soviet Union strength is too weak. The U.S. hasn't thought about what kind of challenge the EU and its currency, the euro, will pose to the dollar 60 years from now.

The public opinion in France, Germany and the rest of Europe is also applauding the general fear of a future war between Germany and France, which was already widespread in France in 1950, but now all is clear. The Germans were originally indignant at the French forcible seizure of the Ruhr and Saar region, and the coal-steel alliance, initiated by the French, immediately smoothed the Germans' hearts. The German-French rapprochement had given Europeans a great deal of confidence in the prospects of peace and prosperity, with only Britain on the sidelines, coldly watching.

In April 1951, the Treaty of Paris was signed and the Coal and Steel Union was born. In addition to Germany and France, Italy, Belgium, Luxembourg and the Netherlands joined in the formation of the "Community of Six Destinies", and six years later, the six countries signed the Treaty of Rome, establishing the European Economic Community and the European Atomic Energy Community on the basis of the Coal and Steel Union, laying the foundation for the future European Union.

Unlike any previous form of international organization or corporation, the Coalition is unique in that it is "supersovereign". By "supersovereignty", the sovereign State cedes part of the ultimate national decision-making power, economic and even political, to the new entity, which will, to a considerable extent, have the character of a State.

The authority of the Coal and Steel Union is the "High Authority", which is composed of a President and eight members who, although from Governments, do not represent the national interests of their countries and are sworn to uphold the interests of the "Community" rather than the national interest. The Supreme Council may exercise three powers: first, to take "decisions" with legal force; second, to make "recommendations" with legally binding final objectives, but States may be flexible as to how they are to be achieved; and third, to express "opinions" that have no legal significance.

The Coal and Steel Union also has a "Common Assembly" that oversees the "Supreme Council". Its "parliamentarians" must be elected by the States, which likewise "represent the people", not the "State". In a structure similar to the separation of powers, the Coal and Steel Union has also established its own "Court of Justice" to arbitrate legal disputes that arise in the event of misconduct by member states.

In the event of a dispute between the Coal and Steel Union and its member States, it would be regulated by a treaty with the force of international law. The essence of this form is the state within a state.

It is no exaggeration to say that without the Coal and Steel Union, there would not be the EU as it is today, nor the Euro as it is today. It is for this reason that the European Union has designated 9 May, the date of the announcement of the "Schumann Plan", as the annual "Europe Day".

In fact, the "Schumann Plan" was not the work of Schumann, but came from another great man, Jean Monnet, known as the "Father of Europe".

"Shadow Government" behind the "Father of Europe"

In the French political arena, where presidents are everywhere and prime ministers walk the streets, there were 24 governments in the short 12 years from 1945 to 1957, just during the Fourth Republic era, with an average of one change every six months. With such frequent and chaotic political situations, it is hard to imagine that the government would have the capacity and time to pursue any economic strategy. Out of the public eye, however, some of the people who actually run the country's grand policy tend not to be so flashy. Jean Monnet is one of France's most heavyweight strategic operators. It was also under his operation that the famous Coal and Steel Union became a great success, recognized by posterity as the chief architect of post-war European integration.

Monnet comes from a wealthy businessman's family and is well-connected. Long before the outbreak of World War I, Monnet, who was in his early 20s, met many important people with the help of his father. These include.

Lord Kindersley, Director of the Bank of England, Partner of Longyear Brothers, Chairman of the Board of Hudson's Bay Company. The Lange family is one of the oldest investment banks and the Hudson's Bay Company was one of the first companies in the world to represent the British in a large territory in North America, the status of the East India Company.

Eric Drummond, later Secretary General of the League of Nations and one of the leaders of the British House of Lords.

John Dulles, later United States Secretary of State, and brother Alan Dulles, Director of the CIA.

Douglas Dillon, later United States Secretary of the Treasury, and the Dillon family is also well known in the United States financial community.

John J. McCloy, later President of the World Bank, Supreme Military Commander of the United States in Germany and Chairman of the Board of Directors of the Chase Manhattan Bank.

And then there's the oldest member of the Astor family in America.

It can be said that Monnet befriended the core of the Anglo-American ruling elite. At the outbreak of the First World War, Monnet was introduced to the French Prime Minister by a "heavyweight friend". The young Monnet proposed to strengthen the unified movement and transport of strategic goods between Britain and France, and was sent to Britain as the French representative on the International Committee for the Supply of Goods, based in London, to coordinate the organization on behalf of France. The British representative who worked with him in England was his old friend Arthur Salter, who later took part in the negotiation of the Treaty of Versailles and the creation of the League of Nations, and whose idea of a "United States of Europe" deeply influenced the course of Monet's life.

After the First World War, at the age of 31, Monnet was appointed Deputy Secretary General of the League of Nations, under the promotion of Sir Caddesley, to help run the day-to-day affairs of Secretary General Caddesley. The League of Nations was originally the product of the Lodz Club, whose ultimate goal was

> "to extend the rule of the British Empire throughout the world; to perfect the system of expansion of the British Empire outwards; to colonize all viable places by British nationals ... to introduce colonial representation in the Imperial Council, to unite the scattered members of the Empire, and thus to establish a world free from war and consistent with the welfare of mankind."

The Rhodes Company has offices in the United States, Canada, India, Australia, New Zealand, South Africa and other self-governing territories, colonies and former colonies of the British Empire. The prestigious American "Council on Foreign Relations" (CFR) is the American branch of the Rhodes Society. The Lodz Club met in secret from time to time in the autonomous territories of the British Empire, planned and deployed in a unified manner, influenced the formulation and implementation of political and economic policies from behind the scenes, and controlled the press, education and propaganda institutions, with the primary goal of unifying the English-speaking countries in the form of a federation, and eventually establishing some form of world government and achieving "one world".

Monnet, as a Frenchman actively involved in the unification of the British Empire, was certainly highly regarded. In 1935, Monnet was appointed by the League of Nations to China as financial advisor to Chiang Kai-shek and to examine the country's economic and financial situation. At the time, Chiang Kai-shek was carrying out the reform of the French currency system, and after the collapse of China's silver standard, the question of whether the French currency should be inverted to the British pound or the dollar was a matter of great concern to both Britain and the United States. As a result, Chiang Kai-shek chose the strategy of keeping his feet on both sides of the boat.

While Murnane was still in Shanghai, China, George Murnane, a partner of the Lange brothers, entered into business with the Wallenbergs in Sweden, the Bosch in Germany, the Solvays in Belgium, the Dulles brothers and the Rockefellers in the United States.

Monnet, in the late 1930s, is considered the most internationally connected Frenchman of his generation.

At the outbreak of the Second World War, and seeing France fall to the ground, Monnet suggested to Churchill that France and Britain should be united into one country, one government, one parliament and one army, and that they should combine their efforts against Germany. Churchill accepted the idea on behalf of the British government, and even Charles de Gaulle, who had no choice at the time, agreed to the merger, but was firmly opposed by the French Prime Minister, Field Marshal Pétain, who later surrendered to the German army and became the puppet emperor of the Vichy regime. After the fall of France, he was appointed by Churchill as a senior member of the British War Material Commission and went to America for help. In the United

States, Monnet again became an advisor to Roosevelt, who advised Roosevelt to change the conventional wisdom and not to determine needs based on the resources already available, and at a time when Europe was facing extinction, the United States should go looking for resources to best meet the needs of war. To this end, Roosevelt embarked on the "Victory Plan" of general military production, in which Monnet played an important role that even the British themselves could not achieve. After the war, Keynes argued that Monnet had made America aware of the importance of the General Military Industrial Mobilization, and that Monet's contribution to Britain in May and June 1941 was extremely important.[63]

On the basis of extensive Anglo-American connections, Monnet was given the power to oversee the implementation of the Marshall Plan in France, and Charles de Gaulle had to draw on Monnet's connections to access American resources and to commission Monnet to develop a five-year plan for France's postwar economic recovery. Despite the fundamental difference between the nationalist and internationalist values of de Gaulle and Monnet, France needed American assistance too badly.

In the early post-war period, Monet's "Monnet Plan", which followed American thinking, was in fact a replica of the "Morgenthau Plan", which advocated the complete "castration" of German industry in the case of Germany. With the shift in the US, Monnet began planning the Coal and Steel Alliance's "Schumann Plan". When Monnet rushed to Britain with the Schumann Plan, Britain's attitude was very lukewarm. The British thought to themselves that the Coal and Steel Alliance would strengthen German and French interests and weaken British influence on the continent, and the British were not in the mood for adult beauty. Monnet had to turn around and return to support the Franco-German coalition and to become the first president of the Coalition's "Supreme Council".

A small circle of central figures has also gradually formed between Germany and France, including former Prime Minister Antoine Pinay on the French side, Jean Violet, the head of French intelligence, Monnet

---

[63] Jacques Cheminade, *FDR and Jean Monnet*, Summer-Fall 2000 of FIDELIO Magazine.

and Foreign Minister Schumann. The German side was joined by Konrad Adenauer, the first Chancellor of Germany, Otto von Habsburg, former Crown Prince of the Austro-Hungarian Empire, head of the Habsburg dynasty and President of the Pan-European Union, and later by Carlo Pesenti, an Italian banker with close ties to the Vatican Bank.[64]

David Rockefeller, the head of the Rockefeller family, describes in his autobiography this more controversial European caucus than the Bilderberg Club

> *"In October 1967, Carlo Pesenti, a banker who owned many important Italian companies ... introduced me to his small circle, where the discussion was mainly about current trends in Europe and world politics... Jean Monnet, Robert Schumann and Conrad Adenauer were the initiators of this circle... The discussions were conducted in French, and usually I was the only American attending the meetings, although sometimes when this group met in Washington, President Nixon's national security adviser Kissinger would come and eat together. All members of the Pesenti circle are active promoters of European political and economic integration."[65]*

There is no doubt that Monnet is the most sold out of these people for European integration. After the success of the first battle of "economic supersovereignty" of the Coal and Steel Alliance, he began to make a bigger move to make the defence of the European countries "military supersovereignty". If a sovereign state loses its economic autonomy, its monetary autonomy, and eventually even its national defense autonomy, the sovereign state is finished. Monet's European Defense Community was eventually rejected by the French de Gaullists. European countries remained at the level of interstate defence cooperation, which was then the newly established North Atlantic Treaty Organization (NATO).

Monnet simply resigned as president of the Coal and Steel Alliance and began to redouble his efforts to set up a rather low-profile organization called the ACUSE (Action Committee for the United

---

[64] Balint Szele, *The European Lobby: The Action Committee For the United States of Europe*, European Integration Studies, Miskolc, Volume 4, Number 2, 2005, p. 109–119.

[65] David Rockefeller, *Memoirs*, Random House Trade Paperbacks, 2003, p. 412–413.

States of Europe). This organization, in close cooperation with the United States Department of State, exerted behind-the-scenes pressure on the various organizations to lobby vigorously, leading to the signing of the Treaty of Rome in 1957 and the creation of the "European Economic Community".

Max Kohnstamm, Vice-President of the Action Committee of the United States of Europe, became the first President of the European branch of the Rockefeller-funded Trilateral Commission in 1973.

The ultimate goal of the Monnet circle is clear: the creation of a "European Republic". This idea of "internationalism" is bound to come into fierce conflict with the "nationalism" of States, which clings to the idea of sovereignty, and it is clear that the public declaration of their political claims to the elimination of sovereign States in the 1950s would have provoked sharp contradictions in European countries, from Governments to the population. Therefore, the elites in Monet's circle can only push this process quietly, and in the face of a strong backlash from sovereign States and social populations, it is even necessary to resort to major crises to "push back" reforms, forcing Governments to constantly surrender their industrial, trade, monetary, fiscal, tax and even defence sovereignty.

The coal-steel alliance is just the beginning, the ongoing euro crisis is just a "crisis lever" and the good news is yet to come.

Such a super-luxurious array of bankers, politicians, opinion-makers, academics, and informants with extraordinary energy are behind the scenes, motionlessly driving the rotation of the international political arena in all its strangeness, and they and the politicians on the stage sometimes cooperate with each other, sometimes bump and bump, and the people of the countries below the stage are watching with fog and excitement.

It is no wonder that in 1969 the American magazine Time called the Monnet circle "the shadow government of Europe".

In December 1963, Monnet was awarded the Presidential Medal of Freedom by President Johnson of the United States in recognition of his "outstanding contributions". Monnet died in 1979, and in 1988 Monet's relics were "invited" by the French Government to the Pantheon, where they were enjoyed for generations.

The dollar goes from scarcity to surplus, the scales of gold power tilt toward Europe

In the early post-war period, the United States continued to run a trade surplus, with dollars and gold pouring into the United States, which at one point had as much as 2/3 of the world's gold reserves, and dollars flowing back to the United States in a steady stream, while Europe was in a serious dollar shortage crisis. That's a big deal for the United States.

The Bretton Woods system was designed with the hope that dollars would flow out of the United States and into the world, giving the United States potential unlimited wealth and control in the grand cycle of international trade. The export of the dollar is an integral part of the United States monetary strategy, for which the United States has developed the Marshall Plan for Europe, the Dodge Plan for Japan, and numerous economic reconstruction plans, including those of the World Bank and the International Monetary Fund. More important means of exporting the dollar, also includes the U.S. multinational companies overseas direct investment, the surging tide of overseas investment dollar, in the capital-starved post-war Europe rampage, the siege of the city to merge assets, triggered the Europeans to cry out in shock. The United States dollar was in the best position at the moment, and it was in Europe at the time.

Since the 1950s, the European economy has been gradually recovering from its post-war ruins. The Marshall Plan brought rolling dollars, the Bretton Woods system established a stable monetary environment, the coal and steel union formed the European Common Market, and on top of all that, after the outbreak of the Korean War, the U.S. military orders flew in like snowflakes, making the European economy start to run at full speed. From 1950 to 1953, the U.S. spent about $30 billion on the Korean War, not nearly as much as World War II, but enough to make Europe and Japan a small fortune.

The United States has not resorted to traditional methods of financing the Korean war, such as a substantial increase in taxes, but has resorted more to "printing money". Due to the unique status of the dollar as the world reserve currency, the United States no longer has to borrow heavily from the United States, as the British Empire did in World War I and World War II, when the United States conducted the Korean War, but the Federal Reserve took the initiative to "monetize" the national debt and inject dollar bills into the world economy, and then did its best to rely on the debt.

The large amount of "bad dollars" created by the monetization of the national debt began to sow the seeds of inflation across Europe with the $3 billion a year in military spending overseas by the United States, as well as mergers and acquisitions in Europe by multinational corporations. Whether people realize it or not, and whether active or passive, as long as he holds dollars, he is the unlucky man who financed America's war debt.

It's as if it's back to the 1920s, when the dual-credit creation inherent in the gold-exchange standard was expanded globally under the Bretton system. As economist Trayvon discovered in 1947, the United States provides the world with two currency reserve assets, gold and the dollar, and the fixed price of $35 for an ounce of gold ties the two together, with gold supply slow and the dollar growing fast. The intrinsic reason for the dollar expansion is that when dollars are exported to Germany, Germany will have to increase the supply of marks due to the increase in foreign exchange reserves; at the same time, Germany will automatically re-deposit dollars into the US banking system, and the US will be able to re-credit itself in the country due to the return of dollars. The process can also go on and on. Rufus, an economic adviser to French President Charles de Gaulle, used a more graphic example to describe the process, where the repeated credit creation of the dollar is like "a band of soldiers marching on the stage, who can appear back and forth between the scenes." The result was inevitably more and more dollars, more and more liquidity, more and more debt bubbles, and more and more serious consequences of the economic crisis; the bursting of the debt bubble caused by the gold standard system in the 1920s led to the world economic depression of the 1930s, the dollar bubble created by the Bretton system that prevailed in the 1950s and 1960s, and the dollar crisis and hyperinflation that ravaged the world in the 1970s; the dollar standard system established after the 1970s, after more than 30 years of credit expansion and debt generation, led to the present world-wide sovereign currency crisis.

Due to the genetic fault of the gold exchange standard, the dollar is bound to grow more than gold, and maintaining a locked price between the dollar and gold becomes a logically unsustainable illusion. This problem, discovered by Triffin in 1947, has largely gone unnoticed by politicians in an era of extreme dollar shortages, when the United

States has up to 2/3 of the world's gold reserves. The so-called "Triffin puzzle" is simply dismissed as an "interesting" academic "brainteaser".

As an international currency reserve asset, the dollar must be exported continuously to meet the needs of countries' economic growth for the expansion of their currencies; at the same time, the development of the world economy also requires that the scale of export of the dollar be constantly expanded to ensure the conduct of international trade settlement. The bottleneck is that when the dollar's output is larger than its own gold reserves, it automatically triggers a crisis in which the world squeezes U.S. gold reserves with dollar bills.

The problem of a severe dollar glut in Europe was stinging when, for the first time in the early 1960s, the dollar in the hands of European countries exceeded the total gold reserves of the United States. How to cope with the surplus of dollars? The problems encountered in Europe in the 1960s were exactly the same as those faced by China now.

The European dollar, a new financial land

The dollar went from being a scarce treasure to a hot potato. Faced with an ever-increasing trade surplus and large dollar reserves brought about by the massive influx of international capital, the choice of European governments, in addition to buying U.S. Treasuries, is to convert them into gold. But the exchange of dollars for gold, which seems similarly hostile to Americans, has not dared anyone else in Europe to follow France's lead openly except de Gaulle, who ate the heart of a bear. But how can the European countries be willing to do so when they are sitting on the US national debt with huge amounts of dollars in their hands?

That's when the bankers had a flash in the pan and they discovered a new financial land, the dollar market in Europe. By European dollars, we mean the dollars that flowed into Europe and roamed around there at the earliest, and they were huge and lacked regulation. Later the Soviet Union, the Middle East and other countries also deposited dollars from oil export earnings in the European banking system, which also formed part of the European dollar. From then on, all dollars outside the United States are referred to as European dollars.

Such a large amount of "free money", except for the purchase of U.S. Treasury bonds, to obtain a small amount of interest income, is in a desperate situation in terms of investment! International banker

Sigmund Warburg is determined to pry open this vast and fertile new financial land.

Sigmund was a rising star of the Warburg family, mainly in London and New York, and was a senior partner at one of Wall Street's most prestigious investment banks, Kuhn Loeb and Co., which in the first half of the 20th century became as famous as Goldman Sachs today. The Warburg family was once talented and smiling on Wall Street. Max Warburg, the previous generation of Max Warburg, was a financial advisor to the German Kaiser Wilhelm II, represented Germany at the Versailles peace talks, after World War I dominated Germany's fiscal and financial power, as a Jewish director of the German Reichsbank, after the Nazis came to power, confronted Hitler in the central bank for five years; Paul Warburg, the chief architect of the Federal Reserve, one of the core decision makers of the United States financial policy; Felix Warburg, also a senior partner of Kuhn Loeb and Co., one of the Wall Street bigwigs; Fritz Warburg, chairman of the German Hamburg Metal Exchange, after World War I represented Germany in a secret peace with Saudi Russia. It could be argued that the Warburg family's power was spread throughout Germany, England, France and the United States.

Sigmund was also a believer in European integration and had deep ties to the Monnet circle. As an international banker, free movement of capital is the eternal ideal, and reducing government intervention is the minimum proposition. He recognized in the 1920s that nationalism was becoming obsolete in Europe and even suggested that the pan-European movement should start with disarmament, pooling the military sovereignty of nations and having an arbitration court to deal with differences. After the outbreak of the Second World War, he moved around in the hope of establishing a political alliance in Europe, uniting Britain and France first, and then establishing a Union of European States with Britain at its core, which would bring military, monetary, transport and communications sovereignty under a unified administration of "supreme authority".

After the Second World War, he admonished the British government to join the European Common Market and articulated to Monnet and Adenauer that London should play a leading role in European financial integration as the financial centre of the European Common Market. When the Coal and Steel Alliance was established, he advocated financial support from the City of London, which unfortunately was not adopted. Sigmund was very disappointed in the likes of Monnet and Adenauer, "who would surely have been grateful to England later if, in the first years of the war, the plan of European unification they led had London as its capital centre." In his view, the only way to achieve European unity was to start with financial integration.

In the case of the United States, he believes that cooperation with the United States goes hand in hand with European integration, and that in order to accelerate European integration, one could even borrow the financial power of the United States to force European recipient countries to abandon trade barriers.

Sigmund has more of the professional depth of a banker than someone like Monet. He saw the significance of Monet's coal-steel alliance to promote economic integration and was able to address practical problems from a concrete financial operational point of view. He has long and tirelessly advised the Coal and Steel Alliance to enter international capital markets for financing, both to expand its resources and scale and to attract private investors from the United States to join the process of rebuilding Europe. After a long effort, his idea finally blossomed, and in 1957, 1958, 1960, and 1962, the Coal and Steel Alliance issued more than $120 million in bonds on the New York capital market.[66]

As the size of the dollar pooling in the European market grew, Sigmund realized with a jolt why dollar financing for European companies had to go to New York. Isn't the European dollar close at hand?

While the EC is focusing primarily on monetary union, Sigmund is thinking about how to integrate Europe's capital markets. On the front lines at Kuhn Loeb and Co. in New York, he knew firsthand how the powerful financial syndicates of Wall Street organized and coordinated large-scale bond underwriting, but Paris and Frankfurt clearly did not have the financial strategic vision to do so.

Four times for the Coal and Steel Alliance's large-scale financing practice in the New York capital markets, cementing Sigmund's belief

---

[66] Niall Ferguson, *High Finance: The Lives and Time of Siegmund Warburg*, The Penguin Press, 2010, p. 201–212.

in the formation of a powerful financial syndicate in Europe. The difficulties are obvious, and while European countries have a common market, it is primarily a trade market, not a capital market. With the diversity of national policies on capital controls and exchange rate adjustments, as well as different legal provisions on monetary and financial matters, it is by no means a simple matter to legally bypass so many regulatory barriers to achieve a unified issuance on the European capital markets in order to issue prehistoric dollar bonds in Europe. What Sigmund is doing, in fact, is linking the whole of Europe's divided capital markets, into one common capital market!

To create a dollar-denominated European bond market, it is paramount that there must be enough dollars in European hands, which is already provided for in the U.S. dollar export strategy by European trade surpluses, multinational investment, and U.S. military base spending overseas. In addition, a large number of wealthy individuals in Europe also have large deposits in dollars, as well as foreign exchange deposits from the Soviet Union, socialist countries in Eastern Europe, etc., which are also held mainly in Europe for fear of being frozen by the American banking system in extreme cases. These dollars are held in the accounts of large corporations, the European Commercial Bank, national central banks and international organizations (such as the Bank for International Settlements).

One might ask, why aren't these dollars deposited directly into a Bank of America account in New York? In addition to the concerns of the Soviet Union and the Eastern European countries, the "Q clause" of the financial sector, which remained in the United States during the Great Depression, severely limited the interest payment limits of United States financial institutions to no more than 1 per cent for 30 days and 2.5 per cent for 90 days for short-term savings.

The next important question is where to start the pilot of European dollar bonds? Sigmund preferred London. This is not only because of London's history as a world financial centre, but also because the Bank of England has adopted a more enlightened policy towards the hot money that the ECB is talking about. These hot money, its deposit time is relatively short, banks can not or do not dare to carry out long-term lending, and at the same time, big in and out is very easy to impact the stability of the foreign exchange market, so the central bank is regarded as a flood of beasts. But where is the money to justify the Bank of England's refusal to deposit when it thinks it's an international banker? The key is how to handle the conflict between short-stocking and long-lending. The Bank of England's response has been to establish a firewall for domestic and international capital flows, in short, a financial special zone similar to the concept of a "free zone", which is of course an abstract special zone. The Bank of England rules that British people cannot buy foreign bonds except in the strict sense of dollar bonds for "real investment" purposes: in this strictly segregated market, British pounds held by British people and foreign dollars held by foreigners, no one is in trouble. Foreigners are free to do as they please in the totally unregulated dollar capital market, and all activities in this market do not affect the domestic capital market in the UK at all. This arrangement is more similar to the Chinese stock market where A and B shares are open to domestic and foreign investors respectively.

Sigmund also resorted to threats plus temptations in order to persuade the Bank of England to back a pilot of European dollar bonds in London. He claims that if the Bank of England does not remove the high stamp duty on foreign bond investment earnings, then he will move Eurodollar bonds to Luxembourg or other markets with more relaxed policies. However, he also stressed that once London becomes the centre of European dollar bonds, a steady flow of dollars will flow to the City of London and it will become the financial centre of the world again. This second half of the sentence was too tempting for the Bank of England to resist. Just as good things were about to happen, the London Stock Exchange jumped in with a bang, rejecting the listing of Eurodollar bonds on the stock exchange. If it can't be listed for trading, then the settlement of the bond for delivery after trading is a big problem. The exchange later made concessions, but insisted that the dollar bonds must be denominated in pounds sterling and that the pre-war exchange rate of the pound sterling against the dollar prevailed, that the actual purchase of the bonds could only be made in Luxembourg and that the dollars used must be claimed from government-controlled foreign exchange lines. Sigmund depressedly asks how financial innovation can be so difficult.

In choosing which company to pilot, Sigmund preferred to issue dollar bonds for the Coal and Steel Alliance, not only to make money, but also for his long-held dream of European unity. In a note to the Bank of England, he mentioned,

> *"This will be a simple dollar bond with no currency options attached. For UK foreign exchange controls, it is a foreign currency bond that UK residents will pay an additional fee to purchase. As a result, residents of the country will not subscribe.*

However, they will get an offer in London and this price will be the base price for the entire European market, which will encourage them to trade through London."[67]

Just as the water was about to flow, the British Foreign Office intervened, arguing that it would be inappropriate to issue European Economic Community bonds in London to help finance them at a time when Britain was being shut out of the European Common Market. The Bank of England was supportive, and although the bonds were not denominated in sterling, the trading was done in London, doesn't that mean London is starting to become the world's financial centre again?

Just as Sigmund persuaded UK regulators to prepare for the opening, new problems were encountered, with all members of the EC having to agree unanimously to get approval for the issue, a process that would take months. As a result, the first Eurodollar bond was not the coal-steel alliance that Sigmund had in mind, but an Italian company that set a record for a debut with a $15 million six-year bond at 5.5 percent coupon value, issued at 98.5 percent of face value. Sigmund led European financial institutions to successful bond sales. From there, the European dollar bond market kicked off with a bang!

The European dollar has finally found a huge investment space on top of the meager gains in US Treasuries. Its significance lies in the fact that the Europeans began to use dollar resources to leverage their strengths and develop themselves without falling into the low-yield trap of dollar-denominated Treasuries and becoming passive bill payers for the financing of the US deficit. This offers a strategically valuable way out for today's China, and for Asia as a whole, with its huge dollar reserves.

Sigmund's attempts have made him the well-deserved father of the "Eurodollar bond".

Monetary Union: the beginning or the end of European integration?

Throughout the 1950s and 1960s, Monnet was undoubtedly the soul of the movement for European integration, and the "Action

---

[67] Ibid.

Committee of the United States of Europe", which he established, absorbed many of Europe's elite figures. In the campaign to unify Europe, Monnet gradually realized that economic integration must come first, and that the establishment of a European Monetary Union was the most powerful lever to pry economic integration.

With regard to monetary unions, there are two schools of thought within Europe: one is the monetary union strongly advocated by the Monnet circle, in which countries surrender their monetary sovereignty and a supersovereign body implements a unified plan for their economic development; the other is the insistence on monetary unions, in which countries establish only a permanent mechanism for stabilizing exchange rates, but the power to issue money remains with the State. In essence, these two schools of thought represent two forces within Europe, the monetary union forces representing the internationalist ideology of Europe, whose ultimate goal is to abolish the sovereignty of nations and establish a unified government of the United States of Europe, while the monetary union supporters are staunch believers in nationalism, believing that the national interest is the ultimate value. The internationalist versus statist battle of currencies has been at the heart of the euro controversy for the past half century. In today's euro crisis, the final outcome of these two power plays will determine the fate of the euro.

The dollar-centric Breton dynasty had a "genetic cancer gene", which was already apparent by the mid-1960s. The devastating impact of the ongoing depreciation of the dollar constitutes an external pressure to establish a European monetary union. In the eyes of Europeans, the dollar has morphed from the umbrella of Europe's economic health and stability to the perpetrator of trade turmoil and currency crises, and the London Economic Conference of 1933 was the center of the US-Europe rivalry and remains a difficult puzzle for both sides to crack. Monetary stability is a prerequisite for economic development in Europe. This is because of the small size of the population of European countries, the lack of economic depth and market capacity to carry the pressure of sustained economic development, so the development of international trade and the expansion of the common market in Europe has become the greatest hope of Europeans. But the irresponsible policies of the dollar have both threatened the external trading environment for Europeans and disrupted the internal common market. The result of the Europeans' repeated dealings with the Americans is a famous quote from U.S. Treasury Secretary Connelly: "The dollar is our currency, but it is your problem."

The impact of the dollar's devaluation on Europe was felt first in Germany.

The German monetary reform of 1948 created a unique central banking system, which is the Bundesbank's model of independence. The ideal of transcending the constraints of state power, which the American and British central banks could hardly hope for in their own countries, finally gave Germany an ideal testing ground in the post-war wasteland. So the U.S.-British design of the German Central Bank, which predates the birth of the West German federal government, a violation of the founding principles and precedents of all nations of the world, was designed to ensure the complete independence of the German Central Bank from the government.

The German central bank was established at the beginning, neither gold nor foreign exchange, credit is still a blank piece of paper. In the face of a completely insolvent banking system in the country, the bank's assets must be completely liquidated while the new mark is exchanged for the old mark at 1:10. Under Nazi Germany, the national economy was fully militarized and economic resources were heavily invested in the war machine, leaving the private economy with little need for credit, while the German wartime economy was rationed and people could not buy anything with money, creating the dilemma of having nowhere to lend the savings of the population accumulated in banks. While banks had nowhere to lend but could not fail to do so, otherwise they would lose their source of income and fall into deficit or collapse, the Nazi government took full advantage of the banks' excess savings and introduced a large number of government bonds at all levels, leaving the banks with no alternative but to use the people's savings to buy government bonds and indirectly finance the war. After the war, there was no more Nazi government in Germany, and the government bonds held by the banks became bad loans. In this case, the German Central Bank provided for a write-off of all debts owed by the Nazi Government to banks. Significant asset losses suffered by banks are partially shared between the central bank and the future federal government by replenishing them with "equalisation claims" issued by the central bank. The "balancing note" is similar to the "central note" of the People's Bank of China, in that it is secured by the credit of the future new government and is repaid by the central bank's own profits, which in turn reduces the portion of the profits due to the future government.

In essence, the "balancing note" is the replacement of the old debt of the Nazi government with the national debt of the new future German government, only to be issued by the central bank on its behalf when the government does not yet exist.

Thus, the assets of Germany's central bank and the entire commercial banking system were based on pure national debt in the early post-war period, with the Deutsche Mark in 1948 being the purest "national debt standard" in the world.

In fact, the credit cornerstone of the national currency is neither the gold standard nor the national debt standard, but the "production standard"! The credit of the national currency is naturally strong and solid as long as the country has a strong productive capacity to create a wealth of goods and quality services. The gold standard or national debt standard is just a symbolic form of the "production standard"! The strength of a country's currency is ultimately determined by its ability to create wealth.

When Germany is full of industrial machinery, huge social wealth is created incessantly, high-quality commodities flooded into the United States market and the European common market, rolling dollars and gold into the German treasury. 1950 Germany did not have any gold reserves, just six years, the German central bank of gold reserves easily surpassed the historical gold power France, but also accumulated a huge amount of dollar reserves.

While the German mark was being praised and vied for, Germany's central bankers began to rise to the occasion, appearing as defenders of the mark and frequently arguing with the German government, with Chancellor Adenauer loudly protesting that the German central bank "is an institution that is accountable to no one, neither to Parliament nor to any government ... the guillotine (of monetary policy) falls on the head of everyone in the street". Adenauer's anger is justified, the backing of Mark's firmness is not the central bank's interest rate policy, but the strong industrial power created by millions of German engineers and skilled workers.

In the early 1960s, the mark began to face increasing appreciation pressure. In order to maintain the demand for currency stability in the Bretton Woods system, the German Central Bank began to be forced to "print marks" to buy large inflows of dollars in order to curb the pressure on the mark to appreciate against the dollar. This is the same problem that China is currently having to issue more yuan to buy dollars in order to keep the yuan exchange rate stable. The rise of the mark has shaken the edifice of the dollar system, as it has created inflationary pressure in Germany, whether to raise interest rates against inflation or to appreciate the mark against inflation, triggering a fierce dispute between the German central bank and the government.

It should be made clear that the appreciation of the mark reflects the growth reality of German industrial power, and that the exchange rate system solidified by Bretton represents the level of economic development of the countries before and after 1945. When the German economy rose from ruins to giants, it was clear that sizing would not be appropriate to use an 8-year-old's shoes on a 20-year-old stick boy. However, an appreciation would result in a considerable potential loss to Germany's currency reserves, especially the dollar, although this loss would not be superficial in an era when the dollar is locked in with the gold price. Fortunately for Germany, gold makes up more of its currency reserves than the dollar, so the extent of the loss of dollar reserves will be greatly reduced. Since the value of the German mark was destroyed twice in 30 years, gold has always held a significant share of the German central bank's money reserves.[68]

However, the appreciation of the mark has created a chain reaction in Europe. As the mark appreciated, so did the Dutch guilder. France and other EC countries are beginning to fear that exchange rate volatility among the Common Market countries will affect the trade and economic balance in the region and ultimately upset the political balance. Thus, in 1965, the EC suggested that the development of the EC would inevitably require the formation of a monetary union, with the objective of exchange rate stability at first, and a gradual transition to a single European currency.

This has led to a half-century-long dispute between the two schools of thought, led by Germany, the school of thought, unified currency is a long process, the integration of national economies is a prerequisite, must first have a common trade policy, common fiscal and tax policy, common economic policy, common livelihood policy, before we can talk about a unified currency. The Germans did not see much viability

---

[68] Martin Pontzen and Franziska Schobert, *Episodes in German Monetary History-Lessons for Transition Countries*, 2007, p. 4–13.

in the existence of a monetary union beyond sovereignty. The other faction, led by France, insists that monetary integration is the starting point for economic integration and that there can be no European economy without a stable exchange rate. In fact, the essence of the argument is whether the monetary union is the beginning or the end, the means or the goal, of European unity.

As the Vietnam War escalated and the dollar's devaluation intensified severely, the urgency of Europe's push for a monetary union in the midst of a rapidly deteriorating currency crisis was greatly enhanced.

The Battle of Gold

> *"France will not be called France unless it is at the forefront; France will not be called France if it is not great. Making France great is the only goal in my heart and the noblest purpose of my life."*

– De Gaulle

In 1958 Charles de Gaulle came to power and France entered the era of the Fifth Republic. It can be said that Charles de Gaulle embodied the characteristics of the French: passionate, arrogant and impulsive, idealistic and fanatical. Since the time of Napoleon, the French psyche has been so unbalanced that the era of glory and splendor seems to have passed away forever, and the cold reality has suppressed the French desire to restore their great country from time to time. France is the victor, but it wins without glory; France is strong, but not strong enough to be European. De Gaulle, whose heart was higher than the sky, was determined to revive France.

Strong nationalist sentiments, undisguised nationalist tendencies, make de Gaulle have no common language with Monet's circle. Europeans often joke about Monnet, calling him "the most influential Frenchman, except in France". De Gaulle's reintegration with Adenauer was not about "giving up French sovereignty" for some United States of Europe, as advocated by Monet's circle; what he needed was a strong European Union under French leadership, with the goal of challenging American world hegemony, and in such a grand vision, even the Soviet Union was a pawn that De Gaulle was prepared to use against the United States. In de Gaulle's mind, "the union of Europe would be done by France and Germany, with France as the catcher and Germany as the horse".

The thing De Gaulle was most disturbed by was the pattern of American and British domination of the world. In World War II, Roosevelt disliked de Gaulle because de Gaulle also wanted to be in firm control of his own destiny, and if everyone was like de Gaulle, then who else could America go and control? Churchill also hated de Gaulle, and even after escaping to England, de Gaulle's arrogance, stubbornness and uncompromising stubbornness were nothing like eating white food in someone else's house. De Gaulle, on the other hand, hated the Anglo-Saxon attempt to dominate France, especially at the Yalta Conference, where De Gaulle was sidelined by the Anglo-Americans and did not get a ticket to this major conference, and where De Gaulle's proud heart was sore.

After de Gaulle came to power and twice kept Britain out of the European Community, the British prime minister denounced "the countries of continental Europe as a raging economic bloc. This is the first time since the Napoleonic Wars". De Gaulle ridiculed the British prime minister in front of officials as "a poor man, I have nothing to offer him".

Why should the Anglo-Saxon currency be poked at as a pillar while the other currencies are just looking at their faces? As long as you can get the dollar off the horse, even if it's a death sentence. De Gaulle not only thought so, but did so.

After two depreciations of the franc between 1957 and 1958, French exports improved and dollar reserves surged. The only way to get to the bottom of the Bretton Woods system is with gold, which is the key to the dollar. At that time, the great and the mighty rise up, and the franc leads the brothers of the mark, the lira, and others to the throne room of money, to see who is the match for the world.

From 1958 to 1966, France used its dollar reserves to demand an average of 400 tons of gold per year from the United States, and France's gold reserves again surpassed those of Germany. Other European countries, under the pressure of the United States Treasury Department, do not dare to easily request the exchange of dollars for gold, the reason given by the United States is that this will damage the financial situation of the world, the subtext of the United States is very clear, whoever exchanges dollars for gold is the "potential enemy" of the world financial order. Of course, the United States on the French act of hatred to the root of the teeth, just a moment to take oil and salt not enter the de Gaulle can not. early 1960s, the United States forced the

European Central Bank to set up a part of the "gold mutual aid total pool", jointly selling gold to stabilize the bottom line of $35 for an ounce of gold. However, the flooding of the dollar continues unabated.

When United States President Johnson came to power in 1964, instead of coming up with concrete ways to cut fiscal spending and improve the balance of payments, he proposed a costly "Great Society" plan and a costly escalation programme for the war in Viet Nam. Johnson's "Great Society" encompasses everything from creating a better urban environment to combating pollution; from waging a war on poverty to increasing employment opportunities to strengthening social security and relief; from universal education to civil rights; from developing the countryside to building highways; from "nurturing orphans" to caring for the elderly; and 115 pieces of legislation. The allocation of funds for health, education and backward area development alone increased from $8.1 billion in 1965 to $11.4 billion in 1966. The escalation of the Vietnam War was a bottomless pit of burning money, beginning in 1965, when U.S. planes began to bomb North Vietnam on a massive scale, and on March 8 of the same year, U.S. ground troops landed in Vietnam, accelerating the steps of the Vietnam War, which reached its peak in 1968, when U.S. troops numbered 530,000. A "great society" would have depleted America's economic resources, and the Vietnam War ended up costing $400 billion! Johnson chose both the cannon and the butter. He confidently believes, "After all, our founding fathers were the ones who beat the enemy with a gun in one hand and built homes with an axe in the other to feed their families." In fact, Johnson wasn't worried about where his coffers would come from because the US could print money and let the Europeans go and help pay the US deficit.

The unbridled spending of the American treasury eventually angered de Gaulle and all the European countries, and in 1965 the Bank of France openly announced that France was prepared to demand from the American government all new inflows of dollar reserves and some of its existing reserves for gold. The French used to exchange dollars for gold, all quietly, not wanting to embarrass America too much. This time, it was a complete public slap in the face to America. European creditors with dollar reserves have been clapping their hands in private. Charles de Gaulle also proposed a global monetary reform programme to strengthen the role of gold in the global monetary system, outlawing the dollar and pound sterling as international reserve currencies and calling directly on European countries to seize power.

In France's view, Britain and the United States occupy both sides of the Atlantic, with the same spirit and horns in each other's hands. In order to break the strong dollar, the European bloc must first break the pound and break its arms.

And at this point, Britain is in crisis.

After the war, Britain's ongoing attempts to restore the sterling zone were met with constant and harsh suppression from the United States. In particular, during the Suez Canal crisis of 1956, Britain was subjected to categorical financial sanctions by the United States, which completely rejected the idea of restoring its colonial empire.

In World War II, the massive exports from the British colonies to Britain created a huge reserve of pounds. The Americans forced Britain to unfreeze these pound sterling reserves in 1947, which triggered a severe pound sterling crisis that wiped out the pound's credit and sent former colonial powers to the dollar. The UK has been forced to freeze its pound sterling reserves again, a huge pound sterling external debt burden that has been weighing down the UK's finances and creating a crisis of confidence in the pound whenever the world economy fluctuates a little. From 1948 to 1982, the UK capital account was in deficit 32 times in 34 years, so much so that during the post-war boom period of industrial equipment upgrading and rapid technological progress, the UK remained cash-strapped and lagged behind major European countries due to historical sterling reserves, pressure from foreign debt and huge overseas military spending. By 1960, Britain's currency reserves were £1 billion, but the external debt owed in pounds sterling was as high as £3 billion, and by the end of the 1960s, the external debt was even as high as £6 billion, becoming the "British patient" in the European economy.

France not only attacked London's sterling reserves with gold, pounding Britain where it hurts, but also used the tools of the French state media to weaken the pound. France's continued practice of converting the pound into gold has resulted in the United States and other "Group of Ten" and IMF organizations loans to defend the pound to nothing. At a critical moment, Germany refused to make a statement in favour of the pound on the grounds that "the German community was convinced that the pound should be devalued", and in November 1967, after a gruelling three-year campaign to defend the pound, the pound surrendered and was devalued by 14.3 per cent. The depreciation of the

British pound immediately spurred a massive sell-off of the dollar in international markets and a rush for gold.

On 17 March 1968, the United States' hard-earned "Gold Mutual" collapsed, and at the end of March, millions of Americans heard President Johnson announce on television that he would not seek re-election. Meanwhile, the U.S. New Year's Day offensive against Vietnam came to no end. The *Wall Street Journal* lamented,

> *"European financiers are imposing peace on us. We, the creditors of Europe, have forced a president to resign, a groundbreaking event in American history."[69]*

At the critical moment when France was victorious and ready to launch a general attack on America's gold reserves, a sudden and dramatic event reversed the entire course of the Gold War. Just five days after the collapse of the "General Mutual Aid Bank of Gold" in the United States on 17 March, students from a Parisian university suddenly took over the campus on 22 March, and more and more universities became involved, turning it into a "May storm" in Paris, which paralysed society for a time.

Although the cause of the incident is unclear, the result is obvious: the gold that France brought back from the United States was forced to return to the United States in good faith. Even de Gaulle himself eventually lost the presidency as a result.

"May storm" in the foreign exchange market set off a huge wave, the franc was a massive sell-off, triggered an avalanche of devaluation. 29 May, the governor of the Bank of France to the Federal Reserve called for help, the Americans replied: "the dollar is not good to borrow for nothing, France does not have gold reserves? It can be sold for dollars." In a desperate situation, the French were willing to sell to the U.S. Treasury at a flat price of $35. The U.S. was in fact desperately short of gold and the price of gold was rising, while the U.S. Treasury demanded a 10 percent price reduction from the French. In fact, the IMF and many other buyers are certainly willing to buy gold for $35. The two sides finally reached a compromise, the U.S. Treasury Department paid $35 to buy, the French in Paris to the IMF to deliver gold, the IMF

---

[69] Michael Hudson, *Super Imperialism-New Edition: The Origin and Fundamentals of U.S. World Dominance*, Pluto Press, 2003, Chapter 12.

in New York to the Federal Reserve Bank of New York their own gold, 1968 to 1969, France was forced in this way to the United States sold $925 million of gold at parity.[70]

The French have been taking dollar reserves and squeezing them against American gold for years for nothing.

In 1971, the dollar "usurped gold" and established the American debt empire

Although the French gold offensive ended in failure, the gold squeeze that France created around the world buried the Bretton Woods dynasty that the United States had built.

On 15 August 1971, United States President Nixon announced the closing of the United States "gold window" and the cessation of the exchange of the dollar for gold. Since then, the Bretton Woods system has become a time-honored term.

Originally, the United States could choose to reassess the ratio of gold and the dollar, just as Roosevelt devalued the dollar against gold in 1934, it was suggested that the dollar be devalued to $72 to 1 ounce of gold, in order to reflect the economic reality of the dollar in the post-war 25 years of excessive hair growth, but the United States is too far away from the appearance of a superficial. Because America no longer needs the nominal emperor that is gold.

The dollar has become the de facto world currency, and whether people like it or not, and no matter how much they complain, the Bretton Woods dynasty has embedded the dollar so deeply into the monetary systems of every country that the more people struggle, the deeper they will get, the more fierce the resistance will be, and the stronger the reaction they will suffer.

For 25 years, the United States has succeeded in using the dollar to sever the link between gold and the world economy, and with the exception of central banks, people have faded away from gold in their daily lives and become accustomed to the dollar. The dollar to replace

---

[70] Charles A. Coombs, *The Arena of International Finance,* John Wiley and Sons, 1976, p. 177–178.

the gold "Li for peach" plan, now it is time for the melon to fall, the water to the canal.

The profound impact that the dollar-denominated system, which replaced the gold exchange standard, would have on the world is still being chewed on until more than 40 years later. The economy was progressing and society was evolving, but the crisis was following suit, and the intensity, breadth and timing of the Great Depression of the 1930s were approaching. The world has recognized that there are fundamental problems with today's global monetary system.

The dollar, as the world's monetary reserve, would result in U.S. Treasuries becoming a de facto global reserve core asset. The more the world economy develops, the more countries' currencies grow hungry for U.S. Treasuries; the more international trade expands, the more pressure there will be on U.S. dollar exports. The dollar is like a planting machine, in the process of circulating the world, inserting the seeds of the U.S. national debt into the financial system of each country, these seeds will germinate and grow, and the growth of the interest on the debt will generate more demand for dollars. The dollar and U.S. debt, in mutual demand, will have an inherent rigid drive for self-growth, until the day comes when one suddenly finds a huge lake of sovereign debt weirs pressing down on each one's head, and that's when someone will exclaim that this lake of debt weirs is doomed to break!

When Trayvon discovered the natural contradiction between the dollar and the gold lock, no one cared, because that was a crisis decades later, not a problem today. When that day came early, people were left to their own devices.

Now, when we find that the dollar is just as inherently contradictory as the U.S. debt, still no one will care. But studying history makes us understand that the day will come!

CHAPTER V

The East Wants to Know, China-Japan Industrialization Tug-of-War

In today's world economic map, the basic posture of the United States, Europe and Asia has gradually formed three legs. It has been said that the 19th century is the century of Britain, the 20th century is the century of the United States, and the 21st century is the century of Asia, and at least in the light of current global developments, there is a real possibility of that.

America's woes lie in the economy, Europe's crisis in politics, and Asia's problems in history.

China and Japan, like France and Germany, are both enemies in history and relatives in reality. In the 60-year post-war economic race, Japan has led the first half, while China has gradually picked up steam in the second half and the two sides are now in a fairly close position. Can China finally get ahead of Japan? Or is it Japan's miraculous resurgence after 20 years of economic stagnation?

It was a race that resembled the post-war 1950s, when both sides were evenly matched.

After receiving $2.4 billion in aid from the Soviet Union, China launched full industrialization with the massive construction of 156 key industrial projects. Japan, on the other hand, is embarking on a difficult post-war renaissance with the direct and indirect help of $4.1 billion from the United States. By at least the mid-1950s, the two sides were not at the same level of development. Japan's industrialization began early, with the accumulation of talent and technology far above China's, but in the post-war period, the Japanese government lost political and economic leadership, and industrial production and foreign trade were still undergoing a difficult recovery. China's industrialization had a poor base, but the Soviet Union's massive industrial assistance with technology and new equipment, and the 18,000 Soviet experts who were deeper into China's technological diffusion, led to a dramatic reduction in the distance between the Chinese economy and the world level in the 1950s.

The inflection point in the economic race between China and Japan came in 1955, a huge gap in economic strategic vision that was magnified by China's own mistakes and reinforced by Japan's full use of the resources of the world market. China lost 20 years in the dramatic shift and acceleration of world industrialization that occurred in the 1960s.

If China does not want to see history repeat itself, then it must carefully review how the strategic gap was created and how it deteriorated.

China gets the Soviet Marshall Plan

The Korean War, which broke out in 1950, not only changed the landscape of Europe, but also brought about a fissure in the fate of Asia. China chose the Soviet Union, while the United States decided to impose "economic exile" on China.

In fact, for China, the choice is not complicated. To develop a backward agrarian nation into a strong industrial nation, China had to seek foreign aid, and the only external forces that could help China industrialize on a large scale in the historical conditions of the time were the Soviet Union and the United States. With the United States' long-standing support for the Kuomintang government and having begun the cold war with the Soviet Union, it is clearly seriously unreliable to expect the United States to provide China under the Communist Party with the technology, equipment, talent and capital necessary for large-scale industrialization. As a result, the Soviet Union became the only external force capable of providing assistance for China's industrialization.

Since the Second World War, all the developing and formerly colonized countries of the world have come to realize very clearly that industrialization is the only way to prosperous and strong nations. However, the industrial economy is far more complex than the traditional agricultural economy, and the technological diffusion brought about by the industrial revolution is not simply a matter of building factories, importing equipment, buying raw materials, organizing production and marketing, but also involves a huge social project that goes along with it, such as the simultaneous development of energy and electricity, steel and coal, equipment manufacturing, petrochemicals, electronics, infrastructure, transportation, commerce and trade, banking and finance, education and training, and many other industries, and this precise coordination mechanism for large industries and a complex system of trade and financial services greatly exceeds the human, material and financial bases available in most agricultural countries. This is why, in the 60 years since World War II, there have been very few emerging industrial powers that have really emerged.

As Stalin's special envoy Mikoyan was impressed by after his meeting with the main leaders of the Communist Party in Singapore in February 1949, he wrote in his report to Stalin that the Communist Party did not know how to stop inflation, how to treat foreign enterprises, how to impose a state monopoly on salt, tobacco and alcohol, how to nationalize the assets of the four major families and the big buyers, how to impose a monopoly on foreign trade. Communist leaders are "very knowledgeable and confident" about general political issues, party affairs, international issues, peasant issues and economic issues, but they do not know much about management issues, "have vague concepts of industry, transport and banking", and do not understand China's enterprise and economic situation, nor do they know what to do. In short, "they are in the closed countryside, out of touch with reality".

During the long and brutal post-enemy guerrilla war and the development of rural strongholds far from the big cities, the quality of the cadres was far from meeting the requirements of industrialization. According to statistics, there were 1.5 million party members in North China in the early 1950s, 1.3 million of whom were illiterate or semi-literate. Nearly 50 per cent of the leading cadres (district committees and above) are uneducated or poorly educated. It takes two to three years for the leaders alone to become literate, and at least five years for ordinary party members.

There is also a serious shortage of core human resources needed for the proliferation of industrialized technologies, and the number of scientific institutions and researchers left over from the Kuomintang era is pitifully small. The Kuomintang government's Central Academy of Sciences has only 13 research institutes with 207 researchers, and only physics, mathematics, biology, geology and humanities are covered. The Beijing Academy of Sciences has nine research institutes, with only 42 researchers remaining. There are less than 200 geological experts in the country, and the total number of engineers and technicians in the country is only 20,000, even in key enterprises like Anshan Steel, there are only 70 engineers, of which 62 are Japanese! Even with these extremely scarce human resources, the level of industrial technology they were familiar with was still decades away from that of post-war Germany. At the same time, there is an even greater shortage of professionals in other sectors that must be matched to these talents in order to make the industrialization machine work, such as the planning of economic systems, the organization of production in modern industry, and the services of trade finance. Clearly, the talent bottleneck is the biggest difficulty facing China's industrialization.

In addition to this, industrialization must require huge capital accumulation, and the capital required by agricultural countries in the process of industrialization can only be derived from agricultural accumulation and external financing. The widespread foreign exchange shortage in developing countries is due to the fact that they have to exchange the slow and meagre natural accumulation of agriculture for the cost of advanced technological equipment abroad, which is too high. In the process of industrialization, the main significance of foreign exchange hard currency lies in the import of equipment and raw materials for the production of technological proliferation. Foreign aid, foreign investment, borrowing of foreign debt are all about the proliferation of valuable technology.

In military terms, the Korean War completely reversed the trend of China's national defence defeat over the past century, deterring the strong enemy on the 38th parallel and consolidating the strategic security zone of industrialization in the northeast and even the whole of China, since then the Western powers have completely abandoned the idea of a large-scale war with China. The military deterrent created by the Korean War made the American forces in the Vietnam War not dare to take a half-step to the minefield at the 17-degree line of latitude north of Vietnam, and forced the mighty Soviet army to reckon with the peace dividends of this deterrent, which China enjoyed for the next 60 years of its industrialization.

On the political and economic front, the Korean War radically altered Stalin's skeptical attitude towards the Chinese government, and his enthusiasm for aiding China in its industrialization increased significantly. Zhou Enlai once said, "It was only when Stalin came to the resistance against the U.S. that he changed his mind about China." Mao also argued that "more or less an important reason for Stalin to believe in the Chinese Communist Party was the entry of the Chinese People's Volunteers into the war." After Stalin, Khrushchev's substantial contribution to China's defense industry, especially missiles and nuclear weapons, in the mid to late 1950s surpassed even that of the Stalin era.

In total, the Soviet Union provided China with up to 6.6 billion rubles, equivalent to $1.65 billion, during the start of China's industrialization in the 1950s, more than the total amount of aid provided by the United States to Germany for the Marshall Plan ($1.45 billion). In addition, under the leadership of the Soviet Union, technical equipment assistance from Eastern European countries to China totalled 3.08 billion roubles. As a result, China has received a total of roughly $2.4 billion in industrialized raw capital from the socialist camp.

It is with this huge amount of industrial capital that China has embarked on an unprecedented industrialization process in its history, carrying out 156 key projects (150 actually completed) in the energy, metallurgy, machinery, chemical and defence industries. The process of transforming the private economy into a State-owned economy, which had been expected to take 15 years to complete gradually, was greatly reduced to five years with the massive entry of external capital, the trade-offs of which are always in dispute. Of course, the money was not a free lunch, and China had to exchange it for agricultural products and industrial primary raw materials.

As an agrarian country that has never experienced the baptism of the industrial revolution, the interrelationship, prioritization and proportional coordination among the various sectors of the complex industrial economy are, for China, the first time for a big girl to get on the sedan chair, and many plausible concepts and fuzzy judgments need to be learned and improved quickly. For industrial systems formed under unnatural conditions, planning is particularly important. The first Five-Year Plan was discussed in February 1951 under the auspices of a six-member team of Zhou Enlai, Chen Yun and Bo Yibo, and it took more than two years of repeated research and revision before the core principles of the Five-Year Plan were distilled and refined. Nonetheless, they ignored such major issues as the proportion of military industry in total investment, the pressure that excessive industrial growth targets put on the concentrated use of human and material resources, how to combine industrial development with China's abundant human resources for handicrafts, how to ensure the supply of food and agricultural raw materials for agriculture, and how finance and finance can ensure that industrialization progresses in tandem with people's living standards. The Soviet Union was by this time a master of the planned economy, and with the assistance of Soviet planning experts, these problems were gradually identified and adjusted.

With a plan, it's just a matter of understanding the principles of what industrialization needs to do, which ones to do first and which ones to do later, what percentage of investment is appropriate, how the chains between the industrial sectors are connected, but the devil is hidden in the details of implementation. Even the best plans, if they are difficult to implement, will end up being far less effective.

Without the Soviet Union's industrial cooperation with Germany from 1922 to 1927, and without a large number of German engineers and military-industrial experts handed over to the Soviet Union, Stalin's attempts to transform the Soviet Union from a backward agrarian state to a powerful industrial state in 10 years could only be an unrealistic fantasy.

Tens of thousands of Chinese engineers were confronted with complex production equipment they had never seen in their lives, completely unfamiliar production processes, Russian technical data and drawings like a celestial book, unknown technical product standards, strict raw material requirements and precise formulations, which were simply the size of two heads. It is not easy to produce advanced products such as high-grade alloy steel, stainless steel, seamless steel tubes, jet planes, tanks, large-caliber artillery, warning radars, automobiles, tractors, ton-ton ships, large-capacity complete thermal and hydroelectric power generation equipment, large-volume blast furnace equipment, combined coal miners and new machine tools among hundreds of new enterprises in just three to five years! After all, it's not as simple as IKEA furniture can be hand-assembled!

But the "devils" of industrialization are hiding in these millions of details. If China's own engineers and technicians had been able to overcome various technical difficulties one by one, I'm afraid that by the time the machine could move, the product would have been obsolete.

The 18,000 experts and engineers from various industries sent to China by the Soviet Union in the 1950s are credited with absorbing the proliferation of industrialized technology in China. In the beginning stages of economic construction, the first thing China felt inadequate was design power. By 1953, there were only 78 design units in the country, each with less than 500 people, and such a meager force could not meet China's needs for full economic recovery and construction. In order to assist China in planning for national electrification, steel development and product variety determination, machinery industry adjustment and new plant construction, ship industry and rail transport, geological survey, etc., the USSR has sent as many as 47 planning expert teams. In 156 large industrial projects, you can often see the figure of Soviet experts, they are not only the "consultants" who sit and talk, but also hands-on help installation and commissioning of practical experts, Chinese engineers are in close contact, understand and discover the details of industrialization problems, and its solutions. Due to the ease with which Soviet experts are familiar with their own equipment, many large projects are built from start-up to production at an amazing rate! For example, the Changchun First Automobile Manufacturing Plant took only three years from start-up to production. No wonder the Central Committee of Finance and Economics has drawn the lesson that

> *"two years of experience have proved that small factories designed by Chinese technicians or small-scale rehabilitated and converted factories are already rife with technical shortcomings in design and wasteful. The design of the huge complex factory, which did not succeed in any way, was halfway back to the Soviet Union. So hiring a Soviet design team was a quick, money-saving, and very surefire way to do that for a number of years when senior Chinese technicians weren't being trained."*

Because the value of intangible assets was omitted from Soviet aid to China, the value of the real technology proliferation that China acquired from the Soviet Union was greatly undervalued. These intangibles should include the cost of patenting hundreds of thousands of core technologies in 156 large projects, the time benefits created by industrial experts in solving technical challenges, the overall combined benefits of design experts in master planning, the decision-making benefits provided by industrial experts in major development strategies, and the knowledge dissemination benefits created by Soviet experts in training large numbers of Chinese engineers and international students. These benefits include: in the oil industry, Soviet experts have rejected the traditional Chinese theory of oil poverty and taught advanced methods of oil field exploration, which has increased the labour productivity of China's oil industry by three times; in electricity, 16 advanced construction methods have been promoted, which have greatly reduced costs and shortened construction periods; in the coal industry, the life of a large number of mines has been extended by 20 to 40 years; in the steel industry, new Soviet technology has greatly exceeded the design level of steel production capacity and cut maintenance time by half; in forestry, new programmes by Soviet experts have reduced the loss rate of timber flow to one tenth of the original rate; in addition, Soviet technology has generated good benefits for China in agriculture and water conservation.

If these intangibles are taken into account, the total benefits of industrial technology diffusion that China received from the Soviet Union are far from the $2.4 billion scale, and I'm afraid an order of magnitude higher!

Industrialization in the land of China in the 50's is no longer a distant dream of the past, but a reality that is taking off!

The Great Leap Forward and the Great Recession

When a person sets his ambition to go from poor to rich and from weak to strong, he will have two choices: one is to accumulate strength and develop steadily, and the other is to fish in the dried up waters and make quick gains. If he is too anxious to develop, devotes all his saved income to his career, works hard every day with no regard for his health, is chronically malnourished, and eventually his health is bound to collapse and a major illness, much of his effort will be wasted.

China in 1957, however, made the second choice.

The early completion of the first five-year plan has brought Chinese society into a state of euphoria at a rapid pace. Socialist superiority was demonstrated through new factories, workshops, busy lathes, a constant flow of industrial products, a wide variety of markets and increasingly rich tables for farmers, giving real hope to a war-torn and poverty-stricken society. The affluence and prosperity brought about by industrialization has suddenly made it seem that the road to catching up with the world's developed countries is not that long. The faster the rate of industrialization, the more realistic the dream of prosperity and wealth becomes.

However, the main basis for industrial development is fragile agriculture. The equipment needed for heavy industry, 85 per cent of which is exchanged abroad for agricultural products, and the raw materials needed for light industry, 90 per cent of which is sourced from agriculture, are also needed to provide food for 100 million urban people and 500 million farmers. This is the common phenomenon that typical agricultural countries face when they develop industrialization.

In China, where industrialization is still in its infancy, agriculture is still largely dependent on the sky for its livelihood. Both natural conditions and climate change can seriously affect agricultural harvests. This was already evident during the First Five. In the five years from 1953 to 1957, there were two good years, two bad years and one flat year. As a result, the Great Desolation Year of 1954 reduced agricultural production, cotton and food supplies were insufficient, and light industries such as textiles grew by only 1%. And as agriculture and light industry constitute almost the entire source of consumer products in China, as consumer goods decline, commerce declines, and the country's fiscal revenues shrink with them. Inadequate fiscal revenue, in turn, affects investment and heavy industry. Thus, the disaster years of 1954 and 1956 directly affected economic growth in 1955 and 1957.

Only when industrialization has reached a certain level can the agricultural machinery, fertilizers, pesticides and large-scale water construction brought about by industrialization be of substantial help to agriculture. Until then, the fragile foundations of agriculture, under the weight of industrialization, were in particular need of care.

A country is like a family, whose income is used for nothing more than consumption or savings. Poor households spend most of their income on daily expenses, with only a small proportion able to save, and a poor agricultural country faces the same problems of accumulation and consumption in its national income. Accumulation is the potential for the future development of the country, consumption is the real-life expenditure of the masses, without which there will be no development impetus, while a lack of consumption will prevent the nation from living a normal life. The ratio of accumulation to consumption is a critical issue. If the rate of accumulation is too high, it is like working on a starving stomach, and over time, one's health is bound to collapse, especially in a poor country like China, which is just living a subsistence life.

Forcing high levels of industrial accumulation would mean that farmers would have to reduce their food rations, which would pose a long-term hidden danger! If industry can't provide enough consumer goods for equitable exchange, farmers will passively slack off and reduce food production, which will be an economic disaster! If we catch up with successive catastrophic years, then agriculture, light industry, heavy industry, commerce and fiscal revenue will suffer catastrophe squared! If industrial accumulation were to be used in the severely deformed industrial sector, with great waste, the situation would be cubic of disaster!

Unfortunately, in the three years of the Great Leap Forward from 1958 to 1960, these three "what ifs" took up all three!

In 1957, the accumulation was only 24.9%, in 1958 it soared to 33.9%, in 1959 it reached an astounding 43.8%, and in 1960 it still reached 39.6%! Such a high rate of accumulation would inevitably seriously upset the fragile balance in agriculture, and farmers would have to reduce their food rations significantly to ensure industrial development. In fact, after peaking at 410 pounds per capita in 1956, farmers' rations did not exceed the then level until 1980, 24 years later. The prolonged stagnation in agriculture has led to the slow growth of the entire Chinese economy.

The "People's Commune" forcibly took the private wealth of farmers, such as farming tools, cattle, chickens, ducks and pigs, to the ownership of the production team, and introduced a big canteen to eat in large pots and pots for no money, resulting in half a year's worth of food being eaten in one quarter. It was no longer possible for the peasants to have the enthusiasm and responsibility for agricultural production that was almost identical to that of the collective farms of Stalin's time. Coupled with successive severe natural disasters, there was a serious decline in agricultural production, the actual production of food in 1958 was 400 billion kilograms, in 1959 it was reduced to 340 billion kilograms, and in 1960 it was even lowered to 287 billion kilograms, the decline in cotton production was even more serious. Hunger is spreading in rural and urban areas on a large scale.

Heavy industrial investment, forced to accumulate at great cost to agriculture, has been spectacularly wasted. Steel production was highly totemized as a sign of industrialization, proposed that steel production in 1958 to double from 1957, from 5.35 million tons to 10.7 million tons, 1959 to double again from 1958, from 10.7 million tons to 30 million tons. "With steel as a platform," the sight of ten thousand horses galloping ahead did appear, and that was the frenzy of the nation's great steel refining. Industrialization is a highly complex system of engineering, and even when Stalin industrialized, he only squeezed more raw capital out of agriculture for the development of heavy industry, but in investing in heavy industry, after all, it was done according to a relatively rational layout of the industrial system. The "Great Leap Forward" overturned the basic logic of all industrial economic development, highlighting steel and leaving the rest behind! Industrialization can only bring benefits if it is coordinated and balanced. As a result, the steel industry was rushed into action and suddenly found that there was a shortage of electricity, and when the shortage of electricity was solved, it faced coal constraints. The "steel marshal" in the lead of the horse turned back, but suddenly found that the large group of men behind could not follow. This, coupled with the large number of substandard products produced by clay-based steelmaking, has resulted in a huge waste of human, material and financial resources, the serious destruction of forest resources, and the development of heavy industry is completely deformed and the relationship with light industry is completely distorted.

The economic crisis began with the abnormal expansion of heavy industry, with excessive accumulation leading to the bankruptcy of agriculture, which inevitably brought down light industry, which had lost its source of raw materials, followed by a vicious contraction of retail sales of goods due to the lack of consumer goods, which led to a huge deficit in the country's fiscal revenues and forced it to reduce the scale of investment, which eventually led to the unprecedented great decline in heavy industry from 1961 onwards, with heavy industry production falling by 46.6 per cent in 1961 compared with the previous year, and by 22.6 per cent in 1962. Steel fell from 18.66 million tons in 1960 to 6.67 million tons in 1962 and coal production fell from 397 million tons to 220 million tons. This is the first serious economic crisis since the founding of the country!

It wasn't until 1965 that the Chinese economy gradually recovered to 1957 levels, and for this mistake, China wasted a whole eight years of precious time!

The "material standard" of the yuan has once again curbed the spread of hyperinflation

Since the founding of the country, the issuance of the yuan has adhered to the core concept of "material standard" in the war years, choosing not to be pegged to the dollar and ruble, nor to gold and silver, forming a completely independent monetary system. In its monetary system, China has drawn on the external characteristics of the Soviet ruble's "plan-based" system to form a mechanism for "plan-driven" money supply and "material regulation" of money circulation.

The Kuomintang shipped the vast majority of its gold and silver reserves when it left the mainland, so it is unlikely that China will establish the intrinsic value of a currency pegged to gold, as the Soviet ruble did. At the same time, the Kuomintang government, after the 1935 French currency reform, used the pound sterling and the dollar as collateral for the issuance of its own currency, resulting in the gradual loss of financial sovereignty and the subsequent inability to dominate China's economic destiny. Therefore, the RMB will not tolerate the ruble, the dollar or any foreign exchange to influence the issuance of its own currency, whether the country is a friend or foe, and the fate of the Chinese currency must be at its own mercy!

China's planned economy, both in terms of actual experience and precision, is far below the level of the Soviet Union, and if the money supply is driven solely by planning, there will be no small deviation, leading to a significant increase in prices. So in the end, the deciding factor in the money supply is not the plan, but prices!

After the final collapse of the three-year Great Leap Forward, China experienced severe inflation. There is no doubt that the source of this price spike is precisely due to the currency overshoot.

In the process of "steel marshal" self-inflation, the scale of China's capital construction presents a "big dry fast" crazy situation, violating the law and the pursuit of super-high goals, reducing the basic requirements of production quality, the result is a large number of unfinished projects, a backlog of low-quality products. However, the funds required for these projects and production have been released by the banks in huge amounts of credit as required by the government's plan. China's banking system is basically modelled on that of the Soviet Union. In the framework of "big finance, small banks", banks are only the cashiers of the government, the government gives the word and the banks pay the money. The industrial production capacity and its products resulting from these investments should have been purchased by the commercial sector with liquidity borrowed from the banks and then sold and, after commercial profits were realized, the bank loans were repaid. However, the scraps piled up in warehouses cannot be sold in the market, and the commercial system has entrenched itself under the mantra of "produce as much as you can, buy as much as you can". There was a serious industrial and commercial rottenness in the banks that ultimately had to be paid for by the state.

The Government, while acknowledging that unsaleable commodities in warehouses are "completed", has inevitably incurred staggering deficits as a result of "fiscal undercollection". In order to guarantee the scale of construction of the "Great Leap Forward", industrial credit in 1960 soared 12 times more than in 1957! In the early 1960s, China's fiscal deficit worsened sharply, and the three years of the "Great Leap Forward" resulted in a cumulative fiscal deficit of 17 billion yuan, equivalent to more than three times the total amount of money in circulation in 1957!

The fiscal deficit forced the Government to start printing money on a large scale, and during the three years of the "Great Leap Forward" the cumulative increase in currency issued amounted to 7.289 billion yuan, while the total amount of money in circulation soared from 5.28 billion yuan in 1957 to 12.57 billion yuan in 1961! At a time when heavy industrial production was severely shrinking and the supply of commodities was extremely scarce due to the collapse of agriculture and light industry, the 25.5 million additional people employed by the "Great Leap Forward" added another 10 billion yuan in purchasing power, exacerbating the sharp contradiction between monetary surplus and commodity scarcity.

The extreme shortage of food and commodities has made the supply of State stores completely inadequate to meet the minimum needs of society, and the Government has had to massively relax the restrictions of the free farmers' market, and when a huge amount of currency has been killed in the farmers' market, the monetary flood of frantic purchases of scarce items has pushed up food prices 10 to 20 times! A catty of rice up to 2 yuan, an egg price of 50 cents, a catty of pork is the sky-high price of 5 yuan, a chicken almost to eat the average worker's small half a month's wages!

This is the most severe nationwide hyperinflation since the superinflation left over from the war era was pacified at the beginning of the country's founding. One of the main reasons for the defeat of the Kuomintang government was its policy of wealth-grabbing with its super-currency devaluation, which triggered a collapse of confidence in the national government among the urban middle class. The lessons of history have made the Government aware that price stabilization has become an urgent and pressing priority.

At that time, there were two kinds of prices in China's commodity circulation market, state-run stores and farmers' markets, and the supply of commodities in state-run stores was planned and controlled, and prices were not high but commodities were in short supply. Farmers' markets have commodities, but they are expensive. The central issue in controlling inflation is to bring prices at farmers' markets gradually back down to slightly higher levels than those in state-run stores. This will stabilize society and reassure the people.

In 1961, China began rationing 18 categories of commodities, ranging from grain, cotton, pork, soap, to cigarettes and matches, and on this basis, local governments introduced dozens and hundreds of local rationing standards for commodities, even vegetables in many places. Urban dwellers supply two taels of pork per person per month, while rations are generally inadequate, and farmers supply only three feet of cotton per person per year. These minimum rations clearly do not meet the needs of a normal life and can only maintain a minimum state of subsistence. But these minimum quantifications have at least stabilized the prices of key commodities.

If the currency overdraft and commodity shortage have formed the status quo of soaring prices, then there are two solutions: one is to recognize the reality of the currency overdraft and let the price of controlled commodities rise, narrowing the huge price gap between state shops and farmers' markets, hoping that the rise in quantitative commodity prices will weaken the incentive for farmers' markets to increase prices; the other way is the classic idea that was tried and tested in the war era and the early days of liberation, since the price rise is caused by the currency overdraft, then the key to lower prices lies in bringing back the excess currency and reducing the currency circulation to adapt to the status quo of material shortage. Either way, the key to success or failure is to stimulate an increase in the supply of commodities, reduce the pressure on the public and stabilize social sentiment.

The first approach, responding to currency over-pricing with price increases, can temporarily stimulate the supply of higher-priced goods, but will lead to a further increase in the money supply, which may not be socially stable. Because the planned increase in commodity prices will inevitably shrink the purchasing power of the public, the government in order to ensure that people's lives will not be more difficult, only to increase wages, which will bring more money supply, the increase in commodities under the stimulus of price increases, under the time lag and the pursuit of more money, may not necessarily produce the effect of price stability. The result is likely to create a vicious cycle of repeated price increases for more water and more noodles, more noodles and more water, and wage increases in turn. Therefore, price increases will not eliminate inflation and are likely to lead to greater inflation.

The second way, to combat inflation by eliminating excess currency, is clearly the cure, and it is a one-step, never-ending solution. At Chen Yun's suggestion, the basic idea of using high-priced commodities to repatriate currency was proposed. The additional provision of "high-priced sweets, high-priced snacks, high-priced restaurants", with no change in the price of quantitative commodities, allows the wealthy segments of society, such as farmers who benefit from selling food at high prices at farmers' markets, democrats with high income security, high-wage workers, and former capitalists with fixed interest rates in industry and commerce, to add an avenue for supplementing their nutrition and improving their lives, thereby consuming their surplus currency in large quantities, without affecting the lives of other groups. At that time, the pricing principle for high-priced goods was "high enough to sell, low enough not to sell". After three years of implementation of this policy, the State has been able to recover the flood of liquidity on a large scale with high-priced commodities, which has had a significant impact in stabilizing prices and ensuring market supply. However, this policy has also generated significant discontent among the lower consumer groups in society.

Immediately afterwards, Liu Shaoqi proposed two price policies for farmers, "high versus high and low versus low". The so-called "low-to-low" means that while the State acquires agricultural products at the planned low prices, it also provides industrial consumer goods at low prices in exchange for the price; "high-to-high" means that the State and farmers bargain, exchanging high-priced industrial consumer goods for high-priced agricultural products and repossessing the surplus currency obtained by farmers at farmers' markets.

Between 1962 and 1964, the total amount of the two schemes was about 4.5 billion yuan over three years, and the total amount of money in circulation was significantly reduced from 12.67 billion yuan at the end of 1961 to 8 billion yuan by the end of 1964. Prices at farmers' markets began to fall gradually and price stability had a clear effect.

But merely stabilizing prices has only solved the immediate problem and controlled the spread of the price spike. Only a substantial increase in the supply of commodities can put out the fires of inflation at its root. This involves adjusting the irrational price system created by the "Great Leap Forward".

The collapse of the agricultural economy was clearly the result of the extreme industrialization policy of transferring agricultural wealth through the use of excessively low prices, and in order to compensate for the loss of agriculture, the State began in 1961 to raise the purchase price of agricultural products significantly, reducing the scale of industrial construction and redirecting the country's economic resources towards agriculture, which in 1961 was 28 per cent higher than in 1960 and 34.8 per cent higher than in 1958.

The jump in the purchase price of agricultural products had a strong stimulus effect on farmers' production motivation almost immediately. Beginning in 1962, with East China as a lead, agriculture in most areas began to see an increase in food production and a decline in farmers' market prices. The rebound from the bottom of agriculture brought about an increase in the supply of raw materials for light industry, a large number of consumer goods began to flood the market, a renewed boom in commercial trade, and a reversal of the trend of fiscal deterioration. By 1965, industrial production gradually recovered and most enterprises began to turn a profit. With the exception of a few products such as coal, where prices have risen, the vast majority of commodity prices have been stable. The prices of lucrative fertilizers, western medicines, and daily hot products produced in Shanghai were generally reduced throughout the country: the general consumer price index fell by as much as 12 per cent in 1965 compared with 1962, the average commodity price fell by 4.8 per cent, and farmers' market prices returned to a normal range with prices in state stores. The "materialist" approach to hyperinflation has again been a great success!

During the five years of economic recovery from 1961 to 1965, the money supply contracted sharply while the supply of commodities increased rapidly and the economy as a whole prospered again amid falling prices. The basic process is to contract the currency to stabilize prices, adjust prices to stimulate production, and further stabilize prices as the supply of goods gradually catches up with the over-issued currency. The practice of the older generation of financial leaders, such as Chen Yun, shows once again that economic prosperity does not necessarily bring about inflation, only irresponsible economic and monetary policies are the biggest accomplices to inflation!

Both Germany's response to hyperinflation in 1948 and China's counter-inflationary approach in 1961 were to reduce currency circulation drastically to reduce the disparity between currencies and commodities in the face of severe commodity shortages and extreme disruptions caused by currency proliferation, which ultimately had the effect of stabilizing prices. In essence, however, the instruments that cut liquidity in Germany and China embody the fundamental differences between the two different currency denominations. Germany is a central bank with a "balanced note" as its core instrument to reduce the size of the banking system's assets and at the same time reduce the money supply, and the "balanced note" is in fact the equivalent of a future federal German national debt. This represents a basic approach to the contraction of liquidity in a "national debt-based" monetary system.

However, the size of China's national debt was negligible in the 1960s, and by 1965, China had become the only country on earth that had "neither domestic nor external debt". Is it impossible to use monetary means to manage inflation without the national debt? Clearly, Treasuries are not the only monetary instrument and may not be the optimal choice. The use of goods and commodities is equally effective in reducing liquidity and in eliminating inflation, without the interest costs inherent in the national debt. In the current plight of national debt faced by European and American countries and the sovereign currency crisis that has arisen out of this plight, is it not worthwhile for countries around the world today to seriously learn from and reflect on the great successes achieved by the "material standard" of the Chinese yuan in price stability and anti-inflation?

What exactly is the nature of money? Is national debt, or foreign exchange, the basis on which a country's currency must be issued? Who actually made this rule? Is there a better alternative? These are all fundamental issues that the world must seriously think about in today's currency crisis!

Reflection doesn't mean we have to go backwards; history has given us the answer to the comparison of the advantages and disadvantages of a planned economy and a market economy.

Strictly planned economy is like planting a tree in a tank, the tank is isolated from each other, the roots can not be connected to the roots, the vine can not be wrapped around the vine, the branches and leaves can not be connected to the branches and leaves, the whole exchange of nutrients in the middle can only be carried out under strict planning regulations, seemingly a lush forest, but the ecological environment does not have an evolutionary function. In these stereotypical man-made forests, weeds cannot grow, flowers cannot bloom, birds are confined to flying high, animals are kept in captivity, wolves, insects, tigers and leopards are extinct, roe deer and roe deer disappear, and the inherent connection between the species that nature has endowed them with is artificially severed, so of course the forest is devoid of life and the mountains are naturally devoid of material production. If planning does not give all groups of people in society an instinctive drive to survive, then shortages can only be the inevitable result of a planned economy.

The Change and Acceleration of Industrialization: China's Missed Opportunity

Until the early 1960s, 90 per cent of the raw materials for China's light industry originated in agriculture, and most of the technical equipment provided by heavy industry served light industry to produce final consumer products. The naturally low growth rate of agriculture necessarily limits the potential for supplying raw materials to light industry and, while directly constraining the development of light industry, indirectly constrains the expansion of heavy industry, leading to low growth in commercial trade and fiscal revenues, and the development of the entire national economy is firmly confined by agriculture to a low growth track.

At this point, only a breakthrough in light industry, especially in the source of raw materials, can break the bottleneck of economic growth.

In fact, the same problems were faced in the process of industrialization in Europe and the United States. The German-French "Coal and Steel Alliance", which made steel the main raw material of industry and coal the main source of power, demonstrated the centrality of steel and coal to world industrial development in the early 1950s. However, the Middle East's dormant sea of oil has completely changed the trajectory of the world's industrialization.

In just five short years from 1946 to 1950, an average of 27 billion barrels of oil were discovered in the Middle East each year, which is nine times the world's annual oil production at the time (about 3 billion barrels)! The West has enjoyed unprecedented economic prosperity in an era of great oil abundance, with oil pouring from the Middle East to the world. Super-abundant supplies brought super-cheap prices, with Western oil prices in the 1960s being just $1.50 a barrel.

The massive and cheap supply of oil has not only brought about the rapid development of the Western automobile industry, but more importantly, the derivatives of oil, which fundamentally broke through the constraints of light industrial raw materials from agriculture! The sudden rise of petrochemical industry, brought about the revolution of the chemical industry: the large-scale production of synthetic ammonia, stimulating the rapid growth of fertilizers, directly breaking through the bottleneck of agricultural production; the use of chemical pesticides, for the prevention and control of agricultural pests and diseases has played a great role; nylon, polyester, acrylic and other chemical fibers, in the textile industry, a large number of alternatives to cotton and animal hides; the emergence of plastic, replacing the daily life, from pots and pans to tables, chairs, benches and other household equipment, in industrial raw materials, from car parts to integrated circuits are inseparable from plastic, in the construction industry, plastic is a large number of alternatives to steel, wood and cement, in the packaging industry, plastic film, plastic bags throughout the market; synthetic rubber in a variety of tires, transmission belt, hose and other industrial supplies greatly exceeded the natural rubber, raincoats, rubber shoes and other household goods, greatly enriching life. In the coatings and adhesives industry, emerging materials are also making a splash.

Since the 1950s and 1960s, the world has emerged in cars, televisions, refrigerators, washing machines, "four pieces" of the consumer goods boom, these products are indispensable to the petrochemicals in the field of light industrial raw materials a major breakthrough. Ethylene, the base product of petrochemicals, has become the darling of the new economic era. In the 40 years from 1940 to 1980, U.S. ethylene production increased from 400,000 tons to 13 million tons, a 32-fold surge!

In modern life, among all the consumer goods that people can see and touch, the direct product of agriculture, has been doubly scarce. Once upon a time, indeed good shirts are so rare, acrylic fabric is very sought after, artificial leather jackets lustrous fashion, liberation brand rubber shoes all over the streets and alleys, tri-plywood large standing cabinet instead of pure wood furniture, synthetic material flooring into the home on a large scale, ultra-white paint to make the room brighter, hard plastic cutting board into the kitchen of a thousand households, shopping in the hands of the housewife of the vegetable market is either a net pocket or a plastic bag, all of this, without the material revolution triggered by petrochemicals, will no longer exist. Consumer raw materials from agroforestry crops have been completely replaced by tens of thousands of new synthetic materials. The revolutionary impact of petrochemicals on light industry has opened up a whole new era of social consumption! It made the process of industrialization, which took a dramatic turn for the worse.

While China was still emphasizing the great role of the "steel marshal" in industry, world industrialization had turned the corner, and a major breakthrough had been made in the field of raw materials for light industry, fundamentally changing the relationship between industry and agriculture, freeing the national economy from its deep dependence on agriculture and natural materials, and pushing the level of industrialization to a new level.

By 1965, China's economy had just emerged from the Great Depression that followed the Great Leap Forward, and then fell directly into the decade of economic stagnation that followed the Cultural Revolution of 1966–1976. Although many of the technologies and ideas of petrochemicals have spread to China, they have not yet been widely diffused in Chinese industry, and the shift from industrial accumulation to agricultural accumulation is far from complete, thus missing a fundamental opportunity for industrialization to change course.

If the petrochemical industry completely solved the dependence of light industrial raw materials on agriculture, bringing about a major change of track of industrialization, then the industrial automation revolution triggered by the rapid advancement of electronics industry and computers, industrialization in a new orbit suddenly increased to the speed of the first universe!

The birth of the transistor at Bell Labs in the United States in 1947, and the advent of the integrated circuit in 1958, brought about a wave of automation with the integrated circuit as the center of the nuclear explosion, Moore's Law as the speed of the shock wave, sweeping all areas of industry.

Automation collects, analyzes, judges and feeds data from the production process, and controls the machine to finally complete the automatic continuous production with ultra-high speed, ultra-accuracy and ultra-intensity, which is beyond the reach of human beings, and the speed and quality of industrial production has been substantially improved. Automation for the first time stripped information from the industrial process, and this great division of labor created a separate industrial branch, this branch with the computer as the brain, the integrated circuit as the backbone, the network as the limb, the vast amount of information as the grain, in the field of heavy industry, created intelligent and digital technical equipment, which, in the light industrial system, raised production efficiency to a level unprecedented since the industrial revolution. The "forest of industry" is no longer a silo of machinery and independent production, but has evolved into a closely connected, highly intelligent and fully integrated "ecological environment". Automation not only liberates human physical strength, but also stimulates the potential of the human brain, from the control of the production process to the promotion of scientific management evolution, from industrial production to the permeation of social life, the information generated by automation will change all areas of social life more profoundly.

In 156 large-scale projects assisted by the Soviet Union in the 1950s, China reaped the enormous benefits of the proliferation of industrialization, greatly reducing the gap with the world economy. However, from 1957 to 1970, at a critical time when the world's industrialization began to change course and accelerate, China's economy was struggling with recession and recovery. The closure and isolation brought about by the "economic exile" of the United States against China has caused deep internal damage to the dynamism of China's industrialization, and the deterioration of Sino-Soviet relations has further cut off access to the latest technological proliferation from the Soviet Union and other socialist countries. Unable to escape the shackles of agriculture's innate constraints on industrialization, China's economy has stagnated for a long time, while political struggles have accelerated the deterioration of its earlier industrialization achievements; factories that were advanced in the 1950s have become obsolete and backward in the 1960s, when world industry was on a wave of dramatic innovation. The major worldwide technological revolution has caused accelerated depreciation in Chinese industry. Firms have contributed major profits, significantly reducing the capital accumulation necessary for technological upgrading. When these valuable industrial profits are funneled into inefficient and wasteful expansions based on old technology, it further distorts the relationship between heavy industry, light industry and agriculture. Although in a closed environment, investment creates the illusion of growth, the entire industrial system is in fact in a state of bankruptcy once it engages in external competition.

To Americans, China is like an "isolated angry giant", which is exactly what the United States expects from "economic exile". However, the international situation changed profoundly and in China's favour in the early 1970s. As the United States increasingly faced the eventual end of defeat in Vietnam, its international reputation hit rock bottom, domestic anti-war sentiment was high, the Soviet Union's influence grew, and U.S. power faced the dilemma of shrinking dramatically around the globe. At this time, the deterioration of Sino-Soviet relations made the United States see the value of China's use, and the two oil crises in the 1970s caused a deep economic recession in the western developed countries, the search for new overseas markets became the most urgent task of the European and American countries.

China seized the opportunity and proposed the "43 Program" in 1973 to introduce US$4.3 billion of petrochemical and steel manufacturing equipment on a large scale within three to five years. China finally understands the importance of petrochemicals for light industry to break away from agricultural constraints, and has prioritized chemical fiber, fertilizer and chemical equipment in the introduction of equipment.

The "43 programme" of the 1970s was the second large-scale plan by China to absorb the proliferation of technology, after the 156 large-scale projects supported by the Soviet Union in the 1950s. Subsequently, a number of additional projects were added to the programme, bringing the total planned imports to $5.14 billion. Using these facilities, a total investment of about 20 billion yuan has been made through domestic support and renovation, and 27 large industrial projects have been built, all of which are scheduled to be put into operation by 1982. The implementation of this plan laid the necessary material foundation for China's reform and opening up in the 1980s.

At a time when China's industrialization is taking off at a rapid pace and with constant setbacks, Japan, China's main rival for a century, is rushing to catch up on the road to industrialization.

Japan's industrial insurance is "castrated", MacArthur's "land reform"

In August 1945, Japan declared its surrender. During the war, 40 per cent of Japan's national wealth was destroyed, directly or indirectly, and the economy was completely bankrupt. As American troops marched into Japan in force, MacArthur, the Supreme Commander of the U.S. Occupation Army, received a clear instruction from Washington:

> *"You are not responsible for the revival and strengthening of the Japanese economy. Be clear to Japanese nationals that you are also not responsible for what particular standard of living Japan should maintain."*

The U.S. occupation of Japan, unlike Germany, where the U.S., Soviet Union, Britain, and France exercised direct military rule over Germany, in Japan the occupying forces exercised indirect rule through the Japanese government, and only in extreme cases could MacArthur have the power to exercise direct rule over the Japanese people. In the face of the question of the emperor's existence or abolition, MacArthur's direct experience of life while in Japan convinced him that the preservation of the emperor's system would favour "indirect rule" in the United States. He also systematically studied the historical experience of the military rule of Alexander, Caesar and Napoleon and concluded that "almost all military occupations breed new wars in the future" and that the Emperor had been incarnated as a god in Japan and that although Japan was defeated, the Emperor's inspiration was "greater than 20 mechanized divisions". Thus, if the emperor is abolished, then the United States will carry the heavy burden of hostility and manage indefinitely the 70 million people facing collapse.

The Japanese government had long been accustomed to being under the command of the military during the war; it was less like a decision-making body and more like an executive body, so that when the American occupation forces replaced the Japanese military, the Japanese government cooperated with the occupation forces with absolutely no obstacles.

America's initial attitude toward Japan was similar to that toward Germany, which was to fundamentally destroy Japan's industrial potential and will to war to start a war again. To this end, the United States has also prepared a Japanese version of the "Morgenthau Plan" for Japan. The U.S. goal was to limit the scale of production of Japanese industry after the war largely to the levels that existed before and after the "September 18" events of 1931, and to reduce Japan's industrial capacity to a level of primary industrialization that would only satisfy the low level of operation of its own economy, without increasing the cost of occupation for the Americans. At the same time, in order to compel Japan to pay compensation to countries that had been invaded in Asia, a large number of industrial facilities would be dismantled as a means of providing in-kind compensation to those affected countries. The U.S. Army established a "blacklist" of Japanese industrial dismantlers, with a total of 1,100 companies appearing on the list, less than the size of the 1,600 in Germany, reflecting both the more thorough strategic bombing of Japan by the U.S. Army and the reality that Japanese industry was weaker than German industry.

In addition to the industrial "castration" of Japan, the United States occupation authorities believe that another major source of the warlords' ability to wage war in Japan is the educational system that has for many years instilled the idea of "militarism" in the youth in the school system. So, following the American occupying forces to Japan, along with a large number of American educators. The United States occupation authorities, while arresting war criminals such as Tojo and other war criminals, have proceeded to rid the educational system of the proponents of the idea of "militarism" immediately. American educators began to chart the direction of the content of ideas in their textbooks, making it clear what kind of ideas should be accepted by young Japanese people.

At the same time, the U.S. occupation authorities are ready to take a swipe at Japan's plutocratic system. However, there are many fishy things in it. The four major plutocrats, Mitsui, Mitsubishi, Sumitomo and Yasuda, are clearly the most important supporting force and financial base of militarism, and the so-called "dissolution of the plutocrats" only breaks up the plutocrats' shareholding companies, but the plutocrat bank, the core of the plutocratic system, remains unscathed. These zaibatsu banking families had centuries of friendship with international bankers on Wall Street and in the City of London, and the Mitsui family had an unusual relationship with international bankers even before the Meiji Restoration. When the knife fell on the heads of the Zaibatsu, there was always an unexpected invisible hand that defused the harshness of the law, not only from the Japanese government, but also from the forces behind the occupation. Just as the

German bankers, while supporting the Nazis, fought the Anglo-American bankers hotly in Basel, they were similarly unduly punished after the war.

While loans accounted for only 12.8 per cent of Japan's pre-war sources of financing for enterprise development, post-war dependence on loans for enterprise development reached 62.8 per cent in 1951. This undoubtedly greatly strengthens Zaibatsu Bank's influence on businesses. When Japan regained national independence after signing the San Francisco Compact with the United States, it amended MacArthur's "Anti-Monopoly Law" in 1953 to allow corporate competitors to hold shares in each other, in effect allowing businesses that had been split up by the plutocrats to regroup. The amended law allowed banks to increase the percentage of shares in enterprises from 5 to 10 per cent, thus forming a strategic alliance of former plutocratic enterprises, centred on plutocratic banks, which not only held shares in these companies, but also provided more favourable loans to plutocratic allied companies, greatly strengthening the plutocratic system as a community of interest. In fact, Zaibatsu Bank is in a sense the equivalent of the former Zaibatsu holding company, playing a central role in the Zaibatsu Group's strategy formulation, tactical coordination and interest hub.

The plutocratic banks are not only raising funds from the residents' savings, but are also gradually borrowing from the central bank. As a result, the plutocracy has been able to mobilize more economic resources, enter more areas, face less competition and have a more flexible organizational system than before.

The most obvious example of this is the Mitsui Group. Mitsui Bank, Mitsui Trust, Mitsui Life Insurance, Taisho Marine Fire Insurance, and other Mitsui-series financial institutions have joined forces to give priority to loans to Mitsui-series companies such as Mitsui Mines, Mitsui Metals, Mitsui Mfg, Mitsui Shipbuilding, Mitsui Fudosan, Mitsui Petrochemical, and Oji Paper. Although the former Zaibatsu holding company did not exist from an organizational point of view, the leaders of the Mitsui family met regularly in the name of the "Niki-kai" for the purpose of exchanging information, and they were as close as the former Zaibatsu corporate group.

Japan's four largest Zaibatsu, Mitsui, Mitsubishi, Sumitomo and Yasuda, together account for 25.4 percent of the country's total capital, while the top ten Zaibatsu account for 35.2 percent. Of the 325 companies originally planned to be spun off, only 11 were eventually broken up, with Mitsubishi Heavy Industries being split into three and then reunited.

It was because of the intact Zaibatsu Bank that, after the end of Japan's occupation, the former Zaibatsu companies, soon regrouped around the Zaibatsu Bank and once again dominated Japan's postwar economic and political scene from behind the scenes.

In 1946, the Soviet Union refused to join the dollar system and the Cold War began to heat up. The U.S. "neutered" the German and Japanese industries and hit the brakes at the same time.

From 1947 to 1950, Japanese industry was dismantled on a much smaller scale, with equipment totalling only $160 million. Japan was able to retain its most important industrial power. The situation was almost identical to that in Germany, and without these preserved industrial strengths, Japan's rapid post-war revival would not have been easy. As the dismantling of industrial equipment involved in war reparations was compressed to insignificance, Asian countries did not receive the necessary compensation for the huge losses of the war, which allowed Japan to shed a heavy burden on its economic development and emerge lightly and quickly.

MacArthur's other major initiative in Japan was the Agricultural Land Emancipation Directive of December 1945, which set off a far-reaching "land reform" movement in Japan. It can be said that without the release of agricultural productivity, it would have been difficult to have the later industrial rise of Japan.

The predicament facing Japanese agriculture was much the same as that of China, and Japan's pre-war industrialization also necessitated the accumulation of capital from agriculture, and when the output of its own agriculture could not meet the supply of industrial raw materials, the rapidly growing imperial industry forced the Japanese government to expand aggressively into China and Southeast Asia in order to obtain supplies of industrial raw materials, food and oil, and at the same time to provide a market for Japanese industrial products to be heavily dumped. In the post-war period, when Japan lost all its overseas colonies and occupations, not only was the source of industrial raw materials cut off, but also the market for consumer goods was lost. The accumulation of industrialization since the Meiji Restoration was worn out in the war. Without "land reform", the continued sluggishness of agricultural production will force the occupying authorities to confront a Japan that cannot feed itself, which will become a permanent economic burden for Americans.

MacArthur's "land reform" in Japan, in which the Government compulsorily acquired land from landowners and sold it to them at fair prices, was a long-awaited reform in Japan, but in the imperial era, when Japanese plutocrats, warlords and landowners were allied, land reform was only a distant dream. It was only after the war that the American occupation authorities had the motivation and strength to destroy in one fell swoop Japan's millennium-old monopoly of most land by the landowning class. For the first time, sharecroppers were given the land of their dreams, and they no longer had to pay half or more of their annual grain rent to their landlords, which greatly increased their enthusiasm for production, and agricultural production reached record highs. For some time after the war, farmers were even more productive than their urban counterparts. Farmers sell their food at high prices in the market, thus earning considerable wealth and accumulating a certain amount of capital. Farmers, who make up half of the population, have been gradually reduced to one-third of the population over the next 20 years, but agricultural production has doubled. It is thus clear that agrarian reform has been a huge boost to agriculture.

It was also the success of the Agrarian Reform that led to an agricultural boom in Japan in 1948 and subsequent years, not only alleviating food shortages and inflation, but also supporting a decade of recovery of Japan's light industry.

However, before there is a real economic recovery, Japan must also address the inflationary dilemma.

Tilting the Production Plan, Bringing Coal and Steel and Inflation

At the beginning of the post-war period in 1945, Japan and Germany were in roughly the same economic situation. During the war, 119 cities in Japan were reduced to rubble, 2.36 million houses were destroyed and 9 million people were displaced. Nearly half of the industrial equipment, roads, bridges, harbour facilities have been damaged to varying degrees. Industrial production declined sharply, amounting in 1946 to only 30 per cent of pre-war levels. During the war, the total amount of money in circulation in Japan soared more than

24 times, and black market prices soared 29 times on average, and the 1945 agricultural failure left rice production at only 60 percent of what it had been in previous years. The severe food crisis, extreme material shortages, and hyperinflation have triggered a series of large-scale demonstrations and continued political instability in Japan.

When the U.S. occupation authorities announced the cessation of Japanese military production, a large number of military industrial enterprises immediately faced a crisis of disruption, and the supporting industrial sectors of machinery, chemistry, metallurgy, etc., basically came to a standstill. Once the military and supporting industries, which account for half of the national economy, cease to function, mass unemployment will follow, coupled with the return of overseas troops and immigrants, the number of unemployed in Japan was once as high as 11.3 million. Material shortages, food scarcity, and inflation have forced the government to impose strict rationing, a measure that will almost undoubtedly spur black market prices to skyrocket.

During the war, the Japanese banking system granted loans to the military industry amounting to half of the total amount of loans, especially an alarming 90 per cent of the military-industrial loans of the six major banks, which were destined to become irrecoverable loans, and the day the war ended, when these banks went bankrupt. In an effort to save the banking system and the overall economic situation, the Japanese government issued a statement the same day it announced its surrender, allowing financial institutions to continue to make new jumbo loans to businesses while allowing bank customers to continue to withdraw money freely. This continued disregard for the existence of bad debts and the issuance of huge loans will undoubtedly exacerbate inflation.

In 1946, the Japanese government was already in danger of being in a stormy situation, and if hyperinflation was not quickly contained, the possibility of revolution and riots would increase with each passing day.

With such vicious inflation, the Japanese people are desperate to take out their bank deposits and quickly buy various black market commodities to protect their hard-earned savings, and a bank run crisis is imminent! How can the banks, with their severely deteriorating assets and liabilities, withstand a run on the population? The Japanese government, at the urging of the plutocrats, asked the American occupation authorities for an urgent response to the inflationary crisis, and MacArthur feared that if the problem continued to worsen, it could lead to mass unrest in Japan and even the outbreak of Revolution II. MacArthur therefore immediately charged the Japanese government to take urgent measures to stop the crisis.

In February 1946, the Government of Japan introduced "financial emergency measures" to issue new yen and recover old yen, and people were required to convert all old yen into new yen by depositing it into a bank savings account within a certain period of time, but only a maximum of 500 yen could be withdrawn for daily expenses, a figure that could barely sustain a life of extreme poverty. By freezing deposits, the government temporarily alleviated the impending bank run crisis and suppressed the spike in black market prices with a sharp reduction in currency circulation resulting from the trade-in. In the short term, the price spike was briefly contained, thus surviving a financial crisis; in the long term, however, no substantive problems were solved.

In contrast to the German monetary reform of June 1948, when Germany traded one new mark for ten old marks, banks cut their assets and liabilities tenfold in both directions and replaced bank assets with "balancing notes" (future national debt), the monetary root cause of inflation was eliminated in one fell swoop, although it created serious social wealth redistribution problems. Although tragic, it is also a kind of radical therapy that is "better for the long pain than the short pain". Japan's "financial emergency measures", on the other hand, were entirely for emergency purposes and did not fundamentally reduce inflationary pressures, but only delayed the outbreak of the problem.

How can this rare "delay" be used effectively to root out inflation? If there is an unwillingness to start with a contracting currency, then a breakthrough must be made by increasing the supply of goods. This is the Japanese Government's "Tilt Production Plan". The main objective of the plan is to concentrate limited resources and increase coal and steel production. Since coal is the energy source for industry and steel is the raw material for industry, the availability of these two materials could lead to the restoration of other industrial sectors.

In 1946, Japan's industrial production was about 30 per cent of pre-war levels, and if production could be restored to 60 per cent, the Japanese Government believed that a large increase in commodities would offset the impact of the surplus currency and thus end inflation. Only by stopping inflation can economic recovery truly begin. To achieve this goal, coal production would have to be increased from

20 million tons to 30 million tons, which would require the occupation authorities to supply the steel sector with heavy oil and iron sand, and then to supply the coal sector with increased steel production, which would facilitate increased coal production, and then to further promote steel with coal.

Guided by this idea, the Government began to pool all its financial resources, and in January 1947, it established a special Treasury for Financial Recovery. The public treasury is financed by the credit of the Central Bank, which is ultimately reflected in the Government's fiscal deficit. Between 1947 and 1948, the public treasury lent a total of 125.9 billion yen, or one-third of the total industrial credit, and the government allocated a huge amount of 85 billion yen (12 per cent of the total budget) to subsidize the spreads of "production-skewing" enterprises. The coal industry received a loan of 47.5 billion yen, or about 38 percent of the total amount of loans from the public treasury. In 1948, the Japanese economy showed the first signs of improvement. Industrial production returned to its pre-war level of 54.6 per cent, with 90 per cent coal and 49.2 per cent steel, largely meeting pre-set targets.

However, the cost of this "tilt towards production" was a larger fiscal deficit and a flood of money, and while steel and coal were available, the raw materials for light industry to produce consumer goods were still limited by the agriculture of 1947. Japan's light industry that year was similar to China's, and with the petrochemical industry yet to be launched, it relied heavily on agriculture as a source of raw materials. At this time, Japan's "agrarian reform" had only just begun, and the effects of increased agricultural production would only gradually manifest themselves after 1948, while the fragile balance between the larger monetary proliferation caused by "tilted production" and the bottleneck of light industry, which was still stuck in a shell, was again disrupted in 1947 and 1948, and inflation, like a wild horse, once again lost control. The increase in wholesale prices in Japan reached as much as 193 per cent in 1947 and 167 per cent in 1948.

The ultimate effect of this policy was that the enterprises of the plutocratic system, using the funds of the state and the savings of the people, regained capital accumulation, recovered some of the strength lost in the war, and their loan burdens were rapidly erased in the vicious inflation, ultimately leaving the disaster of inflation to the people and the savers. This is essentially a robbery of wealth, and a blatant robbery at the direction of the state! As a result, the "March Struggle" of 1948 broke out in Japan, with a nationwide strike of 1 million people on an unprecedented scale in Japanese history. At the same time, civil servants from government agencies and public bodies have also staged mass protests.

Instead of dumping large quantities of consumer goods, "tilting production" has dumped more violent inflation and massive political unrest.

The Americans are out! Isn't this nonsense from the Japanese? Playing with the fire of the fiscal deficit will inevitably lead to the disaster of vicious inflation and social unrest in the end!

The Dodge route, the yen into the arms of the dollar empire

In late 1948, American banker Dodge came to Japan. Dodge had just been in Germany for the June Mark reform, and now he had come to Tokyo in the face of Japan's vicious inflation and the country's fiscal policy, and could not help but be on fire. This is a far cry from the German mark reform thinking he orchestrated.

When Japanese government officials gushed to him about how encouraging the recovery of industrial production had been, Dodge nonchalantly noted, "It would be foolish to boast of higher production indices and increased exports, when in fact it is nothing more than a manifestation of U.S. aid money, (Japan's Ministry of Finance) subsidies and widening deficits." He made a famous analogy: "The Japanese economy is like riding on a bamboo horse, with U.S. aid on one leg and domestic financial aid agencies on the other. By making the bamboo horse's legs too long, there is a danger of falling and breaking its neck, and the horse's legs must now be shortened quickly."

Two views have also emerged within Japan at this time: one is that stability is a necessary condition for recovery and that inflation must be stopped first, and the other is that there can be no stability without recovery and that production must be expanded in order to rebuild the economy. The latter is actually a pro-inflation view. The plutocrats apparently want the country to continue to run massive fiscal deficits so that they continue to receive huge amounts of money and subsidies to achieve greater capital accumulation, and the cost of inflation is naturally borne by ordinary Japanese people. Under the influence of the plutocrats, the Japanese government was slow to cut the fiscal deficit.

The Americans are finally in a hurry!

Having seen the stubborn attitude of the Japanese zaibatsu, the United States Government and the occupation authorities took firm measures and openly came to the centre of the Japanese political scene and, without informing the Japanese Government, announced to the Japanese nationals on 18 December 1948, in the name of the General Command of the occupation forces, the "Nine Principles of Economic Stability", the famous "Dodge Line" in history. The Japanese political class was outraged.

The core of the "Dodge line" is: balance the budget, limit credit, reform the tax system and introduce a single exchange rate.

In his "letter" to Prime Minister Yoshida of Japan, MacArthur demanded, in extremely strong and harsh terms, that the Japanese Government implement the above-mentioned principles to the letter, and as the United States, which provided Japan with huge amounts of assistance, MacArthur believed that it had the right to ask Japan to endure hardship and even to give up part of its freedoms and rights for the time being, and that no ideological and political activities against the "nine principles" would be allowed.

The plutocrats were in an uproar, the political situation in Japan was turbulent, and the Yoshida Cabinet was completely unsettled by the powerful opposition in the Japanese Diet. To this end, Secretary MacArthur gave the go-ahead to simply dissolve Congress and hold new elections, Yoshida's new cabinet finally received an overwhelming majority in the House of Representatives, and the "Dodge Line" was implemented.

As the plutocrats practiced iron-blooded and brutal capital accumulation during the recovery phase of the economy, the wages of Japanese workers were so low that when the House of Representatives was elected, the Japanese Communist Party won in a landslide, with as many as 35 people elected, triggering panic in the United States and the Japanese government. Thus, curbing inflation, raising workers' wages and increasing the real purchasing power of money have been elevated to political issues. Testifying before the U.S. House of Representatives, Dodge noted that "the real problem with economic stability is how people react to politics and society. The important issue for Japan at present is to ensure political and wage stability and to maintain a high standard of living that prevents the development of communist forces, for which it is necessary to raise real wages, and, importantly, to increase the purchasing power of the currency, and, in the final analysis, to increase the food quota and the sale of cotton products."

Here, Dodge's emphasis on food and cotton fabrics is the bottleneck for land reform and light industry. The difficulties of agricultural production and light industry that China experienced in the 1950s and 1960s were also the focus of contradictions in Japan at this time.

Based on Dodge's experience with monetary reform in Germany, he argued that the root cause of inflation was the fiscal deficit, and that the root cause of inflation could not be removed without eliminating it. So he first looked at the reasons for the Japanese government's deficit and found that the 1948 budget had taken the form of a balance only in general accounting, but a huge deficit of 150 billion yen in special accounting. In the 1949 budget prepared by Dodge, taxes were raised substantially and government spending was cut as much as possible, resulting in a "super-balanced budget" that was not only consolidated and balanced without deficits, but also had a huge surplus of 257 billion yen, a surplus of up to 14 per cent of fiscal spending. This huge surplus, while repaying the debt, also provided funds to financial institutions, both curbing inflation and increasing the capitalization of banks.

Since the "Dodge Line" opposed the disguised fiscal deficits of the "revival of the financial treasury", the treasury ceased all new lending from 1949 and began to recover past lending. This move eliminates a major source of inflation.

As Dodge pointed out, U.S. aid and government subsidies are the "two legs of the bamboo horse" of the Japanese economy, so how do you cut them short? Dodge first halted loans from the Reconstruction Finance Corporation, which saved 125.9 billion yen in spending, but the Japanese government doubled financial subsidies to protect the interests of the plutocrats, offsetting Dodge's efforts. Dodge can only think twice about US aid.

Total U.S. aid to Japan was $460 million in 1948, rising to $534 million in 1949, and this aid consisted mainly of U.S. surplus food and oil, medical products, and cotton, which could be sold at a staggeringly high profit in Japan's market for light industrial consumer goods and energy, where there was a severe shortage. At the exchange rate of 1 dollar to 360 yen, United States aid in 1949 was equivalent to 19.22 billion yen, far more than the amount of the "Reconstruction Finance Bank" and financial subsidies.

For such a large sum of money, the U.S. basically let the Japanese government decide how to spend it, but now Dodge wants to use this leverage to realize the intention of the "Dodge Line.

As a result, the United States established a system of "turn-back funds", which required the Japanese Government to deposit the proceeds from the sale of United States-aided goods into a special accounting account to be administered by the occupation authorities. The Japanese Government can only use the "return funds" on a lump-sum basis with the consent of the United States. Dodge set the scope for the use of the funds to be limited to direct investment in repaying government debt and building the economy. In this way, the U.S. has a firm grip on a large portion of Japan's fiscal revenue, forcing the Japanese government and plutocrats to be more subservient politically and economically.

From 1949 to 1951, a total of 316.5 billion yen was spent on "turnaround funds", of which 35 per cent was spent on repaying government debt and purchasing public debt, and 65 per cent on enterprise investment.

Of this amount, 111.8 billion yen was used to repay government debt and purchase public debt, which played a key role in recovering liquidity and controlling inflation. The essence of this policy is similar to the strategy of "high-priced commodities", "high versus high, low versus low", proposed by Chen Yun and Liu Shaoqi at the beginning of the 1960s to raise back the currency, Dodge simply used the U.S.-aided food, oil, medicine, cotton and other Japanese market commodities in short supply as "high-priced commodities", and in the sale of the excess yen, then the funds raised back to pay off the government debt, thus eliminating part of the excess currency and greatly relieving the pressure of inflation, in September 1946, the total amount of Japanese currency in circulation was 64.4 billion yen, at the end of 1947 219.1 billion yuan. The impact of the size of the "turnaround" back into money on currency circulation is evident.

In the enterprise investment, "return capital" did not continue to invest heavily in the "coal and steel" industry gathered by the plutocrats, but vigorously invested in electricity, shipping, telegraph and telephone, national railways and other infrastructure, in the severe austerity "Dodge route", financial investment is the head of the enterprise to obtain funds, and "return capital" accounted for 70% of the financial funds, it can be said that this money has become a powerful tool for the United States to control Japan's financial, financial, industrial.

The essence of American aid is actually the transfer of America's surplus food and commodities to Japan as a "gift", the United States earned the gratitude of the Japanese government; using this "gift" of goods to repatriate the over-issued currency, the purpose of controlling hyperinflation and winning the favor of the Japanese people; finally, the "gift" is then converted into "return capital" investment, as political leverage to suppress the political forces in Japan, and curb the excessive greed of plutocrats. The Americans have taken aid to the highest level of "one fish, three meals"!

The other pillar of the Dodge route is the single exchange rate. For some time after the war, Japan's economy was almost completely isolated from the outside world, the occupation authorities controlled all external economic activity, any foreign trade required the prior consent of the United States, and each transaction involved a different currency exchange rate, thus cutting off the means for the massive export of Japanese goods.

A single exchange rate would unify the chaotic currency exchange situation and integrate Japan's export economy. Due to Japan's lack of domestic consumption power, small market and dependence on overseas sources of raw materials and oil, it will be difficult for Japan's economy to truly develop without expanding foreign trade. The key question is at what level of the yen to the dollar is the real benefit to the Japanese economy.

In 1949, the manufacturing cost of sewing machines in Japan was 24,000 yen, while the FOB price was 40 dollars, which made them internationally competitive.

But in the Dodge plan, the Americans unilaterally set a single exchange rate of $1:360 yen, so that the price of a Japanese sewing machine in the international market would become $66.67, which would be much less competitive. Under such circumstances, the Government of Japan could only offset the adverse effects of the excessive exchange rate through subsidies and ensure the smooth development of export trade. When the first difficult step was taken, with the recovery of the economy, the monthly production of sewing machines increased rapidly from 30,000 to 130,000 units in two years, while production costs continued to fall, and when the government stopped subsidizing, Japanese companies were still able to make profits.

By 1960, the manufacturing cost of sewing machines dropped from 26,000 yen to 4,300 yen, and it was still profitable to sell them for more than ten dollars in the international market, when the competitiveness of Japanese labor-intensive products in the international market became difficult to compete.

The single exchange rate, although not very favourable to Japan at first, will gradually offset the adverse effects of the growing scale of production and declining costs once it has gained access to the world market through which the dollar empire operates, and then the fixed exchange rate will become increasingly favourable to Japan's export trade.

The Dodge route laid down a balanced budget, eased inflationary pressures, and achieved a single exchange rate, all of which only created a runway for the Japanese economy to take off, and the acceleration needed for real take-off came from the Korean War of 1950–1953.

The "Korean boom" has brought Japan a $2.3 billion super war dividend. The profits of the top ten companies in the cotton industry increased 9 to 19 times, 90% of which formed capital accumulation, and the steel, chemical fiber and paper industry achieved similar profit growth. Combined with the $1.8 billion in U.S. aid to Japan, Japan received a total of $4.1 billion in "favor payments" in the 10-year economic recovery period from 1945 to 1955, as part of its choice to submit to the dollar empire. However, with the rapidly expanding international market, the scale of Japanese industry expanded rapidly, and at the same time, Japan absorbed a large amount of new technology from the world, further increased the profitability of Japanese industry, the dependence on the dollar empire won by overseas orders "dividend", far more than the U.S. real silver aid.

"National Income Doubling Plan", the change and acceleration of industrialization in Japan

The foundation of Japan's industrialization was laid during the Meiji Restoration, but by the outbreak of the Sino-Japanese War in 1937, it had been significantly left behind by the Soviet Union's two five-year plans, and by the end of the eight-year war, Japan's national economy had been fully transformed into a war machine, and the depth and breadth of its industrialization had lagged seriously behind that of the United States and Western countries. During the Korean War, the

U.S. considered having Japan produce heavy weapons systems to supply the Korean battlefield nearby, but U.S. industrial experts abandoned the idea after a round trip to Japan because Japan's industrial technology was so far behind that it simply could not meet the needs of U.S. forces.

When 1955 came, China's industrialization, with the help of the Soviet Union, was rapidly approaching the world level; while Japan had successfully recovered from the ruins of the post-war period, but it was a "shallow industrial recovery" centered on light industry, and the technological level of heavy industry was not even as good as that of the most advanced Soviet factories directly introduced by China. If we look at the hardware conditions, China and Japan are roughly at the same level of industrialization.

However, the year also marked a key inflection point in the strategic misalignment of industrialization development between China and Japan. While China still sees steel as central to its industrialization, Japan has become acutely aware of the importance of the electronics industry and petrochemicals, and has made automation its new development goal. This gap in strategic vision widened the gap between China and Japan over the next 15 years to a point where it was difficult to catch up.

The Japanese epiphany over the new industry made them realize how foolish the original act of war was, the ample supply of oil in the world market made the occupation of China's northeastern coal-energy base unnecessary, and the cheap, abundant, high-quality synthetic rubber brought by petrochemicals made the military operation to go south and plunder Southeast Asia's natural rubber an unthinkable adventure. In a sea of thousands of derivatives from petrochemicals, the source of raw materials for light industry is almost fully satisfied. Japan is determined to abandon the founding tradition of military aggression, as it is neither necessary nor beneficial.

Petrochemicals replaced agriculture as the main source of raw materials for light industry, while electronics and automation were the accelerators of industrialization. With these two tools, it was far easier for Japan to conquer the world with industrial products than with sabres and boots, as long as the oil source was guaranteed by the United States.

China, like France, won the war, but lost the economy.

It was with this economic strategy in mind that the Japanese introduced the "National Income Doubling Plan" in 1960. The Ministry of International Trade and Industry (ITI) of Japan had a far more strategic vision of the economy than the planned economy of China at that time, which first specified the types of heavy chemical industry that should be developed as a priority. These include: petroleum refining, petrochemicals, man-made fibers, motor vehicles, industrial machinery, aircraft, electronics industry, etc. These industries are then given absolute protection and development assistance. In order to avoid fierce competition from foreign products in these strategic Japanese industries, the Ministry of International Trade and Industry (MITI) has introduced a variety of trade protection measures such as import quotas, import licenses, high tariffs, and preferential business taxes on domestic products.

When Japan joined the GATT, direct financial subsidies were too strong, and the Ministry of International Trade and Industry (MITI) was inundated with strange tactics for the development of strategic industries. When the shipbuilding industry needs subsidies, the government is not convenient to pay directly, and at this time the Japanese market sugar prices are high and profitable, the government provides the shipbuilding industry with sugar import licenses, so that they can earn the difference in the domestic sugar market, as a disguised government subsidy. This move alone has reduced the export price of Japanese shipbuilding by 20% to 30%.

In order to accelerate the rapid development of strategic industries, Japan began a wave of frantic introduction of advanced technology and equipment. In the system of subsidies for the import of the latest machinery, half of the import price is paid by the Government, the cost of similar domestic manufacturers, and the Government also pays half of the financial subsidies. The introduction of a special depreciation system for enterprise equipment to accelerate equipment renewal and expand capital accumulation. The Government of Japan stipulates that in the year in which an enterprise purchases new equipment, it may take a depreciation charge equal to 50 per cent of the price of the equipment, which is deducted from the total profit and is not subject to tax. With the encouragement of the Government, enterprises are competing to increase investment and upgrade equipment, and in 1961, the proportion of equipment investment by private enterprises in the gross national product was as high as 23%! In addition, government financial institutions, such as the Development Bank of Japan and the Export-

Import Bank of Japan, provide long-term, low-interest loans to strategic industries, and the cost of the loans is deducted upfront from the profits, so they are also not subject to tax.

Through various policy and financial instruments, Japanese enterprises have the lowest tax burden among developed countries in the world, with a total tax burden of 21.2 per cent in 1972, compared with 28.1 per cent in the United States and 36 per cent in Germany.

The Government, industrialists and financiers have taken a close cooperation approach and those industries designated as national strategic are carefully protected and supported by the Government. For these sectors, the Ministries of Tonkin and Greater Tibet provide detailed administrative guidance to enterprises, advising them to reduce production when they believe production is too high and to adjust investment when they believe investment is too much. Businesses are also willing to accept this guidance, and they always flock around the government for the benefits. The government is extremely biased towards some businesses and very cold towards others. Even if it is an opinion or notice from the government, as long as it is from the TPP, any business is afraid that if it does not comply, it may be put out in the cold.

The Bank of Japan's "window guidance" in providing credit is also widely accepted administrative guidance in Japan. It is closely related to the government's policy towards the economy as a whole and amounts to a financial version of economic policy. When banks came to the central bank window, the instruction was a "mere hint" that the central bank had set a ceiling on the total amount of money that could be lent by each bank, but it was always accepted unconditionally. Subject to administrative constraints on the banks' total lending, they will give priority to plutocratic clients. For the Greater Tibetan Province, the availability of funds takes the form of an allocation based on specific policy considerations, with interest rates being only a secondary factor.

Through a decade of development, Japan's industrial structure has shifted sharply towards high profitability. In the industrial sector, the profit margin of heavy chemical industry is higher than that of light industry, which accounted for 51% of Japan's total economy in 1955, 64% in 1965 and 75% in 1975, the highest ever recorded in a developed country. From 1950 to 1969, Japan's industrial production expanded 17-fold, with old products accounting for only 60 percent of the total, while the share of new products, especially electronics and petrochemicals, expanded dramatically.

Japan's economic development model is dramatically different from that of free market competition in the West, with a distinctly planned character. The Japanese government's vision and boldness in supporting strategic industries at this critical juncture in the transformation and acceleration of industrialization is a model of success. Correct strategy, perfect execution, attentive guidance, strong support and careful protection are the key elements for the great success of Japan's strategic industries.

With regard to competition, Japan's perception is very different from that of the West. Japan is a competitive society, but not between individuals, but between corporate groups. Harmony among company employees, dedication to the company, is considered worth promoting by Japanese society, while competition among company employees is discouraged. Therefore, at home, there is competition among Japanese conglomerates, while abroad, it is reflected in cooperation between Japanese companies and fierce competition with foreign companies.

The Japanese economist Doureihara once proudly exalted the Japanese miracle:

> "Mr. Keynes once said in 1937 that, according to past experience, it is unrealistic to raise the standard of living by more than 1 per cent per year on average. Even if there are many inventions that can be raised a little more, our society cannot easily reconcile itself to a growth rate of more than 1 percent. There have probably been one or two times in the last few hundred years when the standard of living in the UK has risen at an annual rate of 1%. In general, however, the increase in the standard of living is, on average, less than 1 per cent in total.' Keynes made these remarks in the gloomy mid-1930s of the 20th century, and he was perhaps psychologically influenced by the pessimism of the time at the time of his speech. However, as history can attest, real income per person grew at an average annual rate of only 0.9 per cent during the glorious half century of the British Empire, from 1860 to 1913. Thus, hardly any economist at the time doubted this Keynesian view ... (but) Japan's growth rate of average real income per capita, at least until 1973, remained almost constant at an annual rate above 8 per cent for 20 years. In the face of this fact, what will Keynes say?"

Even taking into account the strong pound sterling, the pure gold standard enforced in Britain for half a century from 1860 to 1913, and the currency depreciation factor between 1945 and 1971, when the gold standard was in place and the weak dollar, one must recognize that the growth rate of Japanese national income was indeed much higher than in the British era. An objective factor, however, is that the industrial revolution of that year did not rid the country of its natural dependence on agriculture, and income growth of less than 1 per cent was a true reflection of the limits of its growth potential. Without the Industrial Revolution, real economic growth would have fluctuated only up or down from zero, which is why the socio-economy of agrarian societies, for millennia, was essentially at a standstill. It was only after the 1950s, when petrochemicals replaced agricultural raw materials on a large scale, thus breaking the bottleneck of growth in light industry, that the possibility of national income growth at a higher rate became available.

Industrialization had brought prosperity and affluence to the West, and the process of industrialization had brought wars and disasters to the world as countries competed for raw materials and markets. As industrialization began to spread in the East, the scales of power, the world economy and money, began to tip in the East. The way forward for China and Japan, no matter which path is chosen and no matter what setbacks are to be endured, is always to realize the dream of being rich and powerful through industrialization. All countries in Asia will follow this flood of history one by one. The development and growth of the rest of the world will increasingly break with the post-war monopoly of the United States, and the world will increasingly show the general trend of the Warring States era.

CHAPTER VI

The serpentine progression, the path to the euro in the united states of Europe

At the moment, the euro is in serious trouble: the debt crisis in Europe seems to have been defused, the EU internal quarrels continue, the euro disintegration theories are rife. The Americans are somewhat gloating, the Chinese seem at a loss for words, the international financial markets are inundated with bears, and economists are at a loss for words.

Will the euro disintegrate? Will there be a break in European integration? Will the world economy go off the rails?

To find the right answer, we must revisit the history of European integration and take a hard look at the birth of the euro.

The history of post-war European integration is the history of the German-French struggle for continental dominance, and the history of Europe's attempt to rise again under the squeeze of US-Soviet hegemony. Along with this process, there has always been a game between two major forces in Europe, which is the contest between internationalism and statism.

Behind internationalism stands the power of money, with sovereign borders blocking the will for the free flow of capital. Statism, on the other hand, inherited the traditional idea of sovereignty and sought to constrain the rise of the golden power. The European Monetary Union has evolved with difficulty in twists and turns in a repeated game of supersovereign ideas and national interests.

The new paradox of political democracy and financial dictatorship, intertwined with the old paradox of Germany's re-emergence and how France checks and balances it, have together driven the complex process of European integration.

From the birth of the Coal and Steel Union, to the launch of the Viner Plan, from the operation of the serpentine exchange rate mechanism, to the implementation of the European monetary system, from the release of the Delors Report, to the signing of the Maastricht Treaty, from the formulation of the European Monetary Unit, to the establishment of the European Central Bank, the euro in the serpentine progressive road, after half a century of storms and rains, finally repairing the right fruit.

But instead of solving Europe's problems, the euro has brought more problems.

The current euro crisis cannot be overcome without a unified European Treasury. Without a final United States of Europe, the goal of EU integration has not been achieved.

The euro continues to evolve!

De Gaulle's downfall; European integration accelerates as clouds turn

In March 1968, a major worldwide run on US gold reserves broke out, instigated by the French. De Gaulle vowed to pull the dollar from its position as the world's monetary hegemon, to overthrow the Bretton Woods dynasty and reform the global monetary system, and to give Europe under French leadership greater financial power.

At the very moment when the US "gold mutual pool" had completely collapsed and De Gaulle was about to launch a general attack on the US gold reserves, there was a sudden "May storm" in France, and not only was the franc crushed by a desperate attack on the US dollar, but De Gaulle's Not only had the franc been crushed by the US dollar, but the US had also regained a significant portion of the gold that De Gaulle had been squeezing from the US since he came to power.

At the end of May, when the crisis was at its worst, the State apparatus was nearly paralysed as students and citizens marched in Paris with the slogan "De Gaulle out of office". De Gaulle, who had lost control of the situation, suddenly "disappeared" on 29 May without even informing his Prime Minister, Georges Pompidou, and fled overnight to a French military base in Germany. It is clear that, in de Gaulle's view, the sudden "May storm" was intended to force him to step down, while the political and economic situation in the country was largely stable. It is natural for Americans to hate him, but certain political forces in the country, even within his own government, are not happy with his policy of "French supremacy".

During the 10 years that Charles de Gaulle was in power, the ideals of the United States of Europe were largely in place. The super-sovereign "Coal and Steel Union" and the European Economic Community were both created by the "Monnet Circle" before de Gaulle came to power. de Gaulle did not oppose the European Union and supported a rapprochement with Germany, but not by losing French sovereignty, but by making France the driver of the European carriage and letting the Germans pull it. The "Monnet circles" were even more furious at the fact that both of Britain's bids to join the European Community were rejected by Charles de Gaulle. The problem was clear, without De Gaulle's removal, the ideal of a United States of Europe was simply not in play.

Prime Minister Georges Pompidou, was also an active member of the "Monnet Circle".

Pompidou attended the famous Lycée Louis le Grand in Paris in his early years, was a classmate of Senegal's later founding president, Léopold Sédar Senghor, and an alumnus of the great Guy Rothschild.[71] Guy Rothschild later became the head of the Rothschild family bank in France, inherited his ancestral business and became a director of the Banque de France, and held the central bank, as well as shares in numerous companies in the French industrial sector, and was a giant in French finance and industry.

Pompidou graduated from the École Normale Supérieure in Paris and later became a secondary school teacher. In 1944, when Pompidou learned that one of his classmates was already chief of staff to Charles de Gaulle, he immediately wrote to him, hoping to get a half-dozen posts. At the introduction of his classmates, Pompidou's first task was to summarize the various political events in France and to form a one-page summary of the situation, which he sent to Charles de Gaulle daily for his information. In 1946, de Gaulle formed his own party, the Rassemblement Populaire Français, and Pompidou became the main

---

[71] Georges Pompidou, Wikipedia Biography.

liaison between de Gaulle and his party, which had resigned from power.

De Gaulle had been waiting for a chance to make a comeback in East Mountain since he came off the field in 1946, and he ended up waiting a full 12 years. Throughout this time, Pompidou has been de Gaulle's most vocal and unspoken henchman. Despite his absence from the stage, de Gaulle's immense prestige among the French people made it possible for him to take control of France's destiny again at any moment.

The Rothschilds, who have always believed in "always walking with the king", are not only burning the hot stove of the regime, but also have not forgotten the cold stove of De Gaulle, a potential "quality stock". The crisis in the French overseas colony of Algeria was worsening, and the leaders of the French army in Algeria were almost all the same as de Gaulle's old team when he set up the "Free France" government in exile.

In 1954, Guy Rothschild found his former personal mentor, who was not only an old friend of Pompidou's, but also worked at the Rothschild Bank, and Rothschild wanted to poach Pompidou, De Gaulle's heartthrob. At first, Pompidou was a little hesitant; after all, he had only taught secondary school and knew nothing about banking, so he was afraid that he would not be able to do the job at the Rothschild family bank. However, Pompidou thought for a moment that he had been waiting for De Gaulle to come to power for eight years, and God knows if it would come to pass in the end, he might as well go to the famous Rothschild Family Bank to open a bright path for his future life.

It cannot be denied that Pompidou has an extraordinary intellect and ability to learn. He was supposed to be a mere idle in the bank, and Rothschild didn't expect him to achieve much in the financial business; however, in just two years, Pompidou went from being a layman who couldn't read a balance sheet to gradually getting involved in the core business. Just as de Gaulle was impressed with Pompidou, Rothschild had to be impressed with the alumnus. Pompidou is not only able to catch the gist of the business quickly, but often finds the means to break through the problem quickly. As a result, Pompidou's position in Rothschild's bank grew with each passing day, gaining Rothschild's trust. From 1956 to 1962, Pompidou became managing director of the Rothschild Bank and was appointed by Rothschild to serve as a director of several other large companies and to call the shots on behalf of the Rothschild Bank.

In 1958 de Gaulle made his comeback, and Pompidou was called upon to participate in the drafting of the constitution of the Fifth Republic, and continued to advise de Gaulle. In 1962, President Charles de Gaulle proposed Pompidou, who had never had a senior political career, to become Prime Minister of France. Whereas previous French prime ministers were either electoral icons or spent years in politics as government ministers, Pompidou has risen to the top from his position as managing director of the Rothschild Bank. From then on, Pompidou became an important executor of the de Gaulle Doctrine, holding the premiership for six years, the most in four generations of French politics. During these six years, Pompidou has gradually taken control of the main core departments of the French government by selecting and planting his own contacts.

When the "May storm" hit in 1968, de Gaulle suddenly found that the ministers had turned against the President, who was no longer in control of the government, and Pompidou was in power. In a panic, de Gaulle could only play "missing" and did not dare to let ministers know his whereabouts. He ran to the French military bases in Germany to see who the French army was supporting before deciding where to go. When backed by the French military, Charles de Gaulle returned to Paris and announced the holding of re-elections to the Parliament in June, which resulted in a sweeping victory for the de Gaullists. Immediately after regaining support, Charles de Gaulle removed Pompidou from his post as prime minister.[72] The French political scene was in a state of shock, and everyone thought that Pompidou was the staunchest supporter of de Gaullism, and that the two had always had a good relationship but only De Gaulle knew who had caused the "May storm" and why.

For his dismissal, Pompidou "aggrieved", claiming that it was a mistake made by Charles de Gaulle. By this time, Pompidou, who had peacefully solved the "May storm", had surpassed the stubbornly old

---

[72] Dogan, Mattei, *How Civil War Was Avoided in France*, International Political Science Review/Revue Internationale de Science Politique (3), p. 245-277.

Charles de Gaulle in terms of image, with his humiliation, his loyalty, and his lack of regard for personal gain or loss.

Although de Gaullism won the parliamentary elections, the winner was not de Gaulle. The French had begun to call for an era of "de Gaullism" without de Gaulle, and in 1969, de Gaulle's ideas for reforming parliament and local government were rejected in a referendum and, disheartened, he resigned.

Georges Pompidou is naturally the new president the French have been waiting for. With his coyness and tactics, he won the hearts and minds of the people and ushered in his own time.

The "de Gaulle Doctrine" promoted by Pompidou is essentially a "revisionism" that takes away the core of the spirit of "French supremacy". He and his fellow "Monnet circles", freed from de Gaulle, began to move forward with the United States of Europe in stride.

For Pompidou and the group of financial forces behind him, the abolition of sovereign borders, free movement of capital and unregulated finance are the greatest ideals! Letting capital control the state, not the state control capital, is the most important core idea! The whole point of supersovereignty is to abolish it! Europeans united against American oppression was the most convincing slogan.

At this time, the three figures at the centre of the European political scene – French President Pompidou, German Chancellor Brandt and British Prime Minister Heath, all activists of the "Monnet Circle" – have never had a better political time to push for European integration.

In April 1969, immediately after Charles de Gaulle's fall from power, the jubilant British, German and French heads of state gathered in The Hague in December for the EC Summit, which decided to accelerate the process of European integration.

Britain was suddenly welcomed with open arms by the European continent, and in 1973, the EC was instantly joined by Britain, Denmark and Ireland, from its beginnings as six countries to a nine-nation union.

Another major initiative at the Hague Conference was the design of the strategic framework for the European Economic and Monetary Union (Economic and Monetary Union), which culminated in the launch of the Wiener Report in the IO in 1970. Pierre Werner, Prime Minister and Minister of Finance of Luxembourg, was entrusted by the Executive Committee of the European Community with the task of organizing national experts to set up the European Monetary Union Commission to provide a comprehensive monetary strategy designed to protect European interests against the indifference, even deliberate confrontation, of the United States and to balance the economic and industrial power of Germany.

In the Wiener Report, it is proposed that a European Economic and Monetary Union would be established, with some of the key powers of the member States (including fiscal budgets and monetary policy) eventually transferred from national parliaments, governments and central banks to new institutions created within the Community.

The report recommends a three-phase approach to economic and monetary union. The first step is to stabilize exchange rates, establish common guidelines for member economies and coordinate national fiscal and budgetary policies. The task of the last phase is also clear, namely, the permanent fixing of national exchange rates, the achievement of a coherent economic policy among member States and the establishment of a unified central bank of the European Community. However, the report is silent on how to achieve the intermediate transition phase.

The Bank of England, after examining the Wiener Report, concluded that

> *"the European Monetary Union plan is profoundly revolutionary, both economically and politically. Simply put, it is about creating a European federation with a single currency as leverage. All the basic instruments of economic management in member states, including fiscal, monetary, income distribution and regional development policies, are ultimately transferred to the European Federal Authority."*

This is the source of the idea of "European economic government" or "European Ministry of Finance", which has been much speculated in the news, in fact, this is not a new idea that emerged after the outbreak of the European debt crisis, but a plan that was already formulated 40 years ago!

Just as the "Monnet circle" rejoiced, the European integration accelerated heating up the key moment, the dollar and gold decoupled, which brought about a total economic chaos. The process of European integration has been forced to undergo significant adjustments.

The U.S. debt empire is not opening up well, selling grain and grass "loses the wife and the army"

On August 15, 1971, President Nixon announced the decoupling of the dollar from gold, and the dollar "usurped gold to stand on its own feet", opening an era of great devaluation of the currency of the American debt empire.

With "dollars" becoming "no money", the world's currency markets are in unprecedented turmoil. People fled the dollar in a scramble, with a massive influx of capital seeking refuge in the German mark and Swiss franc. In an effort to reverse the dangerous collapse of dollar confidence, Nixon announced tax cuts, a 90-day freeze on wages and prices, and a 10 percent temporary tariff on all imports "to ensure that U.S. goods are not put at a competitive disadvantage by an unfair exchange rate."

The dramatic devaluation caused by the dollar overdraft, which in turn led to a global exchange rate disorder, turned out to be, in Nixon's mouth, a deliberate manipulation of the exchange rate by other countries in an attempt to take away Americans' jobs in trade. It seems that America's accusations of black and white exchange rate manipulation are not an invention of today! But such a logic of putting the cart before the horse is not very interesting even to the Americans themselves. When Federal Reserve Chairman Burns warned U.S. Treasury Secretary Connolly that America's trading partners might retaliate, Connolly contemptuously replied, "Let them be, what can they do?"

But the outrage from Europe was clear and firm, and the Europeans made no secret that their central banks were already very reluctant to hold the dollar, and that if the United States did not agree to re-establish a stable exchange rate regime while removing the unwarranted import surtax, tensions in Europe and the United States would evolve into confrontation.

The dollar's intention to kick gold out completely in one fell swoop was met with a fierce backlash from Europe. The United States had to take a delaying tactic, in December 1971, held a meeting in Washington, D.C., with the participation of finance ministers and central bank governors, formed the "Smithsonian Agreement", the dollar and gold from $35 to 1 ounce of gold, devalued to $38, the dollar against the world's major currencies depreciated 10%.

The world currency markets regained a brief period of calm, and in 1972, the United States, which had failed to defend the Smithsonian Agreement, continued to lower interest rates to stimulate the economy, and the dollar was again plunged into a crisis of massive sell-offs. By February 1973, the dollar had depreciated by a further 10 per cent, to $42.22 against gold. The world is in chaos once again.

In an effort to ease the world's fears about the dollar, the United States is eager to reverse its balance of payments deficit dilemma. In 1972, with Soviet agriculture facing a disastrous harvest, the United States, temporarily disregarding the Cold War rivalry, grabbed the lifeblood of agricultural exports to the Soviet Union in a panic.

Since the U.S. Agricultural Adjustment Act of 1933, in order to guarantee the interests of farmers, the government has been subsidizing agriculture year after year, acquiring large quantities of agricultural products at high prices for U.S. aid abroad. The Soviet Union's agricultural failure coincided with a surplus of U.S. agricultural products, and the two sides hit it off on July 8, 1972, when the U.S. and the Soviet Union announced an agricultural deal in which the Soviet Union would buy $750 million in agricultural products from the United States over a three-year period.

The Soviet Union's agricultural problems are deep-rooted and long-established, and the agricultural disaster of 1972 was far more serious than the government had estimated, when in the summer of that year alone, the Soviet Union made a massive purchase of $1 billion of agricultural products from the United States, of which the purchase of wheat was equivalent to a quarter of all American production!

The Americans turned out to have their own little calculations; the Soviet Union had few foreign exchange reserves, so such a large food purchase would inevitably force the Soviet Union to sell gold on a large scale, as it did in the mid-1960s. According to the Soviet demand for food, at least 800 tons of gold would have to be sold on the market. As a result, world gold prices are bound to plummet and the dollar's position will be greatly strengthened. Therefore, the Soviet Union's purchase of agricultural products was more and more beneficial.

What the Americans did not expect, however, was that the Soviets' surprising appetite for importing American agricultural products would have a far greater impact on domestic market prices in the United States than had been anticipated. Food prices in the United States began to soar, the price index rose by the hour, and the inflation that had swept the country suddenly hit.

More to the chagrin of the Americans, the Soviets did not sell as much gold as the Americans had hoped, but instead turned to the European dollar market to borrow money. In February 1972, the Soviet Union borrowed $600 million for seven years to Italy, the interest rate is only 6%, and in May to the European banks borrowed $1 billion, the interest rate is only 3/8 percentage points higher than the London market interest.[73] The European dollar, which was supposed to be America's inflationary export vehicle, was coincidentally used by the Soviets this time to play a dollar inflationary reflux, paying for American food in European dollars. As a result, the United States is caught in a vicious cycle of less food, more inflation and a weaker dollar.

The sale of food by the Americans to the Soviet Union actually became a "voluntary act" of returning surplus dollars with food, which triggered a domestic inflationary downward pressure on the American economy. This is the kind of altruistic behaviour that only a "responsible power" would employ, but it was never the intention of the United States Government! In June 1973, the United States Composite Price Index rose by 15 per cent and food prices soared by 50 per cent! The United States Government, "at the expense of its wife," was forced to begin to control the export of agricultural products, and the Department of Agriculture ordered that all export orders for food after 3 July will not be able to obtain an export license and will have to wait for follow-up notice when exports resume.

At this point, the world food market began to boil. The skyrocketing food prices have finally triggered an even worse oil crisis!

October 1973, oil crisis derails industrial nations

The devaluation of the dollar and the rise in food prices have kick-started inflation around the world. Food-importing countries, including

---

[73] Michael Hudson, *Global Fracture, The New International Economic Order*, Pluto Press, 1977, p. 70–73.

the Organization of Petroleum Exporting Countries, have been rocked by the shockwaves of inflation.

A further 10 per cent depreciation of the dollar in 1973 caused the Arab States to lose $350 million in foreign exchange reserves, inflation ate up $525 million of the purchasing power of their savings, and the oil-exporting countries were robbed of $875 million of their wealth in 1973.[74]

The oil-exporting countries, angered by the fact that they are not willing to watch their savings being eaten alive by inflation, increased their anger against the United States and Israel with the outbreak of the fourth Middle East war in October. They categorically imposed an oil embargo on the United States, the Netherlands and Denmark until those countries no longer openly support Israel, while declaring that any European country that provides support to United States military bases will also be blacklisted under the oil embargo. So Britain only allowed American planes to take off from the base, but no more landings; Germany refused to allow ships carrying American arms to dock; and Italy demanded that Israel return all occupied areas. There is a total freeze on US military bases in Europe.

Western Europe needs oil and the Middle Eastern countries need industrialization, and it is perfectly logical for the economies of both to be deeply integrated, so that Europe will gradually move away from the orbit of the economic planet set by the United States. As Europe's economy becomes more deeply integrated with the oil-exporting countries of the Middle East and the natural resource-rich regions of Africa and develops autonomously, a more dangerous sphere of monetary power than the British pound was ever able to capture will emerge in front of the United States. The strategic goal of the United States is that Europe, along with the Middle East and Africa, are directly dependent on the United States, and any interdependence between them is to some extent an impediment to American control of the world.

The shadow of the British Empire was too much for the United States that year, and upon realizing the potential for independent European development, Kissinger rushed to Europe in December 1973.

---

[74] Michael Hudson, *Global Fracture, The New International Economic Order,* Pluto Press, 1977, Chapter 5.

Kissinger does not want Europe and the Middle East to overtake their relationship with the United States, and therefore strongly calls for a "joint response to the energy crisis", and for the United States to have "senatorial" powers before Europe negotiates any issues with the Middle East.

Rather than buying Kissinger's account, the Europeans stressed that "the increasing concentration of power and responsibility for world development in the hands of a few powerful countries means that Europe must be united and have an external voice if it is to play its rightful role on the world stage".

In order to pull Europe back into the American orbit, the United States launched the International Energy Agency (IEA) four months after the oil crisis, an agency that was designed by the Americans to be the equivalent of the Organization of Petroleum Importing Countries (OPEC) to counter the influence of OPEC on oil prices. The United States is even prepared to resort to war against the oil-exporting countries of the Middle East if political and economic means fail to achieve their ends. Middle Eastern countries, for their part, have warned Europe and Japan that they will sabotage oil wells, pipelines and port facilities in the event of a military strike, ensuring Western oil disruption for at least a year. The European countries were shocked, and although the impact on the U.S. is great, the U.S. itself has a large number of oil fields that can be developed, in addition to increasing oil imports in Central and South America, Africa and other regions to fill the energy gap. But the European economy, which relies heavily on Middle Eastern oil, is in dire straits. Thus, when the United States Department of Defense threatened that the United States might use military force against Middle Eastern countries if the oil embargo continued, European countries immediately jumped at the chance to use their good offices.

Moreover, the French came to Kuwait to secure French crude oil supplies in exchange for assistance in the construction of petrochemical and refining projects. In Saudi Arabia, the French signed an agreement with the Saudi government to supply 5.6 billion barrels of crude oil over the next 20 years, in exchange for the petrochemical and refinery projects that remain. French oil diplomacy has made a name for itself.

When the Americans proposed the "New Atlantic Partnership" in an attempt to continue to confine Europe to the orbit designed by the United States, Europe once again raised its voice in a unified manner and would cooperate widely with the Arab States. The United States is so popular that it has to cuss out the Europeans for betrayal.

The oil crisis has torn a deep rift in the post-war alliance between Europe and the United States.

A more lasting economic impact than the oil embargo is the price of oil. The oil-exporting countries raised the price of oil from $1.8 to $2.48 a barrel at the beginning of 1971 to $10 a barrel at the end of the year, not entirely because of the sanctions imposed on the West, but also to compensate for the depletion of foreign reserves caused by the devaluation of the dollar, especially the sharp rise in the price of food imports.

Oil has long been more than just an energy source; it is a new basis for economic growth in industrialized countries. The fourfold increase in oil prices will significantly increase the price of raw materials in the petrochemical industry, while the raw materials of petrochemical products, but also the source of raw materials for almost all final consumer goods, such as automobiles, electronics, electrical appliances, textiles, etc., the sudden shortage of oil and the sharp increase in prices, on the developed countries that have been derailed to the oil industry economy, instantly caused great economic internal damage. Just as the food crisis hit China's industrialization at the end of the 1950s, the oil crisis will force fuel costs for industry and transportation to soar, the petrochemical industry to slump, the prices of raw materials for light industry to soar, and the eventual transmission to the market will result in higher commodity prices, higher inflation and stagnant economic development, and the global stagnation of the 1970s is the consequence of the oil industry's economic bottleneck.

The more developed the heavy chemical industry is, the harder it will be hit in the oil crisis. The United States was the earliest and largest industrial country in the petrochemical industry, and during the crisis, U.S. industrial production fell by 14%; in the 1960s, Japan implemented the "National Wealth Doubling Plan", which focused on the petrochemical industry as a strategic industry for development, and in the export-oriented production of consumer goods, encountered a bottleneck in raw materials at home, while at the international level faced with the plight of a sluggish consumer market, as a result, Japanese industrial production fell by as much as 20%. All industrialized countries, while entering a recession or low growth phase. The rapid growth and economic prosperity of the post-war West suffered its first major setback since industrialization changed course.

The oil crisis has forced countries to look for clean energy alternatives to oil, in fact, energy breakthroughs alone will not solve the raw material bottleneck of Western economic growth, which is the dependence of light industry on petrochemical raw materials. Atomic, solar, wind, hydro or tidal power generation, starting with energy alone, attempts to replace oil and spark a new economic revolution, which unfortunately will not get a major breakthrough in economic growth. For two full decades, from the early 1970s to the mid-1990s, developed industrialized countries such as Europe, America and Japan were plagued by low growth, mainly due to the lack of major and fundamental technological and raw material breakthroughs and the lack of a strong economic stimulus similar to that brought about by the great oil discoveries of the 1940s and 1950s.

The industrial revolution of mankind was really just a matter of converting energy from wood to coal and oil, and raw materials from agricultural products and natural materials of the land to synthetic materials based mainly on oil. And a new economic explosion is being birthed in a new technological revolution.

Europe's exchange rate stabilizes, dollar floats and makes waves

In the early 1970s, the world's frequent food problems, inflation, oil crises, economic recessions and the rift between the United States and Europe were, in essence, the result of the devaluation of the dollar.

Americans have finally figured out that even with the abolition of the gold throne, the dollar is still potentially threatened by gold. With gold as a reference, the devaluation of the dollar will be exposed to the world, the price of gold fell again and again, the embarrassment of the weakness of the dollar is repeatedly exposed to the world. A stable exchange rate mechanism, so that the truth of the depreciation of the dollar can not be hidden, so that the trick of sneaking is difficult to hide. Therefore, the United States is determined not only to "ring-fence" gold forever, but also to completely abolish the fixed-exchange-rate system and to completely disrupt world money markets. The more complex economic chaos created by the floating exchange rate will distract attention from the depreciation of the dollar and serve as a distraction and a breakout.

What America wants at this time is a mess of words! Take the currency hullabaloo and beg for a breakout for the dollar!

The United States seeks chaos, while Europe seeks stability.

The free floating of exchange rates has caused the currencies of the countries of the European Common Market to rise and fall and has seriously disrupted trade and economic development. In order to stabilize the situation, the Community, in the spirit of the Wiener Report, introduced the famous "serpentine exchange rate mechanism" in April 1972, which set a ceiling on the float allowed for any pair of currencies within the Community, and the "Smithsonian Agreement" of December 1971, which expanded the float of non-international reserve currencies against the United States dollar from 1 per cent in the Bretton Woods era to 2.25 per cent. Graphically, the exchange rate fluctuations within the Community are like a python in the middle of this "Smithsonian" tunnel. However, when the dollar began to float freely in 1973, the Community's "serpentine exchange rate" was no longer swimming in a tunnel, but rather was floating in a choppy sea.

The Europeans hoped that the impact of the dollar's depreciation would be significantly weakened in the face of the "serpentine exchange rate mechanism". But in the eyes of the United States dollar, the European currencies posed a "one-word long snake formation", but a "one-word beaten formation". The U.S. dollar is high and low, up and down, when to punch, when to kick, completely in the hands of international speculative capital; and the long snake formation of the European currency is like a stagnant position war, can only be defended passively, posed as a beaten face!

The biggest problem with the "serpentine exchange rate mechanism" is that it only locks in the comparative relationship between the currencies of the countries in the European Community, but the monetary and fiscal policies of the countries go their separate ways, which is like lassoing nine big ships in the waves, but the engine power of each ship and even the direction of the rudder are different from each other, once they sail together, they are bound to collide with each other and are difficult to coordinate. When the speculative wave of the dollar came crashing in, the iron rope would be easily broken by the large, violently undulating hull.

In 1973, the German mark was the flagship of the "serpentine exchange rate mechanism", while France and Britain were the main frigates, and in the summer of 1972, the United States sold grain to the Soviet Union, which was expected to sell gold to pay for it, in order to create a trend of falling gold prices and increasing confidence in the dollar, as a result of which the Soviet Union took advantage of the east wind of the European dollar and sent the fire of inflation back to the United States. By early 1973, increasing inflationary pressures had forced the dollar to no longer adhere to the Smithsonian devaluation limits. As a result, in mid-February, when the Bundesbank was forced to raise interest rates under inflationary pressure of 7.5%, the submerged dollar devaluation finally evolved into a raging wave of dollar asset sell-offs.

Britain briefly joined the "serpentine mechanism" in 1972, but was soon beaten out by speculative capital, and in 1973, Prime Minister Heath came to Bonn and asked the pound to join the "serpentine mechanism" again. Germany is naturally supportive, and with the two arms of the pound and the franc, the ability to resist the tidal wave of dollar speculative capital will be stronger. However, the British offer of conditions was a source of hesitation for the Germans, and as the British government failed repeatedly when it tried to peg the exchange rate to the European currency, and as successive governments were brought down for supporting similar policies, Heath proposed that Germany must provide a commitment to support the pound without limit. To the Germans, this is tantamount to asking the Germans to use their own foreign exchange reserves to write a blank cheque for the British, who, with this talisman, are likely to lose their restraint on the deficit. The Germans, unwilling to reject it directly, made a counter-offer, suggesting that Britain should first join the "serpentine mechanism" in order to demonstrate their determination to defend the stability of the European exchange rate by going to war against the odds. As a result, the British backed down.

France would have taken the opportunity of the British rejoining the "serpentine mechanism" to pull out the tempting foreign exchange reserves from the Germans' pockets and create a pool of funds similar to the stable exchange rate, so as to share some of the pressure with German silver if the franc could not hold, but the French dream was dashed as the British backed down. A wave of dollar speculation is crashing overhead.

On 1 March 1973, the "Smithsonian Dike" collapsed and what remained of Bretton Woods' fixed exchange rate system collapsed. The world has entered a chaotic era of free-floating currencies.

When the United States smashed the fixed exchange rate shackles around the neck, began to prepare for the permanent "ring" gold as the king of the currency, to complete the completion of the United States treasury bonds to replace gold, becoming the core assets of the international monetary reserves of the final act.

By 1976, the United States national debt held by governments around the world was $90 billion, so how could this debt be completely eliminated? It's a challenging strategic puzzle. The American way of thinking is to denature these debts into international currency reserves, just as the national debt that underpins the national currency does not have to be repaid.

In June 1974, the United States proposed the establishment of a so-called "Substitution Account" in the IMF, the main function of which would be to convert U.S. debt held by countries into special drawing rights (SDRs),[75] thus completing the leap from U.S. national debt to international currency reserve assets. The denatured U.S. debt, no longer a national debt of the United States, but a core asset in the international monetary reserve, will be permanently embedded in the international monetary operating system and never have to be repaid!

The United States will "ring-fence" the act of gold, divided into four steps: first, the central banks of all IMF member countries, is not allowed to set the official price of gold; second, the value link between gold and the special drawing rights must be severed, so that gold in the central bank's currency reserves, will lose the legal price basis, become "value wandering" assets; third, the United States Treasury Department will hold a gold auction; fourth, the IMF will cooperate with the United States Treasury Department to depress the world gold price. Its core tenet is this: make the price of gold as unstable as possible, so that instability becomes less likely to be a reservoir of wealth, and makes gold less attractive as a currency reserve.

---

[75] Research Department of Federal Reserve Bank of San Francisco, *Substitution Account*, 1980.

At the strong request of the United States Government, IMF members agreed to expel gold from the value base of SDRs, which are no longer tied to the value of gold, but have been redefined as a reference to a "basket" of 16 national currencies. Immediately after, in keeping with the spirit of the US, the IMF decided to sell 1/3 of its gold reserves, half of which was returned to central banks and the other half was sold publicly in the market.

With the abolition of the fixed exchange rate and the "ring-fencing" of gold, the most striking problem in the eyes of Americans is the Middle East countries that have received huge petrodollar revenues due to the oil price boom since the oil crisis.

The surpluses in Europe and Japan were eaten up by rising oil prices, and from 1974 to 1976, $40 billion in oil dividends poured into the pockets of Middle Eastern countries, and the Middle East became a major capital-exporting country. If the Middle East moves closer to Europe and uses petrodollar capital accumulation for large-scale industrial construction, then Europe will be the best provider of industrial equipment and technology, and the Middle East will open its doors to Europe in terms of oil supply and consumer markets. In this way, American interests will be marginalized. The key question is how the U.S. can channel the abundant petrodollars that flow from the Middle East back to the U.S., weakening the intrinsic incentive for the Middle East to move closer to Europe.

The U.S. approach is still to use U.S. Treasuries to channel petrodollars from the Middle East, allowing the Middle East to take over the former role of Europe and Japan and continue to finance the U.S. deficit. To this end, the United States first warned European banks not to accept savings larger than the $15 billion they currently hold, thus cutting off the Middle East petrodollars, and then coerced the Saudis into pouring petrodollars into U.S. Treasuries, using the lure of military cooperation and security guarantees.

After the "usurpation of gold and self-reliance", the U.S. debt empire has experienced a dramatic shock such as the floating exchange rate, the oil crisis, the Middle East dollar reflows, and finally stood firm. In the midst of the chaos, Europe's monetary union has been hit hard.

"The Monnet Circle" dissolves and the European Union languishes

De Gaulle's stepping down was a great boon to the "Monnet circle". With this shareholder wind, Monet's old comrades in arms, German Chancellor Brandt and British Prime Minister Heath, together with French President Pompidou, accomplished the two major events of the enlargement of the European Community and the Wiener Report with a single stroke of luck.

However, the ensuing wars in the Middle East and the oil crisis interrupted Europe's long post-war economic growth, and the advent of the era of floating exchange rates threw Europe into a much larger economic and political vortex. Europe's politicians, exhausted by the economic recession and political turmoil at home, have significantly weakened their willingness and enthusiasm for international cooperation. Germany is concerned about inflation, France is worried about economic growth, Britain's enthusiasm for the "serpentine mechanism" has more than enough to play, Italy and other European Community countries see the leaders of the quarrel, no leader, can only sweep their own door snow, difficult to care about others to the frost.

Faced with the impasse of losing momentum in European integration, Monnet proposed the creation of a "European resource fund" in the hope of breaking the deadlock again from the monetary union, but the German Finance Minister opposed the proposal, arguing that economic integration should take precedence over financial integration. After the oil crisis broke out, Monnet proposed that the European Community should establish a cooperative mechanism for the distribution of oil supplies among the countries of the region, which Germany agreed to, but Britain and France opposed and had to stop.

In May 1974, Destin, of the "Monnet Circle", was elected President of France after the death of Georges Pompidou. Monnet, who is already 80 years old, enlightened the new president, who is less than 50 years old, that "what is most lacking in European affairs is power. Discussions have rules to follow, but decision-making does not." This statement inspired De Stein, who had a similar idea, and with Monnet's encouragement, De Stein proposed a major plan at the Paris EC summit in December, the "European Council" system.[76]

The "Council of Europe", composed of the heads of State of the Community, is the highest strategic decision-making body of the Community, which, although it does not have legislative powers, has the responsibility to direct the direction of major political issues in Europe and to set policy priorities. In the face of a severe economic recession and exchange rate crisis, Europe urgently needs regular meetings of heads of State. The establishment of the "Council of Europe" means that the heads of sovereign States are obliged to provide political services to the supra-sovereign EC.

By this time, the EC had already formed the original prototype of the United States of Europe, with the High Authority of the Coal and Steel Union, under Monet's first presidency, coexisting with the European Economic Community and the European Atomic Energy Community after the Treaty of Rome, and the three supra-sovereign institutions later merged to form the European Community, with their respective powers consolidated into a single European Executives, the predecessor of the present European Commission. It is the equivalent of a cabinet government in a country, responsible for the day-to-day running of the European Community.

Monnet designed the Coal and Steel Union's "Common Assembly", which evolved into the "European Parliament", the equivalent of a national legislative, supervisory and advisory body.

In this way, the "Council of Europe", the "Executive Committee of the European Communities" and the "European Parliament" built the three pillars of the building of the future United States of Europe, and almost all of these institutions took their original shape from the "Monnet Circle", and Monnet and others will certainly be regarded as the founders of the United States of Europe in the future.

In 1975, the "Action Committee of the United States of Europe", formed by the "Monnet Circle", had been in operation for a full 20 years, and Monnet himself was 87 years old. He did not expect the road

---

[76] Pascaline Winand, *Monnet's Action Committee for the United Nations of Europe, It's Successor and the Network of Europeanists.*

to the United States of Europe to be so long, and during the 10 years of de Gaulle's reign, Monnet lost influence in France, although he still enjoyed a high status in Europe and America. In Monet's mind, the United States of Europe was based on a union with Britain and the United States, with partnership on both sides of the Atlantic as its core purpose, and was created not to challenge American hegemony, but to share power with the United States and to dominate the world together. The oil crisis since the 1970s, the devaluation of the dollar, the chaotic exchange rates in Europe, and the recession in the industrial countries have created tensions and even emotional confrontations between the United States and Europe, which Monnet was deeply disappointed by. The laxity of the forces of integration within Europe added to his worries, and as he grew older and less energetic, Monnet felt that his mission had been accomplished. At one point he wanted German Chancellor Brandt to take up his mantle, but eventually gave up on the idea.[77]

Among the staff members who have followed Monnet for years, his secretary, Ms. Linger, is completely unpaid for volunteer service. She worked for Baron Robert Rothschild during the day and continued her work at Monet's office after 5 p.m. Baron Robert Rothschild, also a member of the Rothschilds, did not choose the family's old banking career, but was actively involved in a career as a diplomat. He was the principal drafter of the 1957 Treaty of Rome, and thus one of the founders of the European Community. Throughout the long years, Monnet had maintained close contact with the Rothschild family, and through the liaison of his private secretary, every specific step of Monet's United States of Europe Action Committee had been able to reach the ears of the Rothschild family with timely and accurate feedback and advice.

When Monnet finally announced to all his fellow circle members that he had decided to retire and dissolve the United States of Europe Action Committee, all were extremely shocked. After losing its spiritual leader, the United States of Europe movement wandered for a full decade in loss and disorientation. It wasn't until 1985, after Monet's left and right armies once again raised the flag and became active, that the

---

[77] Ibid.

European Economic and Monetary Union again accelerated sharply, and led directly to the Maastricht Treaty.

In the days of Monet's retirement, the only significant development in the European Economic and Monetary Union was the establishment of the European Monetary System (EMS) in 1979, a concrete result of the 1970 Wiener Report.

At the heart of the European monetary system was the European Currency Unit (ECU), which eventually evolved into what is now the Euro. Germany and France have been engaged in a bitter quarrel around the currency unit. According to the French design, the European Monetary Unit consists of a "basket of currencies" based on a weighted average of the currencies of the European Community countries.

On the basis of the European Monetary Unit (EMU), the float of any country's currency relative to the EMU should not exceed 2.25 per cent, while the Italian lira, which is soft, is allowed to float up to 6 per cent. The new European Exchange Rate Mechanism (ERM) is known as the European Exchange Rate Mechanism (ERM).

This French design is quite clever, and the idea of a "basket of currencies" for the European monetary unit, in the case of a strong mark and a weak franc, is beneficial to the franc. This is because the currency ratio in the "basket" is adjusted only every five years after it has been fixed. In the meantime, if the German mark appreciates too quickly, in order to ensure that the value of the mark in the "basket" does not cross the border, Germany will have to first intervene in the market with its own foreign exchange reserves to lower the mark. In this way, the mark becomes a shield for other countries' currencies. At the same time, the ECU will become an instrument for countries to intervene in the foreign exchange market and, ultimately, in effect, to repay the external debt caused by exchange rate fluctuations in their national currencies.

The Germans strongly opposed such an arrangement, believing that it would "force the creation of the German mark currency out of our control entirely". The Germans understood that when the devalued dollar came flooding in, Germany would be forced to issue additional marks to buy dollars in order to keep the mark from appreciating, while the currency increase was out of control. At the same time, in the intervention to stabilize the European exchange rate markets, it became clear that currency speculators could only save these countries with strong marks when they were able to repay Germany in their own currency through the ECU, which was tantamount to forcing Germany to increase the supply of marks.

Therefore, the Germans insist that the exchange rate stability operation, must inherit the "serpentine mechanism", national currency float can not be relative to the ECU, but the relative exchange rate of any two groups of currencies can not break the ceiling, so that countries can only use their own foreign exchange reserves to adjust the exchange rate. This move, the ploy to turn Mark into a shield, cracked clean. In addition, although intervention in the foreign exchange market short-term borrowing has increased significantly, but Germany insists on repaying the borrowing, must use the dollar, mark or gold, which breaks the idea of other countries trying to "slice" from the mark. Finally, Germany also does not agree to the establishment of a shared "foreign exchange reserve bank".

In launching the European Monetary System, France appears to have achieved a conceptual victory, especially with the introduction of the ECU. But Germany, on core principles, half-steps away. The new exchange rate mechanism, which merely legalized the "serpentine float", did not increase the burden on the Germans, nor did any change occur in the situation where the Mark was dominant.

The European monetary system was established, in fact, as a mark currency area.

Raising the Spirit of Monnet flag again, "European Action Committee" in action

After the collapse of the "Monnet Circle" in 1975, the spiritual drive that had driven the United States of Europe was paralysed, significantly delaying the process of the European Economic and Monetary Union. However, the core cadre of the "Monnet circle" is not sullen and is waiting for the right time to form a new circle again to continue the cause of European unity.

In the early 1980s, Monet's original deputy, Dutchman Max Kohnstamm, gradually became the new cohesive core. He was a long-time Vice-Chairman of the Action Committee of the United States of Europe and, in 1973, became the first Chairman of the European branch of the Rockefeller-funded Trilateral Commission. Kohnstamm, though not as rallying cry as Monnet, had long been involved in the specific work of liaison and coordination, was well acquainted with important

European figures, and he volunteered to take on the task of launching the new circle. The crowd was already in desperate need of a private circle for communication and discussion of European issues, and as soon as Kohnstamm called for it, the old circle of people immediately found a spiritual home and flocked to it.

In October 1982, Kohl replaced Schmidt as the new chancellor of West Germany, and Kohl, also a former member of the Monnet Commission, declared as soon as he came to power that European affairs and European political union were the priority policies of the new government. Kohnstamm felt that the time was finally ripe to re-establish a "new circle". He began to reach out to old comrades in arms, Schmidt, who had just retired from his position as German Chancellor, and Belgian Chancellor Tindermans, a former member of the Monnet Commission and under the influence of Kohnstamm, also began to write to old friends in the former circle who were still active in politics and trade, asking if they would like to join the new circle in order "to ensure that the ideas and methods of Jean Monnet continue to serve as a spiritual guide for the European Union".[78]

In order to reconstitute a new circle in 1984, Kohnstamm began to travel around Europe, visiting old and new friends who were preparing to come to the conference one by one, and bringing with them the theme of the conference and the platform for the future.

On March 13, 1984, Kohnstamm officially launched the new circle in Brussels, attended by Belgian Chancellor Tindermans, former German Chancellor Schmidt, as well as authorities from various countries in the field of finance and trade. German President Karl Carstens, though not present, said he would be involved in the new circle of discussions once he leaves office. A consensus was reached to restore the spirit of Monnet and rebuild a new Commission under the new circumstances. According to Schmidt, the Commission should "develop an overall strategy to awaken a sinking Europe". It was also recommended that Schmidt present a strategic report on the European Monetary System (EMS) and that other members draft thematic reports on the EC, the Unified Market, security and defence, and the accession of Spain and Portugal to the EC. Schmidt concluded with a special

---

[78] Ibid.

emphasis: "It is important to realize that although (French President) Mitterrand has put European issues at the center of his considerations, there is no such consensus within the French Socialist Party." It was therefore necessary to find "some people who could impress Mitterrand and get Mitterrand's tactical support" to get involved.

The best candidate for this is Jacques Delors, the French finance minister. Kohnstamm and Delors first met in 1976, and the two have remained in close contact ever since, with Monet's ideas and powerful circle having an irresistible appeal to the fledgling Delors. A former senior official at the Bank of France, Delors was confident and often outspoken, and his abilities were evident to all, and even Mitterrand held Delors in high regard.

In June 1984, Delors informed Kohnstamm that Mitterrand had agreed to allow him to participate in a new circle initiated by Kohnstamm, and Kohnstamm, to Kohnstamm's surprise, suggested that Delors make the relaunch of European integration a major goal of his work. Later, with the support of Mitterrand and the endorsement of German Chancellor Kohl, Delors was elected "President of the Council of Europe", the equivalent of a Cabinet Prime Minister of the European Community. For Mitterrand, Delors was his agent in the new circle, and the Germans' main purpose in pulling Delors into the new circle was precisely to influence Mitterrand to push for European integration in full force. The tacit agreement was to place Delors in the key position of "President of the European Commission" in order to work together to promote a European economic and monetary union.

The "new circle" was naturally overjoyed at the news that Delors had taken office, and with its own people in key positions, the pace of the European Monetary Union would be much faster. However, with Delors as "President of the Council of Europe", the new circle will need to fill Delors' vacancy with another candidate from the French Socialist Party. As an interim measure, Delors will participate as a "guest" in all activities of the New Circle. When Delors arrived in Brussels as "President of the Council of Europe", the "New Circle" was immediately active in recommending him for the composition of the Council of Europe.

In September 1984, the "New Circle" was officially named "The Action Committee for Europe",[79] and in the mid-1980s the international situation in Europe and the world was very different from that in the 1950s, when the Monnet Commission was established. The threat of the Soviet Union is gradually being lifted, the inner foundation of Europe and the United States united against the Soviet Union is gradually disintegrating, the possibility of the reunification of West and East Germany is no longer a remote fantasy, a unified and powerful Germany will once again appear on the world stage, not only France and other EC countries within Europe are feeling psychological pressure, even Britain and the United States are also worried, the European monetary system has already become the world of the mark, if the unification of Germany is achieved, the territory of dismembered Germany will become a political giant again. At this moment, the "United States of Europe" movement, driven by the Germans, would prompt suspicion in the United States of the emergence of another superpower, and strong nationalism would be stirred within Europe. As a result, the blinding words "United States of Europe" have been replaced by a generalized Europe.

In the process of European integration, it is France that is most psychologically tangled. The French people have long known the Germanic nation's bravery, and the French-led "Coal and Steel Alliance" in the 1950s was a beautiful feeling of tolerance and benevolence for the French people, while the European Union represented a righteous act of European solidarity in the struggle for independence between the US and the Soviet Union. However, in the 1980s, France was already struggling to match Germany's economic power, and the franc had become the mark's heel. The thought of a Germany of 80 million people, politically unified, economically strong, and with a strong currency reappearing on the French border gave the French a chill in their bones.

French President Mitterrand responded by integrating Germany's economic and monetary power with France's military and political position to achieve a more balanced posture for both France and Europe. Germany has the mark and France has nuclear weapons, and further union would be a win-win for both sides, and a step back and a

---

[79] Ibid.

split would be a real disaster. When the French figured this out and the Germans were convinced of this motive, the drive to intensify cooperation between the two sides received a new breakthrough. Delors happens to play a key role in this breakthrough.

Just before Delors was ready to address the European Parliament for the first time on behalf of the "Council of Europe", Kohnstamm wrote a long letter to Delors with a series of suggestions on the content of this important speech. Delors understood this, and in a speech in January 1985, he formally set out the major goal of achieving the European single market by 1992. A few months later, the Heads of State of the "European Council" formally endorsed Delors' objectives and tasked him with completing a detailed report on the implementation timetable. European integration has immediately entered a new phase.

On 6 June 1985, at the first official meeting of the "New Circle", chaired by German President Karl Karstens, Delors presented plans for the future strengthening of the European monetary system. At the luncheon, German Chancellor Kohl had high hopes for the "new circle", and he believed that the most important task of the "European Conduct Council" was

> *"to pass on the historical importance of the European unification process to the younger generation. Only if we continue to inherit this spiritual wealth can we make the process of European unification irreversible".*

In 1986, Delors became more closely associated with the "new circle", and he replaced him in the "new circle" with his close friend Henri Nallett, who had been Mitterrand's agricultural adviser and later Minister of Agriculture. At the meetings of the "New Circle", Delors "lent" the European Commission's team of experts and even translators to Kohnstamm to provide the latest developments in the European economic and monetary field. In addition to this, Delors provides 22,000 European Currency Units (ECU) per year for the activities of the "New Circle", which is funded by the European Commission.

By September 1988, the New Circle had expanded to 92 members from Governments, political parties, business associations, the banking and finance industry and the European Parliament. Thirteen of the members are old men from the Monnet era. The resolutions formed by the "new circle", which reach the German, French, English, Italian, Dutch, Belgian and the President of the Council of Europe directly, are to a large extent directly transformed into lines for politicians on the

European stage. Politicians are able to speak freely and communicate fully in small private circles, in a way that is difficult for them to do in diplomatic settings. The "new circle" pushes the pace of European integration mainly from behind the scenes, with little public publicity in the media, giving politicians ample room to perform in the domestic political arena. These people, because of their high degree of spiritual identity, many of them are old friends who have been working together since the 1950s, trusting each other, lending their strength together, being loyal to each other and never revealing their secrets, forming the Holy Land of faith in the indestructible United States of Europe.

The Delors Commission, a kick in the pants of the European Monetary Union

In 1988, the political infrastructure of the European Community as a fledgling nation was already in place, with the "Council of Europe", the "Council of Europe" and the "European Parliament" forming the three pillars of the future United States of Europe. However, a true state cannot be built without the central bank, the central pillar, which is the most central of all, in any case.

The monetary union, as the main lever for European unity, has played a major role since the 1950s, stabilizing exchange rate relations within the Community and has been a constant driving force for cooperation among European countries.

The most important breakthrough in the European monetary system, launched in 1979, was the formation of the European Currency Unit (ECU), which established the European monetary standard. However, the central bank, a key component of the eventual monetary system, was slow to make a major breakthrough.

Whoever holds the power to issue money is in de facto control!

In this contest of key powers, an external game of national interest between Germany, France and Britain, as well as an internal struggle between the ministries of finance and the central banks of each country, was formed.

To judge the Germans from their humble post-war diplomatic posture and pacifist international image as having forever abandoned the pursuit of the ideal of world hegemony would be to underestimate the strong will of the Germanic nation. Germany is just learning, not getting better!

Germany's aim in supporting European unity was to create a continent of Europe under German control. In the embarrassment of being militarily lame and politically pretending to be a grandson, the only heavy weapon the Germans have in their hands is currency! Germans are exceptionally clear, consistent, coherent and unflinching about what they need to get. Monetary power in Europe must and can only be substantially controlled by the German Central Bank. The advantage of time is on the German side, the EC is in fact already a mark currency area, the German economy is above all European countries, national unity is about to be achieved, the era of political dwarfs is fading away, and the decline of the Soviet Union and Eastern Europe has provided great scope for the imagination of German power to expand eastward. The European continent, led by Germany, is bound to become a world superpower. The German has eaten enough haste over the last hundred years, and this time, it will go about winning its own future with superb patience and perseverance.

France will always be aspirational and ambitious, with grand plans, but not enough execution. After each of its heated quarrels with Germany, the Germans always gave France some relief in the face, but a closer assessment revealed that the Germans had not actually made any substantial concessions. The Frenchman's pleasure in the glory and possession of the symbols of power far outweighs the trivial annoyances that come with the execution of power. France wants the future European Central Bank to do its bidding, but it lacks both the strength and the patience.

Britain has never been out of the "great and glorious" past in its mentality, and in the eyes of the British, the continent of 20th century Europe is no different from the 19th century. Britain imagined that she was still the weight of Europe, and that if she favoured Germany, the ambitions of France would have to be sunk, and if she slid into France, the dreams of the Germanic Empire would be lost. Without Britain's involvement, the continent was bound to be in chaos. As the centre of monetary power in Europe for two centuries, how could London tolerate having Paris or Frankfurt decide its fate?

When the European powers with their hearts set on a course for the 1988 European Monetary Union summit, an exciting drama unfolded.

At the European Summit in Hannover, Germany, in June 1988, Germany and France officially launched the championship final of the ECB, a monetary union event. The summit's decision to set up a panel of experts to come up with the final course of the monetary union, which includes the central bank governors of the 12 EC countries, became the focus of the summit's attention, and the person who will largely determine who the championship trophy ultimately goes to. Chancellor Kohl finally showed his cards, and it was the President of the "Council of Europe", the French super-celebrity Delors, who proposed him! French President Mitterrand smiled and nodded, and British Prime Minister Thatcher followed in bewilderment.

The Germans were quite clever in this move, and Cole was well aware that the French valued reputation so much that the French vanity could be adequately satisfied by the Germans stepping in to lead a panel of experts to develop a programme that would be favourable to the German central bank, destined to be firmly opposed by the French. As long as the substance is in Germany's favor, Cole will wear the laurel on the Frenchman's head with a smile on his face. This is the fundamental reason why the Germans worked so hard to enlist Delors in the "new circle".

Not all are rejoicing at Delors' appointment. German central bank president Bohr is full of grievances. Clearly, Boehl sees himself as the natural leader of the monetary expert group, and he is rightfully the boss among the 12 central bank governors. In addition, the currency issue is the central bank's masterpiece, the finance minister out of Delors, actually want to lead the central bank governors to engage in monetary research, both left the Ministry of Finance to command the central bank of the bad impression, but also a bad precedent for outsiders to lead insiders. He also complained about Mrs Thatcher's lack of sensitive political insight, "She went so far as to welcome the establishment of a panel of experts headed by Delors. She should have known that there were special political considerations in this arrangement." At one point, Ball refused to even participate in the Delors Commission.

On this issue, there is something more or less questionable between Ball's strong aversion to the Commission and his later appreciation of its report. It was precisely because the old hotshot Thatcher saw Poe's firm resistance to the Delors Commission that he did not veto Delors' appointment. The UK doesn't want to see the ECB, but it also doesn't want to single-handedly challenge the entire EC. But then Thatcher regretted it by gullibly trusting Poe.

With the establishment of the Delors Commission, the main work was transferred entirely to the Bank for International Settlements in Switzerland. The Bank for International Settlements, designed to be a central bank for central bankers, is of course, from its philosophy to its atmosphere, from its auxiliary team to its core of experts, a scheme that seriously favours the monetary monopoly of the central bank alone. Who is the boss of the EEC central banks? Still the Bundesbank, of course. In fact, the European Central Bank's monopoly on currency issuance is the German Central Bank's monopoly on monetary power.

Unsurprisingly, in April 1989, the Delors Commission presented the Delors Report with a clear preference that the future European central bank would gain even greater "independence" than the Bundesbank. The report states that the ECB

> "should take a federal form, which we can call the European Central Banking System (ESCB). This new system, which should be given full autonomy, is an institution of the European Community and is not subordinate to any State. The new system consists of a central agency (with its own balance sheet) and national central banks. The new system's mandate is to maintain price stability. The Council of the system must be independent of national governments and the powers of the EC".

The Delors Report also provides a series of policy guidelines such as liberalization of capital flows, financial market integration, permanent currency liberalization, permanent fixed exchange rate, etc. But the content is nothing more than platitudes and nothing new. The most explosive is the "federal" European Central Bank system, which not only represents the complete independence of central banks, but also means that countries will give up "monetary sovereignty". The impact of this report was far greater than that of the 1970 Wiener Report.

The publication of the Delors Report was an immediate source of controversy in various countries and even more so in France. It was only after French President Mitterrand saw the report that he began to realise how much more powerful the European Central Bank was than he had thought. His anxiety and entanglement were overwhelming.

I am not opposed to a central bank, but to some of its modus operandi. The Bundesbank is completely free from government control. While our central bank, the Banque de France, is also independent, it is the Government that determines economic and monetary policy. What will it take to get the French to move forward with the monetary union process? My impression is that the Germans would be willing to push for a monetary union if they believed it would not affect their good, healthy economic situation. However, I am not very willing to commit to this. Without the constraint of political power, the European Central Bank would have the power of national sovereignty, and that would be a dangerous thing to do. The European monetary system is already a mark currency area. At present the Federal Republic of Germany does not have the authority to manage our economy. But once the European Central Bank is established, it will get that power.

The President of the Bank of France, de La Rossier, who participated in the Delors Commission, became the "culprit" within the French Government. Not only because the French government has never been adamant about the independence of the French central bank, but also because he ceded the management of the French economy to the Germans. Looking back on the time, he considers it to be one of the toughest trials of his career.

I was summoned to the Treasury room after the Treasury received the final version of the Delors report. Bérégovoy (Finance Minister), Trichet and a few other officials sat on one side of the table and I was alone on the other. Bérégovoy had a very cold expression on his face. He said the Treasury was shocked and very upset by the findings of the Delors report. He then let Deputy Finance Minister Trichet speak.

The gist of Trichet's speech was that the independence of the European Central Bank, as recommended in the Delors report, was too much, more than that of the Bundesbank. He said I must have made excessive concessions in the Delors Commission discussions.

Bérégovoy then asked me, 'What do you want to say?' I said I heard the word 'concessions'. This is to say that in the process of reaching a monetary union agreement in the Delors Commission, I gave in to certain views or made concessions to certain views. That is not true. I am all for central bank independence, but that in no way means a concession or at the expense of France. The future monetary system will only be possible if the central bank and its affiliated units have independence. Any other institutional arrangement would be unstable. No one forced me to say that, nor did I say it because it was a German view.

It's nothing more than a trick that central bankers have been playing since the 1920s. Central bankers first reach tacit agreement and consensus with each other, then go back and lobby their respective governments to agree to their policies. In the game of political power versus money power, it is the sophisticated politicians who think they have played the bankers, but it is the bankers who end up playing the politicians to death.

When Britain saw the Delors Report, Mrs. Thatcher was so exasperated that she began to realize that it had been a terrible political blunder to put Delors at the head of the Monetary Group, and that the attitude of the German Central Bank's Governor, Pohl, who was adamantly opposed to the Delors Commission, had given her the illusion of serious consequences, admitting that "the greatest damage was that Pohl's position against the monetary union, which was well known, was not expressed at all in the Delors Commission". However, the Governor of the Bank of England, Pemberton, was gleeful.

I recognize that the creation and expansion of a single currency is a perfect plan from a practical point of view. I want people to know that I support the currency union program. It will help the Bank of England regain its independence and help establish a more stable monetary system in the UK. Thatcher's brief instruction to me was to follow Bohr (the head of the German central bank). I wrote a letter to Thatcher, saying that in case Poe agreed to sign it, I could find no reason not to. If I were the only central bank governor who didn't sign off on the Delors report, I'd look extremely ridiculous and ridiculous, and I'd look like a Thatcherian pug.

Germany launched a soft lobbying campaign against Thatcher when it succeeded in doing so. Thatcher, however, had stopped trusting the Germans after taking a big bite out of Poe. So Germany's ally, the Netherlands, struck. The Dutch have never been the answering bugs of the mark when it comes to currency. When the Dutch came to Britain, Thatcher understood at once that they were coming, lobbyists sent by the Germans to persuade Britain to accept the ECB. After a bitter rejoinder from the Dutch, Thatcher insisted that Britain's membership in the European Monetary Union would make it inflexible. The Dutch have responded with a cunning response that joining the European currency is like driving a car with your seatbelt on, it doesn't affect your speed and is much safer. After the meeting, Thatcher's assessment of the Dutchman was, "The rhetoric about the EPRM is rubbish!" When the British Chancellor of the Exchequer suggested that Britain establish a timetable for joining the European currency, the Iron Lady burst into a rage: "That is a particularly harmful suggestion. You must never bring up the subject again, it must be me who says so."

The battle between politicians and bankers dates back at least to the Renaissance in Europe, but it is the first time in the history of Europe that governments have ceded monetary sovereignty, the most central part of national sovereignty, to the bankers in such a thorough manner. In the contest between the gold power and the regime, the gold power gained the ultimate victory. In Europe, it's no longer the state that controls capital, it's capital that controls the state!

Two fronts: German reunification and monetary union

In November 1989, when the Berlin Wall came down and East Germany was about to plunge into the arms of West Germany, the enormous and sudden pressure for German unification turned Cole from the engine of European integration to the brakes all at once.

In the war, the Germans had had enough of fighting on two fronts simultaneously, and now, in the two strategic directions of monetary union and German unification, Kohl preferred to focus on German unification first. This is not only the core issue of the German nation's centennial plan, but also the key bargaining chip to win greater dominance in the future on the battlefield of the monetary union. France, England, and even Germany's Dutch heel, all felt an invisible pressure and a sense of urgency.

In 1948, France had placed the Ruhr industrial zone in Germany under international condominium (in effect, under French control) in exchange for the establishment of the West German federal government. Now, the French are playing the same trick, and Mitterrand has strongly hinted to Kohl that a prerequisite for German reunification is to abandon the mark, accept the euro, and accelerate the pace of monetary union. Otherwise, the French would have served a daunting dish and Germany would have faced the siege and isolation of the "Franco-British-Russian alliance", as it did on the eve of World War I and World War II. Faced with such an extreme threat, Cole had to give in.

Germany was once again forced to fight on two fronts simultaneously. The European Monetary Union, united with Germany, had been bound together by the French. Every inch of progress on the road to unification will have to be accompanied by a weighty compromise on the monetary union. The price of German reunification was the abandonment of the mark. Mitterrand saw this concession as a great victory for France, and Kohl played the tragedy of the German people being forced to part with Mark to the point where the whole audience was moved to their senses. With the BoE dominating the ECB's big picture, the real loss for Germany is not the abandonment of the mark, but the loss of the opportunity to win more concessions from France.

It was still Thatcher who saw things more clearly when, in March 1990, at a banquet in London with France's top 10 industrial giants, she said: "Germany is already the dominant force in Europe's economy and, when unified, will be the dominant force in European politics." She argues that "European integration is not a check on Germany. France needs to join forces with Britain to counter the German threat." The Iron Lady once again reiterated her consistent view that European integration was "a Europe given to Germany as a piece of iron", which would strengthen Germany's dominant position.

Thatcher was indeed worthy of a distinguished statesman, and she saw very soberly that the future trend of a united Europe would be a growing German power, and that Britain was far more strategically far-sighted in its guard against Germany than France. In Thatcher's view, France was just a dowry for Germany, and would end up sending people and treasure with them. However, she is also a super realist. She would never tolerate the Germans running the British economy through the ECB on the one hand, and wants the benefits of the exchange rate mechanism in the European Monetary System on the other. In her words, "Britain expected to join the European exchange rate mechanism in order to use the status of the Deutsche Mark to create some sort of gold standard-like mechanism to help Britain control inflation". In other words, the Iron Maiden turned down a marriage contract in euros, but craved a bride price with a stable exchange rate.

In October 1990, the United Kingdom decided to join the European Exchange Rate Mechanism. The Germans had a double whammy, the reunification was officially completed on 3 October, and Britain received the bride price of the Exchange Rate Mechanism. One step further, the British Empire, which had not even managed two world wars, would be integrated into Europe under German domination. Germany's ambassador to the United Kingdom was eager to find Thatcher, since the United Kingdom accepted the bride price, Germany naturally wants to strike while the iron is hot, as soon as possible to promote the United Kingdom to marry the future of the euro wedding.

Thatcher:

> *"Germany is now united. Cole must have been very happy. He can now implement more domestic policies."*

German Ambassador:

> *"Chancellor Kohl will continue to advance European integration, including the creation of a European Monetary Union."*

Thatcher:

> *"What did you say? Do you want me to go to Her Majesty and explain to her that in a few years her avatar will no longer appear on our bills?"*

Thatcher's cold realism rivals that of Churchill back in the day! There was no semblance of ambiguity or wandering in the defence of the national interests of the British Empire. The British did have a fight with the Germans, who were both highly sensible, clear-eyed in their goals, persevering and never wavering. There is still a gap between France and Britain and Germany in terms of self-control and judgment, which is why France has only been in the Napoleonic era for a while for the last 200 years, and has been pushed around constantly by Britain and Germany for most of the rest of that time.

In any case, Kohl, who at this time was known as the most successful politician in Europe, greatly underestimated the difficulties of reunification at a time when he was fulfilling in his hands the historic and ambitious task of unifying Germany. The biggest mistake Kohl made during the process of German reunification was the severe imbalance in the exchange ratio between the East and West German marks, which not only caused 20 years of economic sequelae for Germany, but also nearly upended the European monetary system.

On February 6, 1990, without consulting the Bundesbank, the Ministry of Finance and the Reichstag, and without informing the rest of the EC, Kohl suddenly announced the shocking news that the West German mark would supply East Germany. World opinion was outraged that the mark had long since ceased to be the currency of the Germans and that it was the cornerstone of the monetary stability of the European Community. The news, on the one hand, sent shockwaves through the currency markets and, on the other, almost immediately calmed the tumult in East Germany.

After the fall of the Berlin Wall in November 1989, the situation in East Germany largely spiraled out of control. People were cheering, and there was a massive influx of West German "tourism", less than 20 million East Germans, as many as 10 million people crossed the border to visit the long-awaited capitalist "paradise", East Germans were deeply shocked by the advanced and prosperous West Germany. Social opinion in East Germany formed a one-sided voice, which was to hasten the unification with West Germany. In such an atmosphere, all efforts and attempts by the East German government to transform existing social mechanisms were immediately submerged in a wave of denial. The people had no mind to work, demonstrations of all kinds were taking place, the government was on the verge of paralysis, and the East Germans had fallen into a general frenzy of desperation to live at once as richly as the West Germans, when it seemed that as soon as unity was achieved, wealth and prosperity would immediately and automatically come.

Since 1951, the government has insisted on equating the East German mark with the West German mark, despite the growing productivity gap between the two. The collapse of confidence in the social system was directly reflected in the black market price of the currency. It was later acknowledged that the size of the East German external debt had been exaggerated and that the economy was not as bad as thought. However, the collapse of confidence accelerated the devaluation of the East German mark and undermined the foundations of the East German economy.[80]

In order to stabilize the East German mark, in November 1989, Kohl reached an agreement with the East German government that the West German central bank would offer 3.8 billion marks for East German tourists at a 3:1 exchange ratio, and since this ratio was far more favorable than the black market price, the great lure of arbitrage drove more East Germans to West Germany, who exchanged the West German mark for 3:1 and went back to dump it at a higher price. As a

---

[80] Jonathan R. Zatlin, *Rethinking Reunification: German Monetary Union and European Integration.*

result, the supply of West German marks was met with a frenzied "demand" from the East Germans, which was probably Kohl's "monetary ploy", that when the West German marks were in full swing in East Germany, Germany would in fact complete its "economic reunification" first, and that other countries would insist on opposing German reunification, and would not be able to reverse the process of national reunification bound by the strong bonds of monetary interests.

The East Germans fell into a monetary misunderstanding in which they took the West German mark for granted as wealth itself, without realizing that the value of money lies in the productivity behind it. The idea of giving up hard work and getting rich just by having money pervaded the entire East German society. East Germany's own economy, with such a general mentality, is increasingly sinking. At the same time, the demand for West German marks is growing. The call for monetary unification has created a huge social problem in East Germany. The East Germans shouted, West Germany if we don't send Mark over, we'll move over there!

And that's where the pressure is on Cole to launch Mark Redemption in a hurry.

On July 1, 1990, Kohl's declaration of the mark-to-mark ratio was not 4:1 or 3:1, as everyone had guessed, but a staggering 1:1![81] If East Germans had started working diligently, the burden on the West German economy would have been gradually reduced, but that was far from the case later. When "monetary affluence" suddenly arrived, the East Germans were far less hardworking than the West Germans had been for 20 years after the war. The brilliance of the German mark, until the birth of the euro, was not completely revived.

Germany was forced to fill the economic hole in the East German economy by printing money, with the inevitable result of inflation. By August 1991, inflation in Germany was approaching a rare 5 per cent. The central bank was forced to raise interest rates in a big way. Just three years ago, interest rates in Germany were 3 percent lower than in the United States, and for more than a year after German reunification,

---

[81] Ibid.

they were 6 percent higher! This is the biggest currency posture reversal on either side of the Atlantic since WWII!

Soaring interest rates in Germany have created a mess in the currencies of the EC countries. Countries were forced to follow Germany in raising interest rates, which resulted in a further worsening of the recession of the early 1990s. The UK, which had just joined the European Exchange Rate Mechanism (ERM) before it had a chance to feel the benefits of exchange rate stability, let the pound come under saturation attack from the likes of Soros and was forced out of the ERM under the pressure of German rate hikes. Italy, Spain and France were also successively bloodied by exchange rate speculation mobs.

In December 1991, in the midst of recession and crisis, the heads of Europe gathered in Maastricht, the Netherlands, to co-sign the Maastricht Treaty, and the EC became the EU. The central bankers, led by the Bundesbank, drafted the charter of the European Central Bank, according to the Delors Report's tonal door. The Mayo places the final completion of the monetary union in 1997 or 1999. Countries' fiscal deficits, inflation, interest rates, debt and other indicators will become the threshold of whether or not to enter the euro empire.

The birth of the euro has finally entered the countdown.

Euro Empire Genesis

Although the ECB is in theory a supersovereign institution, in practice it is difficult to escape the infiltration of sovereignty consciousness, and in 1994, the dispute between Germany and France resumed around the establishment of the European Monetary Agency, the preparatory body of the ECB.

First there is the question of the address of the ECB, which will mean whose sphere of influence the ECB is in in the future. Germany has been forced to propose Frankfurt as the best option, which is the seat of the German Central Bank, and the ECB is located under the watchful eye of the German Central Bank, facilitating the exertion of tangible and intangible influence. It was a substantial arrangement, and German Chancellor Kohl uncompromisingly refused to consider other cities such as London, Amsterdam, and Bonn. The French were ultimately unable to hold the line.

In the way the European Monetary Agency operates, the Germans insist that the Monetary Agency must have the function of open market operations, essentially playing the role of central bank intervention in the foreign exchange market, but the French are concerned that a large number of foreign exchange transactions will make Frankfurt replace Paris as the largest financial center on the European continent, and therefore propose to use the model of the European Central Bank and national central banks to operate jointly, trying to "decentralize" the open market operations. However, since the Germans provided the main currency reserves for the currency board, it was ultimately money that spoke.

In 1995, Chirac won the French presidential election and de Gaullism again gained political clout. Chirac, while not as distinctly French as de Gaulle, was sensitive to the question of French sovereignty. He's not an opponent of the euro, but he's a skeptic to say the least. Chirac, in particular, is always worried about the ECB's enormous power. Once the ECB is operational, France's national sovereignty over currency, exchange rates, and interest rates will be lost, and the fate of the French economy will be decided by those in Frankfurt, a very tangled situation for Chirac, who believes in nationalism. With Chirac's support, French Finance Minister Dominique Strauss-Kahn proposed a European "economic government" to provide a political check on the ECB. This is the same Kahn who later became president of the IMF and was taken down by the US over the scandal.

On this non-critical issue, the Germans were willing to make concessions. This is the "Euro Group", which was established in 1997. The "Eurogroup" is made up of EU finance ministers, who regularly discuss economic issues, especially exchange rate issues, with officials of the European Central Bank. The French hope to use the "Eurogroup" to infiltrate the political power of statism into the core of monetary power under internationalist control. Kahn expressed France's political imperative to strengthen government regulation of the ECB, "Without the existence of substantial and legitimate political institutions, the European Central Bank will soon be treated by the public as the only institution responsible for macroeconomic policy."

The Germans are clinging to the real power of currency issuance, and the so-called checks and balances of the "Eurogroup" against the ECB are merely non-binding "regular exchanges". The Germans, on the other hand, were much more practical, not only eating the "fat meat" of the right to issue money, but also sticking their chopsticks in the "fiscal power" of the pot.

In 1995, the Germans proposed a Stability Pact that would impose fines on countries with fiscal deficits of more than 3 per cent of GDP. This is pissing off Chirac of France. What? The Germans are still coveting the French budgetary power? A system of fines would not only make it impossible for France to use its financial power to stimulate the economy and improve employment any longer, but would also leave it in a state of derogatory disrepute by EU countries and world public opinion if it had to do so, with the franc subject to the bloody slaughter of speculative capital in the exchange rate market before the euro was launched. To Chirac's screams, the Germans lowered the bar a bit, changing the Stability and Growth Pact to the Stability and Growth Pact, and the effect of the harsh punishment was diminished.

The dispute between Germany and France over the appointment of the ECB president culminated in November 1997, when the central bankers of the EU member states unanimously proposed Duisenberg, the head of the European Monetary Agency, as the incoming ECB president. In practice, however, the ultimate power to decide on the choice of governors remains in the hands of French and German politicians. Duisenberg is the representative of the Netherlands, which has never been the heel of the Germans. In fact, the ECB's "constitution" has fully implemented and strengthened the Bundesbank's system, and whoever is in this position can only implement the Bundesbank's policies. This is determined not only by the power of the German economy and currency, but also reinforced by all the soft support systems that Frankfurt has to offer. However, the French could not take the plunge and insisted on putting Bank of France Governor Trichet in this position.

So-called supersovereign internationalism is pervaded by statism from the bone. The fact that there is only one power and a whole bunch of people vying for it, and that the competitors are all recommended by the sovereign state, creates a logical trap that cannot be escaped.

In May 1998, European heads of state were at loggerheads over the choice of the President of the European Central Bank, and almost unhappily broke up. Germany and France went their separate ways, with the French insisting that if Duisenberg were to become governor, he would have to leave in July 2002, six months after the start of the euro note. During the 12 hours of debate, the German, French, English and Dutch heads of state comically spat at each other.

> **Chirac:** *"Who made us have to spend all our time talking about how many more weeks he could work?"*
> **Cole:** *"You ask 'who', he didn't just come off the street, you know that by heart."*
> **Chirac:** *"He (Duisenberg) is a cow!"*
> **Cole:** *"I don't like it when people say that about him. I believe he has both virtues and talents. It is necessary for us to discuss this with respect."*
> **Chirac:** *"It was the media that called him that and we learned he had the nickname. I can't let the media call me that. We have accepted the fact that the ECB is set up in Frankfurt."*
> **Tony Blair** *(British Prime Minister, presiding): "There's not much point in us having this discussion."*
> **Chirac to Blair:** *"It's not serious either. You are such a wise and rigorous man, but the procedure is not wise and rigorous at all."*

After Chirac threatened to veto Duisenberg's candidacy and Kohl announced that Germany was ready to leave early, there was another scramble and finally a compromise was reached, and on 3 May 1998, Duisenberg was officially appointed President of the European Central Bank. For his part, Duisenberg immediately issued a statement that if he did not complete his eight-year term as governor, it would be entirely "voluntary" and that he would not resign, at least until the introduction of European paper money.

On January 1, 1999, the much-anticipated euro was finally born after nearly half a century of difficulties. The funny thing is that people still refer to the euro as a "frail and sickly premature baby".

EU national currencies, based on the European Currency Unit (ECU) of 1 euro, are converted at the market exchange rate as at 31 December 1998. The euro, at this time, is also an abstract, intangible currency, mainly used in the financial markets, banking and electronic payments. It was not until January 1, 2002, when the new euro banknotes and euro coins were introduced that the euro officially became the legal tender of the euro area.

The euro is derived from the European Monetary Unit (EMU), which is made up of a "basket" of European national currencies, the currency reserves behind each national currency are still mainly foreign exchange and national debt, so the euro is, in essence, the national debt and foreign exchange reserves of the member States as collateral, the currency issued.

This creates a problem inherent in the euro, where the national debt of member States is closely linked to their respective economic development and fiscal policies, and thus the root cause of the value of the euro comes from the economic and fiscal health of each country. The value of the euro cannot be guaranteed without control over the economies and finances of States. The crux of the euro's current predicament lies here.

The euro has been opened and there is no turning back, and a unified European Treasury is a prerequisite for ensuring its continued development. The current euro crisis provides an opportunity for "crisis-induced reform". The forces driving European integration have long since taken root, and the establishment of the European Treasury is not a question of whether it will or not, but when.

When a unified European Treasury finally appears on the horizon, will the birth of a United States of Europe be far away?

CHAPTER VII

The debt drive, the fragility of the American age

S ince the establishment of the "American debt empire" in 1971, the American debt, as a core asset, has been implanted in the monetary systems of the world. While U.S. debt went to Germany, Japan and France, real savings from those countries went to the United States. These savings were looted when the dollar depreciated significantly against national currencies. When the Germans and Japanese found out, they could only tolerate it because they needed strong military protection from the United States; when the French found out, Charles de Gaulle was furious and vowed to crush the dollar system; when the Europeans finally figured it out, the Middle Easterners, who were rich in oil, took over; when the savings of the Middle Easterners were almost siphoned off, the United States stuck the syringe of American debt, the "savings sucking blood", on the Chinese, who were both rich and poor.

The global surplus dollar is gradually creating a large "financial heterogeneous space" internationally. These "rootless" dollars, wandering around without regulation, are making money at an alarming rate, swapping tangible assets for huge bubbles, and robbing society of wealth with high leverage.

The globalization of finance is essentially the globalization of dollar-denominated debt, which has resulted in financial assets growing much faster and larger than real wealth, meaning that a significant portion of those assets, due to the lack of a wealth counterpart, are really just huge debts. The stagnation of the world economy will gradually deplete the cash flows that support these debts. When the risk of default increases, a large number of asset holders will inevitably concentrate on selling to cash out, which will lead to a plunge in asset prices, a paralysis of the financial system and a subsequent recession of the real economy, the recession in the United States in 1990, the global financial tsunami in 2008 and the debt crisis in Europe in 2011 were the inevitable result of the collapse of the debt-driven economic growth model.

Debt currency, the "cancer gene" of economic growth

The flow of money implies the transfer of assets behind it. Under the pre-1971 Bretton Woods system, the exchange of dollars and commodities would eventually manifest itself in the transfer of gold assets, which was the root cause of the depletion of the United States gold reserves and the worldwide run on the dollar as a result of the growing United States balance of payments deficit.

After the establishment of the US debt empire in 1971, the core assets behind the dollar became pure US debt, and the flow of the dollar simply meant the transfer of US debt assets. U.S. debt, in effect, became the ultimate means of payment for the transaction of major goods and services on the international market!

For the United States and the world as a whole, such a major change in the monetary mechanism would inevitably lead to an alienation of the economic growth model.

In the gold standard era, the driving force for economic growth came from the investment accumulated in national savings, while in the US debt standard era, the instinctive impulse for economic expansion gradually shifted from investment to debt. The core idea of capital and credit has changed from savings accumulation, to debt creation.

The investment-driven and debt-driven models of economic growth represent a world of difference in economic worldviews, with the 1990 recession in the United States, the 2008 global financial tsunami and the 2011 debt crisis in Europe having their roots in the fragile economic growth path that the world has been on since 1971. The current world financial crisis is a total liquidation of 40 years of a debt-driven economic growth model!

What is savings? What is an investment? What is consumption? What is wealth? Today's society has become increasingly rusty with these most basic concepts, words that are used so often in everyday life that people often don't bother to delve into them. Put aside the dizzying concept of money and return to the most primitive state of the economy and everything will be clear at a glance.

In primitive societies, if a hunter used a simple pike to hunt, he would have to take at least three hare a day to survive, and he would have to run after the hare, which would be physically exhausting, while harvesting very little prey. Soon he discovered from his companions that hunting with a bow and arrow and being able to shoot prey at a distance not only increased concealment and improved hunting efficiency, but also saved a lot of physical strength by not having to run at a rapid pace. With any luck, it was also possible to shoot up to the elk and have a great meal.

This hunter decided to make his own bow and arrow too, but it would take no short time. He would first go over the mountains to find tough, lightweight wood, then shade the felled wood to make a tight wood, and then make a bow out of the wood. He also had to find a very elastic cowstring and repeatedly smash it to make a bowstring. In the end, he also had to spend a certain amount of time making many arrows. At last count, hunters find it takes at least five days to complete the technical upgrade of hunting tools. During this time, he couldn't go hunting anymore, so he couldn't work on a hungry stomach, so the hunter went up early and hunted hard, and when he finally accumulated 15 rabbits, enough food for five days, he was able to start making the bow and arrow.

The 15 rabbits that are guaranteed to survive without hunting for five days are the hunter's "savings" and the making of a bow and arrow is the hunter's "investment". "Investment" is aimed at achieving more efficient hunting results, provided that there are sufficient "savings".

As a result, the hunter's "investment" has paid off handsomely, with the use of a bow and arrow that allows him to shoot more than five rabbits a day and, with luck, one elk. In addition to a full stomach, the hunter is able to take the extra prey and exchange it for much-needed clothing, and this is when he begins to "consume". Thus, the essence of consumption is an exchange! The premise of consumption is that the hunter must have surplus savings.

In the end, the hunters left more than enough food, the necessary bow and arrow improvement "investment", the necessary subsistence "consumption", and this is the "wealth" that the hunters had accumulated. Prey cannot be stored for long periods of time, so hunters need to find a means by which they can store their wealth for the long term, just in case they need it in the future. In the market trading, hunters find that gold and silver are very popular, and all people are willing to exchange their goods for gold and silver, which can be stored for a long time, but also easy to cut, carry, and calculate, everyone's sought after goods become "currency". The best feature of liquidity is that there are people who want it whenever they want it, so "liquidity" is best. Gold and silver then fulfilled all the requirements of the hunter for storing wealth, which is long term preservation, readily convertible and easy to use.

Gold and silver, from discovery, to mining, to smelting, to manufacturing, are equally labor-intensive, so that this particular currency, gold and silver, is exchanged with other fruits of labor in market transactions, and this exchange is an exchange of honest labor. The magic of gold and silver in trading is that it abstracts the complex exchange of commodities of different natures into pure and simple numerical ratios, thus reducing transaction costs, expanding the size of the market and promoting the social division of labor. Gold and silver have gradually become the most accepted "honest money" in the market, serving as a medium of exchange, a measure of value and a store of wealth.

If the maker of gold and silver, who adulterates the currency, and substitutes it for the good, uses the adulterated gold and silver in the marketplace in exchange for the honest labor of others, then that person is committing fraud! This currency, is the currency of fraud! If caught by the market, those who make fake gold and silver will be beaten up. If this person is the government, in control of the violent machine of the state, and the market participants are unable to resist, everyone is not willing to be defrauded, so fraud against fraud, the quality of goods will deteriorate and the trading order will be in chaos. The weakening of money as a store of wealth, the disintegration of the willingness to save in the long term, the prevalence of short-term behaviour, the rise of speculation and the spread of social impatience. Money is a contract of wealth, and to destroy the value of money is to destroy the contract of social equity of wealth, with the end result that market transaction costs rise, impeding economic development and stifling wealth creation.

The assets behind the dollar, replacing honest gold with the white bars of debt, are fundamentally disrupting the market economy, dismantling social equity, accelerating the division between rich and poor, and eroding the moral foundation!

When debts become money, this "rabbit-feeding" white paper will flood the banking system, and the so-called "savings" will no longer be the accumulation of the fruits of people's honest labour, but "rabbits" that do not exist now, and may not exist in the future. How could a hunter go hungry for the "investment" of making a bow and arrow? Where would there be real savings for honest exchange "consumption"?

The U.S. debt empire itself is increasingly short on savings, both to overdraft consumption and to borrow money to invest. The economic model on which it relies for growth is nothing more than "borrowing" other people's savings and enjoying a higher quality of life while making quick investments in financial assets to "make money". The American debt is used as evidence to borrow the savings of other countries, which Americans never seriously intend to repay, and when the "white bond" devalues the hunter, the real savings of the hunter holding the white bond will be gradually deprived.

U.S. debt, as a core asset, is embedded in the monetary systems of countries around the world. While U.S. debt went to Germany, Japan and France, real savings from those countries went to the United States. These savings were looted when the dollar depreciated significantly against national currencies. When the Germans and Japanese found out, they could only tolerate it because they needed military protection from the United States; when the French found out, Charles de Gaulle was furious and vowed to crush the dollar system; when the Europeans finally figured it out, the Middle Easterners, who were rich in oil, took over; when the savings of the Middle Easterners were almost siphoned off, the United States inserted the syringe of American debt, which "sucks the blood out of the savings", into the Chinese, who were rich but not poor.

After the 2008 financial crisis, Bernanke went on a money-printing spree that could neither increase Americans' "real savings" nor promote "real consumption" in the market, let alone "real investment". After all, printing money does not create a "hunter's rabbit" out of thin air. The only thing it does is make countries that have lent their real savings to the United States suffer a significant loss of savings.

In 1976 the world held $90 billion in U.S. national debt, and in 2011 that number reached $4.5 trillion! That's a 50-fold increase in just 35 years! Would anyone still believe that such an asset could be preserved? So in another 35 years, what will that number be? How many national currencies will countries create with such a currency reserve as collateral? The real savings of society, in the inflation of money, are constantly diluted and transferred, and eventually more savings are accumulated into the hands of the 1%.

When the American debt empire "blood-sucking" addiction, the blood-forming function of its own economy is weakened. Instead of spending a major portion of borrowed foreign savings in the U.S. real economy to strengthen the competitiveness of industrial products and improve the trade deficit, it was spent on unprecedented financial wealth creation. While Wall Street reaped staggering profits, what was left was a declining competitive industrial economy, a shrinking middle class with shrinking incomes, a vastly increasing number of poor people, and an over-indebted state and society. All the prosperity that comes from spending on debt is a mirage, and when the debt is unsustainable, the prosperity will be a thing of the past.

In the early 1970s, the U.S. debt empire banned gold, scrapped the fixed exchange rate and tied up oil pricing, but the dollar was far from winning. Mistrust of the dollar has led to a scramble to own gold, silver, oil and other commodities, with inflation like a blazing fire sweeping through all corners of the world and the American debt empire in turmoil.

The "SDR alternative account": a bloodless financial coup

When the collateral assets behind the dollar went from heavy gold to light U.S. debt, all dollar holders had an instinctive reaction of "wealth loss". The source of the U.S. debt is the U.S. fiscal deficit, and the long-standing "benevolent neglect" of the deficit problem by Americans has long broken the hearts of Europeans.

The sequel to the fiscal deficit is the growing inflation caused by the overdevelopment of the dollar. From 1958 to 1964, although the problem of the United States fiscal and balance-of-payments deficit was gradually exposed, Americans still held large gold reserves and confidence in the dollar remained, so that inflation was almost zero; in 1964, confidence in the dollar began to falter, as foreigners held more dollars than the United States gold reserves for the first time, and over the next four years, inflation rose to 2 per cent; in 1968, inflation rose to 4 per cent when the strategic defence of the United States gold reserves, the "gold mutual fund", completely collapsed. When Nixon announced the complete decoupling of the dollar from gold, inflation soared to 10 percent from 1972 to 1978, and by 1979, inflation reached a staggering 14 percent!

The two oil crises in 1973 and 1979 caused the price of oil to soar more than 10 times, as the most important energy and industrial raw material for the European and American economies, the price of oil soared, causing the entire economic train of industrialized countries to seriously derail. The dollar is fire, the oil surge is the wind, the floating exchange rate is oil, fire by the wind, the wind to help the fire power, fire on top of oil, inflation and recession with a prairie effect sweeping the world.

Pulled out the gold, a monetary magic pin, the world economic system immediately turned upside down and chaos into a pot of porridge.

Intractable, chronic hyperinflation distorts people's economic thinking and subverts society's notions of wealth. Going into debt was no longer a bad idea, as inflation was diluting the pressure to pay it off; overdrafting was quickly becoming the rage, enjoying the purchasing power of money now, as it would continue to rot; savers became fools, and the frugal became the old-fashioned ignoramus; the tradition of honest effort was abandoned, and speculation in wealth was widely celebrated; all long-term planning became anachronistic, and all short-term behaviour became mainstream. Hyperinflation has disintegrated the traditional moral values of society and destroyed the industrial spirit of the founding of the United States.

When the dollar depreciated and inflation prevailed, the profit-seeking nature of capital led to more capital flowing into speculation for quick gains and away from the long, arduous and risky nature of industrial investment. From 1947 to 1973, productivity growth in the United States was 3 percent, while from 1973 to 1979 it plummeted to 0.8 percent. Inflation, ever the natural enemy of productivity!

Internationally, the dollar, while tied to oil pricing, is reluctant to hold dollar-denominated assets any longer, even in the Middle East oil-exporting countries, in an era of hyperinflation as the dollar depreciates. The Europeans have long shown their impatience with the dollar, and the Japanese are secretly preparing to move dollar assets. By 1979, the world was on the brink of abandoning the dollar.

In August 1979, the oil countries issued a stern warning that they were seriously considering abandoning the pricing of oil in dollars in favour of IMF special drawing rights (SDRs).[82] The news undoubtedly alarmed the United States, and if oil pricing gave up on the dollar, the US debt empire would be in great danger of falling apart on the ground. Who else would want to keep holding on to the dollar when the world is already severely overstocked? A collapse in dollar confidence would cause everything non-dollar to go crazy and hyperinflation would be out of control.

The newly established European Monetary System (EMS), led by the Germans, has become an island of monetary stability in the midst of the dollar's devaluation and is in danger of being swallowed up by a wave of speculation. German Chancellor Schmidt has gone to the extreme of rage, telling the Americans in no uncertain terms that the long-standing "benevolent neglect" and inaction of the United States on the easing of the dollar is enough for the Germans! Europe has had enough too!

Anthony Solomon, Deputy Secretary of the U.S. Treasury, exclaimed in an internal memo:

> "At present, the U.S. faces an absolutely extreme and dangerous situation in the international foreign exchange markets... The main reason why the dollar is under tremendous pressure is this: it is almost universally believed that there will be a serious conflict between the U.S. and Germany over exchange rate policy and that cooperation between the two countries has broken down. The U.S. side wants the dollar exchange rate to remain stable or appreciate, yet Germany wants or expects the dollar exchange rate to depreciate... A massive avalanche of private money has long been unusually nervous and ready to flee the dollar. The pressure on the dollar is likely to cross the tipping point... Consistent with the current foreign exchange market situation and investors' psychological expectations, the United States is no longer confronted with a specific tactical problem, but with the potential for the situation to deteriorate rapidly into a full-blown devastating crisis."

In the midst of the worst crisis the dollar has faced in this post-war era, the Fed has even foreseen a real fear that the building will collapse.

---

[82] Research Department of Federal Reserve Bank of San Francisco, *Substitution Account*, 1980.

In the face of the world's abandonment of the dollar, the U.S. urgently formulated a backup plan to "rescue the dollar", which is through the IMF's plan to replace the dollar with special drawing rights (SDR). The core of this plan is to replace the US dollar with SDR and invest in US Treasuries with the recovered dollars.

This plan by the Americans is tantamount to "electrifying" the dollar and abandoning its status as an international reserve currency in order to defuse the world's anger against the dollar. However, the actual dominance of the American debt empire remains firmly in the hands of the Americans! In the past, there were other investment options for countries' dollar reserves in addition to buying U.S. bonds. In this way, SDR is just a skin, the lining is still U.S. debt, not medicine! The dollar standard has become the "SDR standard" in name, and the collateral for currency issuance is still US Treasuries. In the end, the U.S. national debt will become the real asset behind the world's unified currency and will never have to be paid back![83]

In 1979, the world currency faced a major inflection point. The Bretton Woods system under the Dollar Regency in 1944 was a time when the Dollar was in full swing, and the United States had the highest gold reserves and the most powerful military power in the world. In such a powerful background, the United States does not dare to hastily abolish the imperial throne of gold, but has taken the Xu Tu slow progress, "hostage gold to make the vassals" strategy, finally conquered the world's currencies. Today, the U.S. debt empire is on the rocks, the dollar is a street rat, and everyone is crying foul. At home, the economy is in decline, unemployment is high and inflation is rampant. In the international arena, the European backbone has appeared, Japan leaps to try, the Middle East pro-European anti-American, Russia tiger eyeing prey, not enough international support, the dollar "power down" easy, SDR commanding the hard![84]

At this point, the only way out of the U.S. debt empire is to take a shot at inflation, first stabilize the dollar confidence, and then take the long view of everything.

---

[83] Ibid.

[84] Ibid.

It is highly noteworthy that although this package was not ultimately implemented, it was prepared long ago around 1980 as a backup in the event of the collapse of the dollar.

Since the financial tsunami in 2008, the concept of "SDR alternative accounts" has once again surfaced in the international arena. The world's anger at the dollar's two rounds of quantitative easing is no less than the embarrassment the dollar suffered in 1979. For Asian countries with large dollar reserves, how to get out of the dollar's predicament has risen as a national strategy. The United States has now reintroduced the "SDR alternative account" programme, claiming to provide a solution to the problem of reserve currency diversification and alleviate global economic imbalances, when in fact, the new bottle is just old wine.

Until now, the IMF has been a limited pool of national currency reserves, mainly to provide recipient countries with "excess" liquidity from other countries to meet immediate needs. In other words, the IMF can only use existing funds, not create credit. Thus, the IMF is not yet the world's "lender of last resort" and there is a critical gap in the positioning of the world's central banks. In the future, the IMF cannot rule out the possibility of evolving the "basket" of SDR currencies into a concept similar to the European Currency Unit (ECU), while at the same time acting as the "world exchange rate police" and restoring the fixed exchange rate system. If the IMF is given a credit-creating function, it will become a magnified version of the "European Central Bank". Further down the line, I'm afraid the SDR will be upgraded to "World Euro". The monetary sovereignty of each country will be forced to be handed over to the IMF.

This will be a bloodless international financial coup!

Neoliberalism, the cry of the 1% rich

The petrodollar is a double-edged sword, and high oil prices have contributed to the stagnation of the US industrial economy while strengthening international demand for the dollar. The U.S. real economy's position in the global marketplace is losing ground to fierce competition from Europe and Japan. Corporate profits are shrinking, productivity growth is stagnating and capital structure is deteriorating due to high inflation. The industrial strength of the United States has been weakened most severely since the war. The dollar crisis further weakened the mechanisms by which Wall Street dominated the distribution of world wealth, and by 1975, the share of social wealth held by the richest 1 per cent of the American population had fallen to its lowest point since 1922.

The 1% of the wealthy have decided that the rules of the game must be completely changed to tip the scales of wealth distribution back in their favor. The American ruling elite, with the Rockefellers at its core, was determined to fundamentally overturn the welfare state system that had been established in the United States since the Great Depression of the 1930s, as well as the various restrictions on the expansion of wealth by the wealthy.

In the mid-1970s, John Rockefeller published *The Second American Revolution*, in which Rockefeller made clear the need for a radical reform of government, reducing its powers and "transferring the functions and responsibilities of government, to the greatest extent possible, to the private sector". In the book, Rockefeller deliberately selects economic cases that highlight the fact that government regulation of finance and business is unnecessary, that support for social welfare is a waste of money, and that only the unrestricted pursuit of profit by corporations, and the financial system that goes along with them, is the driving force behind America's growth. President Reagan famously said in the 1980s, "Government can't solve problems, government itself is the problem."[85] These words are the central idea of the Rockefeller book, without which Reagan would not have been chosen by the Golden Power group, I'm afraid.

The idea of the "second American Revolution" has sounded the American media's attack on the government, with inefficiency, incompetence, waste, deficits, inflation, and the government becoming the culprit of the economic recession. 1% of the rich are ready to burn the government's regulatory shackles on the financial industry and transnational corporations, taking advantage of the American people's discontent with inflation and unemployment. To put it bluntly, government redistribution of social wealth and support for public welfare prevents the freedom of the 1 per cent of the rich to seize more

---

[85] William Engdahl, *Gods of Money: Wall Street and The Death of the American Century*, Wiesbaden, 2009, p. 276–279.

wealth, who want a pristine forest of the weak and the strong, where the government cannot restrain the rich from squeezing the wealth of the poor, but has an obligation to prevent the poor from rising up against it.

In 1976, the "Second American Revolution" entered the implementation phase. The Trilateral Commission, an elite organization funded by the Rockefellers, could be described as a "central division" that sent senior cadres to the United States Government. With the support of the Trilateral Commission, the unassuming Governor of Georgia, Jimmy Carter, was elected President. Presidents without a background tend to be more docile, especially when major policy changes need to be introduced, and such weak presidents are needed. As a result, before Carter was even in the White House, the bigwigs had placed 26 "Trilateral Commission" cadres in key government positions, most of whom Carter had never even met. Carter's entire foreign policy and major domestic policies came largely from the Trilateral Commission. It was during Carter's tenure that the government began to deregulate the financial industry and a great deal of financial innovation began to emerge. When Reagan was elected president, he vowed to make deregulation and privatization the focus of his administration. It was during the Reagan era that the financial revolution erupted, with the result that the gold powers revolutionized the government!

In academia, the spirit of the "Second American Revolution" is enriched by the ideology of "neoliberalism", which embodies the main aspirations of the 1 per cent of the rich.

The University of Chicago, the home of monetarism, itself developed with funding from the Rockefellers, and the monetary policy that monetarism has shaped has contributed much to the 1% of the rich. Friedman, the monetarist guru, was sent to personally tutor President Reagan and, at the same time, to "open a small foxhole" for British Prime Minister Thatcher, the 1% of the rich need to unify in thought and action to coordinate the financial mega-changes in the United States and Britain. Friedman's monetarism began to take hold, arguing that "inflation is ultimately a monetary phenomenon" and that the core of anti-inflation was tightening the money supply. The dollar is the central tool of the 1 per cent of the wealthy to rule the world and distribute wealth, and must be firmly defended without hesitation. To that end, a significant rate hike and appreciation of the dollar was necessary. Because the main forms of wealth for the rich are financial assets, a strong dollar is a prerequisite for stable financial markets. Therefore, a strong dollar is in the core interest of the 1% of the wealthy in the US.[86]

A distant echo of monetarism is the school of supply that strongly calls for tax cuts and welfare cuts. They claim that with a big tax cut, the U.S. economy will "magically" explode into massive productivity, while welfare cuts will force workers to lose their lazy dependence and work hard to increase production. In fact, the biggest beneficiaries of the tax cuts are, of course, the 1% of the rich, while the victims of the welfare cuts are clearly the 99% of the middle class and poor. In the 1980s, when the whole supply school was in its heyday, the "magic" productivity explosion was not finally seen, and the American industrial economy, which was full of German and Japanese goods, never recovered the international competitiveness of the early 1970s.

Both the monetarist and the supply school, which is strongly opposed to government intervention, strongly call for privatization. With these theoretical foundations in place, America's ruling elite is poised to start in several directions and reclaim the power of wealth distribution.

With such a layout, the distribution of wealth in society would clearly benefit the 1% of the rich.

All of this has to start with tightening the currency and strengthening the position of the dollar. At this point, the position of Federal Reserve Chairman becomes all the more important. Paul Volcker is an ideal candidate.

Volcker's currency "chemotherapy", the U.S. debt empire turned to peace

On October 6, 1979, Federal Reserve Chairman Paul Volcker, who had just been in office for two months, convened a secret meeting of the Open Market Committee at the Federal Reserve Building to discuss how to move the knife on inflation. Volcker was a Rockefeller who started his career with the L.A. family's Chase Manhattan Bank (the predecessor of today's JP Morgan Chase) and was selected by the L.A.

---

[86] Ibid.

family's top minister, Robert Roosa, to train at the Treasury Department.[87] This Rosa was the general architect of the use of U.S. bonds to hedge European dollar reserves in the 1960s, when Europeans were forced to accept U.S. Treasuries instead of gold as the main investment option for foreign exchange reserves, Rosa can be considered one of the founding fathers of the U.S. bond empire. Under Rosa's tutelage, Volcker, who served as Under Secretary of the Treasury during the Nixon era, personally planned and participated in the "coup" to abolish gold. After the success, Volcker was promoted by the Rothschild family to the key position of governor of the Federal Reserve Bank of New York, holding the "military power" of the Federal Reserve.

In order to effectively stem inflation, Volcker decided to fundamentally change the Fed's approach to controlling the dollar's money supply by directly controlling the money supply (MS) and no longer using interest rates to indirectly regulate the currency.[88] Direct control of the money supply means holding the MS growth in check and liberalizing interest rates, no matter how high they soar, which are more like "chemotherapy" that kills cancer cells directly, which is cool and violent. The idea is to hold the interest rate, liberalize the currency and let the credit expand as it should. Indirect control is like taking traditional Chinese medicine, which focuses on nourishment, and is effective by stimulating the inner function of the economy. Direct control of the money supply has the advantage of being quick and forceful, although the side effects on the economy will be significant, as interest rates will fluctuate dramatically.

Why do conventional means of interest rate control fail? The root cause of this is also the dollar's excessive overpayment! The long and huge balance of payments deficit of the United States since the 1960s has meant that the United States has been printing dollars to export overseas, sourcing supplies from other countries, paying for the operation of costly overseas military bases and the cost of the war in Vietnam, resulting in the formation of an alarming force of European

---

[87] Joseph B. Treaster, *Paul Volcker: the making of a financial legend*, John Wiley & Sons, Inc. 2004.

[88] Steve Solomon, *The Confidence Game: How Unelected Central Bankers Are Governing the Changed World Economy*, Simon &Chester, 1995, p. 139–140.

dollar speculation, the size of which swelled rapidly from $315 billion in 1973 to $4 trillion in 1987! These "rootless" dollars, wandering abroad, have evolved into a "financial heterogeneity" that transcends sovereign frontiers. While they are stored within the financial systems of sovereign countries, their inherent drivers of expansion are divorced from the need for credit expansion for economic growth in each country, and manifest themselves primarily in the greed of transnational speculative capital for profit. They rampage between countries, they are not regulated by any sovereign central bank, and they rapidly reproduce themselves in a separate financial space.

This is the most significant change in the international financial landscape since the 20th century!

It was because of the European dollar that the American banking system changed dramatically in the 1970s. Under the orthodox fractional reserve system, the Central Bank requires commercial banks to "freeze" about 10 per cent of their deposits as reserves, which may be deposited with the Central Bank or held by the banks themselves to meet the occasional withdrawal needs of savers. When banks lend, the reserve ratio puts a constraint on their credit expansion. However, when European dollars can be borrowed conveniently and cheaply, banks are no longer bound by resident deposits and reserves, and they tend to lend first and then borrow from the European dollar market to meet reserve requirements or withdrawals by depositors, a financial innovation known as "managed liabilities".

The Fed, under the weight of the European dollar, suddenly found that traditional interest rate policy could not constrain the expansion of the money supply, with a steady stream of dollars pouring into the U.S. banking system from overseas, and banks were not short of money!

Once Volcker understood why interest rate policy was failing, he turned his full attention to the money supply, especially MS growth. The so-called MS is the sum of the cash in the hands of residents and their deposits in a checking account at the bank (Checking Account). Checking accounts are very popular in the United States, and people generally put money in checking accounts that they will soon have to spend, such as rent, mortgage payments, utility bills, and daily living expenses. So, MS represents the total amount of money that people are about to consume, which has a more direct impact on inflation.

Volcker designed an inflationary "chemotherapy" program, he locked the MS growth target between 4% ~ 6.5%, with "high energy money" as a means of regulation, if the credit expansion caused by speculative demand, more than the MS control target value, the Federal Reserve will contract the "high energy money", resulting in bank lending funds tight, the federal funds rate will automatically rise, curbing speculative credit expansion. When MS growth falls back into the target zone, interest rates will automatically slide as well.

To intensify its efforts, Volcker also announced an increase in the rediscount rate from 11 per cent to 12 per cent, and called for an 8 per cent reserve rate for banks' European dollar borrowings, large term savings and other "liability management" tricks.

When the first session was over, Volcker found that the federal funds rate had soared from 11.5% to 14%, speculative credit was still expanding at an accelerated pace, and by January 1980, inflation had reached 17%! From February to April, the federal funds rate continued to soar to 18 percent and the bank's lending rate to premium customers rose to 20 percent in tandem!

As a result, instead of killing inflation, Volcker's first course of "chemotherapy" left the economy on its last legs.

In the second quarter of 1980, the United States GNP plunged by 9.4 per cent and the unemployment rate rose from 6.1 per cent to 7.5 per cent. The money supply MS growth target, which had been planned to be locked in a range of 4–6.5 percent, has now exceeded 15 percent!

Faced with such a bad situation, Volcker was at a loss for words. In fact, the problem still lies with the European dollar. The soaring U.S. interest rates, on the overseas "financial heterogeneous space" has produced a strong arbitrage stimulus, a large influx of European dollars, not only to fill the "chemotherapy" caused by the currency shortage, breaking the MS ceiling, but also accelerated the speed of currency flows, stimulating the increase of inflation.

Inflation depends not only on the size of the currency, but is also greatly influenced by the velocity of money flows, which are far from as simple as the textbooks assume. It's like the quick-drop capability of the U.S. Army that allows a million troops to move quickly across the various theaters to flex the fighting power of five million troops. Faster currency flows will allow a dollar to play the role of a few dollars. Volcker apparently did not anticipate the abrupt change in the speed of currency flows caused by the accelerated influx of European dollars.

When the federal funds rate reached a staggering 18 percent, all those indebted faced extinction, they had to speed up their debt payments, the assets of the banks automatically shrank as they were paid off, and the corresponding money supply MS began to gradually decline.

The pivotal moment has come. As long as Volcker sticks with it, an 18% interest rate is like a mega-dose of "chemo" that, after enough time, will have a lethal effect on inflationary cancer cells, thus wiping out inflationary expectations, and a sustained decline in MS will eventually lead to a decline in interest rates. At this point, however, the economy was twisting and turning in agony, the people were crying out for help, and politicians were beginning to break into a rant. The U.S. Congressman issued a stern warning: "Volcker, you will be the first person to be paraded and brutally beaten!"

It's a big gamble! Don't you dare keep betting! If it doesn't work within six months, Volcker will become the most pathetic Chairman in the history of the Federal Reserve, with no face, no credibility, and will eventually be whipped by society for an eternity.

Volker's hand went soft and the credit began to loosen.

At this time, any retreat will be market super amplification, the Fed's anti-inflation determination was interpreted as "but err", so the entire market inflation expectations immediately turned over, speculative psychology again salted fish turn over! Over the next two months, the federal funds rate plummeted by half, to 9 percent, and with inflation still as high as 11 percent, both long-term and short-term rates fell to negative levels.

The credit expansion in the markets is boiling over again and the Fed is out of control all at once!

By the summer of 1980, the economy was recovering rapidly from the credit expansion and inflation was making a comeback. The growth of the money supply MS surprisingly surpassed 22.8%, twice as much as inflation. Volker's first course of "chemotherapy" was a complete failure.

Anti-inflation, no economy; anti-inflation, no dollar! After weighing the pros and cons, Volcker has renewed his anti-inflationary resolve.

Beginning in the fall of 1980 and continuing until the summer of 1982, Volcker initiated a second anti-inflationary "chemotherapy", and on 25 September 1980, Volcker raised the rediscount rate again to 11 per cent and the federal interest rate back up to 14 per cent. President Carter's dream of re-election became Volcker's first stab at inflation.

A full year of high interest rate policy, the dollar exchange rate began to soar, especially after Volcker started the second "chemotherapy", the market began to believe that this desperate man is playing for real. At this point, under Volcker's bullying, Germany and Japan began to lower interest rates. To further reinforce expectations of a stronger dollar, Volcker tightened the money supply again in May 1981, and from May to November, MS's growth rate dropped to zero for the first time, while the federal interest rate climbed to 19%! The European dollar accelerated back and the dollar's appreciation accelerated. This time the European dollar has not triggered a dramatic expansion in total money supply because no one is lending anymore.

In the year since then, the dollar has soared 34%!

Volcker's second round of "chemotherapy" not only continued to tighten the money supply and maintain high interest rates, but also opened up a second battlefield of "appreciation against inflation". US imports as a percentage of GNP is about 7%, and the downward effect of the price of imported goods due to appreciation should not have affected the overall price level of the US too much, but Volcker has understood the essence of anti-inflation, which is to fight psychological war! In an environment of high interest rates, there will be intricate psychological changes in people's perceptions of falling prices for imported goods. At a time when more and more people are paying off their debts and money supply growth is almost zero, the fall in import prices will lead people to believe that further price increases are a bit of a stretch. The exchange rate appreciated at this point, and it had the effect of setting off four or two pounds!

The Fed's composite estimate of this is that a 10 percent appreciation of the dollar would result in a 1.5 percent drop in inflation, half of which would likely be due to a drop in the price of imported goods and the other half would be purely psychological. And a 34% appreciation of the dollar would bring inflation down 5.1%. From 1980 to 1982, inflation in the United States fell from 13.5 per cent to 6.1 per cent, of which the appreciation of the dollar contributed about two thirds of the 7.4 per cent decline.[89]

Volcker's second round of "chemotherapy" thinking is to stick to the goal of money supply, maintain high interest rates, forcing people to repay their debts, reduce MS; at the same time, high interest rates lead to the return of the European dollar, strengthen the dollar appreciation expectations, forcing Germany and Japan to cut interest rates, leading to a sharp appreciation of the dollar; in the money supply reduction and high interest rates of "negative currency pressure", the exchange rate appreciation of the price decline effect, will be the market psychological high times amplification, ultimately reversing inflation expectations.

However, the massive tax cuts, the huge deficits, the Star Wars program, and the economic theories of the supply school that President Reagan embarked on, have Volcker worried that the valuable opportunities won by the victory in the anti-inflation war will not last long.

Borrowed Prosperity

The economic boom of the Reagan era was, in the final analysis, the result of "overdrafting" in three ways: borrowing from the future, borrowing from foreign savings, and "grabbing" cheap raw materials from the Third World.

For nearly three years, from the fall of 1979 to the summer of 1982, Volcker, with religious fervor, wielded the monetary baton to shatter inflationary expectations, while smashing the real economy into a deep concussion. From 1980 to 1985, the dollar appreciated dramatically by 50 percent! This is the most violent currency earthquake in modern economic history for a major country! As a result, the industrial economy of the United States has been wiped out. Unemployment has soared to 10.8 per cent, the heavy chemical industry has had its backbone broken, nearly one third of the workers in the steel industry have been laid off, automobile factories have closed down, production lines for equipment manufacturing have been largely idled, the

---

[89] Ibid, p. 148.

petrochemical industry has been drastically reduced in size, mines have been abandoned and even agricultural products have lost their international competitiveness.

Five years have passed and people have not even seen the "miracle", the United States is full of more Japanese cars, factories with more advanced German equipment, stores shelves full of cheap Asian consumer goods. Finally, the rebound in industrial employment has been made possible by Reagan's "Star Wars" military orders. The supply school, which claims to be at odds with government intervention in the economy, stumbled out of a deep recession with the most intense government deficits of the post-war period.

The period from 1983 to 1988 was the golden age of Reagan-era economic mythology. On closer examination, one finds that Reagan's economic prosperity was "borrowed" from the future. During this time, the U.S. fiscal deficit reached over $200 billion per year, representing more than 5 percent of the GNP. The US net domestic savings rate has fallen to 2.5 per cent from 6.5 per cent in the 1970s, and the huge fiscal deficit is responsible for eating away at domestic savings. A country's net savings is the "hunter's rabbit", which is the prerequisite for consumption and investment. Consumption, is when the hunter takes a portion of the savings rabbit and exchanges it with someone else; investment, is the other savings that the hunter consumes to make the bow and arrow. Since the end of the Second World War in the United States, net investment has been 7 per cent of GNP, and successful investment leads to more efficient output, so investment provides the impetus for economic growth. But during the eight years of Reagan's administration, net investment in the United States fell to a mere 5% of the GNP. The supply school had confidently promised that their policies would raise the US savings rate and increase net investment, which clearly blew the whistle!

When Reagan was elected President of the United States, the total private and public debt of the entire United States was $3.87 trillion, and by the end of the 1980s, that number had become $10 trillion!

With insufficient domestic savings, the Reagan administration not only overdrafted into the future in order to maintain the standard of living of American society, but also borrowed huge amounts of foreign savings overseas, to the tune of 14% of total U.S. savings! In 1984, foreign purchases of U.S. fixed-income assets (mainly U.S. Treasuries) jumped threefold to $37.4 billion. Japan's capital flows to the U.S. in one year alone amounted to a staggering $50 billion!

American scholars flirt that the US finally found its comparative advantage in the 1980s, and that was exporting US Treasuries!

The inflow of foreign capital reinforced the appreciation of the dollar, lowered the price of imported goods, stimulated U.S. consumption and widened the U.S. trade deficit. As a result, the U.S. current account was in surplus in 1980, and since 1984 the U.S. has been running an annual deficit of $100 billion, skyrocketing to 3 percent of GNP! American industry has been forced to move outward on a massive scale, and the core industrial assets that create national wealth have been fundamentally weakened.

Borrowing money from the future, borrowing money from foreigners, and instead of being used primarily for reinvestment in the industrial economy, the borrowed money was used by Wall Street to create a large bubble of rapidly expanding financial assets. Industrial investment in long-term capital in the United States has been largely abandoned, with export growth from 1983 to 1984 only half of what it was during the previous economic recovery, and imports twice as high. No wonder the American media commented,

> *"The 'miracle' of the supply school is finally here: it's that foreigners provide the bulk of the goods and most of the money. If the US policy in the 60s and 70s was 'spend and tax high', then the 80s was 'spend and tax high'."*

After Volcker controlled inflation, the U.S. economy began a strong 5 percent recovery, but U.S. industrial employment never recovered to 1970s levels. 1985–1986, the U.S. industrial equipment utilization rate fell again.

At a time when the U.S. industrial economy is in tatters, Wall Street is reaping the rewards. Volcker lowered the rediscount rate seven times in a row in the six months from the summer of 1982 to the end of the year, and the federal benchmark rate fell straight from 14 percent to 8.8 percent. The bond market and stock market are starting to enter a big bull market. From 1982 to 1987, Wall Street's stock market skyrocketed by 200%! The myth of financial wealth creation began to take hold in the United States.

The year 1984 was a turning point in the United States' financial megatrends, as domestic capital began to shift massively from banks to bond markets and international capital inflows shifted from Europe to Asia. By 1985, Volcker found that the U.S. money supply had begun to expand explosively again, but U.S. inflation had fallen from 4.4 percent in 1984 to 3.5 percent in 1985. MS has become increasingly inaccurate as an indicator of inflation, thanks to a plethora of financial innovations. The banking industry began to enter the money market on a large scale at the end of 1984, and the interest component of checking accounts increased significantly, indicating that money tended to "invest" rather than "consume", and that MS's expansion was no longer indicative of an accumulation of "consumer impulses ready to spend money immediately". As a result, the Fed quietly abandoned the goal-oriented monetary policy of MS growth starting in 1984.

The expansion of the money supply since 1984 has been diverted from the expansionary demand for credit generated by real economic growth and increasingly reflected in the demand for financial transactions stimulated by financial innovation; before the mid-1980s, the market value of US equities as a share of GNP was usually in the range of 8–20 per cent, but by 1986 this share had risen sharply to 100 per cent! This phenomenon suggests that credit expansion has escaped the constraints of real economic growth and has become the inevitable result of self-inflation of financial assets. The American debt empire has entered a new phase of development, and the dollar has since become an instrument "derived from financial transactions and subordinated to them for their sake".

The globalization of finance is essentially the globalization of dollar-denominated debt, which has resulted in financial assets growing much faster and on a much larger scale than real wealth, meaning that a significant portion of assets, due to the lack of a wealth counterpart, are really just huge debts. The essence of the freakish boom in financial markets is the debt-driven self-inflation of financial assets; before the 1980s, the total debt of private, non-financial corporations and the government in the United States was about 140 per cent of the GNP, and by the mid-1980s it had surpassed 165 per cent, the highest level of debt since the Great Depression of the 1930s! At the same time, the number of poor people in the United States has grown from 24 million in 1979 to 32 million in 1988.

Under the interaction of the European dollar, the banking system's off-balance sheet asset business has experienced an unprecedented boom, with financial innovations such as interest rate swaps, currency swaps, credit guarantees, floating rate mortgages, asset securitization, leveraged buyouts, futures and options on financial products, and so on, and in 1982 alone, as much as $230 billion of savings in the banking system flowed into the booming bond market. The central bank's monetary policy "braking system" for excessive lending in the financial markets is gradually failing, and systemic risks are increasing day by day.

In the anti-inflation war waged by Volcker, a large number of third world countries, such as Mexico, Argentina, Brazil, Nigeria, the Congo, Poland and Yugoslavia, were also "killed", all of which had the misfortune to fall into the "debt trap" of the United States dollar. in the 1970s, the petrodollars brought about by the oil boom flowed back from the Middle East to the "financial heterogeneity" of Wall Street and London. In the strategy of the "Second American Revolution", the redistribution of international wealth is a major concern for the rich 1 per cent, and the transfer of raw materials from third world countries to developed countries at low prices is a strategic objective that must be achieved.

With the petrodollar, international bankers began to lend on a large scale to third world countries in desperate need of importing expensive oil, but the U.S.-British banks made it a condition that the interest rate on the loans would have to fluctuate with the London Bank Offered Rate (LIBOR).

The high interest rate "chemo" anti-inflation campaign by the United States and the United Kingdom has had the wonderful effect of killing a few birds with one stone. The IMF, as the "international debt police" of the dollar, was pushed to the front line of the debt, and the contemporary "Sherlockians" want to cut off several times the "fresh flesh" from the third world countries, and the IMF's prescription for the third world dollar debtor countries is just a "laxative" prepared by Wall Street doctors, the more you eat, the faster your body collapses. the IMF requires the debtor countries to cut imports to the limit, the fiscal budget shrinks to a barely subsistence level, the currency devaluation to the export of raw materials jumped to the low price, so that the economic resources of the developing countries to the developed countries in an unprecedented transfer. As a result of the IMF debt restructuring, developing countries, which in 1980 had a dollar debt of only $430 billion, by 1987 owed $1.3 trillion in new debt to the contemporary "Shylocks", not including the $658 billion in principal and interest already paid. The countries of the Third World have suffered far more heavy losses than the two world wars combined.

In 1987, world raw material prices actually fell back to 1932 levels! The low raw material prices that started in the early 80's lasted a full 20 years! It was not until the beginning of the 21st century, when China's economy began to prosper, that this trend was reversed.[90]

For nearly 30 years, the 1 per cent of the wealthy have enjoyed a "harvest of meat" unheard of in modern economic history from the American middle class and third world countries, and the distribution of the world's wealth has reversed the pattern of the first 70 years of the twentieth century, accelerating its concentration in a tiny minority; the Occupy Wall Street movement, which began to spread rapidly around the world in September 2011, is the reason why the 99 per cent of the poor, no longer the silent majority, are ready to demand, in their own way, a rational redistribution of society's wealth, realizing the long-term damage done to their vital interests by the "golden world".

The neoliberalism of the Reagan era reduced the United States from being the world's largest creditor to the largest debtor in a matter of years. It was the stunning war-consumption of World War I that yanked the British Empire from the throne of the world's creditor hegemon, and it was the United States that used the power of the emerging creditor nations to force the European debtor nations to accept the hegemony of the dollar. In almost the same amount of time, neoliberalism reenacted the great reversal of the global debt-to-debt relationship caused by World War I. When Britain became a debtor nation, the British Empire declined, and when the United States became the largest debtor nation, the hegemony was instead more solid. This suggests that debt has replaced debt as the new scepter of world domination and that investment has given way to indebtedness as the main driver of economic growth, opening a dangerous era for a debt-driven economic development model.

Dollar on Ice and Fire

By 1985, when Volcker finally brought inflation down to 3.5 percent, the dollar had largely emerged from the 1979 worldwide dollar crisis. The monetary strategy of high oil prices tied to the dollar has

---

[90] F. William Engdahl, *Gods of Money: Wall Street and the Death of the American Century*, Wiesbaden, 2009, p. 292.

propped up the faltering U.S. debt empire and saved the dollar from the confidence panic of losing its gold, while the U.S. economy has paid the heavy price of hyperinflation and a severe recession. To make matters worse, the Soviet Union, a major oil exporter, made a fortune during the oil crisis of the 1970s, strengthening its military power to fight Star Wars with the United States. Having stabilized the hegemonic base of the dollar, the U.S. vacated its hands and prepared to pack up the Soviet Union.

From 1981 to 1984, the Soviet government's only means of earning hard currency from exports was the export of oil; in 1975, Soviet oil production was 93.1 million tons, and by 1983 it had grown to 130 million tons, but since the late 1970s, the Soviet Union's over-exploitation of oil had led to a lack of subsequent production capacity; in 1985, for the first time in history, Soviet oil production fell by 12 million tons due to the increase in extraction costs and the lack of funds, which coincided with the critical point in time when the United States conquered inflation.

As early as 26 March 1981, President Reagan, in his private diary, addressed the question of how to take advantage of the Soviet economy and its dependence on Western loans to deal a fatal blow to the Soviet economy, and in November 1982, President Reagan issued a directive on national security (NSDT-66) that clearly set out the secret mission to inflict damage on the Soviet economy, and in March 1985, in a secret message to the United States Embassy in London, Secretary of State Schultz mentioned that "the Secretary of State is extremely interested in the study being conducted by the State Department on the impact of the plunge in oil prices".[91] In September, the United States began to pressure the Saudis to dramatically increase their oil production to below $20. In April 1986, Vice President Bush Sr. came to the Saudi capital, Riyadh, to admonish the King that "market forces, not OPEC, are the best way to set oil prices and production".[92] This translates as a strong implication that Saudi Arabia is fully committed to increasing oil supplies and crushing world oil prices.

---

[91] Ibid, p. 295–296.

[92] Ibid.

As Saudi Arabia ramped up production, "market forces" caused the price of oil to plummet from $35 a barrel to below $10 in the spring of 1986. As a result, Soviet exports collapsed, Western lending channels were closed, food imports were lost, urban food supply quotas were tight, corruption was rampant through the back door, and anti-government sentiment among the Soviet population was growing. At the same time, oil broke off as the aid link that bound the Eastern European countries, causing them to centrifuge away from Germany under the pressure of huge Western debts, accelerating economic collapse and finally inducing the disintegration of the Soviet bloc.

The industrial economic base of the United States and the West after the war was heavily dependent on the supply of oil, and low oil prices brought economic growth and market prosperity, and soaring oil prices sent the economy into inflation and development stagnation. The anti-inflationary results achieved by Volcker's monetary means had lasting effects only reinforced by the 1986 oil price crash.

Inflation fell to 2 percent in 1986 and interest rates fell back deeply with it. Wall Street is boiling over.

But just as the U.S. stock and bond markets are booming, a huge volcanic lava of money is quietly gathering explosive eruptive force beneath the surface of financial markets.

The dollar's appreciation in the early 1980s was so far removed from the fundamentals of the US economy. Under the weight of the strong dollar, the US trade deficit has widened rapidly, the industrial economy has suffered an unhealable injury, and US manufacturing output needs to expand by at least 30 percent to rebalance the economy, but the strong dollar stands in the way of economic balance. The financial asset bubble on Wall Street inflated rapidly when large amounts of hot money from overseas poured into the United States, attracted by the high exchange rate of the dollar. Cheap credit is as cheap as cheap oil, making American consumers revel in debt. U.S. businesses, spurred by emerging financial instruments such as junk bonds and leveraged buyouts, have embarked on an unprecedented merger boom of unprecedented scale, with junk bond issuance alone reaching the staggering figure of $170 billion in the 1980s.

The fatal problem with corporate leveraged buyouts is that they replace years of hard-earned capital funds with debt. Not since the Great Depression has such a high level of indebtedness been achieved in the capital formation of American businesses. More fundamentally, there is also the fiscal deficit that the U.S. government cannot contain, which is both the gospel and the curse of dollar hegemony. Since the United States has chosen the path of a debt currency, since debt has become the root of power in the American debt empire, and fiscal deficits are the inevitable result, since surpluses will redeem the debt and thus dismantle the basis of that power, how can one expect the American treasury to truly move toward frugality and responsibility?

The UK deregulated its foreign exchange in 1979, and Japan followed suit in 1980. Since the United Kingdom is the largest market for the dollar in Europe and Japan has rapidly increasing dollar reserves, these two countries have opened the floodgates for the free flow of international capital, and the world's financial markets have since become even more volatile and dark. With insufficient savings in the U.S. and an excess in Japan, the serious imbalances in the world economy were exposed in the 1980s.

In 1986, the U.S. economy was on the verge of another recession, but Washington failed to realize the magnitude of the problem.

By this time, the Reagan administration's Secretary of the Treasury had been replaced with James Baker, the rising star of the U.S. ruling elite, and the Baker family had four generations of ties to the Rockefeller oil empire, as well as deep ties to the Bush family. He was entrusted with the task by Reagan despite having previously opposed him in the campaign. Baker understands that the dollar must depreciate, but is reluctant to confront Volcker's most pessimistic prediction that the dollar will repeat the nightmare of the 1978 world sell-off frenzy. If this most pessimistic scenario were to occur, Walker's parachute would be to be forced to raise interest rates and stop the free fall of the dollar. And a rate hike is Baker's big pet peeve, as he has learned from Volcker's anti-inflationary insanity of categorical rate hikes, which would be another economic holocaust. His hardcore brother, Vice President George W. Bush, Sr. has decided to run for president in 1988, and the recession will destroy Bush, Sr.'s prospects, while he will also cut off his political life. Baker is determined to achieve an orderly devaluation of the dollar with his own set of methods.

To this end, Baker proposed a two-stage programme: first, the establishment of a similarly enlarged version of the European Exchange Rate Mechanism (ERM), which would allow the major currencies to float between 10 and 15 per cent against the dollar, in the hope that this would force other countries to defend the dollar and avoid a possible collapse. Then, a mechanism for coordinating the economic policies of each country was established to eliminate the imbalance between the U.S. economy and Europe and Japan. In other words, Baker is whimsically hoping to come up with a monetary system that is bigger and more complex than the eurozone. Central bankers who have been through the twists and turns of the European monetary union are shaking their heads, not to mention the fact that Baker wants to create a world monetary union led by G5 finance ministers and played by central bankers. Because once the exchange rates of countries are tied, monetary policy must revolve around them, and central banks must commit themselves to the need for interest rate policy to serve exchange rate changes, how can central bankers bow down to the dictates of the finance minister?

On September 15, 1985, the powerful Baker simply shrugged off the central bank governors and convened a secret meeting of the finance ministers of the five countries to discuss the U.S. proposal, which was the "Plaza Agreement" reached a week later. This agreement does not specify specific requirements for the central bank; all Baker wants is the trend of a depreciating dollar. The central bank governors were relieved. As a result, Baker's "Square Deal" itself had a huge market impact, with the dollar depreciating by 12 per cent against the mark and 8 per cent against the yen a week later, and by January 1986 by about 20 per cent.

Baker's confidence was boosted by his initial victory, and in January 1986, in order to protect the gains from the dollar's depreciation, Baker continued his efforts to persuade Germany and Japan to introduce economic stimulus and to cut interest rates at the same time as the United States. Baker's idea is that everyone cuts interest rates together, the dollar doesn't rebound, and the economy benefits. The fiscal stimulus, in turn, is counting on Germany and Japan to increase imports into the United States and rebalance the U.S. economy. Baker's fiscal stimulus package was rejected on the spot, and the Germans claimed that it wasn't forcing inflation on us, that Germany could tolerate high unemployment at 9%, but that the bitter lessons of history made Germany never tolerate inflation.

After hitting the wall, Baker turned around and asked Volcker to cut interest rates, which Volcker flatly rejected. As a result, Baker took advantage of the change of two Fed governors, for Bush Sr. to insert "his own people", the recruitment condition is "dare not say no to Volcker". After the changeover, Reagan Bush Sr. outnumbered Volcker at the Fed. At the Fed meeting on February 24, 1986, Volcker was suddenly "cornered". Most of the directors recommended that the rediscount rate be reduced from 7.5% to 7%, Volcker in the complete absence of psychological preparation, abnormal anger, surprisingly fell out of the door, this is the first time in the history of the Federal Reserve "coup".[93] Baker is also surprised to see the extent of the flip-flopping. He does not want to "abolish" Volcker, but to force Volcker to give in by "admonishing" him. He knew that Volcker's share of Wall Street, if it went public, the stock and bond markets would collapse the next day, and other central banks would sit back and watch the dollar fall off the cliff, by which time, Baker would be out of pocket. Baker had to compromise, and although Volcker did not say anything, he hated the "coup d'état" to the bone.

"The depreciation of the dollar after the Square Deal" did not result in a soft landing for the U.S. economy, the depreciating pressure on the dollar increased sharply, and the plunge in the dollar that Volcker feared was already showing clear signs, with data from the second quarter of 1986 showing that foreign central banks had stopped buying U.S. debt and that private capital inflows from abroad were shrinking. Yields on US long-term bonds are already on red alert.

Baker became anxious, the Germans were far more difficult to deal with than the Japanese, who were adamantly unwilling to engage in fiscal stimulation, and Baker had to offer the United States to reduce the fiscal deficit in exchange, and the stubborn Germans remained unmoved. The US dollar plunged sharply in the dark cloud of market depreciation, and as a result broke through the umbrella of the "European Exchange Rate Mechanism" (ERM), which Germany has painstakingly operated, German companies faced with the dollar depreciation, panic, have stopped investing, the momentum of German economic growth instantly collapsed.

The Germans had no choice but to accept the "Louvre Agreement" of February 1987, in which Baker demanded that interest rates be lowered to the level of the United States in order to form a protective net against the free fall of the dollar. In return, of course, Baker

---

[93] Steve Solomon, *The Confidence Game: How Unelected Central Bankers Are Governing the Changed World Economy*, Simon & Schuster, 1995, p. 309–310.

promised to reduce the US fiscal deficit to 2.3 percent of the GNP. Volcker was rather dismissive of Baker's promise, "You would have lost faith then, knowing full well that you could not achieve that goal. Why not say an ambiguous number?" Baker admitted this privately, but since President Reagan publicly stated that he wanted to achieve the 2.3 percent deficit reduction goal, he could not have sung the opposite tune publicly. The US naturally failed to deliver on this promise, because when it came time to state it, Baker wasn't going to take it seriously. On the "Louvre Agreement", the British comment was most spot on, "This is the direct descendant of the 'Square Deal', when we all thought the dollar should be devalued, and now we all agree that the dollar needs stability".

After the "Louvre Agreement", the dollar continued to fall, and the central banks used their milk to block the dollar from being pelted in the face, and by September 1987, the countries had eaten a suffocating 70 billion dollars! In fact, they had to print the local currency to buy dollars. Central banks, whose central reason for claiming independence is their refusal to print money for government deficits, are at this very moment printing money wildly for the deficits of the US government.

Even that didn't stop the global stock market crash of 1987 triggered by the collapse of the dollar.

Greenspan: The Last Savior of the Financial Markets

Volcker left because future President Bush Sr. felt he could not be trusted. In June 1987, Volcker knowingly offered to resign, abandoning the embarrassment that would come with asking for re-election. Greenspan came in with a roundness that made one think he might be more obedient than Volcker, Wall Street liked him, Washington accepted him, and Greenspan was more of a seasoned politician than an earth-eater like Volcker. Volcker took office just in time for the collapse of the dollar in a major crisis, is considered to be in critical command, Greenspan inaugurated once again encountered the dollar out of control crisis, eight years of history just finished a cycle, the dollar rose wildly that year, is now falling wildly down.

Baker was already in shock when, at the annual meeting of the World Bank and IMF on September 30, 1987, Baker unexpectedly proposed the use of commodity prices, including gold, as an indicator of inflation to reduce exchange rate volatility, and many on the Bush

Sr. campaign team suggested reconsidering the monetization of gold. Obviously, when the dollar gets out of hand, the benefits of a fixed exchange rate and a strong currency will make politicians tick. Central bank governors were even more dismayed by the statement of the Chancellor of the Exchequer, who went so far as to propose a more radical "permanent and adjustable exchange rate mechanism". The Bretton Woods system, represented by gold, is the Treasury as the power of the central mechanism, central banks are only a supporting role, while the European Exchange Rate Mechanism (ERM) gradually handed over the exchange rate power to the central bank, to the euro era, the European Central Bank is complete monetary centralization, the British Chancellor of the Exchequer's proposal is the way of Bretton Woods, central banks can not agree?

When the report of the US trade deficit far exceeded expectations came out, even the Japanese, who were most cooperative with the US debt empire, began to sell US dollar assets frantically, and the US 30-year Treasury yield should break the psychological mark of 10%. At this point, Treasury yields are approaching four times the yield of stocks!

The biggest hope for a scorched-headed Baker is for other countries to cut interest rates and push for economic stimulus to give the dollar some breathing room. And the U.S., with interest rates at best unchanged, a highly indebted economy and a badly bubbled stock market, cannot withstand the stimulus of a rate hike. The stubborn Germany is the biggest headache for Baker, who is not willing to stimulate the economy, but is prepared to raise interest rates, and even gave Baker the idea that the United States "should have a recession", so as to solve the problem of imbalance. Baker was so angry that he nearly turned his back.

On Sunday, 18 October 1987, Baker, who was full of thoughts about how to force the Germans to give in, inadvertently said on national television that the United States would not "sit back and watch the trade surplus countries raise interest rates and squeeze the hopes of global economic growth, and they want to expect the United States to follow suit".[94] This is interpreted by the market as the "Louvre

---

[94] Ibid.

agreement" of cooperation faces a breakdown, Germany and Japan to raise interest rates and the United States does not follow, then the dollar is bound to accelerate the plunge. In that case, who would dare to hold US debt assets? People are dumping US bonds like crazy, US bond yields will skyrocket and the appeal of stock returns will be gone!

On Monday, the New York stock market blew up a storm of stock plunges, erupting into one of the biggest crashes in history. The Dow Jones has retreated 508.32 points in one day, down 22.6 percent! The stock market crash swept across the world, with London, Frankfurt, Tokyo, Sydney, Hong Kong and Singapore all suffering strong shocks, with stocks falling by more than 10 per cent. The stock market crash frenzy has caused great panic among stockholders in Western countries, with many millionaires reduced to abject poverty overnight and thousands of people having mental breakdowns and jumping to their deaths. The day was dubbed "Black Monday" by the financial community and "the worst day in Wall Street history" by the New York Times.

Greenspan had just taken office when he encountered such a major crisis, knowing that everyone would compare him to Volcker, and the time had come to make a name for himself! He decisively declared that "in fulfilling its role as a central bank and in support of the proper functioning of the economy and the financial system, the Federal Reserve today reaffirmed its commitment to guarantee liquidity in the financial system." This statement actually indicates that the central bank is ready to use money printing machines to save the stock market, a statement that implies that the Federal Reserve is not only the lender of last resort to the banking system, but also becomes the final savior of the financial markets.

The stock market has temporarily stabilized the panic, but the dollar will come under more downward pressure as the Fed's bailout has caused long and short term US interest rates to fall in unison, thus widening the gap with German rates. As the world turns its attention to Germany, will the Germans step in to save the dollar and the world stock market?

On 22 October, the German central bank met as usual. Governor Ball set the tone for the meeting by making the unassuming first comment, "Baker got in trouble, we just responded". The council members then proceeded to analyze the domestic economic situation in Germany in a slow and methodical manner, paying little attention to the global stock market disaster. When invited to speak, German Finance Minister Stoltenberg, who was so anxious that he stressed the importance of international cooperation, "It was wrong to raise interest rates (before the crash)," was shocked by the global stock market crash, and his frequent attendance at international conferences made him empathize with the anxieties of other countries. But Poe is unmoved, and he doesn't trust the government to determine the market. Eventually, the Bundesbank announced that it would not cut interest rates and even hinted at a rate hike under certain circumstances.

The world's stock markets are in disarray, and Baker is gnashing his teeth in hatred as he finally learns about the rock-solid independence of the Bundesbank! Even if the sky were to fall, as long as the Bundesbank feels it is right, no one could shake their resolve. By comparison, Greenspan is much better at talking.

On the same day, the German central bank's statement immediately triggered a new plunge in the dollar and the European exchange rate mechanism was in crisis. Things soon stabilized, though, and it turned out that the Japanese were sweeping the market with a staggering appetite for $2 billion a day as U.S. stocks plummeted, and the dollar temporarily gained support. However, the gap between interest rates on US long and short term bonds and international market levels is still widening, as if a high hanging sword is always hanging over the dollar exchange rate and international speculators are still hovering like vultures over the ailing dollar. In theory, the central bank does not have a direct responsibility to manipulate the foreign exchange market, and as the defender of the market economy, Greenspan should stand idly by and watch the market fight between short and long. The United States often accuses other countries of trying to manipulate the exchange rate, but when someone dares to move on the dollar's head, the Fed will not hesitate to pull the butcher knife.

At the end of 1987, under the circumstances of the dollar crisis is still accelerating, Greenspan decided to launch a "dollar short hanging war", the total attack was scheduled for Monday, January 4, 1988, while the foreign exchange traders of various countries just returned to the trading table, killing them by surprise. This time Greenspan personally organized it, the Japanese and German central banks agreed to join forces, and the Federal Reserve Bank of New York became the main trader. The challenge for Greenspan is to reverse market expectations of a falling dollar. The international foreign exchange market has a whopping $64 billion in daily trading volume, and if central banks go hard against the market, the billions or tens of billions of dollars of intervention money will soon be swallowed up by the market. Greenspan knew that in the battlefield of forex trading, the most important way to win is psychological warfare. At the right time, a high-profile shot was taken to crush the most important dollar shorts with the momentum of a Tarzan, prompting a reversal of the sheeple effect, and the so-called defeat was like a landslide, and the rest of the work will be solved by the market automatically.

Monday, January 4, Asian markets are about to open, just after the holiday of foreign exchange traders are still in the holiday lethargy, their brains on the market direction has not yet had time to form a clear judgment, the dollar still seems to be in the weakness of the decline. At the moment, it's still Sunday night in New York, and foreign exchange traders at the Federal Reserve Bank of New York are keeping a close eye on the movements of overseas markets, "like the race gate at a racetrack before it opens and the restless horses nervously feel any movement around them that would be a signal for them to start galloping".

Waiting for the market to officially open, the traders of the Federal Reserve Bank of New York immediately called the banks of Japan and other Asian countries to ask for quotations, the Asian foreign exchange traders were astonished, they almost never received a direct quote from the foreign exchange traders of the Federal Reserve Bank of New York, and no matter what the price of the dollar, see the goods! This suggests that today's market is unusual and is likely to be a major move by central banks to join forces. That's the kind of high-profile strike that Greenspan wants to make first and shock the market. The Fed's laying orders are surging out, gaining momentum, and pushing the dollar intermittently higher on both FX futures and spot. The big dollar shorts in Asian markets quickly sensed that something was up and they immediately pulled their legs and ran for their lives. The foreign exchange market in the small and medium-sized retail investors are not sure, only to see the short large is retreating, the foreign exchange market at a time people turned over, chaos. Immediately afterwards, the major media began to race to report the strong rally of the dollar in the foreign exchange market, further amplifying Greenspan's expectation of market psychological shock, the sheeple effect immediately reversed. European and U.S. markets expanded the battle along the way, and dollar shorts were killed in a bloodbath. In just two trading days on Monday and Tuesday, short orders in the international foreign exchange market for the dollar were nearly extinct. The dollar gained 8.3 percent against the yen and rebounded as much as 10.4 percent against the mark in two days. The stock market in New York soared 4 percent, while the price of 30-year U.S. Treasuries rose sharply at the same time.

Later, the Federal Reserve revealed that Greenspan in the foreign exchange futures market under the odd soldier is a kind of "innovation". Greenspan's strategy of winning with a positive fit and winning by surprise, coupled with psychological warfare, public opinion warfare, air traps, and a major assault on Asian markets, was a major success in the dollar defense war. The actual amount of money that central banks actually put into intervention was surprisingly small, totaling less than $4 billion, with the Bank of Japan probably contributing $1 billion, the Bundesbank about $800 million, and the Federal Reserve only $685 million. With such a low cost and such a great effect, it can be said that the central banks have intervened in the foreign exchange market, the most impressive performance.[95]

In this battle to defend the dollar, Greenspan's superiority over Volcker comes to the fore. Greenspan simply do not need to raise interest rates to protect the dollar's stupid approach, but used the foreign exchange futures this strategic air power, in the dollar short behind the bombardment, and in foreign exchange, stocks, bonds several major battlefield concerted combat, and achieved a low-cost high yield of strange and good results. If Volcker fought the costly, deadly Vietnam War, Greenspan fought the precision strike, non-contact Gulf War. Since then, the strategic tactics to strengthen the position of the dollar, no longer rely on the traditional interest rate hike, but in foreign exchange, futures, stocks, bonds, commodities, media, rating agencies, economists, geopolitical, military, diplomatic and other areas to carry out a highly coordinated "over the limit war". in May 2011, just as the world generally bearish on the dollar, long on gold, the United States suddenly launched a new dollar defense war, once again embodies the essence of this strategy.

But Greenspan's dollar defense war also exposes a larger problem, is central bank intervention in the foreign exchange market, or is it a

---

[95] Ibid.

free market economy? The central bank as a foreign exchange market referee, should have been to the game of short and long sides of the wall to maintain the market order, but now actually directly off the field, and is holding the football directly into the goal of one side.

The so-called exchange rate manipulation, Greenspan is the first prize!

The information revolution, why is life short?

From Reagan to Bush Sr. the entire US economic growth of the 1980s was largely based on debt expansion. Inflated assets bring inflated debt, which is ultimately financed by the real economy. At a time when the real economy can no longer provide sufficient cash flow and foreign savings borrowing is facing drying up, the bursting of the asset bubble will highlight the ugly liabilities that were previously masked by the boom. The recession then becomes an inescapable nemesis.

When the Japanese stock market crashed in 1990 and the economy plunged into a prolonged depression, America's most important source of foreign savings was cut off. Germany was busy with national reunification, with domestic funds being diverted to the East German region to revive the economy and unable to export any more savings. This could be a disaster for the American debt empire, which relies heavily on foreign savings.

The rate of expansion of liabilities of US companies has significantly outstripped the growth of tangible assets such as equipment and plants, resulting in a decline in corporate net assets from 94.5 per cent of GNP in 1980 to only 74.3 per cent in 1988, with the profits generated by tangible assets no longer able to support the huge debt. When the asset bubble burst, the pressure to repay corporate debt principal and interest doubled. The $200 billion junk bond market is plunged into a winter of lost liquidity. Commercial real estate is in dire straits, general real estate is in dire straits and the $1 trillion mortgage-backed securities market is in danger of being wiped out. Overdrawn consumers are forced to tighten their belts and accelerate debt repayment. Real estate shrinkage, consumer loan delays, corporate debt defaults, leading to a dangerous banking system, nearly a quarter of the banks have been in the mortal coil, they control $750 billion of problem assets, the Federal Reserve nightly alarm. Even more deadly, the U.S.

government's fiscal deficit has reached an eye-watering $400 billion, or 6.5 percent of the GNP! An industrial country that was once incredibly powerful has become an "economic patient" that is gradually losing its competitiveness in the world market; an industrial country that was once the world's largest exporter of capital has become an "economic paralysis" that makes it difficult to live on its own without foreign savings and blood transfusions; a middle-class paradise that once gave 99 per cent of ordinary people the hope of a rich life through hard work has become a paradise where only 1 per cent of financiers who take advantage of speculation and risk have privileges.

This is the full legacy of the US debt empire's transition to a debt-driven economic growth model from the 1980s!

Greenspan is facing the first post-war debt implosion recession, and this is only the early stages of the development of such a crisis, not knowing how many times simpler it is than the far deeper debt crisis of 2008! After all, the size of the total U.S. debt at this point is only 180 percent of GDP, much smaller than the 300 percent in 1929 and 350 percent in 2008.

Reducing debt so that businesses and consumers can reload lightly is the only way out of the crisis. Nonetheless, the 1990–1991 recession was more complicated and the recovery period longer than other post-war recessions, and real estate prices in 1990 did not gradually recover until 10 years later. The whole economic boom didn't start to pick up again until the mid-1990s.

And the driving force behind this economic boom is the reverie-inducing age of the information revolution.

Human scientific and technological progress often takes a long time to accumulate, and when technological breakthroughs in scattered fields converge towards a common focus, there is a sudden explosion of productivity. The same is true of the information technology explosion. After World War II, the emergence of semiconductors opened the curtain of the information revolution, the invention of the integrated circuit in 1958, the computer to the center of the information revolution, microprocessors, networks, satellites, optical fiber, lasers and other areas of technological breakthroughs in the field of communications to form a convergence effect, and laid the foundation of Internet technology. When the first graphical browser, Netscape, appeared in 1995, the first high point of the information revolution was reached with a bang.

This process is very similar to the post-war petrochemical industry on industrialization produced a major push, oil and chemical industry in different fields respectively accumulated decades of research results, when thousands of technological breakthroughs in the Middle East found cheap oil under the convergence effect, immediately triggered the outbreak of petrochemical industry, fundamentally breaking through the bottleneck of industrial energy and raw materials, bringing about the European and American post-war economy 20 years of sustained prosperity.

The enormous impact of these two major technological revolutions on economic output is evident from the productivity data of the United States for more than 100 years, with the United States experiencing three periods of high productivity during the 111-year period 1889–2000: the first, from 1917 to 1927, with a 3.8 per cent increase in productivity; the second, from 1948 to 1973, with a 2.8 per cent increase; and the third, from 1995 to 2000, with a 2.4 per cent increase. The interval between the three productivity bursts, roughly 20 to 25 years, is exactly one generation.[96]

Both petrochemicals and information technology have had a direct and far-reaching impact on all aspects of human society. The various new materials created by petrochemicals have transformed almost everything that humans can touch, and the vast amount of information brought about by information technology has provided a nearly limitless experience that the human brain can perceive. What they have in common is that they break through the old supply bottlenecks and give rise to a series of new industries that penetrate all corners of the traditional sphere and create new products and services that are generally accepted by society, which will greatly increase the productivity of other industries when they provide them with raw materials, equipment or services, and grow at a very high rate when they form new industries. They touch the nerves of the economy at all levels, they bring together inventions in numerous fields of science and technology, and they have a permanent and irreversible impact on the quality of human life.

---

[96] Laurence H. Meyer, *A Term At the Fed: An Insider's View*, Harper Business, 2004, Chapter 9.

However, what is the reason for such a huge gap between the continued impetus of petrochemicals to world prosperity for a full 20 years, and the remarkable contribution of information technology to economic growth, which seems to have lasted only five years?

The reason is a change in the pattern of economic growth! During the two decades of the post-war economic boom, the world economy, under the Bretton Woods system, maintained a stable exchange rate regime and the intrinsic value of money, and the driving force of economic development in all countries was based on real domestic savings and a relative balance between investment and consumption. The "financial heterogeneous space" created by the vast capital without borders is still small, and the power of speculative capital is not yet in place. Investment is a practical contribution to the creation of inventions, the improvement of technology, the saving of raw materials and the reduction of energy consumption, and economic prosperity is based on the steady growth of the real economy. This model of investment-driven economic growth creates significant and real social wealth in a stable monetary environment. Under a relatively equitable mechanism of social wealth distribution, the poor and the rich, the ruling elite and the middle class, are able to share the fruits of economic growth, resulting in a socially balanced production and consumption that allows economic prosperity to be sustained over time. It is thanks to this that the 20-year expansion of the petrochemical industry has given a sustained impetus to industrial economic prosperity.

After 1980, the United States and the United Kingdom spearheaded a paradigm shift in economic growth, with the investment-driven model of healthy development being replaced by a fragile, debt-driven growth model. The prolonged overhaul of the US dollar in the 1980s created an unprecedented "financial heterogeneous space", in which a group of greedy and huge financial monsters with a super-hungry appetite for profit and normal returns from the real economy simply could not satisfy their rapidly expanding appetite for self-inflation. They generate money at an alarming rate, replacing tangible assets with huge bubbles and robbing society of wealth with high leverage. They break the normal growth cycle of the industry, they use "financial hormones" to produce the fruits of technology that are not yet ripe, they disregard the economic logic of coordinated growth of the industry, their key to making money is that everything must be faster, faster and faster.

The misfortune of information technology is that, at a far from mature stage, it has encountered a frenzied over-investment of capital and, while information technology is still gradually penetrating into other industries and has not yet formed considerable benefits, it has formed a serious surplus in its own industry chain that cannot generate sufficient returns. Overinvestment has created irreparable waste of savings, and the bursting of the bubble has covered the glory of the information revolution. The ill effects of uprooting the seeds have pushed back the good prospects of the information age by more than 10 years.

After the NASDAQ collapse in 2000, the US debt empire unleashed an even bigger real estate bubble, a financial crisis much larger than the 1990–1991 debt bubble, and pushed the recovery of the information revolution into the more distant future.

The economy is going to grow, and the technological revolution is going to spread like wildfire. However, with a debt-driven growth model, the next boom will also be a short-lived blip!

CHAPTER VIII

The Dragon Has Regrets, China Model 3.0 Upgrade

In the 30 years before the reform and opening up, China's industrialization followed the path of the Soviet Union, the era of "China Model 1.0". China studied the planned economy of the Soviet Union very seriously, but because the fundamentals were too poor, people's brains were too active, and the quality of the population did not meet the requirements of a strictly planned economy, it did not end up being so rigid as to be immutable. As a result, the Soviet master went from rigid to zombie.

After the reform and opening up, China's intellectual elites suddenly found the West to be like the world of bliss, with all ideas so new, all products so advanced, all systems so reasonable, and all cultures so fashionable and trendy that they regretted that they had been backward because they had worshipped the wrong master. Now that the door is open, they are determined to take the West as their teacher, especially the American model as the ultimate "other shore", and start the exploration of the sensational "China Model 2.0". They did not hesitate to plunge into the deep, swollen waters of globalization and swim hard towards the "other side". The closer you get to the other side, the more excited you become, as if all difficulties will automatically disappear when you reach that new land.

Suddenly, the financial tsunami of 2008 drowned the "other side" and the American master also fell into the water and struggled. After the tide receded, Occupy Wall Street was filled with protesters on the other side. What to do? The intellectual elite hesitated, and some insisted on continuing to swim to the "other side", imagining that when they got there, everything would be perfect again. More people have begun to swim backwards, discovering that "turning back to the shore" is the better option, and they have gradually identified the beacons of national and ethnic interests in the treacherous tide of globalization, and they are determined to start a new journey of exploration.

When the two masters, the Soviet Union and the United States, got down, the hard-working student of China: suddenly found the loss and anxiety of losing the way forward. For the past 170 years, China has been an accustomed student, never prepared to be Mr. Thought. However, reality has pushed China to the forefront of the world's tide, with the US in recession, Europe in debt crisis, and Asia's trading partners all staring at China's moneybags, counting on China to kick-start its stimulus policies again and save the world from fire and water.

This time, China's choice of path will affect the economic map of the world! China's model, which will attract the attention of all nations, is that China's destiny is inextricably linked to that of the world, for the first time in recent history!

History might call China's choice: "China Model 3.0".

"Tough start to the toss"

The origin of what the West calls the 30-year "Chinese miracle" is in fact a severely aged and fragile industrial base.

The dividends of industrialized technology diffusion, which had brought China rapidly closer to the world level at the time in the 1950s, have largely stagnated in the ensuing two decades, amidst old capital and political unrest. Instead of getting better, the huge disparity between accumulation and consumption, which is the result of a serious imbalance between heavy, light and agricultural industries, is getting worse. China's industrialization, following the "economic exile" of the United States and its hostility to the Soviet Union, lost access to cheap and rapid technological diffusion. With just 30 years of China's own technological accumulation, it is impossible for the Chinese, no matter how smart and diligent they are in a closed environment, to catch up with the 200 years of industrialized sedimentation in the West. This precipitation is reflected not only in the industrial technology itself, but more importantly in the entire industrial system, which is matched by a pool of human resources, production organization, infrastructure, equipment manufacturing, raw materials and energy supply, as well as by financial institutions, capital markets, legal norms, research and innovation, education and training, health care, social service systems adapted to the industrial economy and, above all, the agricultural base.

Lacking the guarantees of an integrated system, industrialization alone, like steelmaking, without regard to the coordination of other industries, is not only lacking in momentum, but also has endless consequences. The setback to industrialization in emerging countries is often to see only the industry itself and not the complete social service system that is needed behind it, and then, after the economy has "hit the high wall", it has to turn back and make up for it.

At the beginning of the reform and opening up, the biggest bottleneck constraining industrialization was agriculture. Eighty percent of China's population are farmers, who need to provide not only the food they need for themselves and the urban population, but also the main raw materials for light industry before the petrochemical breakthrough. These two mountains weighing down on agriculture are already overwhelming, and if the accumulation ratio reaches more than 25 per cent, the agricultural economy will be suffocated and industrialization will be paralyzed. In the 10 years after 1970, the accumulation rate exceeded 30 per cent every year, and in 1978, when the "foreign leap forward" was launched again, the accumulation rate reached 36.5 per cent, which is close to the level of the three-year great leap forward (39 per cent)!

The so-called accumulation is the "rabbit" resources invested in making bows and arrows in the story of the hunter told earlier, and if this percentage is too high, the lack of savings will force the hunter to work on an empty stomach. And China's economy, especially the rural economy, has basically been in a state of severe overdraft since 1957. Moreover, over-investment has also contributed to the lack of sufficient rural savings in exchange for industrial consumer goods, severely depressing the improvement of the quality of life and market prosperity. This, coupled with a distorted price system, makes it impossible for farmers to receive reasonable compensation for the fruits of their labour in terms of consumer goods, which greatly reduces their incentive to produce.

The revitalization of agriculture is a life or death test for the success of China's reform and opening up!

In 1979, in order to reverse its long-standing debt to agriculture, the Government began to raise the purchase prices of 18 types of agricultural products by 30.5 per cent for grain, 25 per cent for cotton and 38.7 per cent for oil and grease, and in the same year raised the prices of eight types of foodstuffs, including livestock, aquatic products and vegetables. In the six years since then, the purchase price of agricultural products has risen almost every year and farmers' incomes have gained a historic boost. At the same time, the reform of the rural economy, with family contracting at its core, was officially launched, with farmers regaining the right to manage their land and the autonomy to market their agricultural products. The policy of "guaranteeing the State, leaving enough for the collective, and the rest for itself" has created a great temptation for the peasants, whose enthusiasm for production has been fully released, agricultural production has continued to grow, and their net income has been rapidly increased. The spell of the shortage economy was broken by the rapidly increasing rural consumption capacity, which strongly stimulated the light industry boom, and the market became increasingly well supplied.

The frenzied momentum of the "foreign leap forward", which began in 1978, was finally contained in 1981. Investment in heavy industry was squeezed and economic resources began to be sharply tilted towards agriculture and light industry, with the cumulative share falling below 30 per cent. By 1984, the ratios of heavy industry, light industry and agriculture were gradually harmonized, and China's economy was at its best since reform and opening up. The first salvo of the reform was to give farmers direct access to the benefits. Spurred by agricultural growth, light industry began to gain momentum, the countryside prospered in tandem with the cities, and reforms that gave the people real and tangible benefits won the hearts and minds of the people.

At a time when the situation was improving, the chronic "investment hunger and thirst" in heavy industry resurfaced, and investment in fixed assets under universal ownership surged to 21.8 per cent in 1984 and 39.3 per cent in 1985, with even more dramatic expansion of investment under collective ownership. In the euphoria of the boom in production and sales, wage bonuses for industrial companies began to be dissipated, bank credit gradually got out of hand, and in the fourth quarter of 1984 the size of credit increased by 164% year-on-year, and bonuses doubled! Policy compensation for past long-standing agricultural deficits has allowed farmers' incomes to grow faster than agricultural output. Several factors combine to cause the sum of accumulation and consumption to exceed national income, and the fiscal deficit becomes a major problem. The large deficits led to a severe currency over-issuance, which increased 2.5 to 3 times between 1983 and 1988! This led directly to double-digit inflation in 1988.

Anti-inflation, or price liberalization? It's a poignant question.

In the case of serious currency over-issues, the liberalization of prices, which is like the people who have been frightened by double-digit price increases, blew the "rallying cry" of the bank deposits and the mad rush to buy goods!

Inflation, whenever and wherever it may be, is always the mortal enemy of true productivity.

What is the currency? Money is a contract of social wealth! People believe that in the future, when they need it, they can exchange this contract for products or services of the same value, and they believe that the "counterparties" who have never met in the market will not default, and that the currency, the contract of wealth, will hold tens of thousands of market participants, within the framework of "not knowing each other, but trusting each other". A stable currency that reduces transaction costs across society, promotes the social division of labour and stimulates wealth creation. To undermine the value of money is to undermine the integrity of the wealth contract, and is tantamount to dismantling the foundation of mutual trust throughout society! The devaluation of the currency will eventually increase the transaction costs in the market and hit wealth creation.

Inflation, transforming money into an instrument of fraud, a deed of wealth, into a voucher for bad debts. Playing fraud in the market will only bring more fraud, the wind of good faith will be gone, speculation will prevail, long-term planning is replaced by short-term behavior, prudent savings is replaced by uncontrolled overdraft. The prevailing impetuousness of society is the inevitable result of inflation.

Any society that is fair and honest should have zero tolerance for inflation! Whoever, whatever excuse is used to advocate inflation, is a destroyer of honest money and a trample on the moral bottom line of money.

In this regard, the "stubbornness and stubbornness" of the German central bank against inflation, although not perfect, can be a model for all countries.

Many people assume that China's economic development is necessarily accompanied by inflation because the economy is becoming more monetized, but this is by no means a logical explanation. What once didn't want money entered the market, and while it created demand for money, it also increased the supply of commodities, and this matching monetization process, should not affect the trading price of other commodities. The phenomenon of monetary overdraft stems mainly from the monetization of fiscal deficits and the monetization of inflated financial assets.

The major source of the severe inflation that occurred in 1988 was the fiscal deficit. And the fiscal deficit is rooted in the age-old problem of inefficiency, waste and duplication of construction. China seems to have fallen into a strange circle, whenever the pursuit of high speed development, the coordination of the economy is bound to go wrong, and in the end, the desire for speed will not achieve. And when the desire for growth is reduced, the economy grows healthier and faster. This can only illustrate the problem that industrialized societies are highly complex, beyond the cognitive limits of those who plan the economy. The constant "toss-up" of economic overheating and emergency cooling repeatedly illustrates the insurmountable contradictions of the old system.

There's a classic line from the movie Jurassic Park, "Life Finds a Way!" Just as the reform of the city's economic system was mired in a swamp and had to be trudged through, a new, never-before-noticed bright spot began to quietly shine brighter and brighter on the screen of China's economic radar.

China's first-stage rocket of economic take-off – rural industrialization

If China's explosive economic growth during the 30 years of reform and opening up was driven by a two-stage rocket, rural industrialization has taken on the heavy burden of the first-stage rocket.

In the early 1980s, the agricultural economy acquired a rare capital accumulation in a policy of tilting the country's economic resources; in the 1950s, China's industrialization began with Soviet technology and capital input, while in the 1980s, rural industrialization began with the spread of urban industrialization. The industrialization of the countryside is an unprecedented initiative in the world in the 200 years of the Industrial Revolution. China's countryside is both a land of large populations and vast poverty, and a magical place of great vitality and explosive potential. The Chinese Revolution began in the countryside and eventually formed a prairie fire, with the strategy of "surround the cities with the countryside and finally seize power", a strategy that the

West could not have imagined, but which has been a great success in China.

In fact, it is all based on the simple and profound reality that the majority of China's population is in the countryside, and China's destiny is inevitably tied to the countryside. In ancient times, there could be no dynastic change without armed rebellion with peasant participation; in recent times, there could be no complete revolution without peasant participation; and in economic construction, development without most peasants gaining substantial benefits is fragile and unsustainable growth. Ignore the countryside and it will become an insurmountable obstacle to development; focus on the countryside and it will become an unstoppable source of power. The roots of China's development lie in the countryside, and the source of China's strength also lies in the countryside. This simple "Avenue" is also the initial impetus for China's economic take-off.

The planned economy, because of its inability to understand the high complexity of the industrial economy in a deep, thorough and comprehensive manner, has always had structural irrationalities in its planning, which are magnified by the inherent contradictions in institutions and mechanisms, making it possible for State-run industries to occupy only the "big cities and traffic lines" in the market, leaving huge vacancies in the market hinterland, resulting in the phenomenon of the so-called "shortage economy".

When the countryside gained a modest capital accumulation, rural enterprises with flexible mechanisms and a keen sense of the market came into being. They used second-hand equipment eliminated by urban industries, state-owned enterprises retired but still rich in "residual heat" technicians, targeting the huge gap in the consumer market, quickly started production machines, with low prices, poor quality products quickly captured part of the market share of consumer goods.

These enterprises are large hundreds of people, small to a few people, most of the fixed assets are just tens of thousands or hundreds of thousands of yuan, in the orthodox economic statistics, they are just the same size as individual households, can be called the "guerrilla" in the market economy. They are of low quality, poorly equipped, weakly financed, small in number, and even lack of bank loans for "air force support", compared with the "national army" of state-run industries, simply shabby to the point of being unappealing. However, the spectacle plummeted, the titular "national army" can not actually beat the "guerrillas", millions of township enterprises to the posture of ants and soldiers, in all areas of the market, gradually eat into the "national army" sales share. The building materials, metallurgy, wine making, garment, textile, chemical and other industries, which are in high demand in the market, are in full bloom, gradually forming a major force in China's economic sector that cannot be ignored.

The main key to victory for the "guerrillas" is "strategic and tactical flexibility". Strategically, the "guerrillas" are entering the field of small investment, quick results, high return, a certain resource advantage, product market demand is strong. Tactically, the management of the "guerrilla" operation has shown great flexibility, practicality and efficiency, allowing the operator to make timely decisions in accordance with the market. The internal structure and staffing of enterprises are also determined according to the actual needs; there are no restrictions on staffing and recruitment targets; cadres can go up and down; workers can go in and out. In the employment system, there are generally contract workers, temporary workers and hired workers, with a small number of unproductive staff. If they do a good job, they stay, if they don't, they go home. Businesses can choose employees, and employees can choose businesses. With regard to the distribution system, wages are generally determined by the enterprises themselves, most of which are linked to production and efficiency; the level of wages fluctuates according to the size of the contribution and the profitability of the enterprise; the remuneration can be high and low; the income of the employees is in a different class; the more you work, the more you get; and the focus on efficiency fully mobilizes the motivation of the employees. More importantly, the "guerrillas" rely on the strong support of the local community, sufficient land resources, low labor costs, and the local government to form a community of interests, forming a solid "base", can attack, retreat can be defended, and large room for maneuver.

In the approximately 16 years from 1980 to 1996, rural industrialization created an astonishing 130 million jobs, accounting for one-third of agricultural employment and half of the surplus agricultural labour, with exports of 60.8 billion yuan and a total output of 1.8 trillion yuan! Between 1980 and 1988, the share of the national light industrial products market supply capacity increased, the contribution of township enterprises accounted for 32%; in 1988, the output of major consumer goods, township enterprises provided electric fans accounted for 45.5% of the country, silk fabrics accounted for 68.7% and nylon velvet accounted for 52.1%. By 1997, the tax paid by township enterprises accounted for 17.7 per cent of the country's total fiscal revenue and 35.8 per cent of local fiscal revenue. Where rural industrialization is advanced, it is also where local revenues are better. In addition to its contribution to fiscal revenue, township enterprises have also taken on the important task of subsidizing and building agriculture with work, and have financially supported the development of local agriculture; from 1978 to 1997, township enterprises built agriculture with work and subsidized agriculture to the tune of 73.66 billion yuan, and rural industrialization has played an enormous role in supporting agriculture.

At the high stage of rural industrialization, about one-third of farmers' income comes from township enterprises. During this period, farmers' incomes doubled almost every five years, and their contribution to GDP topped out at more than 50%, at one point supporting half of the Chinese economy!

Arguably, from the early 1980s until the mid-1990s, rural industrialization was the central driver of China's economic growth, with rural affluence and new purchasing power injecting a powerful dynamic into the urban economy. A consumer revolution that has lasted for more than a decade has erupted, centered on household appliances and consumer goods. Contrary to perception, it is not the urban boom that has driven the countryside, but the hundreds of millions of peasants who have joined the flood of industrialization through a unique model that has created enormous social wealth through higher productivity. When rural areas exchange this staggering new "savings" with cities, they are stimulated to meet this demand with newer products, better services, more means of production, more advanced infrastructure, and faster energy and power growth. The success of rural industrialization has far exceeded the expectations of those in the planned economy.

At the same time, the industrialization of cities is undergoing painful and dramatic transmutation, and the reform of state-owned enterprises is deepening day by day. After a short period of adjustment from 1989 to 1991, Deng Xiaoping's southward tour in 1992 rekindled the passion for economic reform in China, this time, the market economy completely replaced the planned economy and became the basic state policy of China. The Asian financial crisis of 1997–1998 caused a temporary headwind to China's economic growth.

By this time, the fuel for the first-tier rocket of rural industrialization had also been gradually depleted. As the shortage economy becomes a thing of the past, and as international competition begins its powerful penetration in China, the weaknesses of rural industrialization are exposed day by day, and the difficulties of firms in terms of size, technology, capital, talent, information, channels, institutions, etc., become less and less room for maneuver. The experience of "guerrilla warfare" has passed and the era of "three-dimensional warfare" of capital, technology and information without borders has begun.

In the absence of a new rocket boost, China's economy began a clear downward trend in the late 1990s. The productivity gains of rural industrialization have reached their limits, and the new "savings" of farmers that can be exchanged with cities have begun to shrink, while urban productivity gains have not yet reached new limits. When a larger exchange between the two sides was not possible, China's consumer market began to cool rapidly and corporate profits shrank. The weakness in commodity trading has led to a weak money supply. At this time, financial transactions were far from being the main demand for money supply, and in this context, the fog of deflation and recession began to pervade the Chinese economy, exacerbated by the Asian economic crisis, which undoubtedly worsened the terms of trade around China.

Starting in October 1997, China's general retail price index began a 27-month decline until the end of 1999, while the consumer price index continued to decline for 22 months from March 1998. The deflation that people usually complain about is not, in essence, a monetary problem and cannot be solved by monetary expansion. The root cause of deflation is the stagnation of social productivity growth. In China, it was almost synchronized with the stagnation of rural industrialization in the mid-1990s.

Ultimately, the overall productivity of China's industrialization will not produce a fundamental breakthrough without the stimulus of another strong external technological diffusion.

At the time, Chinese residents had already saved as much as 5 trillion yuan, and it was suggested that by spending those savings to buy a house, an economic recovery could occur. This is using the commoditization of real estate to achieve the exchange of houses for savings, thus pulling the huge real estate industry chain and promoting economic growth. This is effectively monetizing housing, encouraging mortgage lending while at the same time engaging in massive monetary creation to stimulate economic output with monetary increments while offsetting the effects of deflation. If we analyze this policy and the effect of the government releasing money by raising the purchase price of agricultural products to stimulate the consumption power of farmers in the early 1980s, we will find that the effect was even greater that year; the policy in the early 1980s inadvertently produced two benefits: first, the farmers' income increased, leading to an increase in food production, when the farmers exchanged with the cities, not only solved the supply of raw materials for light industry, but also stimulated the demand for consumer products; second, the initial formation of capital accumulation in the countryside, which set off an unexpected tide of rural industrialization, which flourished in the following decade or so, 130 million people joined the army of raising labor productivity, a large amount of wealth creation in turn stimulated the prosperity of urban economy. And the monetization of real estate, although it can play a pulling role on the relevant industries and ease the danger of economic downturn, but it is not yet able to break through the bottleneck of the whole society to further increase productivity.

The second major revolution in social productivity came in 1999, when China joined the World Trade Organization (WTO).

China's second-stage rocket for economic take-off – globalization

Until 1999, the first 20 years of China's reform and opening up, industrialization was largely confined to the narrow space of the domestic market. It is said that the main reason for the narrow domestic market is low productivity and inability to create enough wealth to form a large domestic market exchange.

After acceding to the WTO, China immediately entered an almost limitless world market space. Just as in post-war Japan, the narrow domestic market was unable to further improve industrial productivity, and once the vast international market was opened up, Japanese companies began to expand their production scale rapidly, while production costs plummeted and labor productivity increased to eye-popping levels. Following its accession to the WTO, China began to experience a similar abrupt change in productivity.

Since 2000, most of the world's top 500 companies have been in China, and today almost all of the world's famous brands are in production in China, a rare opportunity for technology diffusion. 156 major projects in the 1950s, with Soviet aid to China, played a crucial role in the start of China's industrialization. It was with the hands-on help of tens of thousands of Soviet experts that China first figured out what modern industry was all about and how an industrialized society should function. Thousands of technical patents were transferred to China almost free of charge, and countless technical problems were solved by Chinese technicians one by one in a set of detailed drawings and the experience of Soviet experts. However, such a good thing as a pie in the sky may only happen once in a hundred years.

Regardless of what the TNCs' intentions are when they come to China, they are bound to employ a large number of Chinese employees, which is tantamount to China using the TNCs' technological capital investment to provide domestic technologists with "hands-on" opportunities to absorb Western technology. These young researchers have learned a great deal of advanced technology on the job, and even if it is not the most core research, they are still able to learn the basics of what is at the cutting edge of today's technology, how to conduct scientifically regulated experiments, how to use advanced instruments and tools, how to write standard research reports, how to retrieve cutting-edge research results, how to coordinate the various research departments, etc. They won't be working in multinationals forever, and when they do, the proliferation of these technologies will permeate large areas of Chinese companies. Without transnational corporations coming to its door, China fears that it will not have the opportunity to give millions of researchers such systematic and advanced training. The long-term benefits to China's future from this alone far outweigh the short-term profits that multinationals can make in China.

Before that, the gap between China's technical personnel and the world's advanced industrialization level has been too big, whether state-owned enterprises or private enterprises, the huge disparity in science and technology research and development with the world level, causing the biggest bottleneck in China's economic development. In this case, no matter how radical the corporate reforms are and no matter how well the corporate system is perfected, it is unlikely to break through the huge bottleneck of technological accumulation. Even Huawei, which attaches the most importance to technology research and development in China, insists on spending 10% of its sales revenue on research and development every year, with more than 25,000 researchers and 7 to 8 billion yuan of funding every year, and after years of hard work, not a single original invention has been made! If this situation continues, even if the total size of China's economy exceeds that of the United States, the world's top 500 companies are all Chinese, still can not get rid of the basic pattern of China under the control of the United States!

According to the World Intellectual Property Organization, Chinese inventors filed 203,481 patent applications in 2008, second only to Japan (520,054) and the United States (400,769). It may seem like China's inventions are taking a "big leap forward", but when analyzed carefully, it's not so at all. More than 95 percent of China's domestic patent applications are accepted by domestic intellectual property offices, most of which are only under the banner of "innovation" and in fact make minor changes to existing designs. A more convincing way to judge would be to obtain the recognition of patent applications and grants accepted by countries outside China, in particular the patent offices of the United States, Europe and Japan. As a result, of the 200,000 patents in China in 2008, only 473 patent applications were accepted or granted by the above-mentioned three patent offices, compared to 14,399 in the United States, 14,525 in Europe, and 15,446 in Japan; in 2010, only 1% of the total number of Chinese patent applications were accepted or granted by foreign patent offices!

China's use of multinational companies to cultivate technical talents is a bit like the cuckoo bird laying its eggs in its nest, just as China vigorously encouraged study abroad back then, many people complained that the study abroad policy led to the brain drain. The use of transnational corporations to cultivate talents has scaled up this "study abroad" model by an order of magnitude. Whether these "study abroad" talents eventually choose to start their own businesses or enter other sectors of the economy, they are bound to become a force for the future of the economy.

Globalization has cultivated talents for China, and the proliferation of technologies resulting from the proliferation of these talents can only gradually penetrate into the domestic economic system, and it will take time to finally create a truly original technological breakthrough.

The globalization of the economy has also brought advanced corporate governance structures and business models to China. In the process of connecting with the world, people are phasing out the old and inefficient ways of organizing production, removing another important constraint that has long constrained the efficient functioning of the economy. When Walmart and Carrefour opened their chains in China, traditional businessmen and ordinary people saw what an advanced business model was. In the past, people only knew indirectly, through the medium of television and newspapers, what a highly integrated and efficient system of commercial circulation looked like, and when these chains came to their doorsteps, people were able for the first time to directly experience the convenience and affordability of modern commerce and to gradually understand how this complex system was actually constructed. Copying and imitating business models has also brought about a dramatic change in China's economic landscape.

Since 2000, the "Made in China" revolution, with the east wind of foreign investment, in the Bohai Sea, the Yangtze River Delta and the Pearl River Delta region to form a world-class manufacturing center, in more than 100 production and manufacturing areas occupy the throne of the world's first, "Made in China" labeling piles of shelves around the world. The second-stage rocket of globalization has pushed the Chinese economy to a new "cosmic speed".

The explosive growth of the export-oriented economy has created enormous new wealth for China. Continued years of massive foreign investment, along with a staggering trade surplus, have pushed China's foreign reserves from over $160 billion in 2000 to a dazzling $3 trillion in 2011 in one fell swoop! Figuratively speaking, China's export economy is more like that of the hunter who, with the help of the technology of other hunters and with the strong stimulus of massive external demand, dramatically improved the accuracy and range of his bow and arrow, thus achieving a great harvest of hunting, although he was forced to lend half of the harvest to others, but still left with half of the additional "savings". When he took these savings to the market and exchanged them, it greatly stimulated the market.

Similarly, when the huge new "savings" generated by China's export sector was exchanged in the domestic market, it stimulated all sectors of the economy to start expanding production supply, thus triggering a chain reaction of consumption throughout society and accelerating productivity gains in all production and service sectors. From daily necessities to household appliances, from the Internet to telecommunication services, from automobile consumption to high-end luxury goods, from real estate to steel and cement, from equipment manufacturing to petrochemicals, from energy and electricity to coal metallurgy, from transportation to infrastructure, all industrial chains of industrialization and urbanization are simultaneously in full swing, rapidly producing a variety of goods and services and participating in the increasingly violent market transactions. The profits that rolled in were magnified into a larger wealth effect in the stock and financial markets, where the money supply flew in tandem with exchange rate appreciation, and house prices soared in tandem. The tremendous success of China Model 2.0, prior to the 2008 financial tsunami, created a boom unprecedented since the founding of the country.

Many believe that China's economic growth has three sets of wagons: exports, government investment and consumption. In fact, there is an inherent logical dependence on all three, with exports being the real driver, higher productivity and broader markets creating incremental savings, while driving government tax revenue growth and forming the basis for investment. Consumption is an exchange, which likewise stems from incremental savings. Thus, exports with higher productivity are the real rocket that will propel the economy off the ground.

The globalization of the Chinese economy since 2000, unlike the rural industrialization after 1980, has far surpassed the latter in depth, breadth, durability and sophistication. Rural industrialization is at a low level, and productivity growth is not based on scientific and technological progress, but is largely due to the market gap left by the planned economy.

However, the second stage of the rocket also has serious side effects, which are: China has increased its productivity, but only got a fraction of the profit; China has opened up completely, but it is difficult to enter other countries; China makes famous products, but no one knows about Chinese brands; China has a large economy, but few original technologies; China's GDP is growing rapidly, but it does not enjoy much; China has earned huge savings from trade, but the United States has borrowed most of them; China has a large amount of dollars, but the world cannot buy good things; China has sacrificed the environment to depress the quality of life, but the West has eaten meat and put down bowls to curse the mother. In short, China appears to be very rich, but in fact it is very poor.

In the vortex of globalization, the most puzzling question for the Chinese is, what do we want for others to be satisfied? And the American way of doing things is, I did it, you like it or not.

There is a difference between being good and being self-improvement. The good and strong compete for the judgment of others, while the self-improvement of the self-improvement is all that matters. A good and strong person appears to be confident, but in fact has an inferiority complex that is rooted in the lack of an internal value system and has to rely on external standards of judgment. Self-improvement people don't care what others say, because these people don't think anyone is qualified to judge themselves from the bone of their being. Today's China is very strong in many ways, and is very concerned about international evaluation, and is afraid of losing face in front of foreign countries. The root of the problem lies in the fact that China's intrinsic value system has not yet matured, and foreign faces have become the judges of Chinese dignity! A person without personality will not be charismatic, and a country without personality will not be appealing.

China's two main export categories: commodities and savings

As early as the 1980s, American scholars said that the United States had finally discovered its "comparative advantage", which was to export U.S. Treasury bonds. Beginning in the 1950s, first the Germans, then the Middle East oil exporters, then Japan and now China, took on the burden of exporting domestic savings to the United States.

The export sector is like a hunter, whose prey is the export of foreign exchange, and whose prey, in whatever form it takes, is in essence China's new savings. When China buys U.S. Treasuries, it actually means that domestic savings are flowing to the United States. Hunters could have used these savings to better their bows, to exchange more other goods in the marketplace to improve their own quality of life, and to stimulate greater domestic consumption and create more jobs, but now the hunters' additional savings are being borrowed in half, which amounts to a simultaneous erosion of the domestic capacity for new technological advances, the scale of consumption, and the opportunities for employment.

When these Chinese savings flowed into the U.S., they did not enter the U.S. industrial arena to help American hunters modify their bows and arrows, increase the level of hunting, repay borrowed foreign savings with more trophies, and balance America's trade deficit. This borrowed money actually flowed into the US financial sector, pushing up asset prices in the US. From the "9/11" incident in 2001 to the Iraq war in 2003, the Federal Reserve cut interest rates 13 times in a row in an attempt to stimulate economic growth, but the result was the creation of the largest real estate bubble in the 200-year history of the United States, Chinese savings became the bubble of the United States real estate orgy and the smoke of the Iraq war.

The real estate bubble fueled the flames of financial innovation, and Americans were able to cash in on some of the appreciation in their homes with ease. If an old American woman bought a house for $400,000 last year, and this year the price has risen to $500,000, the bank will encourage her to spend $100,000 of the year's appreciation in the form of a "value-added mortgage" discounted to $70,000, without any increase in income, the old American woman has gained an extra $70,000 in spending power for nothing, she began to spend wildly, renovating the kitchen, renovating flower gardens, watching movies, going to restaurants, traveling around, shopping malls, when she spent the money, it stimulated American consumption, bringing employment and economic growth. The result, more prosperous economic indicators, brought a bigger stock market bubble and rising real estate, and older Americans had more spending money the next year. As a result, older Americans stopped saving, and for the first time since the Great Depression of the 1930s, the savings rate in the United States increased negatively for three consecutive years from 2005 to 2007, so why save? Anyway, with old Chinese women working and saving frugally, the savings will go into the pockets of old American women anyway, so wouldn't such a model make everyone happy? China's old lady is responsible for saving, America's old lady is responsible for consumption, China's economic growth and America's economic prosperity, is not this kind of "Sino-American" cooperation the "heaven and earth" of America?

China's export-led economic growth has been a perfect match for the asset-inflated boom in the United States. In essence, it is the U.S. asset inflation that is pulling China's economic growth, and it is the U.S. asset bubble that is fueling China's second stage rocket. It's just that there's an explosive question in the middle of this: can asset inflation continue indefinitely?

Don't forget, every time the old American lady uses a real estate ATM to withdraw money, she increases her debts, while her income growth is far from keeping up with her ballooning debts, behind the ballooning assets is actually the ballooning debts, and the increasing debt burden makes the old American lady's debt service increasingly stressful, and she has to count on the interest rate to stay super low forever, because her financial situation is at the limit of stress. What finally came was the Fed's seven consecutive rate hikes from 2004 to 2005.

What if the Fed continues its ultra-low interest rate policy? Then the real estate bubble will be bigger and the bursting of the bubble will be even more deadly. The "debt lagoon" of old Americans finally began to crumble in 2007, more old Americans defaulted on their collective debt in 2008, and America's asset-inflated boom came to an end!

Bernanke tried to "reflate assets" by printing money to restore the wonderful asset-inflated prosperity. But does printing money lead to real savings growth? Can real investment and consumption be created? In addition to the original heavy debt burden, the American old lady has increased the huge social cost of saving Wall Street, the soaring national debt for the American old lady's "debt tiger stool" added a big brick, the American society's pain index soared to the highest level since the 1930s, unbearable Americans have rushed to the streets, igniting the world storm of "Occupy Wall Street". High unemployment accompanied by crippling debt, coupled with shrinking financial assets in retirement accounts, has overwhelmed any thoughts of further overdraft spending by older Americans. The Federal Reserve's ultra-low interest rate policy, round after round of quantitative monetary easing, can not dispel the bank loan managers such as the fox as the birds of a feather, also can not boost the old lady in the United States to speculate in real estate desire and ability.

This is the end of an era, this is the end of a pattern!

Since the 1980s, the debt-driven economic growth of the United States has brought about a ballooning of asset values, and this new economic model has earned the United States a happy-go-lucky good time in the first seven years of the 21st century, providing ample fuel for the secondary booster rocket that will take China's economy off. Now that this wonderful economic "perpetual motion" has been extinguished, "China and the United States" are bound to begin to split.

What to do with the savings that the old Chinese lady lends to the old American lady? The Fed's method is QE1, QE2, and in the future QE3, or even QE (n+1). The essence of the so-called quantitative easing of money is to dilute the purchasing power of the currency, disguised as offsetting the pressure of indebtedness, and the main purpose of the dollar's devaluation against other currencies is eating away at the savings of other countries!

In addition to the significant loss of real savings that the second stage rocket brought to China's economic growth, what's more serious is that the fuel for the second stage rocket is gone! China's ability to add new savings is facing an increasing depletion. Without significant new productivity gains, there is no source of new savings, and no real investment and consumption is possible. The biggest effect of the Chinese government's fiscal stimulus and investment push will inevitably be inflationary pressure, which will simply keep the economy running and not lead to real prosperity!

China Model 3.0: Forming the world's largest consumer market!

The need for China to transform is not only a requirement for its own economic development, but more importantly, it has no choice but to do so. This raises a number of important questions: what exactly is China Model 3.0 supposed to achieve? And what is the path? How can this new path be achieved?

For nearly 170 years, China has been a diligent and good student, first following the example of the West, then the East, then the Soviet Union, and finally falling in love with America. China has learned from all the countries of the world and found that there is a problem with replicating any model in China, and China must and can only follow its own path and learn from the experience of other countries.

It must first be made clear that China is not Germany or Japan, much less the Four Little Dragons of Asia, and that only the United States is a reference for China in the positioning of national goals. The export-oriented economic development model is by no means the fundamental way forward for the big countries. Learning from the American experience should draw primarily on the era of the industrial rise of the United States prior to 1971, particularly the decisive path to leapfrogging the United States in the 19th century. In contrast, the US model of debt-driven economic development since the 1980s has been very harmful and should be carefully avoided.

At the heart of America's rise to power is always being in control of your own destiny! Under the guidance of this founding spirit, all domestic and international policies of the United States are based on the principle of pragmatism, and whatever is in the interest of the United States is used when it is useful and discarded when it is not, without the slightest ambiguity. The United States is arguably the most "clear-cut" of all countries, with a clear and uncompromising vision of what it wants, and an almost paranoid insistence on achieving it, while always pushing through options that are not in its interest.

In the course of its economic rise, the United States insists on always being in control of its own destiny, which is reflected in the fact that the United States deliberately protects its own domestic market, ignores the so-called free trade theory of the British desperately "selling", and implements the idea of high tariffs, high wages, heavy technology, strong industry and big market. The promoters and advocates of free trade and the theory of comparative advantage are none other than the world hegemonic powers themselves, whose aim is to perpetuate into a system the enormous competitive advantage they have acquired. No country that is catching up cannot be compelled by such harmful doctrines to cut its own meridians, and the principle of globalization that China must establish is to use what is good for me and discard what is bad for me.

When America, guided by this pragmatism, developed into the largest market in the world, she had her destiny firmly in her hands! The reason Roosevelt dared to subvert the 1933 London Economic Conference and allow the dollar to devalue to destroy Europe's monetary stability was because U.S. exports accounted for only 3% of the total size of the economy, and even by 2010, 77 years later, only 8.8%! When the British expelled American power from the continent in the 1930s, Roosevelt rightfully rejected the false name of being a "responsible power" and subverted the pound sterling empire, which was his real intention. After World War II, the United States ignored Europeans' desire for monetary stability, or was it because the U.S. domestic market was large enough and European countries had limited market space that monetary stability was far more important to Europe than the United States. It is in America's interest to have the dollar devalued while not being dependent on European markets, which of course America has no qualms about.

When debt was a weapon, the United States smashed the British Empire with the baton of debt, and when the United States became a debtor nation, it turned debt into power, and chased the creditor nations with the scepter of debt. Whenever China reduces its holdings of U.S. Treasuries, or even just underbought them, there is always something rare and odd going on around China. For example, the President of the United States suddenly announced a meeting with the Dalai, or sold arms to Taiwan, or incited trouble in the South China Sea, or encouraged Japan to assert itself in the East China Sea. Once China significantly increases its holdings of U.S. Treasuries, the environment around it will be quiet for a while. This is US debt diplomacy! In fact, the US is collecting protection money from China through the national debt. No? That's what's keeping you awake!

Why is the United States so tyrannical? Because it calculates that China is more dependent on the US than the US is on China, without the US market, Chinese manufacturing would collapse and the mass unemployment would be a nightmare for Beijing every night. In the final analysis, the reason why the baton of debt or debt can be waved freely in the United States is that all countries need the United States market, and whoever is rejected by the United States market amounts to "economic exile". With the euro challenging the dollar, the source of strength is not the currency, but the unified mega-market of the EU! When EU countries don't have to rely on the US market, Europe can truly control its own destiny. This is exactly why Roosevelt was very scornful of Churchill's Pound Zone that year.

The sad thing about Japan is that although it has its own strong production capacity, it is not born with a huge domestic market. After its original attempt to occupy the raw material base and huge market in Asia by means of war, Japan was forced to defect to the United States, the dominant player in the world market, without which Japan would have been nothing.

China's vulnerability also stems in large part from its heavy reliance on international markets, with exports accounting for 26.8 per cent of GDP in 2010, compared with 8.8 per cent in the United States, and it is clear who is more dependent on whom. In such an unreciprocal situation, China can't remain unchecked by the United States and can't truly control its own destiny!

All powerful people and successful people in society may have different personalities, temperaments, hobbies, etc., but they always share one characteristic, and that is "their own destiny, their own control"! No powerful man has ever achieved ultimate success by leaving his destiny in the hands of another master. When a country, especially one as large as China, sees exports as the main driver of development, it is tantamount to giving away the mastery of destiny! When 26.8% of GDP is directly dependent on external markets for economic activity, China cannot be a manipulator of its own destiny, much less a world-class power!

High dependence on external markets can only make China's economy more fragile, make Chinese diplomacy harder to hold on to, and add to national security concerns. Not only does it bring about fierce trade frictions with other countries and dangerous political confrontation, it also prevents China from developing real cohesion and rallying power. Now, the vast majority of what China can produce for export could move to India, Mexico, Vietnam or other countries in a decade, just to see who is cheaper. When China's currency appreciates, labour costs, world raw material prices and environmental pollution deteriorate to a certain critical value, multinational corporations will abandon China as if they were abandoning their jobs, without the slightest hesitation or mercy. Staking the fate of the country on such a growth model is dangerous and disturbing!

The core of China's future development model should not hesitate to give top strategic priority to the development of the domestic market, to steadfastly reduce export dependence to a safe zone below 10 per cent of GDP, and to shift the main resources of the national economy away from sending them to foreign markets and towards the domestic market. The social wealth created by the Chinese, who consume labor, time, energy, resources, land, raw materials, food, electricity, and are under pressure from traffic congestion and environmental pollution, should be enjoyed by Chinese consumers themselves as a priority.

The rise of the United States in those days revolved around the idea of high tariffs, high wages, heavy technology, strong industry, and big markets, with big markets at its center. Without the protection of high tariffs, the infantile industrialization of the United States will be destroyed by the British manufacturing industry, the lack of a strong productive society, will not be able to form a large consumer market; without high wages, there will not be more spending power, and will not be able to form a prosperous market, it can only become the polarization of the capitalists' profits by suppressing workers' incomes, as in Britain, the awareness of human capital, so that the United States realized that high incomes are necessary for the quality of workers, health, mental state, enthusiasm for work, and the motivation for innovation are guaranteed. Wages are not only costs, but also capital, and long-term investment in human capital will be able to bring about higher returns; heavy science and technology can produce technological innovation, accelerate the increase in productivity, realize the creation of social wealth on a larger scale, form huge savings, and ultimately bring about a larger market size and more investment; strong industry has always been the key to the rise of the United States, strong industrial productivity is the prerequisite for creating a prosperous market, without a huge production capacity, the United States could not replace Britain, nor could it become the "arsenal of democratic countries" in the two world wars, after the war to establish the "new order under American rule".

In addition to high tariffs, the U.S. strategy of high wages, heavy technology, strong industry and big markets is perfectly applicable to China today.

Replacing the international market with the domestic market, swapping Chinese consumption for American consumption, and shifting export resources domestically will dramatically alter China's relations with all nations, trade conflicts will become trade peace, fierce rejection will be transformed into warm cooperation, hostility to China will be bowed by the lure of the Chinese market, and the alliance of political siege and military containment will be unstoppable. The biggest market, means the biggest power!

The key question to creating a world's largest consumer market is where to start. Can the scale of production generated by the export industry, which is oriented to the world market, be able to absorb the excess production capacity by hard-to-start domestic demand?

The answer is: it's up to the man!

China's third-stage rocket of economic take-off – the second industrialization of agriculture

The bottlenecks that have caused China's economy are often the way out.

Experience since the founding of the country has shown that a prosperous country is a prosperous country and a rich country is a smooth industrialization, as was the case in the 1950s and again in the 1980s. Conversely, the countryside is in decline and economic development is bound to suffer from growth bottlenecks.

The structure of China's population dictates that peasants will remain the dominant group in the country's future, and economic growth that ignores the countryside is neither moral nor sustainable. The widening of the economic gap between urban and rural areas is also a hidden cause of social instability. After the agricultural economy fell into slow development in the mid-1990s, the rate of growth of farmers' incomes doubled from every five years to every 10 years. Although the government abolished the agricultural tax, various apportionments and invisible expenditures have kept the economic resources of agriculture, which is constantly under a state of blood loss. The accumulation of valuable agricultural capital, which had been formed in the first 15 years of reform and opening up, gradually disintegrated in the latter 15 years.

If the rural economy is not kick-started, domestic demand revitalization is just an empty phrase. It is impossible to create a large domestic market without income growth for the majority of the population in a society.

However, the growth of farmers' incomes should never be achieved through financial subsidies or transfer payments, and the development of an agricultural economy with the mentality of saving the poor rather than the needy is bound to fail. Effective and sustained growth must and can only come from a significant increase in productivity! Farmers must improve their standard of living by creating more wealth.

With the prospect of a long period of economic sluggishness in Europe and the United States in the future, the breakthrough to kick-start domestic demand will be to initiate the process of the second industrialization of rural areas. Only industrialization can bring about higher productivity than agriculture, and only by going deeper than the first rural industrialization can the rural economy be truly revitalized.

Modern urban industrialization, especially informatization, high-technology, and advanced business models, should again spread technology on a large scale to the countryside. If rural industrialization in the 1980s was a demand for farmers to proactively look to the cities for technological diffusion, then this time it should be up to the government and cities to proactively supply the countryside cheaply.

What is most needed in the countryside right now? That is, to reduce the loss of profits in the marketing and distribution of agricultural products. Starting from the circulation link of agricultural products modernization, squeezing out the inefficient and high loss of middlemen layer by layer of exploitation, realizing the direct connection of agricultural products from land to urban residents, most of the circulation profits that should belong to farmers are returned to farmers, which will quickly increase the net income of farmers and release considerable consumption energy. This not only enables the efficient and low-cost distribution of agricultural products, but also ensures food safety at source. Such a business model could be a reference to Wal-Mart's chain model, which gives priority to opening market access to private enterprises, capping the profits of such enterprises and letting them gain growth potential at scale. In the financial and capital markets, ad hoc green channels for the listing of agricultural companies, encouraging such companies to list on a priority basis. Hearing this "Sesame Open" capital mantra, a large number of funds will be crowded in, and after fierce competition, the best choice will be made.

If Alibaba can provide 6 million SMEs with information on demand in the international market, then why can't there be companies willing to provide information on market demand to hundreds of millions of farmers? Data mining with strong market information will allow companies to make high profits while solving the most troubling information deficiencies for farmers. Don't forget that information agitation can also create new business opportunities. Because of the significant strategic value of this data collection and analysis of national farmers, governments, research institutions, banks, brokerage firms, and funds everywhere will also be interested clients. At present, China's rural areas with access to the Internet are expanding rapidly, and the penetration rate of mobile phones in rural areas is also increasing, so that areas with conditions can start the informationization process first, while areas that do not have conditions for the time being can be gradually resolved by government-led private capital. The Government only needs to read the "sesame open door" again, not worried about no private capital to actively intervene.

The first rural industrialization did not industrialize agricultural production, distribution, deep processing and intensification, but filled the market gap of urban industrialization; the second rural industrialization should focus on the industrialization of food with Chinese characteristics.

High-tech modern agriculture will significantly increase productivity and reduce water, fertilizer and pesticide consumption. The most famous case is the Israeli drip technology, where an Israeli farmer stumbled upon a leaky water pipe in 1962 and his crop grew exceptionally well. The reason is that continuous infiltration of water into the soil at the same point is the most effective way to reduce evaporation, efficient irrigation and control water, fertilizer and pesticides. This discovery was immediately supported by the government, and the world-famous drip irrigation technology came into being in 1964, and for 30 years, Israel's agricultural water use was largely stable, but agricultural output doubled by five! The principle of drip irrigation is simple, yet allowing water to drip evenly onto each plant is very complicated. The rigid, anti-clogging plastic tubes, connectors, filters, and controllers developed in Israel are the result of high technology. In Israel, "water is the lifeblood of agriculture", not in the sense of digging ditches, but in scientific irrigation and efficient water use. Drip irrigation makes every inch of land high tech, and computer controlled drip irrigation systems for water, fertilizer and pesticides are typical of the spread of modern industrialization to agriculture.

Israel's "drip irrigation technology" has turned the desert into an agricultural oasis; Japan's "one village, one product" campaign has turned the countryside into a paradise on earth with a beautiful environment and a developed economy; South Korea's "new rural construction" has narrowed the income gap between urban and rural areas; and the Netherlands' "efficient use of land" has created the miracle of being the world's third largest exporter of agricultural products on a narrow land with the highest population density in the world. Each of these countries faces a similar predicament to that of China, but agriculture has taken an unprecedented leap in productivity, underpinned by the proliferation of technology, informatization and modern commerce, which has allowed farmers in these countries to approach or exceed the incomes of urban residents. As the saying goes, it is up to the man, and as long as the Government is willing to tilt economic resources in favour of the countryside on a large scale, it is not inconceivable that productivity in rural China will increase.

Higher productivity will generate more consumer demand, stimulate the emergence of rural services, attract a large number of surplus rural labour, and create a situation in which the agricultural population is divided, with agriculture, agricultural industrial clusters, urban part-time workers and rural services going hand in hand; at the same time, speed up urban construction, abolish the household registration system, allow land management rights to be sublet and circulated, and increase agricultural intensification.

One of the root causes of rural backwardness is the severe lack of infrastructure. Water, electricity, and transportation all form bottlenecks in agricultural development. Inadequate educational resources, poor health care and monotonous cultural and recreational practices have exacerbated the conditions for the second rural industrialization. The quality of the population, in particular, is a constraint on productivity growth. The Americans understood this as early as the 19th century, and Japan has been implementing education for all since the Meiji Restoration. China also now sees the serious consequences of strategic short-sightedness. If there is no more determination now to tilt resources in favour of rural human capital on a large scale, this heavy debt to the quality of the population will be doubled in the future in the form of profitable compensation.

All visions of a second industrialization of the countryside require money, and money in staggering numbers, and without the investment of funds, everything is empty talk. In the next five years, the scale of investment in water projects alone will reach 2 trillion yuan! This is a compensation for the stagnation of rural water development over the past 20 years. Thus, the scale of funding required to initiate a second rural industrialization will be at least several times greater.

The key is how should such a large sum of money be raised? At the moment, land grants are the dominant idea, but they are not the best option. Pushing up land prices, is the idea of monetizing land and real estate, in the absence of a substantial increase in productivity, ultimately can only lead to a more serious over-issuance of the currency, in the promotion of asset bubbles and speculation prevalent at the same time, inflation and house prices, the rise of raw materials, will also squeeze the profit margin of industry, thus suppressing the real wealth creation, weakening the source of economic growth. The idea of land appreciation and fantasizing about wealth falling from the sky is the same as the idea of an old American woman using her house as an

ATM. American old ladies can overdraw their savings to Chinese old ladies, while China can only create "fake savings" by printing money.

Part of the capital for the second industrialization of the countryside can be borne by the capital market, those with short investment, high returns, can be listed on the business model, do not need the government to contribute money, as long as the policy of giving enough temptation, profit-seeking capital is there. As for long-term investments in rural infrastructure and education and health care, capital markets generally do not intervene, and short-term capital seeks returns of at least 10 times over three years, which are not attractive to investments that take 5 to 10 years to bear fruit.

For long-term investments in rural areas, a more reasonable approach than land grants is to issue "special agricultural bonds" or local agricultural bonds. This agricultural debt is fundamentally different from local financing platform debt. In 2010, China suffered direct losses of hundreds of billions of yuan due to floods and droughts, and even greater losses due to indirect production shutdowns and disruptions in business flows. The construction of agricultural water projects will reduce the losses of disasters, which directly increases social profits and productivity, the cash flow it creates, although not as intuitive as the benefits of the project, but the total social benefits are obvious and lasting, the interest payments on the agricultural debt of the treasury, will be overcompensated by taxes from the increased economic profits of the whole society.

It may take 10 to 20 years for investments in education and health care in rural areas to generate returns. However, such investments can convert rural populations from indebtedness to capital in the long run, and the benefits will become increasingly evident over time. For such investments, consideration could be given to issuing special ultra-long term (20 years or more) bonds that provide tax relief on investment returns and encourage investors not only to pursue economic returns but also to create social benefits.

There are two kinds of debt: one is productive debt and the other is consumer debt. The former is like muscle, while the latter is like fat. Productive indebtedness, if the investment outlook is clear and the debt ratio is within safe limits, will play a positive role in economic development.

The comprehensive benefits of issuing agricultural bonds can be seen in two ways: first, it can absorb on a large scale the currency that has been severely over-issued for a decade and reduce the serious impact of asset bubbles and speculation caused by liquidity flooding; second, it can increase the depth and variety of the interbank market, improve the construction of the financial system and make the stock and debt markets more balanced. In the short term, the ratio of national debt to GDP may rise sharply, but that's nothing to be alarmed about, agricultural debt is benign debt and is fundamentally different from the overdraft consumption patterns in Europe and the US. Agricultural investment will improve rural infrastructure, reduce the operating costs of the agricultural economy, increase agricultural productivity, create incremental agricultural savings, stimulate output in the urban economy, gradually absorb overcapacity in the outward-looking economy, increase the size of the domestic market and increase fiscal revenue.

The core starting point is the growing size of the domestic market, increasing China's power to control its own economic destiny!

The second battleground for job creation and market expansion

The difficulty of financing for small and medium-sized enterprises, under the tight monetary policy, has highlighted the current situation of the serious irrational allocation of financial resources in China. Small and medium-sized enterprises (SMEs), which create the most jobs, contribute the most tax revenue and play an important role in the national economy, are in crisis because they cannot access credit from the banking system. In the helplessness of not being able to obtain funds from normal channels, SMEs have to rely on super usury underground money banks to maintain the demand for liquidity or bridging loans; and in the event of a slight accident, usury traps with annual interest rates as high as 30%, 50% or even 100% will easily destroy a business that has been diligently operated for years and has a good reputation. The indiscriminate spread of underground money banks has gradually formed a potential crisis of Chinese-style "subprime lending" chain reaction.

The call for solving the financing difficulties of small and medium-sized enterprises has been going on for many years, and the root cause of the delay in solving the problem lies in the natural preference of commercial banks in a market economy to "suspect poverty, love the rich and avoid risk". This is similar to the prevailing "loan scarcity" mentality of commercial banks in the United States after the financial tsunami, not that there are no companies and individuals in the United States who want to get loans, but that banks, after suffering heavy losses, have developed a paranoid aversion to risk, resulting in the shrinking of consumer and mortgage lending in the United States.

A further example is the Great Depression in Germany in the 1930s, when 30 per cent of the population was unemployed on the one hand and a large amount of idle industrial production capacity on the other, and when money came in to combine the two, it would create new savings, which would stimulate production expansion in other areas, market exchange would take place and the German economy would come back to life. But Germany's commercial banks have refused to provide credit to kick-start the economic recovery process. Banks have always been overly cautious in times of crisis and abusive in issuing credit in bubbles. It seems largely unreliable to expect private banks to activate the German economy. The Nazi Government, which had just come to power, believed that "our economic problems are not due to a lack of means of production, but to the fact that the means of production that are available are not being used to their fullest. To reduce unemployment, the most urgent task today is to make use of idle means of production." The solution is to "invest in productive loans". The German government decided to move away from the traditional theories of credit creation by banks and not be constrained by gold and foreign exchange and to create a new form of currency by the government, the famous "Mefo Bill" (job creation bill). The German Government pays short-term bills of exchange with an interest rate of 4.5 per cent for a period of three months directly to government purchasers and provides that the bills of exchange may be "discounted" at all banks in the country, and that the banks may take them to the Central Bank for "re-discounting" for cash or hold them to maturity. This move amounts to the direct issuance by the Government of Reichsmarks secured by "job creation drafts", completely bypassing the risk-averse banking system and injecting the Government's will to create jobs directly into the German economy through these drafts. Once the idle labour force was combined with the idle means of production, the German economy immediately began to revive, and in just five years it had achieved almost full employment, unemployment had fallen to 1.3 per cent, gross national product had doubled, and it was once again a strong industrial country in Europe.

This example illustrates that when the commercial banking system, for various reasons, is reluctant to provide credit for job creation, governments can bypass the banking system and inject the will of the state directly into the economy through the instrument of financial innovation.

China is currently facing a similar paradox, with job-creating SMEs going bankrupt due to an extraordinary lack of capital, while commercial banks prefer to hedge their bets by lending money to large state-owned enterprises that are not short of it. The problem here is that if the market economy principles of commercial banks are respected, the government will not be able to require banks to lend directly to SMEs, otherwise there will be complex entanglements between banks and the government in the future. At the same time, small and medium-sized enterprises are too small to raise funds through the issuance of bonds, on the one hand, the law does not allow, on the other hand, no broker is willing to earn a few million yuan of underwriting fees and laborious efforts. If a number of small and medium-sized enterprises are pooled to issue "pooled bonds", there will be further credit rating problems and operational problems such as what to do with other enterprises if one of them defaults. Also, investors find it risky and are reluctant to invest.

At this point, the Government is in fact faced with a strategic analysis that if increasing the size of the domestic market is given the highest priority, then creating more jobs will directly increase the consumption capacity of the domestic market. Financial innovation is necessary if the dilemma of financing SMEs is to be addressed. The basic features of this innovation are twofold: one is bypassing the banks and the other is government support. The goal is that SMEs that are willing to create more jobs will be able to access low-cost funding.

In this area of financial innovation, job creation drafts, short-term commercial paper, and junk bonds are all approaches worth exploring in depth.

In the case of foreign direct investment, increased employment that generates tax revenue and technology diffusion would naturally be welcome, but there could be some adjustments in the approach. Since China's foreign exchange reserves are clearly overstretched, these foreign currencies now don't even know what to buy, and more foreign currencies coming into the country are instead increasing the burden on China's foreign exchange reserves. What is most valuable to foreign companies is not their foreign exchange, but their technology, management, brand and international marketing channels.

In other words, when it comes to attracting ordinary foreign investment, the Government can say "welcome". But we don't need you to contribute money, our foreign exchange investment company is willing to invest, you take technology, management, brand, channel into the stock, we do the big shareholder, you do the small shareholder.

If it is really a good money-making project, foreign exchange investment companies or domestic investment companies will compete for shares, so that the foreign exchange reserves have one more way to use in the country. Why are foreigners willing to come? The Chinese foreign exchange was in short supply 30 years ago, and foreign direct investment was the right thing to do. But 30 years east, 30 years west, China is now worried about too much foreign exchange. Foreign exchange reserves are used domestically by exchanging foreign exchange for a controlling stake in foreign capital. Since it's not easy for China to find good assets overseas, can someone else turn down a good investment delivered to their doorstep? To put it bluntly: we come to drive, and they act as horses.

For those MNCs that are already operating in the country, if they are making good profits and have a monopoly on China's leading industry, they should take the opportunity to buy back their shares. The aim is to reduce monopolistic foreign investment to a non-monopoly status and to turn large foreign shareholders into small shareholders. Aren't you worried that you can't spend your foreign exchange reserves? You can't buy good assets abroad, and you can't shear some wool at home? They have been making money for so many years that it would have been time to give some of the profits back to Chinese society.

The repurchase of TNCs' stakes in China from foreign exchange reserves should, of course, be carried out on a "voluntary" basis, and the key issue is to find ways to get foreign investors to voluntarily sell their stakes at a reasonable price. In fact, the government can cite the various "rhetoric" that Chinese enterprises have encountered in overseas M&As and use it in the opposite way. For example, the ubiquitous national security concerns, the fashionable environmental protection, and the tax verification. The solution is always more difficult!

Is real estate a wealth bubble or a pillar of economic growth?

To answer that question, it's better to look at the simplest hunter's tale and analyze it more clearly.

The hunter hunts in the traditional way, thus forming a "savings" of his prey, and when he uses these savings to "invest" in bow and arrow manufacturing, he is increasing his productivity. And higher productivity brings more prey, enabling him to exchange these remaining "savings" in the market. If he needs a garment, then the garment maker is "stimulated" by production to speed up the production of the garment and meet the needs of the hunter, thus increasing the productivity of the garment. As both hunters and dressmakers generate an increasing surplus of savings, their incremental savings are exchanged in the market, which in turn stimulates more industries to accelerate production, resulting in a wider range of productivity gains.

As a result, economic growth began to "spread" from the sectors that had pioneered productivity gains to peripheral industries, leading to a general increase in social productivity. In this process, high-productivity sectors play the role of "economic locomotives", while low-productivity sectors are stimulated by their demand to generate growth and then gradually increase their own productivity.

If the hunter is the "engine of economic growth", then the development of the garment and other industries is the "pulled" sector. The general increase in the productivity of society as a whole has created a large amount of surplus wealth, thus creating the need for "wealth cellars". Before hunters made bows and arrows, there was no surplus wealth in society, the land of the entire tribe was not worth much, and who cares about land development if they can't even fill their bellies? It is only when there is a demand for "wealth cellars" in society that gold, treasure, jewelry, and also the land, play the role of a container for the overflow of wealth. Thus, the land began to appreciate in value. Increasingly affluent hunters and garment makers gradually developed a demand for housing, and real estate developers were "stimulated" to build houses, which in turn "stimulated" the masonry, wood, furniture and other industries.

In this chain, hunters are the source of demand and the driving force is bow and arrow manufacturing. Only a revolution in productivity is the true source of wealth creation.

The whole idea of relying on land appreciation and real estate development to pull the economic chain is questionable. Land appreciation and real estate development is a natural consequence of increased productivity, not its initial cause. Reversing this logic has the wrong economic effect.

Without a revolutionary breakthrough in productivity, the one-sided pursuit of land appreciation will result in higher costs for the industrial sector. The monetization of land and real estate, then, leads to an increase in the money supply that exceeds the increase in productivity, with the result that general inflation, the rise in the cost of land, raw materials, energy and labor, accompanied by fierce competition in market prices, will squeeze the profits of the entire industrial sector that has not yet achieved a breakthrough in productivity. The end result is that the unprofitable industrial sector, without the necessary "savings" to accumulate, loses the ability to improve "bow and arrow manufacturing" and weakens the potential for productivity gains.

The growth of total GDP is not the real purpose of economic development, and healthy economic growth must be oriented towards increasing productivity. The GDP generated by real estate and its industrial chain, which was supposed to be the result of productivity growth, has now become the cause of productivity suppression. Hundreds of millions of tons of steel, cement and raw materials are frozen in "ghost buildings" full of speculation and with an unusually high vacancy rate, which, like the big steel refineries of the 1950s and the "foreign leap forward" of the 1970s, is a waste of precious economic resources, which is tantamount to depriving hunters of the accumulation used to make bows and arrows, and putting them in a state of idleness and waste.

The monetization of land and real estate has spurred a credit-creation binge, and the increasingly devalued purchasing power of money has distorted the rational distribution of wealth in society. It transfers the wealth of savers to the pockets of a few on a large scale, and it sets a bad example of "get rich quick". In the midst of the great change in the flow of wealth, land appreciation easily surpassed the meager profits of industrial production, quickly destroying the will of the industrialists to work hard, and shaking the determination of industry to continuously improve "bow and arrow manufacturing". Since buying a piece of land to sit and wait for appreciation is faster and more profitable than boring, painful, brain-deadening and risky technological innovations, who wants to continue to be down-to-earth and diligent in industry? This short-sighted and impetuous social atmosphere has made "Made in China" increasingly shallow-rooted and vulnerable to wind and waves.

The rapid appreciation of land and the abnormal development of the real estate industry are destroying the potential of industrial productivity growth from both material and spiritual aspects. The GDP they create is high in toxins, side effects and foam, and is a "high pollution" industry in economic development.

Normal real estate development is conducive to improving the quality of life of the whole society, bringing about healthy economic growth, promoting social consumption and expanding the size of the domestic market, which should be encouraged. However, the monstrous real estate boom is by no means a blessing for China.

After 11 September 2001, the information technology revolution in the United States was cut short by excessive capital speculation and the process of productivity explosion came to an abrupt end. In the absence of new technological breakthroughs, the United States has embarked on an "asset bubble" model of stimulating the real estate boom to fuel economic growth. Excessive credit expansion and financial innovation eventually led to the worst economic crisis since the Great Depression of the 1930s. Japan's monstrous real estate boom after the mid-1980s triggered 20 years of economic stagnation, and the Asian Four Little Dragons' real estate bubble was severely punished by the 1997 Asian financial crisis. The hand that squeezed the real estate bubble cannot go soft!

There is no need to overthink the Western "high opinion" that the bursting of the real estate bubble will trigger China's financial crisis. All financial crises are a chain reaction of liquidity depletion caused by debt defaults, which in turn destroy the assets of financial institutions. Injecting enough liquidity, bailing out financial institutions, and stopping the spread of defaults isn't hard, the US has done it, Europe is preparing to do it. The hard part is that the persistence of high debt suppresses the desire and ability of consumers to expand their credit. Without credit expansion, there will be no lasting momentum for economic recovery, and it will be difficult to generate a virtuous cycle of employment and production. And the fact that the government has no power to forcefully adjust the debt-bonding relationship in society is the crux of the matter!

In the United States, under the system of "gold power", Washington is implementing the policies of Wall Street, and debt is the most central asset for banks. So the debt is "sacrosanct"! As a result, the U.S. government used the most irrational and wasteful way to save the financial crisis. The root cause of bad bank debts is that lenders are not able to afford the debt burden caused by defaults, the simplest and most efficient way should be, the United States government with rescue funds to directly cancel the bad debts, the debt relationship is written off, so that consumers without debt pressure will be able to mount lightly, the economic recovery will soon be back on track. But the bankers don't agree, how can banks make money by reducing consumer debt? The bankers insist on taking government money to capitalize the banks and keep the debt-ridden consumers as slaves to the debt, even more so before they can get the government to keep subsidizing with the treasury, two houses being the obvious example. The result is that government money makes up for the bank's losses, the debtors continue to be pressured by high debt, the government subsidizes when they can't pay, and all the government money comes from overdrafting future national debt, the pressure of the soaring national debt is ultimately borne by taxpayers. Rather than declining, the ratio of total debt to GDP of the economy is increasing. Consumers, burdened by greater debt, have lost the ability to expand their consumption, the economy is in a quagmire, and there is little hope of a job recovery.

The fundamental difference between China and the West is that the debt-debt relationship can be forced by the government to restructure. In the early days of the Jinggang Mountain base, economic development was in decline due to heavy peasant debt. The policy proposed by the Red Army was that "all debts owed by workers and peasants to Tendong should be abolished and not returned". When the heavy shackles of peasant debt were lifted, the economy of the base soon prospered.

The abolition of the debt-debt relationship means a redistribution of social wealth, which is in fact a social revolution! The cornerstone of Western society's domination is the interests of financial groups, and changing the debt-bonding relationship is tantamount to "ruining their lives", which, of course, will not work.

In China, since the government is the center of social power, in times of crisis, everything can change! Including debt-debt relationships, which can be adjusted at any time, making it difficult for a Western financial crisis to occur in China. And this institutional difference is difficult for Western scholars to understand. If the real estate bubble bursts, the government can directly buy property and rent it cheaply to low-income people, not only to build a bottom for asset prices, but also to save the cost of building a large number of low-rent housing. As the economy recovers, real estate prices will recover in a healthy way and the banking system's bad loans will ease considerably.

Get rid of the dollar, the yuan needs a cure

The concept of "foreign exchange reserves", invented by the Governor of the Bank of England, Norman, at the Genoa Conference in 1922, has been a dubious and ineffective monetary system. The British lacked gold after the First World War, so came up with the currency "water into oil" trick, put forward the pound and the dollar together as the central bank's currency reserves, supporting the issuance of national currencies, which is the essence of the gold exchange standard system. National currencies are pegged to two core currencies, the pound sterling and the United States dollar, which in turn promise free exchange for gold. This monetary system contributed to the flood of world liquidity in the 1920s, which culminated in the Great Depression of the 1930s.

The Bretton Woods system of 1944 upgraded the global version of the system, with the core currency becoming the dollar and the dollar reserve becoming the cornerstone of national currencies, resulting in the collapse of the global monetary system in 1971.

After the birth of the American debt empire in 1971, and especially after the use of monetary "chemotherapy" by Federal Reserve Chairman Volcker to consolidate the dominance of the dollar in 1979, the dollar reserves again prevailed, until the birth of the euro.

In fact, there is an insurmountable logical contradiction inherent in the use of sovereign national currencies and the national debt of the assets behind them as the basis for the issuance of the world's currencies, the famous "Triffin dilemma" of those days, which still applies today. Logically, the dollar system will collapse again sooner or later, and none of the countries that use the dollar and U.S. debt as core assets for foreign exchange reserves will be spared. It's a question of when, not if.

Knowing this clearly, it would be a violation of the principle that "a gentleman does not build under a wall of danger" to use the dollar reserve as the basis for issuing the yuan. Holding U.S. debt is tantamount to exporting domestic savings and suppressing the expansion of the domestic market. Holding dollars, that is, indirectly holding U.S. Treasuries behind dollars, is also equivalent to financing the U.S. deficit.

But what exactly do these dollars buy? The scale of China's accumulated foreign exchange reserves is so large that it suddenly finds itself holding a huge surplus of dollars in its hands, when in fact it can't buy anything good except US Treasuries. At this point, shouldn't China ask, in turn, if this export generation still makes sense? The true purchasing power of dollar assets is depreciating every year, doesn't that amount to pouring a portion of the exported goods directly into the Pacific? Is China consuming resources, energy, manpower and material resources in order to get jobs, just to dump its products into the sea in batches? Is it possible to do something meaningful? Some argue that China must continue to buy U.S. Treasuries or the U.S. Treasuries assets it now holds will shrink. The logic is also flawed, if you held a stock in a losing company and you knew it would lose money in the future, would you choose to continue buying like crazy to maintain the stock price? Unless you're ready to pull the high shipping! But the most unfortunate thing is that you suddenly find out that you are actually the biggest, last and dumbest catch.

Before 1994, refinancing was the main mode of renminbi investment, and from 1983 to 1993, it accounted for 70 to 90 per cent of the renminbi's base currency investment. During this period, the renminbi was highly relevant to the country's economic development, as refinancing was a loan received by domestic financial institutions from the central bank, which was channelled into the domestic economic cycle, and the independence of renminbi issuance was gradually weakened by the gradual changes in the mechanism of renminbi issuance after the exchange rate convergence in 1994, the increasing share of foreign exchange, the increasing reliance on foreign exchange reserves as collateral for the renminbi's base currency, and the gradual erosion of renminbi issuance.

The issuance of the yuan is increasingly tied to the credit of foreign currencies, especially foreign governments, independently of the level of economic development of the country. In this context, China's economic development model has undergone a significant change, from reliance on the domestic market to reliance on the international market. In the 1950s, Chen Yun proposed that the renminbi should be pegged neither to the US dollar, pound sterling and gold, nor to the Soviet ruble, because the older generation had witnessed the serious consequences of the increasing colonization of the national economy after Chiang Kai-shek's French currency was pegged to the pound sterling and the US dollar, and monetary sovereignty fell by the wayside, and the financial frontier was lost.

Throughout the history of currencies, the rise of any great power's currency has been to use its own wealth as a monetary reserve to provide the blood of credit to its own economy or to the world economic cycle dominated by it. When the British Empire dominated the world, it used gold as its currency reserve; when the US dollar ran the world, it used US treasury bonds as its currency base; when the euro came into being, it used European treasury bonds as its basis of issuance; when the RMB ran the world in the future, would it be able to fight under the wings of US treasury bonds for a long time?

Foreign exchange reserves, is a sign of currency marginal countries being dominated by core currency powers, not by any means a symbol of monetary independence, it does not represent the strength of the currency, but simply reflects the depth of currency dependence.

The issue of foreign exchange accountancy is not a technical detail, but a choice of strategic direction for China's currency.

In order for the renminbi to regain dominance of currency issuance and for domestic credit creation to serve the domestic economic cycle, it is necessary to cut off foreign exchange access to central banks. The specific approach is to establish a "foreign exchange equalization fund", which will issue special "foreign exchange bonds" on State credit, raise RMB funds, and play the role of "buyer of last resort" for foreign exchange in the Chinese interbank market, block the channel of foreign exchange flow to the central bank, and eliminate the substantial increase in base currency investment solely for the purpose of acquiring foreign exchange. At the same time, this "foreign exchange bonds" can also greatly enrich the variety of the bond market and provide new investment options for insurance companies, banks, funds and other investment institutions.

The main responsibilities of the "foreign exchange parity fund" include: to intervene in the exchange rate market to achieve exchange rate stability of the renminbi; as the largest concentration of foreign exchange, lending to institutions that demand foreign exchange, as long as the lending proceeds exceed the cost of issuing "foreign exchange bonds", the fund can naturally make profits. The fund itself does not make direct foreign exchange investments, which can be outsourced to CIC or other newly formed foreign exchange investment companies, it only deals with foreign exchange investment management companies as a lender.

As for the foreign exchange reserves that already exist at the central bank, they can be resolved gradually in batches by means of asset swaps. For example, in order to raise large-scale construction funds for the second industrialization of rural areas, the State can issue special, ultra-long-term "agricultural bonds" on State credit, which can be used to replace foreign exchange assets and link the renminbi closely to domestic economic transformation. Similarly, new bond varieties such as "employment creation bills" issued to solve the employment problem, "national innovation bonds" to develop technological innovation, "health care bonds" to improve the difficulty of access to medical care in China's urban and rural areas, "low-cost housing bonds" to solve the housing problem, "national resource reserve bonds" to guarantee the source of raw materials for economic growth, can be used to replace the central bank's foreign exchange assets in batches. In this way, the yuan will truly become "the people's currency", "serving the people" and the Chinese economy.

Only by getting out of the dollar's predicament once and for all will the future internationalization of the RMB have a solid and reliable economic foundation and finally be in firm control of its destiny!

CHAPTER IX

The Age of the Warring States, tensions on the Horizon

For the past 10 years, the relationship between "China and the United States" has relied on the bundling of interests – Chinese production, American enjoyment, Chinese savings, American consumption – which is a prerequisite for the United States to tolerate Chinese economic prosperity. Over the next decade, the United States faces a high degree of overlap between three major cycles: debt deleveraging, weak consumption due to ageing, and productivity-boosting bottlenecks, and is bound to fall into a prolonged economic downturn. The debt-driven model of bankruptcy in the United States, Europe and Japan are similarly unpromising, and the prolonged downturn in developed countries makes China's outward-looking economic model unsustainable, and China will be forced to undertake economic transformation. The decline in domestic savings growth and the tilt towards the domestic side would undermine the basis for "China-US" cooperation. In the United States' view, China's utilization value is shrinking.

A sluggish U.S. economy can make its confidence fragile, and hegemonies that lack confidence tend to become more sensitive and aggressive. If China's economy continues to prosper, the U.S. will take full advantage of the East and South China Sea issues to deplete China's strength and even provoke localized wars to weaken it; if China's economy lands hard, the U.S. will take advantage of the momentum to pick up this biggest potential rival. "America's Pacific Century" is a major proclamation of its national strategic transformation.

The basis of China's economic prosperity is actually quite fragile, with oil, raw material supply and sea trade routes basically in the hands of the United States, and a highly externally-oriented economic model that relies heavily on the European and American markets, none of which is a problem when the interests of both sides are tied together;

however, everything will become a problem when the common interests of the United States and China are weakened.

Before the external environment deteriorates, China should be proactive, learn from the European experience, actively promote the Asian Economic Community, transform potential Asian rivals into allies with a community of interest, and use the Asian dollar's monetary strategy to integrate Asia's political and economic resources, while steadily promoting the internationalization of the yuan. In fact, the currencies of externally oriented economies are unlikely to become the dominant world currency, as the experience of the yen and the mark has shown.

China should lead the Asian dollar process and use the currency leverage of the Asian dollar to pry Asia's full cooperation, and eventually form a triumph over the dollar and the euro.

The "Sino-American" Dilemma

In 2009, Neil Ferguson, a leading British financial historian, coined the term "Sino-American" in his book The Ascent of Money to describe the economic "marriage" between China and the United States. People in the eastern part of the "China-America" region (China) are saving, while people in the western region are consuming and importing from China, which depresses the inflation rate in the United States, China's saving lowers the interest rate in the United States, China's labor curbs the wage cost in the United States, and the result is a prosperous economy in the "China-America".

Indeed, in this economic "marriage", China has been able to access the vast United States market and the United States-dominated world market, and the investment boom in China by multinational corporations has brought about derivative effects in terms of capital, technology, management, markets and brands, increasing the overall productivity of Chinese society and becoming a second-stage rocket that has propelled the Chinese economy to take off. In this sense, China has reaped huge economic dividends. In return, the U.S. asked China to "share" a significant portion of this dividend with the U.S. By buying U.S. debt, the savings created by China flowed back into the U.S. capital markets, pushing up the value of U.S. assets while depressing U.S. interest rates. On top of the loose monetary hotbed, financial innovation has transformed asset appreciation into an "ATM" for U.S.

consumers, stimulating the U.S. economic boom, which has led to more demand for Chinese products.

However, the "Sino-American" model of prosperity is neither solid nor sustainable. The price of "market for savings" in the United States is the inevitable rising level of indebtedness in its economy as a whole, and the bottleneck of debt-driven economic growth is the increasingly acute contradiction between consumer incomes and indebtedness pressures, which will eventually become unsustainable and lead to collapse. The essence of the so-called imbalance in the world economy is the debt-driven economic model of the developed countries, which has led to widespread bankruptcy worldwide.

Over the past 10 years, Wall Street has created a huge asset bubble, with the 1% super-rich enjoying 20% of national income, twice as much as Reagan's "neoliberal" enlightenment in the 1980s! At the same time, the 1 percent of wealthy people account for 43 percent of the wealth of society as a whole, the largest wealth imbalance since the founding of the United States! "The Occupy Wall Street movement is challenging precisely this irrational system of wealth distribution. Induced by the wealth effect, America's best science and technology talent went to Wall Street, and patent applications for inventions in almost all areas of technology in the U.S. showed negative growth of over 20 percent. At the same time, 40 per cent of U.S. corporate profits come from the financial sector, and high-tech manufacturing shows a long-term declining growth trend. The American hunter's interest in bow and arrow making is dwindling, while his obsession with appropriating the savings of other hunters is growing, and the means and techniques are constantly being pushed out in a variety of ways. This is actually a hidden "tax" on other countries through dollar means, the more trouble the United States, the heavier the "hidden tax burden" of developing countries.

After the crisis, Obama proposed the "House on the Rock" economic recovery strategy, trying to change the foundation of the U.S. economic edifice from a financial "quicksand" to an industrial "rock", returning to manufacturing, innovation and exports is the core of the strategy. "House on the Rock" concept, from a 2009 Obama speech at Georgetown University. In this well-prepared speech, Obama quoted a biblical parable that a house built on sand will fall down and a house built on rock will still stand. Obama's thinking is certainly good, but adjusting the economic growth model means rebuilding the country's wealth distribution system, the financial power groups must spit out part of the fat from their mouths.

The United States needs not only strong political will and the consensus of the ruling elite to adjust its economic model as an institutional guarantee, but also a realistic and realistic basis and economic resources. And for at least the next 10 years, the United States will lack the necessary conditions for economic transformation. This critical period coincides with the most adverse crossover of the three major economic cycles in the United States.

First, the economic "unleveraging" cycle would take at least 10 years to effectively remove the huge asset disaster caused by the "debt overhang". The information technology revolution, which began in 1996, brought about a great leap in the productivity of American society, creating an amazing wealth spillover effect, which in turn stimulated the recovery and prosperity of the real estate industry. Until 2001, U.S. real estate, and its downstream industry chain, was essentially in a period of reasonable growth. However, beginning in 2002, in order to replace the engine of information technology growth that had been turned off, and in response to the strong demand for economic resources in the post-9/11 "war on terror", the United States launched a means of stimulating the real estate bubble, easing the money supply, intensifying financial innovation and accelerating the siphoning off of other countries' savings, creating an artificially dazzling economic boom with the dual benefits of cannons and butter.

When the asset bubble finally burst in 2007, home prices fell as much as 33%, more than the intensity of the Great Depression of the 1930s, and U.S. home prices are likely to continue to fall 10% to 25% over the next five years. The bursting of the asset bubble resulted in heavy losses to the U.S. financial system, with the banks' off-balance sheet assets, stock bond commodity markets, and financial derivatives trading in tatters, and the value of pension health insurance funds, individual investments, and retirement accounts in ruins, bringing the total financial system losses to an astounding $9 trillion!

The U.S. real estate bubble of the late 1980s took six or seven years from bursting to coming out of the doldrums, and the bursting of the real estate bubble in 2007 was far greater than the real estate crisis of the early 1990s in terms of size, magnitude, and intensity, as well as in terms of hazard profile, amount of loss, and durability. This time, it will take the United States no less than 10 years to get out of the asset price slump, and the process of the financial system's complete removal of bad and troubled assets will be long and painful.

The Fed's quantitative easing policy is nothing more than an attempt to "reflate assets" and help the financial system to eliminate the toxic junk of assets, part of these harmful assets are absorbed by US bond holders and thus flowed overseas, while other parts are borne by the US economy itself, manifesting itself in government deficits, chronic unemployment, persistently weak consumer demand, fragile economic recovery, etc. Detoxification and detoxification of toxic waste, in whatever form it takes, is a long process.

The process of removing the enormous pressure on the economy from the "debt lagoon" is known as "unleveraging". From the experience of the Great Depression of the 1930s in the United States, the disparity between total debt and GDP in 1933, as high as 299.8 percent, proved to be an unbearable collapse "level" of the economy, without cutting debt levels, the economic engine will be difficult to restart. It took the United States more than a decade to reduce its total debt-to-GDP ratio to a safe zone of 120% to 150% after World War II, and in 2008 the United States again exceeded the crisis threshold (358.2%), the worst debt ratio in the United States in nearly 80 years!

The U.S. bailout method is a wrong way of thinking, not only did it not lower the dangerous debt ratio, but the size of the national debt soared to a level roughly comparable to GDP, the water level of the "debt overflow lake" is actually higher than before the crisis. The U.S. economy cannot function normally and sustainably without a significant drop in total debt below the safe 150 percent of GDP line. Without at least 10 years of painful "unleveraging", it will be difficult for the total debt level of the United States to recede into a safe economic operating zone.

Second, the age structure of the U.S. population predicts a cycle of shrinking consumption over the next decade or so. The 77 million "baby boomers", the median population in the early 1960s, have already reached the age when consumption is shrinking (47 years old being the peak).

The Baby Boomers in the United States have never been in the habit of saving money, and the first half of their lives are just in time for the United States to become the hegemonic empire that dominates the world, and they are generally super-optimistic about the future, with spending and extravagance becoming the norm, and recklessness and indulgence being the characteristics of their generation. They don't have the grizzled memories of the Great Depression of their fathers, or the brutal baptism of World War II where you die and I live, everything is so smooth and everything is so brilliant.

When the "baby boomers" generation born in the early 1960s, after 47 years of luxurious living, came to the onset of the financial tsunami, at this time, just as they began to gradually go downhill from the age of peak consumption, economic prosperity suddenly disappeared and a wave of unemployment swept in. They find that their pensions in the stock market have suffered serious losses, and their bank accounts have never been "as thin as their wings" due to their year-round extravagance, while their indulgent habits and overspending have left them long in debt. In such a scenario, their consumption will plummet off the normal aging consumption curve in response to the brutal economic cold spell ahead.

2009 is exactly at the edge of the cliff on the population consumption curve, one step forward, is the "consumption waterfall", and then is a sharp decline in the consumption cycle, the duration of which goes straight to 2024. This will be a 14-year long cycle of declining consumption. With a high level of indebtedness, the U.S. consumer market is in for a long ice age!

Neither monetary policy nor fiscal policy will have a noticeable effect on an aging generation; after all, these policies will not bring one back to childhood. It is unrealistic to encourage older people to borrow boldly to spend, and the year-on-year contraction in consumption will deprive the "green shoots" of the current seemingly bright economic recovery of fertile soil for credit. After all, consumption drives 72% of U.S. economic growth!

More seriously, Europe's demographic cycle coincides with that of the U.S., and both economic sectors in Europe and the U.S. will simultaneously fall into a long-term consumption ice age. This will be an unprecedented catastrophe in the economic and ecological environment for all emerging market countries with European and American markets as the main export targets and serious overcapacity.

Third, a new revolution in productivity also requires time and technology accumulation. During the 111-year period 1889–2000, the United States experienced three periods of high productivity, the first from 1917 to 1927, with productivity growth of 3.8 per cent; the second from 1948 to 1973, with productivity growth of 2.8 per cent; and the third from 1995 to 2000, with productivity growth of 2.4 per cent. The interval between three productivity bursts, roughly 20 to 25 years, is exactly one generation. It is no coincidence that the cycles of such technological concentrated breakthroughs coincide with demographic cycles, and if one's spending power is age-dependent, then so is one's creativity.

In general, a relatively fixed proportion of the most creative people in a society, an increase in educational attainment only changes the starting point of the creative geniuses, not their proportion in the total population. A person's most creative age is between 25 and 40 years old, and on average should be in their early 30s, when their experience, intelligence, and energy are at the peak of their lives. The "baby boomers" generation was born at the median point in the early 1960s, while the innovative geniuses among them reached their most explosive age in the early 1990s, and by 2011, they were approaching 50 years old, and their ability to innovate was bound to decline dramatically. And with the next generation born around the median point of 1990, they have the potential to bring about a new productivity revolution in the period between 2020 and 2025.

When the three cycles of economic unleveraging, population consumption and productivity breakthroughs are considered together, it can be seen that the next real cycle of prosperity in the United States should occur after 2020, with 2024 being a key turning point. Before then, however, there will be a "lost decade" for the United States economy. This decade will also be the best time for China to catch up with the developed countries in the first half of the 21st century. After that, the problem of aging in China will worsen rapidly.

The so-called "rise of China" actually has a window of time, just like the launch of a rocket; the best "window of time" to miss a launch can only wait for the next opportunity. China's next "window to rise" will probably come in the second half of the 21st century.

History has left China with a rather stingy time for its rise, if it cannot take advantage of the decline in European and American strength within 10 to 15 years to achieve a rapid economic take-off, so as to get rid of the "Western gravitational pull" and reach the "third cosmic speed", then after 2025, China will again fall back into the orbit of the world economy dominated by Europe and America. China's dream of a strong nation will have to wait another 30 to 50 years!

10 years of danger after 2012

The next 10 years will be a decade of profound changes in the pattern of major Powers, as well as a decade of dangers and challenges. The basis for cooperation between "China and the United States", built over the past 30 years as a result of geopolitical and economic interests, will undergo fundamental changes.

The U.S. economy will also face the heavy burden of an aging population as it suffers from debt deleveraging, while stagnant productivity struggles to generate new sources of wealth. As a result, the general trend in the United States economy will be one of economic fragility, heavy debt, sluggish employment, depressed consumption, fiscal deterioration and high deficits, much as in Europe and Japan. Without productivity gains, there will not be sufficient incremental savings to stimulate real and sustainable consumption and investment.

The United States has only two options before it: either to transform its economy and rebuild the "house on the rocks", but the difficulty lies in political resistance and economic weakness, a strategy that is not only difficult to implement but also slow in coming to fruition; or to restart the engine of asset inflation and restore the debt-driven boom of the past 30 years. Not only would there be little political resistance, but the suffering of the economy would be shared by other countries.

There is no doubt that the second path is more in the fundamental interests of the ruling group of the United States, the "golden world", and is therefore a natural choice for the United States. However, there is a problem here, and that is that both the asset inflation and the debt bubble have come to an end, and American consumers are no longer able to support greater debt pressure.

This is the inevitable contradiction between the wonderful ideals of the American ruling elite and the harsh reality. To achieve "asset reflation", domestic savings in China and other developing countries must be "extracted" with greater intensity. China's continued export of domestic savings is a fundamental condition of the U.S. willingness to tolerate China's development, and is the basis of the "China-US" marriage. However, this creates a logical dead circle, China's main drive to create domestic savings comes from U.S. consumption, which in turn depends on Chinese savings, and in the case of unsustainable

U.S. asset inflation, the "China-U.S." community of interest also comes to an end.

For China to transform its economic model, it must and must inevitably shift the main resources of its national economy from overseas to domestic markets, and China's export orientation in terms of commodities and savings will also change. The expansion of China's domestic market is bound to be accompanied by weakening export dependence and shrinking demand for U.S. Treasury debt, which will seriously threaten the strategic interests of the U.S. debt empire. While a booming Chinese market could stimulate U.S. exports, that stimulus is, after all, too small relative to the size of the U.S. economy.

The birth of the eurozone has gradually squeezed the dollar out of circulation on the European continent, greatly compressing the dollar empire, and the dollar in circulation abroad is facing an increasing surplus, which is the root cause of the worldwide commodity and oil price boom since 2000. The lack of international demand for U.S. bonds has forced the Federal Reserve to gradually become the biggest buyer of Treasuries. If China weakened its U.S. debt purchases, the financial ecology of the United States would deteriorate even more.

As 77 million "baby boomers" retire over the next decade, the U.S. Social Security and Medicare systems will face an inevitable collapse. In these two areas alone, the welfare guarantees promised by the United States Government create a super "hidden liability" of $100 trillion. Heavy Medicare spending will put an unprecedented strain on U.S. finances, and huge fiscal deficits over the next 10 years are inevitable. By 2020, by the most optimistic estimates, the size of the U.S. national debt could also easily top $23 trillion, a figure that will only worsen if the U.S. economic recovery is not as optimistic as the government estimates.

Over the next 10 years, the United States will need staggering amounts of money to cover its fiscal deficit, a need that will far exceed the limits of countries' export savings!

At the heart of America's economic woes is a lack of savings, and when there is not enough real savings to supply, the Fed can only fire up its money printing machines to create the illusion of monetary wealth, with the consequence of the continued depreciation of the purchasing power of the dollar, and the continued collapse of the dollar's credit. This is a self-accelerating process of deterioration, where the more the United States lacks savings the more it needs to print money, and the increasing proliferation of money accelerates the flight of capital away from dollar assets, causing the United States to lose the ability to attract savings from other countries.

Can another Volcker emerge in the US to save the dollar with high interest rates and high exchange rates? The answer is no. The United States in the early 1980s was still one of the world's largest creditors and largest savers, able to withstand the short-term drastic shocks of high interest rates and exchange rates. But the United States of America in the next 10 years, under the pressure of super-indebtedness, the "economic torpedoes" fired by high interest rates and high exchange rate policies, will be the first to sink the American economy itself, which is tantamount to economic suicide!

Everything will return to the world monetary chaos of the 1970s, and the root of the problem will be the same: the foundation of the world monetary edifice created by the US national debt standard, which was originally built on a "quicksand". The world will finally realize that today's world monetary system is not free from the spell of the "Triffin dilemma".

The supply of dollars by the United States to the world as a reserve and trade currency and the supply of United States national debt as a reserve asset of the world monetary system is the same logic that led to the collapse of the Bretton Woods system as a result of the mismatch between dollars and gold assets, and the same inherent mismatch between dollars and United States debt assets, which is the irreconcilable contradiction between the demand for unlimited expansion of dollars and United States debt and the limited growth of United States fiscal revenues.

For the world economy and trade to continue to grow, the United States must be required to supply more dollars, and the core asset behind the dollar is U.S. debt, which must therefore continue to grow. However, the dollar is the currency of the United States, the U.S. debt is a liability of the U.S. government, and the growth of the U.S. debt is subject to the growth of the U.S. government's fiscal revenue, and when the size of the U.S. debt reaches the limit of what fiscal revenue can support, the entire world monetary system will face collapse.

Where is the limit of US debt? That is, interest payments on U.S. debt as a percentage of fiscal revenue must not exceed a tipping point!

As Harvard professor Neil Ferguson points out in The Decline of Empire, historical experience has shown that when 20 per cent of a country's fiscal revenue is spent on interest payments on national debt, the country faces a serious crisis and hyperinflation is inevitable. When that ratio exceeds 50 percent, the empire will be on the verge of collapse.

In Spain, between 1557 and 1696, the heavy debt burden led to 14 defaults on the national debt, which led to the decline of the Spanish Empire; in France, on the eve of the bourgeois Revolution of 1788, 62% of the fiscal revenue was used to pay the principal and interest on the national debt, which led to the collapse of the dynasty; in the Ottoman Empire, in 1875, 50% of the fiscal revenue was used to pay the principal and interest on the national debt, which led to the near dissolution of the empire; in the British Empire, on the eve of World War II in 1939, 44% of the fiscal revenue was used to pay the principal and interest on the national debt, which led to the inability to meet the challenge of Nazi Germany.

The U.S. will also face a crisis in which interest payments on the national debt inevitably cross the threshold. According to the U.S. Congressional Budget Office, interest payments on the U.S. national debt accounted for 9 percent of fiscal tax revenue in 2011, reached 20 percent in 2020, surpassed 36 percent in 2030, and are on track to reach 58 percent in 2040!

Can sovereign credit exist in any country where the mere payment of interest on the national debt takes away a large part of its fiscal tax revenue? Congressional estimates are only the most optimistic projections, as it took an ultra-low interest rate policy in the United States, with the Fed stepping in directly to buy Treasuries, to artificially drive down the 10-year Treasury rate to around 2%. Based on the average yield of 5.7 per cent on U.S. Treasuries over the past 30 years, a total crisis of the dollar and the world monetary system will likely occur between 2020 and 2030.

It can be said that China will face unprecedented opportunities and dangers in the next decade or so. A person whose confidence is fragile will tend to be extraordinarily sensitive and aggressive; likewise, a world hegemonic state whose strength and confidence are declining will be more dangerous. The U.S. policy of returning to Asia is not just a verbal proclamation; it could be a major reorientation of national strategy. If China succeeds in its future economic transformation and continues to "contribute" domestic savings to the U.S., the U.S. is likely to adopt a "no-huddle" strategy towards China, accommodating its further development in a tangled mindset. However, if China refuses to buy U.S. debt on a large scale, the U.S. will not be able to continue to "sit back" and watch China succeed. The disputes around China will become more and more explosive, and even China will be forced to engage in one or more local wars, thus escalating the smokeless "currency war" into a smoke-filled "currency war"!

Who can save the euro?

If America's problems are economic, Europe's problems are political.

As the axis of power in the EU, Germany and France have fundamental conceptual differences. Politically, France has always wanted to be the "motorist" of the EU, while Germany continues to be the "horse" of the EU economy. For half a century after the war, Germany, under the psychological pressure of the guilt of World War II, diligently displayed the usual low-profile and uncompromising attitude of the "horse", which, however, was by no means the nature of the German nation. As Germany completed its reunification and took firm control of the European Central Bank's currency issuance, Germany gradually emerged from the shadow of war and began to take the reins of the "motorist" more and more tightly into its own hands. France's political supremacy has been increasingly dismantled by the fall of monetary power, and without the support of the ECB, France is powerless on almost all issues. In order to balance the balance of power, French President Sarkozy urged the "euro group" upgraded to "European unified Ministry of Finance", trying to restrain the power of the European Central Bank under German leadership, but the effect remains to be seen.

Luxembourg Prime Minister Jean-Claude Juncker said of the "Eurogroup":

> *"I believe that the Eurogroup can do its job without severely constraining the ECB... It is a waste of time to argue for monetary policy and the ECB. France was unsuccessful in pushing their idea. President Sarkozy's proposal for stricter political control of the ECB could not be supported by any of Europe's finance ministers, and even if the leaders of some*

countries may share this view, it will not go away because the Germans are firm."

Economically, Germany is a classic "bow and arrow" dictator, believing that wealth is rooted in production creation, while France is more concerned with the rational distribution of wealth. In the words of Jean Peyrelevade, the French bigwig behind the financial sector,

> *"The German public is aware that industrial output has a healthy structure and is essential for economic growth and increased purchasing power. In France, however, support for increasing productive capacity is not popular. German companies have a 20% higher profit margin than France. The policies that Sarkozy pushed reflect his consistent view that the key to economic growth is to increase people's purchasing power through income distribution and cutting personal tax burdens. Sarkozy believes in his policies, but he will make a big mistake".*

Sarkozy failed to realize that productivity gains are the root of all wealth creation, that income distribution only works with higher productivity, and that making a big cake is a higher priority than dividing it evenly. While the French mentality of enjoying life is certainly admirable, the German choice to work hard is even more admirable. France's struggle for dominance in the EU with Germany is doomed to failure, and as former British Prime Minister Thatcher long ago pointed out, France is nothing more than a dowry for Germany, ultimately putting a complete Europe into German hands. In response, former German Chancellor Gerhard Schröder was unapologetic:

> *"If France's political goal is to treat the creation of the euro as part of a plan to weaken Germany and thus reduce our (German) so-called economic dominance, then the opposite will happen. Increased German competitiveness means that Germany is stronger, not weaker. It can be said that this is obvious and necessary because we are the strongest economy in Europe".*

The power struggle between sovereign states is only one bright line in the story of the EU and the Euro, but behind the surface of the political and economic struggle, the directors of the "United States of Europe" process are always working on a darker line of plot. On the surface, it seems that the "unified European finance ministry" is designed to restrain the power of the European Central Bank and the Germans, which will inspire more people in EU countries to worry about Germany and weaken their resistance to the "unified European finance ministry", and then, in the sound of a "hoodwink", dutifully surrender their own budget and tax policy sovereignty to the super-sovereign EU. The politicians may be acting and are quite engaged, so much so that they often forget whether they are in the play or out of it.

In fact, the planners of the "United States of Europe" made a strategic mistake in their push for a European monetary union, which is not as big as it gets, but as close as possible to the economic level. In the initial period, the euro countries should be limited to Germany, France, the Netherlands and the Rumania, first completing internal economic integration and then introducing a unified Ministry of Finance. Due to the small size of the alliance and similar level of economic development, communication costs are relatively low and achievable. If everything works well and the rules are ripe, then include Italy, Belgium, which have bigger financial and debt problems that will take at least a few years to digest. Further expansion can only be considered afterwards. As a result, the Eurozone is now a hodgepodge of good and bad people with different opinions, and Germany will spend a lot of valuable time trying to coordinate, and time comes at a cost! If we want to make the eurozone really strong, we should give up when we give up. Not knowing the trade-offs can only be a self-defeating mess.

In the same way that the "Central America" phenomenon has emerged in which the people of the East (China) are responsible for production and the people of the West (the United States) for consumption, the European Union has also emerged as a "North-South Europe", in which the countries of the North, led by Germany and the Netherlands, are responsible for production and creation, while the countries of the South, represented by Greece, Italy and Spain, are responsible for consumption. The problems that have arisen in the southern EU are the same as those in the US, which have gone down the road of no return to a debt-driven economy driven by asset bubbles. They took advantage of the low interest rates and low inflationary environment gained by joining the eurozone to strongly stimulate the real estate bubble, using asset appreciation to drive consumption booms. In the first decade of the eurozone's existence, the Spanish economy grew by an average of 3.6 percent, Greece by 4 percent and Ireland by 6 percent, much more than the northern EU. The rise in asset prices is bound to be accompanied by the expansion of liabilities, and the boom in consumption is not born of productivity gains, but merely a stimulus to asset inflation. Their consumer demand drove Germany's economic expansion between 2004 and 2008. As a result, serious economic imbalances have emerged within the EU, with countries such as Spain, Greece, Italy and others experiencing serious worsening trade and fiscal deficits, while countries such as Germany and the Netherlands have accumulated huge trade surpluses.

When the 2008 asset bubble witnessed a widespread worldwide collapse, the debt-driven growth model of the Southern European Union declared bankruptcy. When the tide of prosperity receded, what was left was a wreck of unpayable debt. In an era of asset bubbles and consumption sprees, these countries have opted to abandon industry and buy high-quality, inexpensive industrial consumer goods from northern European Union countries, thereby weakening or even permanently losing considerable "bow and arrow" manufacturing capacity. High debt, a shrinking economy, high unemployment, depleted tax revenues, and fiscal bankruptcy are precisely the full liquidation of the wrong model of economic growth.

The key question is, who should step in to save the southern EU countries? The whole of Europe is looking at Germany, which has a lot of money in its pocket, hoping that Germany will "contribute" to the domestic savings generated by exports and help everyone to get through the crisis. Shrewd Germans would never take their savings lightly to save others.

Looking back at the history of the European Union for more than 50 years, Germany has always been a country that is very much "in the know", with a clear view of its own interests and a tightly guarded approach. The basic premise of Germans saving other countries is that other countries must first deplete all their financial resources and Germany is never stupid to save other countries! Britain and France have repeatedly tried to "take advantage" of Germany, and each time they have failed to do so after hitting a wall.

Britain briefly joined the "serpentine mechanism" in 1972, but was soon beaten out by speculative capital, and in 1973, Prime Minister Heath came to Bonn and asked the pound to join the "serpentine mechanism" again. Germany is naturally supportive, and with the two arms of the pound and the franc, the ability to resist the tidal wave of dollar speculative capital will be stronger. However, the British terms were a source of hesitation for the Germans, the British government failed repeatedly in its attempts to peg the exchange rate to the European currency, and successive governments were brought down by their support for similar policies, so Heath offered the promise that Germany must provide unrestricted support for the pound. To the Germans, this is tantamount to asking the Germans to use their own foreign exchange reserves to write a blank cheque for the British, who, with this talisman, are likely to lose their restraint on the deficit. The Germans, unwilling to reject it directly, made a counter-offer, suggesting that Britain should first join the "serpentine mechanism" in order to demonstrate their determination to defend the stability of the European exchange rate by going to war against the odds. As a result, the British backed down.

When the European Monetary System (EMS) was launched in 1978, France proposed the creation of a European Currency Unit (ECU) with a "basket of currencies" at its core, with national currencies floating up to 2.25 per cent with the ECU as a reference point. This French design is quite ingenious, and with the mark strong and the franc weak, the idea of floating relative to the ECU favors the franc. This is because the currency ratio in the "basket" is adjusted only every five years after it has been fixed. In the meantime, if the German mark appreciates too quickly, in order to ensure that the value of the mark in the "basket" does not cross the border, Germany will have to first intervene in the market with its own foreign exchange reserves to lower the mark. In this way, Germany's foreign exchange reserves will become a shared resource for the European monetary system. At the same time, the ECU will become an instrument for countries to intervene in the foreign exchange market and, ultimately, in effect, to repay the external debt caused by exchange rate fluctuations in the national currency.

The Germans saw through the French intentions at a glance, insisting that the exchange rate stability operation must inherit the "serpentine mechanism", national currency float can not be based on the ECU, but the relative exchange rate of any two groups of currencies can not break the ceiling, so that countries can only use their own foreign exchange reserves to intervene in the exchange rate first. This move cleared the way for the French ploy to calculate German foreign exchange reserves. In addition, Germany insists that when repaying borrowings resulting from exchange rate intervention, countries must pay in dollars, marks or gold. At the same time, Germany does not agree to the establishment of a shared "foreign exchange reserve pool". As a result, at the insistence of Germany, France only had to give way.

The establishment of a monetary union was originally a strategic choice to maximize Germany's interests, pulling in Britain and France was at the heart of the construction of the monetary union, and Germany adopted an attitude of zero appeasement towards British and French attempts to access German domestic savings, if Britain and France did not exhaust their entire financial resources to obtain funds from Germany? Not even a door!

There are two steps that must be taken to save the southern EU: the first is to stabilise Europe's financial system and the second is to reactivate its economic engine.

The Southern European Union, in the course of the bursting of the asset bubble, has incurred asset losses on the scale of at least Euro2 trillion, and these bad financial debts have flooded the banking systems of these countries and have spread throughout the eurozone in the form of national and corporate bonds. While Europe's financial problems have not had a magnifying effect similar to that of the huge US financial derivatives market, it is never easy to digest a rotten debt of this magnitude.

One is to print money through the ECB and use inflation to write off the bad debts, which goes against the Germans' almost paranoid anti-inflationary mindset and will also result in a loss of German savings; the other is to create a European Stability Fund (EFSF), which will take over the bad debts.

There is a renewed dispute between Germany and France over the operating mechanism of the European Stability Fund, with a single focus on whose savings are being used to fill the hole. The French proposal to convert the European Stability Fund into a bank is reminiscent of Keynes's vision of the IMF back in the day, where countries with no money always wanted a credit overdraft and the main role of banks was to create credit. The French are counting on the fund's banks to go out and buy the rotten assets, take them to the ECB to collateralize the funds, and then continue to buy them, gradually transferring them from the banking system to the ECB's balance sheet, which in effect amounts to the ECB monetizing the toxic junk, with the final bill payer still being the German savers.

The Germans, of course, are not doing it, and what they are proposing is a leveraged guarantee fund model in which the European Stability Fund guarantees 20 per cent of losses, raises money to amplify it several times, and absorbs the savings of other countries in the market, which would protect German wealth and put the savings of other countries at risk. Considering that Greece's debt is reduced by up to 50 per cent and the European Stability Fund guarantees only 20 per cent of losses, it is clear that the investment risk is significant.

The trouble also lies not only in the short-term risks of financial investment, but in the fact that the model of economic development of the southern EU countries has collapsed, a prolonged recession has become inevitable and debt-servicing capacity has been fundamentally undermined. While it is relatively easy to stabilize financial systems, it is by no means easy to restart the economic engines of these countries, as the saying goes, "save the poor, not the needy". Under the euro system, these countries can no longer stimulate exports by devaluing their local currency, and their own industries have gradually disintegrated in the face of the significant competitive advantages of German industry, on which they are increasingly dependent for domestic consumer goods. Without monetary and tariff protection, without fiscal and tax support, it will be harder for the southern EU countries to start "bow and arrow manufacturing" again and compete with the powerful German industrial products. All they can do is keep cutting fiscal spending and suppressing consumer demand, and the economy will go in a vicious cycle of austerity. The rotten debts of the southern EU countries are like cutting leeks, one crop will grow and another will grow. In fact, it's probably a bottomless pit of losses.

Now, whether it is the United States or Europe, "monsters" greedy eyes are on China's savings, China's foreign exchange reserves have become the eyes of others, "the meat of the Tang monk". The "monsters" offer all sorts of temptations, such as yuan-denominated financing, granting China a market economy status, counteracting dollar hegemony, etc., which sound attractive but are often flashy and untrue.

Yes, the United States began its first dollar expedition after World War I with the hegemony of its dollar creditors, but it ended in failure, because the basis of monetary hegemony lies in the size of the market it dominates, and in the face of the separation of the sterling and franc zones, the first expedition of the dollar failed to return. Only in World War II did the destruction of European nations against each other create a historic opportunity for dollar domination. The current situation is that the size of the euro area is much larger than the pound sterling cut off, outflow of the yuan overseas is difficult to form trade settlement of the cut off sphere of influence. Until a sufficient domestic market size is formed in China, Chinese savings should stay at home to play a greater role. When SMEs are on the verge of widespread bankruptcy due to lack of capital, channelling domestic savings to Europe inevitably creates a "moral hazard".

The market economy status does not eradicate the anti-dumping problem in trade, the trade conflict between Japan and Europe and the United States in the 1980s, Japan does not have a market economy status problem, the root cause is still a conflict of interest, the market economy status is just one of the many pretexts to wage trade war.

The anti-dollar hegemony rhetoric is also very suspicious, the European and American financial system is originally the balance of interests of the major families in the past 200 years, after repeated games, there are contradictions and conflicts of interest between them, and there is also the basic consensus that the gun is the same as the outside. For an outsider, I'm afraid their common interests outweigh their internal conflicts.

China's role in the European debt crisis should still learn more from the savvy Germans.

China's Near and Far Worries

The Chinese economy in 2012 will soon feel the cold tide of simultaneous cooling of the three major developed economies in Europe, the United States and Japan, the second stage of the rocket that the Chinese economy took off – globalization, has run out of fuel. It would be a state of glide that loses power, more like what happened after the first stage of rural industrialization rockets died in 1997–1999. In the short term, China's economy is facing weak external demand, weak internal credit expansion, sluggish consumption, falling prices, shrinking profits, sharp debt problems and worsening asset conditions, all of which will suddenly make 2011 an even more intractable deflationary predicament for the inflation-plagued Chinese economy.

The traditional thinking is that China's economic development has three carriages: exports, investment and consumption, which can still support China's economy to continue to grow at a high rate if exports go wrong. This analysis ignores the logical subordination between the three. Economic growth is driven by productivity gains, and the logic of growth is that sectors with the fastest productivity "acceleration" create sufficient incremental savings to provide an economic base for consumption and investment as demand spreads to slower sectors. In the three carriages, the sector that has really brought about the rapid increase in productivity is export, which is oriented to the world market, based on technology and equipment close to the world level, at the expense of low labor and resource costs, relying on the support of local governments in all aspects of close cooperation, with the best production organization mode as the guarantee, with the industrial cluster effect as the driving point, to create a quality and low price in the international market is invincible "Made in China" myth. Without the productivity miracle created by the export sector, there would not have been sufficient incremental domestic savings to finance the Government's huge infrastructure investments and thriving market consumption. From this perspective, exports are the real locomotive of China's economy, while investment and consumption are "stimulated".

While Europe, the United States and Japan are facing the debacle of the debt-driven model, they also have debt dilemmas, ageing populations and productivity bottlenecks that cannot be solved in the short term and that will not be achieved in 10 years if they are to re-energize their economies. The economic woes of developed countries have created a huge drag on China's export sector, a new problem unprecedented in 30 years of reform and opening up, and the export economy has been exacerbated by the huge appreciation of the yuan.

The export sector will of course have full penetration into emerging markets and will be quite productive. At the same time, the capacity of developed countries' low- and middle-tier markets can also provide a minimum guarantee of a base figure for exports. As a result, China's export sector will be able to maintain a still large size, although incremental growth will gradually diminish and the function of the economic rocket booster will weaken.

The rate of productivity increase represents the basic trend of social progress, while the "acceleration" of productivity implies major technological breakthroughs and advances in production methods. Thus, productivity "acceleration" is far more meaningful than economic scale. This is the root cause of why China's GDP in the 18th century was 1/3 of the world's, yet it still ended up being passive and beaten.

As the export-boosted rocket dies down, the growth of real domestic savings will gradually slow down, which will lead to weaker consumer demand. With regard to consumption, people often fall into the misconception that stimulating consumption will lead to economic growth, which completely reverses the logic of the relationship between the two. When a farmer takes 100 eggs to the market to trade, he asks for a change of clothes, which is what he is spending with his savings. Consumption is essentially an act of exchange, and consumption presupposes production, without which there would be no consumption. To generate more consumption, more must be produced. If the farmer increases his egg production by increasing his productivity, he enriches the market supply when he takes 200 eggs to the market to trade, and he asks for more than just clothes to be exchanged, which stimulates economic growth. Stimulating consumption will not lead to sustained economic growth, and only increased productivity will lead to more consumption and thus economic growth.

Can stimulating residents to spend the large amounts of money in the bank lead to economic growth? Deposits are the monetary embodiment of savings, and farmers' eggs are the real savings. The essence of savings is a measure of how long people can continue to survive in society when they are no longer engaged in production. A deposit is merely a delayed consumption, the essence of which is still product exchange. In the absence of productivity gains, spending bank deposits is tantamount to shortening one's "social life", which can sustain the economy but does not lead to real growth.

Consumption must stem from a significant increase in productivity in one sector of the economy, creating a large number of new, cheaper products that require more exchange in market transactions to stimulate development in other sectors. The explosive development of the economy was always driven by the emergence of new industries, when the petrochemicals emerged in the 1950s and information technology swept society in the 1990s, new products and services created new consumption in market transactions, stimulating more new demand. Because of starting from zero, productivity gains are more prominent in new industries.

When China's consumer market begins to weaken, the idea of stimulating consumption, as tempting and inflammatory as it is, cannot be blindly generated, but is by no means a cure for the problem.

Economic cooling and deflation will intensify if governments adopt a do-nothing approach. At this point, the calls for fiscal stimulus will be deafening. The question is, how rightly should the government stimulate the economy, and many of the measures taken since 2009 will not have a sustainable effect in future economic woes; they are nothing more than attempts to extend the life of a second stage rocket. Increased government investment can sustain economic growth, but China's debt problem will become acute if it is spent in areas that do not increase productivity, or in sectors of the economy that are difficult to generate benefits in the short term. Ultimately, unsustainable debt can only be solved by monetary increases, which will add to the inflationary trouble in a cooling economy. Deflation and inflation may go hand in hand, but will occur in different areas. Continued low prices in the consumer market and ballooning prices in the asset sector could put China's economy in a difficult situation.

The key to economic transformation is to ignite a third-stage booster rocket, and government investment must be spent in the right areas to have a sustainable effect. A number of prerequisites must be in place for the areas that can drive China's continued economic growth: first, there is a great potential for productivity acceleration; second, there are significant scale effects that benefit the majority of the population in society; and finally, there is a wide range of industries involved and a comprehensive pull on all sectors of the economy.

Of the three sectors of the economy that meet these three conditions, agriculture clearly ranks first. The core of the second rural industrialization is informatization, intensification, high technology and urbanization. Low rural productivity is the potential advantage of its "acceleration". Large-scale government investment in rural and agricultural infrastructure will improve the basic conditions of the agricultural economy, reduce production costs and increase the profits of the agricultural economy. At the same time, the investment of economic resources in capital markets will produce productivity "accelerations" in agriculture that are much higher than in other economic sectors. More than half of China's population still lives in the countryside, and they will create massive new savings on a massive scale based on productivity gains. As healthier, greener, safer, richer and more nutritious agricultural products flood the market, farmers will demand the exchange of better quality, cheaper, more energy efficient, more diverse and innovative industrial consumer goods, thus stimulating the light industrial sector to increase its own productivity. While the light industry is increasingly thirsty for raw materials and equipment manufacturing, it will in turn drive the development of heavy chemical industry. More affluent rural areas would naturally generate a desire for urbanization to further improve the quality of life, which would not only improve the distorted distribution of the population and alleviate the "urban disease" of over-concentration in large cities, but would also generate more sustained demand for all industrial sectors.

The third stage of the rocket will ensure that China gradually forms the world's largest consumer market, gaining a real power base for the great powers and putting China's destiny firmly in its own hands!

Asian Economic Community

America's problem is economics, Europe's problem is politics, and Asia's problem is history!

Asia's history is no shorter than that of Europe, and its political wisdom has always been a source of confidence for Asians. The rich and profound cultural accumulation, the long-standing Confucian tradition and the spirit of openness and tolerance in Buddhism have laid a solid platform of civilization and faith for the Asian Economic Community.

China faces serious challenges in economic transformation in the next decade, and stability and cooperation in East Asia is an indispensable external guarantee for the Chinese economy. If Europe's generational enemies, Germany and France, can put aside their former grudges and become the two driving forces of the European Community, can China, Japan and Korea, which also have a century-old grudge, untie the knot of history and become the forerunner of the Asian Economic Community?

The key to the German-French rapprochement was the establishment of a community of interest in the "Coal and Steel Alliance". Since coal and steel were both indispensable materials for national warfare and the primary source of energy and raw materials for industry in the 1950s, placing the economic lifeblood of the two countries under the "coal and steel alliance" of "super-sovereignty" would fundamentally eliminate the intent and ability of both sides to wage war, the purpose of the Schumann Plan being "to make war not only inconceivable, but also materially impossible". It can be argued that true reconciliation will be difficult to achieve without a complete bundling of the interests of both sides. More importantly, the Coal and Steel Union has explored a realistic and viable "supersovereign" economic model, laying the foundations of the European Common Market. Without a market large enough to compete with the United

States, Europe cannot gain the ultimate power to dominate its own destiny.

No major war has broken out in Europe since the end of the Second World War, bringing to an end nearly 500 years of fratricidal warfare, and Europeans today enjoy the rich dividends of peace. Peace, as opposed to war, is always a civilizational advance.

The Coal and Steel Alliance, created by the Europeans more than 60 years ago, is a more realistic, if not more urgent, reference for Asia today. Asia, though long removed from war, has never been removed from a war mentality. The bitter hatred between China, Japan and South Korea in recent times has not faded with time, but has instead clashed with fierce sparks of vengeance in their respective folk. The three countries are on guard against each other and are on guard against each other, consuming considerable diplomatic, military and political resources.

Historically, Britain's basic strategy for keeping the continent in check has been to provoke wars between continental European countries. If France was strong, it would draw Russia, Germany and other countries to establish an anti-French siege; if Germany was strong, it would support other European powers to besiege Germany, and in the midst of the mutual consumption of the European continent, it consolidated Britain's position of world hegemony. After the rise of the United States, the British strategy of "combining the strong with the weak" was brought to a higher level. During the Cold War, Europe was placed in the first line of siege of the Soviet Union, which not only controlled Europe but also consumed the Soviet Union; during the period of isolation of China, the United States brought together Japan, South Korea, Australia, the Philippines and other countries, with Taiwan as the core of the first island chain, and strangled China's sea passage. Hegemonic states always try to stir up disputes between other states in order to divide and conquer.

Now that China has "unfortunately" become the second largest economy in the world, it has never been a good time for the oldest two, and the vigilance of the boss and the jealousy of the oldest three make it easy for them to form a united front against the oldest two. Germany at the beginning of the 20th century, the Soviet Union in the Cold War, and Japan in the 1980s, without exception, have all been defeated by the Anglo-Saxon English-speaking peoples, who have failed because they were too strong and eager to challenge the bosses, and because they failed to break the strategic military, political and economic encirclement established by the bosses and the older three.

The United States has ended the wars in Iraq and Afghanistan, which, combined with regime change in numerous countries in North Africa and the Middle East, have led to an unprecedented strengthening of its control over global oil resources. For China, which must rely on imports for more than half of its oil each year, the Americans have a firm grip on the lifeblood of the Chinese economy, and their extreme dependence on overseas markets, especially those in Europe and the United States, has made China's ostensible prosperity actually built on a rather tenuous foundation.

Secretary of State Hillary Rodham Clinton, in her Foreign Policy of 11 October 2011, made a major policy statement on "America's Pacific Century", claiming that the politics of the future will depend on Asia, that one of the most important missions of the U.S. foreign policy strategy over the next 10 years will be to target significantly increased investments in the Asia-Pacific region, that the relationship with China is one of the most challenging and influential bilateral relationships the U.S. has ever had to manage, and that there is no guidebook for the development of U.S.-China relations, yet the stakes must not fail.

It is clear that the US has begun to shift the focus of its global strategy towards China's perimeter, and its intentions to guard against and contain China have been made clear. Japan, India, Australia and the South China Sea countries, encouraged by their own interests and the United States, gradually began to form a united front that was very unfavorable to China. A situation in which East Asian countries are fighting over oil resources in the East and South China Seas is no longer out of reach. Once China was forced into a localized war, it undoubtedly fell into the strategic trap of the United States, repeating the historical mistake of French and German sandpipers fighting each other and British fishermen gaining.

To break this historical destiny, the East Asian countries must break out of the traditional way of thinking and boldly learn from the successful experience of the European Monetary and Economic Union and turn their differences into peace for the sake of peace in the Asia-Pacific region.

Each of the three major East Asian countries, China, Japan and South Korea, is fatal, China's vulnerability lies in its economy, Japan's vulnerability lies in its politics and South Korea's vulnerability lies in its military, and all of these weaknesses are linked to the United States. If the three East Asian countries unite, their respective weaknesses will be protected by a strong alliance, and it is the common aspiration of all Asian countries to create a common market in Asia with the three countries at its core, free from the domination of Europe and America over the destiny of Asia.

Rather than engaging in this zero-sum game, countries are competing for nothing more than benefits, and the benefits should be shared. Deng Xiaoping put forward the concept of "putting aside sovereignty and developing together" a long time ago, which is a strategic principle in the fundamental interests of Asian countries. It is time to flesh out this idea and be brave enough to put it into practice. The Diaoyu Islands dispute between China and Japan and the Dokdo issue between Japan and South Korea involve not only sensitive sovereignty disputes, but also the vital interests of the huge undersea oil resources, the stalemate between the parties has nearly destroyed the peaceful environment of the Asia-Pacific region, bringing the economic development of countries to the brink of derailment.

If the Coal and Steel Alliance has been validated by European practice, then this model of "supersovereignty" can also be replicated in the contested regions of Asia. If an institution similar to the European Union's "Asian Economic Community" is established, with the "oil union" as the starting point, the disputed submarine oil resources will be ceded to this new institution of "supersovereignty", so as to fundamentally resolve the sensitive and irreconcilable contradiction of sovereignty and form a mechanism for joint investment, joint development and benefit-sharing among all countries, so that the interests of all countries will be deeply bound and the outbreak of war will be "neither conceivable nor achievable" and the people of Asia will be able to enjoy peace dividends forever.

Through the establishment of the "Asian Economic Community", China will break the political, economic and military siege of the United States, Japan will be assured of a reliable supply of oil, South Korea will have a joint security commitment from China and Japan, and ASEAN and India will have access to a unified Asian market. This would be a strategic alliance of great interest to all Asian countries!

In fact, the purpose of remembering history is not to live in it, but to prevent it from repeating itself! What Asians are most sensitive to is sovereignty, in fact, behind sovereignty is the power of the state to dictate its own destiny! It's the interests that concern Asians most, in fact, the benefits that are shared outweigh the competing interests themselves!

If Asia was once the birthplace of the oldest civilization of mankind, then the wisdom of Asians should not be lost to Europeans! If Asia's history has suffered at the hands of the great powers, then Asia today must never again surrender its fate to any hegemony!

Asia as a whole will have an unprecedentedly high status and independence on the international stage and a strategic landscape that is at odds with the United States and Europe.

Building the Asian dollar market: Hong Kong is a bridgehead

The first task of the "Asian Economic Community" should be to start with the "oil alliance", to completely remove the fuse from the gunpowder barrel of war in the Asian region and to bind the fate of the Asian countries in a community with the great ties of interest of submarine oil. This is a large and risky investment, where does the money come from?

The answer is the Asian dollar market!

The European dollar, as it is known, first referred to the dollars that flowed into Europe and roamed around there, stemming primarily from Europe's trade surpluses with the United States and U.S. dollar military spending at European military bases, which grew in size over the years. Later, the Soviet Union, the Middle East and other countries also deposited dollars from oil exports in the European banking system, further expanding the "financial heterogeneous space" of the European dollar, and later, the dollars of other countries and regions also flocked to Europe. Later, all dollars in circulation outside the United States were referred to as European dollars.

International banker Sigmund Warburg first started hitting the European dollar, so large and unregulated that the dollar money, used solely to invest in U.S. Treasuries, yielded too little. In the early 1960s, he pioneered the European dollar bond, a new investment instrument, using idle or low-yielding European dollars to finance European enterprises and EC projects, the significance of the European dollar bond is that Europeans began to use dollar resources, borrowing power, while developing their own, did not fall into the low-yielding trap of U.S. Treasury bonds, becoming the passive payer of U.S. deficit finance.

Over the last decade, the Asian region has become the world's largest dollar reserve, with trade surpluses continuing to bring rolling dollars back to Asia every year that seem to have no better place to go than to buy US Treasuries and low-yielding bonds of other sovereigns. In fact, this issue was cracked by Eurodollar bond innovation back in the 1960s.

Why should dollar savings in Asia necessarily flow to financial markets in the United States or Europe? Why should I only invest in low-yielding European and American Treasuries? If Asia's economy is developing significantly faster than Europe and the United States, won't these funds stay in Asia to find opportunities for high returns?

High-yield, low-risk, sovereign credit-grade projects, doesn't "oil alliance" fit the bill perfectly? At that time, Sigmund Warburg initially wanted to use the "Coal and Steel Union" project to carry out the first European dollar bond issue, the "Asian Economic Community" can directly issue dollar bonds, the funds will be used for the exploration and development of subsea oil in the Asian region, which is the EU has not yet done the EU bond model. "The dollar bonds issued by the Asian Economic Community will be guaranteed by the foreign exchange reserves of each country and will have a credit rating equal to that of the sovereign credit of Asian countries, which will allow for further financing of projects in other Asian countries and regions in the future, fully revitalize the huge dollar assets of Asia, make a direct contribution to the economic development of Asia, and obtain higher and more reliable investment returns.

Hong Kong is in the best location, with a well-developed legal system and an abundance of financial talent, and in the 60 years since the war, it has accumulated a wealth of experience in the international financial markets, making it the London of Asia! At present, Hong Kong's positioning as a world financial centre is still unclear, should it vigorously develop its stock market, real estate finance, trade finance, or RMB offshore centre in the future? The Hong Kong Government appears to be indecisive. In fact, the Asian Dollar Convergence Centre and the Asian Dollar Bond Issuance and Trading Centre are the big moves for Hong Kong! There are currently trillions of dollars of assets in Asia, which will soon exceed the size of $10 trillion in the future!

Any other business would be a piece of cake if this big deal was held in its hands.

Hong Kong's main rivals will be Tokyo and Singapore, and if China pushes for an "Asian Economic Community", Hong Kong will clearly be the preferred centre of financial operations, just as Germany and France pushed for the birth of the European Community, but Paris and Frankfurt failed to become the hub of the European dollar, and London, which is more financially regulated and internationalized, remains the most active core of the European dollar. The conditions in Tokyo, Beijing, Seoul, Shanghai and Singapore are not as good as those in Hong Kong, with the degree of internationalization and experience in the financial market being the most critical differences.

With the issuance and trading of Asian dollar bonds as the core, supplemented by RMB, Japanese yen, Korean won and other currency-denominated bond varieties, Hong Kong will become an international financial hub that can compete with New York and London in the future!

The unprecedented institutional innovation of China's unique "one country, two systems" design for Hong Kong has given Hong Kong a distinctive international character among all Asian cities, and its psychological and geographical proximity to Asian countries is justified.

Asian Monetary Union: Strategic Direction of the Asian Monetary Fund (AMF)

The financial turmoil of 1997, which exposed Asian countries to a fierce exchange rate storm, has had a devastating impact on Asian financial markets that is still haunting. The economic development of Asian countries, which have generally adopted an export-oriented economic model, urgently requires stability in exchange rate markets in order to hedge against international trade risks. In the absence of a joint exchange rate mechanism in Asia, countries generally rely on the International Monetary Fund (IMF) as a last resort. However, after experiencing the financial turmoil in 1997–1998, everyone has a bitter memory of the nature of the IMF "rescue", the IMF rescue mechanism under the leadership of Europe and the United States, rather than putting out the fire, it is more like robbery.

After learning the hard way, Asian countries have proposed to establish the Asian Monetary Fund (AMF). Of course, it is entirely conceivable that this initiative was immediately opposed by the IMF and the US Treasury. However, with the establishment of the Arab Monetary Fund and the Latin American Reserve Fund, it is only a matter of time before the AMF is established, and the outbreak of the financial tsunami in 2008 and the European debt crisis in 2011 have again highlighted the need and urgency of the AMF.

The AMF is currently positioned as an exchange rate stabilization fund, but does not contain a long-term plan similar to the European Exchange Rate Mechanism. This is one of the reasons why the AMF has struggled to gain the attention of Asian countries; it is merely a tool to save the day, rather than a central part of future monetary strategies. If an Asian common market is to be established, then the eventual single currency of Asia is a logical necessity, and stabilizing exchange rates is only one step in the process.

The first phase is the establishment of the Asian Exchange Rate Mechanism (AERM, Asian Exchange Rate Mechanism), which is similar to the European "serpentine exchange rate mechanism", the main purpose of which is to stabilize the exchange rate of countries within the framework of a mechanism. To this end, a common reserve fund needs to be established. Indeed, in the aftermath of the Asian financial turmoil, the Chiang Mai Initiative has proposed that Asia allocate $120 billion from the foreign exchange reserves of countries as emergency aid to help countries in distress to stabilize their exchange rates. Of these, China and Japan both contribute 32 per cent of the total reserve pool, Korea 16 per cent and ASEAN countries 20 per cent. The amount of funds contributed by countries within ASEAN also varies, with Indonesia, Malaysia, Thailand and Singapore all at $4.77 billion and the Philippines at $2.64 billion. When the financial crisis struck, the five ASEAN member States could tide over the situation with funds equivalent to 2.5 times their national contributions. However, during the 2008 financial tsunami, when some countries in the region faced liquidity difficulties, the reserve fund scheme was difficult to implement because of the lack of an independent regional monitoring entity.

The debt crisis that erupted in Europe in 2011 is likely to hit Asian financial systems again in the coming years, and the Asian exchange rate mechanism should be accelerated. However, the political attitudes of Asian countries determine the pace of the process, and the establishment of the Asian Exchange Rate Mechanism within five years is possible if countries can agree on a strategy to establish an Asian community.

At the heart of this mechanism is the stabilization of exchange rate fluctuations in Asian countries, and only relative stability of the region's currencies can effectively promote the growth of international trade and lay the foundation for the eventual realization of a unified Asian common market. The key to it is to determine the maximum relative float of currencies between countries, and when the exchange rate of any pair of currencies floats beyond that limit, countries that fall below the lower limit are obliged to use their own foreign exchange reserves to intervene in the market to restore exchange rate stability to their currencies. In the most extreme distress, the AMF's foreign exchange reserve fund will initiate an emergency rescue. This rescue amounts to a foreign exchange loan, which the recipient country is obliged to repay when it emerges from the crisis.

The second phase of the AMF's mission is to build the Asian Monetary System (AMS). This depends first and foremost on the establishment of the Asian Community and the advancement of the Asian Common Market. When Asian countries reach a consensus on tariffs, subsidies, agriculture, free movement of capital and people, the unified Asian Currency Unit (ACU, Asian Currency Unit) will serve as the monetary unit for intraregional trade settlement, the ACU is also made up of a "basket" of Asian currencies, which occupy a weight equivalent to their economic and trade status, together forming a benchmark for the value of Asian currencies, adjusted every five years to reflect changes in their economic status.

When the ACU is created, the Asian exchange rate mechanism will be adjusted from a maximum float between any pair of currencies to a float of national currencies relative to the ACU, which will place greater responsibility on the large foreign exchange reserve countries in order to attract more countries to participate.

The ACU will assume the historical role of the anchor of the value of Asian currencies and will be the basis for the birth of the Asian dollar in the future.

The third and most critical phase of the AMF is to fix the exchange rate between national currencies and the ACU. After a certain period of preparation, the ACU will be used as the currency benchmark for the Asian dollar when political conditions and the economic environment permit, and mature countries can take the lead in converting their currencies to the Asian dollar.

The AMF should have promoted the Asian dollar and the establishment of the Asian Central Bank from the beginning of its existence with a long-term view, if only as a supporting role for the Foreign Exchange Relief Fund and the IMF, which is clearly too low positioning, the AMF should play a central role in promoting political alliances and economic integration in Asia, not a "driven" institution. This requires that the AMF should be the most active, effective and active communicator between governments, central banks, ministries of finance, research institutions, academic organizations, media and the public.

Also, the advance of the Asian dollar should take a lesson from the euro, rather than wait and see. China, Japan and South Korea can take the lead in establishing an exchange rate stability mechanism, China and Japan's foreign exchange reserves are comparable, South Korea is not weak, these three alliances will not produce disputes and tug of war over who will save whom, to avoid Germany in the process of promoting the European exchange rate mechanism, always worry about their own foreign exchange reserves will be France and other countries' concern of "slimming". Indeed, the slow pace at which the European Exchange Rate Mechanism is moving is largely due to this German apprehension and endless bargaining, which has wasted a great deal of valuable time. Once a political consensus is reached between China, Japan and South Korea, and the euro's experience in operational details is readily available, the Asian Exchange Rate Union should advance much faster than Europe.

After a period of stable operation, the exchange rate alliance between China, Japan and Korea was gradually opened to the ASEAN 10 and other Asian countries. These countries have joined the Exchange Rate Union (ERU) largely for its own sake: first, in the hope that the exchange rate mechanism will be of great help in the event of an unpleasant situation for their currencies; and second, in the desire to enter a larger Asian common market. At this point, a certain threshold of compliance needs to be set.

The toughest time was in the early days of the launch of the exchange rate union, and this difficulty was not so much the trouble caused by the operational details, or even the political will of China, Japan and South Korea, but the enormous pressure from the United

States. Can and dare to stand up to this pressure and fight to dominate their own destiny is the biggest question mark about the success or failure of the Asian Monetary Union and the biggest question mark about Asia's destiny!

RMB, or Asian dollar? That's a problem

For China, would pushing for internationalization of the yuan bring more benefits, or would pushing for the Asian dollar yield the best results? This is a critical issue.

Historically, the pound and the dollar have been the major world reserve currencies, while the mark and the yen, even in their economic heyday, never held more than 10 per cent of the international reserve currency position, as was destined by the export-oriented economic development model of Germany and Japan.

Due to the limited capacity of their own markets, Germany and Japan had to use the world market as the main expansion space for economic growth, and the process of exporting products was inevitably accompanied by a return of international currency. Conversely, for a country's currency to serve as the world's main trade and reserve currency, it must export its own currency on a sustained basis, only through trade deficits and overseas investment. If Germany and Japan become trade deficit countries, exporting large amounts of marks and yen, importing foreign products will soon flood their relatively small domestic markets, while their own industrial capacity will be dismantled, thus burying their status as economic powerhouses. Japan has been promoting yen investment and yen lending overseas as early as the 1980s, and its efforts over the past 30 years have not produced significant progress, making it difficult for the yen to go out. The main reason people are willing to hold the yen is the desire to buy goods in the Japanese market in the future, and if the domestic market is not large enough, the incentive to hold the yen will be greatly diminished.

As a result, a country with a small domestic market, no matter how strong its economy, is unlikely to have a currency that is a major international currency. International currencies can only be played by countries with large markets.

The British Empire used to have a huge market size that spanned $1/5^{th}$ of the continent of the earth, a quarter of the world's population, and the deficit caused by the export of sterling was large in absolute terms, but not a large share of the total economy of the British Empire. In the 1930s, the United States foreign trade accounted for only 3 to 5 per cent of the total economy, and its huge domestic market made the United States not care about fluctuations in the exchange rate of the dollar. The export of currency has to be capitalized, and countries with large families can first withstand this pressure and then enjoy its benefits.

China's current situation is that domestic consumption accounts for only 1/3 of GDP, and overseas markets are the mainstay of China's economic growth. This outward-looking economic pattern and small domestic market capacity are destined to make it difficult for RMB internationalization to achieve a substantial breakthrough until China's economic transformation is successful. The best effect would be nothing more than that the mark and the yen's position in the international currency that year would not be enough to bring greater real benefits to China.

China's economic prosperity is heavily dependent on overseas supplies of oil and raw materials, as well as demand from European and American markets, and there is a fragile side to the foundation of this prosperity. If the debt-driven model of the European and American economies is unsustainable, how can China's economic prosperity be sustained if localized wars cause disruptions in the supply of oil and raw materials? At the same time, the supply of the RMB and the US dollar are tightly tied together, before the completion of the RMB "scraping the bone to cure the poison", is not the internationalization of the RMB or the re-export of the US dollar in the guise of the RMB? On a relatively fragile economic basis, with a relatively small domestic market size, would the going out RMB be a strong and robust currency? The appreciation of the yuan has brought more excitement from currency speculators than from the sincere trust of the world's nations.

The stronger the internationalization of the renminbi, the more vigilant and aggressive the U.S. will be towards China, the more eurozone countries will be happy to see the renminbi become the main target of U.S. strikes, while Asian countries will be vigilant against China's attempts to establish a "new order of the renminbi".

In the face of immature strength, a high-profile attack by the yuan is likely to leave it alone, inviting a siege from the currency hegemonists in the absence of allies.

Therefore, the high-profile internationalization of the yuan prior to the success of China's economic transformation is a radical strategy.

Relatively speaking, the Chinese led effort to push the Asian dollar appears to be radical, but is conservative.

If the U.S. and European economies remain sluggish for a long time and China is forced to undergo economic transformation, China will be unable or unwilling to continue to provide domestic savings to the U.S. and will lose its use in the eyes of a pragmatic, supreme America. Over the past decade, the U.S. tolerance of China's economic prosperity has been based on Chinese production for U.S. enjoyment and Chinese savings for U.S. consumption, and once common interests are lost, the "China-U.S." marriage is bound to break down.

The new "Pacific Century" strategy proclaimed by the United States has in fact locked China as a strategic rival without naming it, and a series of recent conflicts over territorial sea issues in Asia have intensified, showing the United States' pre-emptive momentum. In the game of "Asians versus Asians", the United States is reaping very high profits at very low cost. The United States, while holding China's oil supply, sea access and market-dependent economic lifeline, has instigated Asian countries to rob China of its interests, putting China in the dilemma of "no war, no peace". Over the next 10 years, the fragile self-confidence caused by the prolonged economic downturn in the US will make the US more sensitive and aggressive towards China.

China needs more allies and fewer adversaries in the sharp and complex game between the US and China. The establishment of a united front in Asia to turn potential adversaries into friends with interests is a "taiji pusher" to resolve the oppressive siege of the United States. In this sense, the promotion of the subdollar is not only a monetary strategy, but also a geopolitical and military one.

By uniting Japan, South Korea and the 10 ASEAN countries, using the "oil alliance" as a starting point and the monetary mechanism as a lever, the concept of an Asian common market will be mobilized to turn confrontation into cooperation and conflict of interest into benefit sharing. The Asian Common Market needs a common currency, and a common currency will expand the common market. If Japan's technology, China's production, South Korea's innovation, and ASEAN's resource advantages are combined, the Asian dollar will become one of the world's top three currencies, relying on such a large unified market.

It won't be hard for the US to hit the yuan because it will offend only one country, China, but to hit the Asian dollar will offend all Asian countries, and the costs and benefits will be hard to match. The Asian Community and the Asian dollar, not only provide Asian countries with more room for development and more autonomy, but also provide an effective umbrella for China. Politically, China relies more heavily on Asia; economically, the common market can provide more room for economic transformation; militarily, China has no rivals in Asia, only allies, and the U.S. military advantage will be effectively neutralized.

The Asian dollar strategy is indeed a strategy for China to protect itself, and is worth sticking with, no matter how long it takes or what difficulties it encounters. In the short term, the results of the RMB internationalization strategy are not promising, while the sequelae are numerous. However, there is no fundamental conflict between the two strategies, conservative and radical, and a steady push to internationalize the renminbi and kick-start the Asian dollar process could well go hand-in-hand. There may be only one ultimate effect of RMB internationalization, and that is to increase China's leverage in the Asian dollar system.

The Germans abandoned the mark, but they now control the euro; the Germans abandoned the protection of their own market and ended up dominating the big market across the EU. The so-called "shed gain" means that without shed gain, there can be no gain, and without shed small gain, there can be no gain. The Chinese also need to learn well from the Germans in how to pursue their interests.

The Warring States Era of the Dollar, Euro and Asian Dollar

The dilemma of the dollar is that sovereign currencies cannot, in fact, permanently carry the burden of the world's currency. The world monetary edifice, built with sovereign debt as a core asset, will eventually collapse as sovereigns become overburdened with tax revenues. History has proven repeatedly that the eventual collapse of the dollar system is actually a logical necessity.

The question is, who can replace the dollar as the new world currency when the dollar system is untenable? Euro, Renminbi, or Yen, or any other currency? The answer is that there is no substitute for the dollar for any sovereign currency. The dollar will be the "last emperor" of the era when the sovereign currency will be the world's currency.

In the final decades of the Dollar Empire, the world economy will experience repeated sharp bumps in the face of an increasingly volatile currency crisis. The trend towards regionalization of currencies, represented by the euro, will continue in Asia, the Middle East, Africa and South America. Such a regionalized currency would in turn severely squeeze the circulation of the dollar and accelerate its decline.

The dollar empire, like all the last emperors, will naturally not sit back and watch the dollar disintegrate; it will use all its political, economic and military resources to suppress these "currency revolts". Perhaps this crackdown can have some effect, and the world's "monetary gangs" are temporarily dormant. Behind this brief calm, however, brewed a larger crisis of rebellion. More rebellion sparked more repression until the dollar empire was exhausted. At this point, the conflict between the "sovereign monetary faction", which had always existed within the dollar empire, and the "world unitary monetary faction" began to intensify, and the political scales gradually tipped in the latter direction.

If the dollar goes to the "power down" the final moment, the United States has long been ready for the world's currency "spare tire" will emerge, which is the IMF's special drawing rights (SDR). in the late 1970s, when the dollar is in the stormy and dangerous moment, "SDR alternative account" was about to be put into operation, if not the Federal Reserve Chairman Volcker quickly, in a crisis to save the dollar, the world is afraid to have been living in another currency space.

The SDR is highly aligned with the European Currency Unit (ECU), which is a monetary reference unit consisting of a basket of currencies. Replacing national sovereign currencies with SDRs is as simple and painless as replacing European currencies with the euro, as long as the exchange rates of national currencies are fixed to the SDR. As long as the US continues to dominate the IMF, there is no fundamental difference between calling the shots in dollars or SDR. Giving up the dollar would give the United States a more powerful SDR, which, of course, the United States would have to share with its European partners in exchange for Europe giving up the euro, something that the "sovereign monetarists" in the United States, who have long been accustomed to dictating, would not tolerate.

Currently, SDR has a major flaw, and that is that there is no RMB in the currency basket of SDR, and given the size and potential of the Chinese economy, the game cannot be played without bringing China on board. Maybe China will come up with a new monetary system of its own, and there will be trouble. In order to join the SDR, the RMB must be freely convertible, which will be the starting point for the future interest of Europe and the United States in articulating the benefits of free RMB conversion from all possible angles with all the hard words and threats.

The question is, what does joining the SDR's currency basket mean for China? If according to the design of Europe and the United States, the IMF will become the future world central bank, SDR as the world unified currency to replace the sovereign currency of each country, the United States and Europe are naturally the major shareholders with veto power, while China and other countries are the small shareholders who play along. China is losing the right to issue currency while not getting a greater counterweight to power. In this way, it will be Europe and America that will dominate China's destiny.

The United States gives up the dollar, Europe gives up the euro, they will both gain more dominance, they give up, but get more, China and other countries give up, and there is nothing left.

If the emergence of a unified world currency is the great trend of world economic development, the so-called unstoppable vastness, then China should strive to dominate this trend, not be dominated by it.

China must recognize that the RMB as a sovereign currency will not be able to replace the objective laws of the dollar, and at the same time will not be accepted by other countries, in the face of the situation of the weak RMB and the will of European and American currencies, China can only integrate the power of Asia under the shield of the Asian dollar, in order to counteract the sword of the dollar and the euro, forming a three-pronged posture. Without the Asian dollar, the currencies of Asian countries will be broken by the United States, and eventually the Asian currencies of the stragglers will be completely absorbed by the IMF. With the Asian dollar, and then a broader currency alliance with South America, Africa, the Middle East, and other regions to build each other's horns, greater currency leverage will be gained.

If the time comes for a unified world currency in the future, Asia will have at least one third of the world, and the power will be equal to that of Europe and the United States, with the same shares and the same power, sharing the world!

Whether or not the world's currency landscape is properly understood today will not only determine the future fate of the RMB, but also that of China and Asia!

The strong, always their own destiny, are at their own mercy!

Testimonials and Acknowledgements

In early winter, when I finally put away my pen, but could not put away my rushing thoughts, the night in Xiangshan was so long and silent. With their eyes closed, the fragments of history are scattered in the gutter of memory and cannot be cleared away, and the inspiration that emerges from time to time is like an electric current that stimulates the brain in desperate need of calm, and the words of passion chase, collide, and squeeze each other, eventually converging into a mass of viscous expression of desire in the uncontrolled consciousness. The all-night work, which lasted for more than half a year, once stopped, seemed to fall immediately into a state of mental weightlessness, which was more painful than even the joy of liberation.

Remember a quote from Steve Jobs:

> *"If you know your life is coming to an end, if every day when you stand in front of the mirror and ask yourself if what you have done today will leave you without complaint or regret, if the answer is yes every time, then this thing is your birthright."*

As I tried to stand in front of the mirror and torture myself with the same questions during my days at Fragrant Hill, I felt that maybe I had really found my calling in life.

I remember when I was very young, my parents and teachers said I wasn't strong, when in fact, I never cared about those comments. Growing up, I realized that being good and being self-improvement are two personalities. The good and the strong compete for the evaluation of others; the self-improvement people only care about the evaluation of the self: the good and the strong appear to be self-confident, but in fact have an inferiority complex, the root of the inferiority complex is that they lack their own internal value system, and have to rely on external criteria; the self-improvement people never care what others say, because they have in their bones a compass of self-value positioning. When society overestimates your value, you should walk on thin ice and be cautious; when your value is undervalued by society, you should be calm and relaxed, laughing and watching the clouds go by.

Stick to what you see. I am not afraid of sarcasm and sarcasm; I am not afraid of being short and long; I am not trying to make a success of a moment; I am not trying to be a straw man or an inappropriate person. It's been a lifelong belief of mine. This belief has strengthened me during my time at Fragrant Hill.

My research and writing have convinced me that I am creating a value for society. A person's value depends on how much he contributes to society, not how much he has.

This book came out without the care and help of many friends, without whom I would have done nothing.

Zheng Yingyan undertook much of the specific and tedious preparation for the birth of this book. Without her fruitful work communicating with the publisher, I would be bogged down in a plethora of transactional details and unable to focus on research and writing. Together with the publisher's responsible editor, she sifted through nearly a hundred draft book cover designs to find the colors and patterns that best fit the author's personality. She strongly advocates the rejection of the eye-catching and flashy popular style of domestic financial books, emphasizing the classic and atmospheric texture. She objected to a large amount of text on the cover and insisted on simplicity and plainness. She has worked hard to ensure the quality of the book after months of tireless communication with the publisher in terms of details such as book design style, paper texture, book pricing, promotion, time schedule, etc. After this ordeal, the head of Yangtze River Literary Publishing House sincerely admired that if she became a professional publishing agent, it would save the publisher a lot of trouble.

President Kim and President Lai of Yangtze River Literary Press gave me the utmost support and encouragement in my writing, and their enthusiasm and attentiveness warmed me through the hard work. The publisher's Mr. Lang Shiming is the most dedicated editor I can imagine, and his close cooperation with Zheng Yingyan has almost completely shielded me from all trivia. Publishing as a service industry, they have allowed me to enjoy almost perfect quality service.

Professionally, I have benefited from many learned predecessors and teachers.

At a financial seminar, I benefited from Bank of China Vice President Wang Yongli's observation that real positions in the dollar will never flow out of the US banking system. In a later exchange, Mr. Wang gave me a comprehensive overview of the flow and settlement details of virtual dollar positions outside the United States, and I have repeatedly read his expository articles in this area. It was with his inspiration that I sought out Jacques Rueff's book "The Original Sin of Western Money", a book by the famous French economist, and found that Mr. Wang Yongli's views were the modern embodiment of Rueff's thesis. This view was incorporated by me in the section on the inherent flaws of the gold exchange standard in Chapter 1.

Mr. Zhang Yuyan of the Institute of World Economics of the Chinese Academy of Social Sciences has been one of the scholars I follow most, and I have been enlightened by his many views on the currency circulation domain, the historical impact of silver flows on the rise and fall of Europe, the relationship between the rise and fall of ancient Chinese currencies and regimes, and the internationalization of the RMB. These observations have had a profound impact on some of the conclusions in the book.

Mr. Xia Bin of the Development Research Center of the State Council is also a scholar whom I have great respect for. On New Year's Eve this year, when everyone was at home, Mr. Xia Bin and I were talking about his book China Financial Strategy 2020 in an empty cafe, and his holistic vision and in-depth analysis were convincing. Many of his ideas have influenced my thinking about China's future financial strategy in the book.

I must read every article by Mr. Yu Yongding of the Academy of Social Sciences. I brought up the idea of the Asian dollar at a recent seminar led by Mr. Yu Yongding, who had been involved in Asian economic and monetary cooperation for ten years, and lamented with a bitter smile that the realization of the Asian dollar would not be easy. Although we don't share the same view on this issue, it fuels my interest in gaining a deeper understanding of the realities of the dilemma of realizing the subdollar.

What I should be most grateful for, and feel most indebted to, are the wives and daughters who are far away, who have sacrificed more than I could ever hope to make up for in the service of my ideals. My daughter, Jinjin, used to not be able to read Chinese, but in order to be able to read books written by her father, she is working extra hard to learn Chinese well, and she is now able to write me daily emails in Chinese, and I am so moved by her efforts. Father is a constant idol in my daughter's heart, and in order not to disappoint her, I must keep moving forward.

Author.
11 November 2011,
Xiangshan, Beijing

Other titles

Omnia Veritas Ltd presents:

THE CURSE OF CANAAN
A demonology of history

by

EUSTACE MULLINS

Liberalism, more popularly known as secular humanism, can be traced in an unbroken line all the way back to the Biblical "Curse of Canaan."

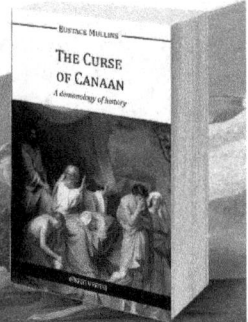

Humanism is the logical result of the demonology of history

Omnia Veritas Ltd presents:

THE RAPE OF JUSTICE

by

EUSTACE MULLINS

AMERICA'S TRIBUNALS EXPOSED

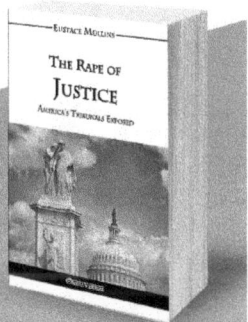

American should know just what is going on in our courts

Omnia Veritas Ltd presents:

THE SECRETS OF THE FEDERAL RESERVE

by

EUSTACE MULLINS

HERE ARE THE SIMPLE FACTS OF THE GREAT BETRAYAL

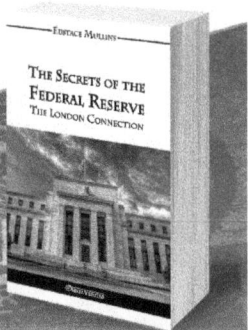

Will we continue to be enslaved by the Babylonian debt money system?

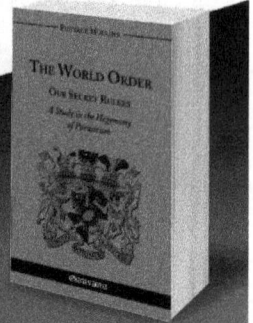

www.ingramcontent.com/pod-product-compliance
Lightning Source LLC
Chambersburg PA
CBHW060324100426

42812CB00003B/873